Beyond Chief(
Complexity in Airica

Recent critiques of neo-evolutionary formulations that
focus primarily on the development of powerful hierarchies have called for a broadening of the empirical base
for complex society studies. Redressing the neglect of sub-
Saharan examples in comparative discussions on complex
society, this book considers how case material from the
subcontinent can enhance our understanding of the
nature, origins, and development of complexity. The
archaeological, historical, and anthropological case materials are relevant to a number of recent concerns, revealing how complexity has emerged and developed in a
variety of ways. Contributors engage important theoretical issues, including the continuing influence of deeply
embedded evolutionary notions in archaeological concepts of complexity, the importance of alternative modes
of complex organization – such as flexible hierarchies,
multiple overlapping hierarchies, and horizontal differentiation – and the significance of different forms of
power. The distinguished list of contributors includes historians, archaeologists, and anthropologists.

SUSAN KEECH MCINTOSH is Professor of Anthropology
at Rice University, USA. She has conducted archaeological research in Mali, Senegal, and Ghana, and is co-
author of two monographs on Jenné-jeno, Mali, widely
recognized as the earliest urban site documented in sub-
Saharan Africa.

NEW DIRECTIONS IN ARCHAEOLOGY

Beyond Chiefdoms

Pathways to Complexity in Africa

Edited by

SUSAN KEECH McINTOSH

CAMBRIDGE
UNIVERSITY PRESS

CAMBRIDGE UNIVERSITY PRESS
Cambridge, New York, Melbourne, Madrid, Cape Town, Singapore, São Paulo

Cambridge University Press
The Edinburgh Building, Cambridge CB2 2RU, UK

Published in the United States of America by Cambridge University Press, New York

www.cambridge.org
Information on this title: www.cambridge.org/9780521630740

First published 1999
This digitally printed first paperback version 2005

A catalogue record for this publication is available from the British Library

Library of Congress Cataloguing in Publication data

African perspectives on political complexity / edited by Susan Keech
McIntosh
 p. cm.
1. Political anthropology – Africa. 2. Social archaeology – Africa.
3. Archaeology and state – Africa. 4. Africa – Politics and
government. 5. Africa – Antiquities. I. McIntosh, Susan Keech.
GN645.A367 1999
306.2´096–dc21 98-38081 CIP

ISBN-13 978-0-521-63074-0 hardback
ISBN-10 0-521-63074-6 hardback

ISBN-13 978-0-521-02269-9 paperback
ISBN-10 0-521-02269-X paperback

Contents

Figures

Tables

Contributors

RAYMOND ASOMBANG
Department of Arts and Archaeology
University of Yaoundé
Cameroon

NICHOLAS DAVID
Department of Archaeology
University of Calgary

JUDY STERNER
University of Calgary

JAMES DENBOW
Department of Anthropology
University of Texas at Austin

IGOR KOPYTOFF
Department of Anthropology
University of Pennsylvania

PIERRE DE MARET
Université Libre de Bruxelles
Belgium

RODERICK MCINTOSH
Department of Anthropology
Rice University

SUSAN KEECH MCINTOSH
Department of Anthropology
Rice University

PETER ROBERTSHAW
Department of Anthropology
California State University, San Bernardino

DAVID SCHOENBRUN
Department of History
University of Georgia

AIDAN SOUTHALL
Department of Anthropology
University of Wisconsin, Madison

ANN B. STAHL
Department of Anthropology
State University of New York, Binghamton

JAN VANSINA
Departments of Anthropology and History
University of Wisconsin

Preface

This book project had its origins in my own frustration at the paucity of African models, African-inspired theories, and African case studies in the archaeological literature on the development of complexity. When Antonio Gilman asked me to organize an archaeology session at the 1992 annual meeting of the American Anthropological Association in San Francisco, I used the opportunity to showcase what that continent has to offer to ongoing debates about the origin and nature of complex societies. If archaeology was to live up to its claims to be a comparative discipline, it needed to take Africa, especially sub-Saharan Africa, seriously and systematically into account.

The papers at the invited session entitled "Intermediate-level Societies in Africa: Archaeological and Anthropological Insights" ranged widely over the continent and included presentations by anthropologists and historians as well as archaeologists. A number of the papers in this volume (those by Southall, S. McIntosh, Schoenbrun, Robertshaw, and Denbow) were originally presented at this session. Igor Kopytoff was also scheduled to participate, but circumstances prevented it. Fekri Hassan participated in the session, but in view of the strongly sub-Saharan focus of the rest of the papers, it was decided to strengthen that focus for publication and exclude ancient Egypt – arguably the best-known African complex society. Subsequently, papers presented by Ann Stahl and Nic David at the Complex Society Group's meeting in San Bernardino in October 1995 were added, and additional papers solicited. Not all of the additionally solicited papers actually materialized, leaving the coverage of some themes and areas envisioned for inclusion rather threadbare. But even in ideal circumstances, it is

unlikely that any group of twelve authors could adequately represent the various regions of a subcontinent two to three times larger than the contiguous United States, let alone satisfy everyone's wish list for gender, national, ethnic, and disciplinary diversity among the contributors. In the end, it seemed enough to provide some sense of the variety of anthropological, historical, and archaeological case materials available for the study of complexity in Africa, selected with an eye to their resonance with certain themes that have emerged in the recent archaeological literature.

I am indebted to all the people who read part or all of my introductory essay in preliminary or more advanced draft and provided useful, encouraging and/or cautionary remarks: Nic David, Brian Fagan, Antonio Gilman, Stephen Houston, Ben Nelson, Simon Ottenberg, Thurstan Shaw, Aidan Southall, and Ann Stahl. My debt is particularly large to those stalwart individuals who read through more than one draft version: Tim Earle, Igor Kopytoff, Rod McIntosh, Pete Robertshaw, David Schoenbrun, and Jan Vansina. Although I have not patched all the holes that they found, I am deeply grateful for the collegiality, insightful comments and editorial surveillance. The chapter was significantly improved as a result of their input. Thanks also go to Joe Tainter for long and thought-provoking conversations about complexity along the road between Bandelier and Jemez as well as in Albuquerque.

Four people in particular encouraged me to move ahead with publishing this collection: Ivan Karp (who suggested a more anthropological, rather than archaeological, orientation for the volume, however); Ann Stahl, who uttered just the right words at a critical juncture in

1994; Norman Yoffee, who encouraged me to take the project to Cambridge University Press; and Rod McIntosh, who provided endless support and childcare while I wrestled with the introduction and editorial tasks. I am grateful for their confidence in the project. My children, Alex and Annick, graciously forbore my absences and preoccupation with "the book," but have made it quite clear that they don't need another book project in my future any time soon!

More than anything, the completion of this volume is a testimony to my long-time research collaboration with my husband, Rod McIntosh, who first suggested almost two decades ago that standard neo-evolutionary models for the development of complexity did not easily accommodate the massive mound complex of Jenné-jeno, where we began fieldwork together in 1977. In the intervening years, as chiefdom studies were on the ascendant and hierarchy was on everyone's lips, it seemed quixotic at times to continue to develop the idea that a settlement cluster on the scale of Jenné-jeno was not centrally organized under a paramount chief. Isolated as we were in a department with no other archaeologists, we each served as the other's major source of support in the belief that alternative models for complex social organization were necessary for archaeology to fulfill its promise as a comparative discipline. Africa's role in this project would necessarily be a large one, we felt. But the time was not yet right.

With the rise of interest in multiple sources of power (as the influence of Foucault gradually trickles into the mainstream of archaeology) in the 1990s, a more receptive climate for such ideas seems to be emerging. People who work on complex societies far from the traditional areas (Maya, Peru, Europe, Polynesia, Mesopotamia) that have historically dominated discussions on complexity now share a sense that archaeological discourse on complexity has expanded considerably to include a much greater range of variation in patterns and trajectories of complexity. There is a sense, articulated in the title of a session at the 1998 Society for American Archaeology meeting in Seattle, that the discussion of non-hierarchical models of complexity need no longer be conducted in whispers. Perhaps, then, the time is finally right for a book such as this.

1
Pathways to complexity: An African perspective

SUSAN KEECH MCINTOSH

Over the past decade, sub-Saharan Africa has virtually disappeared from the screen of archaeologists engaged in broadly comparative, theoretical discussions on the emergence of complex society. Prior to the 1980s, the subcontinent was represented with some regularity at important archaeological conferences and discussions on these issues (e.g., Cohen and Service 1978; Friedman and Rowlands 1978; Moore 1974) even while the actual archaeology of sub-Saharan complex societies remained nascent. Since then, the visibility of Africa in comparative theoretical discussions has declined considerably, despite the surge of interest in societies organizationally intermediate between small-scale, non-stratified and locally autonomous groups and the internally differentiated state (e.g., Arnold 1996; Drennan and Uribe 1987; Earle 1987, 1991c; Gregg 1991; Price and Feinman 1995; Upham 1990) and despite the abundance and diversity of such societies throughout the subcontinent at the time of European colonial expansion. Sub-Saharan regions are represented briefly, if at all, in some widely cited works (Earle 1987, 1991c; Ehrenreich et al. 1995; Haas 1982; Price and Feinman 1995; Renfrew and Cherry 1986; Trigger 1993 is a notable exception). Ironically, the archaeology of complex societies in Africa has grown remarkably during this same period (see, e.g., Shaw et al. 1993).

The primary objective of this volume is to reintroduce an African perspective into archaeological theorizing about complex societies. This is a daunting task because the subcontinent is vast (over three times the size of the United States) and in historic times has exhibited an astonishing diversity of sociopolitical formations. Thus, any attempt at general coverage will necessarily suffer from incomplete and unsatisfactory geographic representation, and leave a host of relevant topics and potential insights unexplored. Nevertheless, it is possible to identify certain themes emerging from the recent archaeological literature that find a particular resonance in the African comparative material. The ongoing effort to broaden archaeology's focus beyond preoccupation with the development of vertical control hierarchies (with the Polynesian chiefdom as prototype) to include less hierarchical, more decentralized or horizontally complex configurations is one such theme (Arnold 1996; Crumley 1987, 1995; Ehrenreich et al. 1995; Nelson 1994; Spielmann 1994). A growing interest in the initial emergence of hierarchy, rather than with its elaboration into more state-like formations is another (Arnold 1996; Price and Feinman 1995; Upham 1990). Related to both of these is the critique of deeply embedded evolutionary notions which continue to subtly influence and shape archaeology's conceptualization of what constitutes complexity, and how it can be identified and studied (Rowlands 1989b; Morris 1997; Yoffee 1993). Emerging from this critique is, again, the growing concern with documenting variability in both the forms and, especially, the developmental trajectories of complexity (e.g., Blanton et al. 1996; Drennan 1996; Feinman and Neitzel 1984; Yoffee 1993). Virtually all the contributors to this volume engage critically with one or more of these issues. The result is, I hope, a persuasive argument for considering Africa central to any and all comparative discussions concerning the diverse forms of and pathways to complexity.

In this chapter I aim to outline in a general manner some of the ways that African case material can contribute to archaeological discussions of these issues. Certain recurrent aspects of African society, such as the co-occurrence of vertical hierarchies with multiple, horizontally arrayed, ritual associations, and particular notions of ritual power and leadership, offer opportunities to reconsider how we think about power and how it is used in crafting polity. I also attempt to reinsert Africa into the evolutionary critiques of the past decade or two. I begin with a brief consideration of why it is that Africa has been absent from the discussion table for so long.

Missing Africa

It is not possible here to tease out all the factors contributing to the neglect of Africa over the past decade even by archaeologists who style their approach as explicitly comparative. However, one can identify several factors that may have played a role. Among these are various

problematic aspects of the African ethnographic literature. Much of the earlier literature, for example, observed
the state/stateless classification scheme introduced by
Fortes and Evans-Pritchard in *African Political Systems*
(1940). Fortes and Evans-Pritchard focused on the distinction between stateless (acephalous) societies in which
a system of competing lineage segments provides the
framework of the political structure, and state societies, in
which a centralized administrative organization is
present. The latter category embraced political systems
that in other classifications would range from simple
chiefdoms to early states (as, for example, Taylor's [1975]
classification of sixteen "states" in central, eastern, and
southern Africa as non-ranked, ranked, and paramount
chiefdoms). As archaeology broadened the scope of its
complex society inquiries to focus less on the state and
more on its presumed antecedent formation, the chiefdom, the task of sifting the vast literature on African
"states" for relevant examples became daunting and was
further complicated by frequent colloquial usage of the
term "chief" for village headship in autonomous villages.
Following Sahlins (1968), Service (1962), and Carneiro
(1981), archaeologists use the term to indicate supralocal
authority. So the fact that the chiefdom, as a separate,
widely used taxonomic category, does not exist for Africa
the way it does for North and South America and
Polynesia, did little to facilitate the inclusion of the continent in discussions on chiefdom-level societies.

It can be argued that this taxonomic elision is a good
thing, sparing Africanists the endless caviling about the
proper boundary between chiefdom and state that besets
other regions. In this sense, the African "state" corresponds to Johnson and Earle's (1987) "regional polity."
Some argue that the term chiefdom should never be used
in an African context, not only because it is freighted with
unacceptable evolutionary stage implications, but also
because so many chiefdoms in Africa were, like tribes, the
result of colonialism and capitalist penetration (Southall
1988a: 169). Although the terms "tribal" and "tribe" have
been rehabilitated in North America, where they are considered acceptable when referring to native American
groups, in Africa, the pejorative implications of the terms,
arising from earlier evolutionary and colonial usage, are
still considered offensive (Southall 1970, 1996). As
Southall (1988b: 55) observed, the African counterpart of
"orientalism" is "Africanism," whereby a state in Africa is
always referred to as a tribe (see also Rowlands [1989a:
261–4] on "primitivist" discourses on Africa). The
classificatory dilemmas leave us with "intermediate-level"
or "middle-range" as the least objectionable category for
an enormous diversity of African societies. This suits our

purposes very well, for one point that emerges from
several of the papers in this volume (Kopytoff, David and
Sterner, Vansina) is how easily and fluidly a variety of
African societies move back and forth from lineage to
village headship to regional chiefship and kingship. From
the point of view of process, it is perhaps more useful to
investigate this apparent cycling without a priori subdivision. In addition, eschewing "chiefdom" liberates us from
the assumptions built into the term, equating complexity
with the emergence of chiefship (i.e., Carneiro's [1981: 45]
definition – following Oberg 1955: 484 – of chiefdoms as
polities united under the permanent control of a paramount chief).

In addition to classificatory muddles, the historical
development of theory in African ethnography is another
factor potentially discouraging non-Africanist interest.
The influence of *African Political Systems* can again be
cited. It introduced structural functionalism, which dominated anglophone ethnographic research in Africa for
over two decades. As Earle (1987: 288) has pointed out,
this static and ahistorical perspective offered little to
archaeologists interested in diachronic change and cultural evolution. Furthermore, when a new generation of
ethnographers took advantage of fieldwork opportunities
opening up in Melanesia and attempted to apply African
lineage models, the discovery that African lineages did not
exist elsewhere in the world became, in the words of
Parkin (1990: 184, 196) "wholesale denunciation of the
relevance of African ethnography for other areas and
increasing uninterest in its findings" (but see also Karp
1978). In Melanesia, the creation of exchange as a key
tool for understanding society filled the vacuum left by
the failure of descent theory there (Strathern 1990).
Melanesian exchange studies, coupled with studies of
chiefdoms and social stratification in Polynesia, opened
up a rich theoretical vein for archaeology in the 1960s and
1970s, replete with big man and chief models with a
materialist bent that could plausibly be operationalized in
archaeological terms (e.g., Sahlins 1963). Ironically again,
it was precisely during this period that Africanist anthropology became much more involved with issues of process
and historical change, particularly with regard to African
paramountcies and kingdoms, which were the privileged
focus of post-independence research (e.g., Fallers 1964;
Forde and Kaberry 1967; Goody 1971; Lloyd 1960, 1968,
1971). However, by the 1980s, the Oceanic hegemony in
archaeological theories of intermediate-level societies was
well established, and African societies were discussed
within analytical and classificatory frameworks originally
formulated with Polynesian and Melanesian societies in
mind (e.g., Service 1975). It should be noted, however,

that a number of "non-aligned" (in the sense of not identified with evolutionary, functionalist, materialist, or Marxist paradigms) Africanist anthropologists from Europe and Israel provided discussions of interest in a series of volumes on the early state (e.g., Claessen 1984; papers in Claessen and Skalník 1978, 1981; Claessen and van de Velde 1987; Claessen and Oosten 1996; Eisenstadt et al. 1988b).

Further disincentives to seek theoretical insights from African ethnography were supplied by a burgeoning post-colonial literature that sought to re-situate in the context of wider regional and international economies, politics, and history, societies depicted by ethnographers as isolated and timeless. *Population and Political Systems in Tropical Africa* (Stevenson 1968) is an early example that is frequently cited by non-Africanist archaeologists interested, presumably, in its focus on the functional correlation of population density and political centralization. Targeting Fortes and Evans-Pritchard's (1940) troubling claim that African case studies indicated an inverse correlation between these two variables, Stevenson re-evaluated several of the *African Political Systems* case studies, concluding that the density/centralization anomaly disappeared when historical data were taken into account. High density, acephalous societies such as the Tallensi of Ghana were relics of earlier states, and some low density states, such as the Bemba of Zambia, had higher population densities prior to the arrival of the British, while others, as in the case of the Ngwato, were artifacts of British rule and not indigenous states at all. Although Stevenson's historical methodology was deeply flawed, making many of his conclusions suspect (Goody 1970, 1977; Ottenberg 1970), he laid open for interested archaeologists the problematic nature of ethnographic data from Africa.

The debates on the extent and impact of the slave trade on African societies across the continent further developed the idea that Africa had been fundamentally transformed in recent centuries (e.g., Inikori and Engerman 1992; Lovejoy 1989; Manning 1990; Rodney 1972; Wolf 1982), resulting in social configurations on the eve of colonial conquest that, while genuinely African, were not necessarily "traditional" (examples of in-depth studies of the transformations include Ekholm Friedman 1991; and Harms 1981). The colonial presence altered social formations in yet other ways, creating named, bounded "tribes," altering trade patterns, formalizing informal or contested indigenous hierarchies, promoting local headmen to chiefs, and chiefs to kings in the interests of indirect rule, supported by the ability of the colonial governments to aggregate support through the distribution of "prebends

and benefices" (Fried 1975; Lemarchand 1977: 12; Mamdani 1996: 44–6; Southall 1970, 1996; Stone 1996: 67–8). While it may seem that the African case material represents societies so altered by centuries of contact with powerful, expansionist economic and political systems as to render them of limited use for archaeological theories applicable to periods prior to the emergence of such systems, the recent reinsertion of historical concerns into anthropology makes it clear that the problem is global and not Africa's alone (e.g., Roseberry 1989; Sahlins 1985; Wolf 1982). Africa, Latin America, North America, Polynesia, India, China are all implicated. One cannot label African case material as too problematic and then turn to North America or Polynesia for analogies uncomplicated by history.

Archaeologists, whose interpretations of the past are of necessity based primarily on analogies from the present, have not yet fully appreciated the impact of the breakdown of the concept of timeless, "traditional" society. Various historians, among them Hobsbawm and Ranger (1983) and Vansina (1989, 1990), have demonstrated the truth of Coquery-Vidrovitch's assertion (1976, quoted in Mamdani 1996: 39) that "the static concept of 'traditional society' cannot withstand the historian's analysis." Ann Stahl (1993) has considered the implications for archaeology, pointing out that, even in cases of direct historical continuity with the archaeological case of interest, it is no longer possible simply to assume continuity and persistence between past and present. Earlier practices of uncritical projection into the past accompanied by more or less extensive mapping on of ethnographic details to the archaeological case cannot be sustained. Rather, continuity must be treated as an empirical question requiring investigation by methods that facilitate the identification of change (discontinuity) as well as persistence. With the realization that all ethnographic/ethnohistoric case materials utilized by archaeologists must be subjected to careful source side criticism following rules of evidence established for ethnohistorical, historical, as well as anthropological sources (Vansina 1989; Wood 1990, cited in Stahl 1993: 247), any rationale for particularly avoiding African comparative materials due to their problematic nature disappears.

Whatever the full account of Africa's declining contributions to theory over the past decade may be, my purpose in the remainder of this chapter is to outline the valuable contributions that the sub-continent can make to the theoretical concerns that have emerged in the recent archaeological literature. In drawing on case material for this discussion, I have not followed the prescription for source-side criticism alluded to above. It is simply too time consuming in view of the wide range of examples discussed. Readers are thus alerted that the literature is taken somewhat at face value in order to make a number of general points.

I suggest that Africa challenges deeply embedded evolutionary notions of complexity as differentiation by political hierarchization and provides an instructive counterpoint to formulations that locate power centrally in individuals and focus analysis primarily on the economic strategies used by these individuals to maintain and expand operational power. It provides a rich corpus of material relevant to an understanding of societies in which central authority, often of a ritual nature, is paired with a power structure that is diffuse, segmentary, and heterarchical, as well as societies in which considerable complexity is achieved through horizontal differentiation and consensus-based decision-making. The distribution of power among several corporate entities (e.g., lineages, secret societies, cults, age grades) can be regarded as a strategy that has successfully resisted in a variety of ways the consolidation of power by individuals. Understanding how and why resistance is effective requires exploration of African ideologies and constructions of power, which in some cases differ significantly from Western notions. Where effective resistance is encountered, is fission the only response to population increase, or can scale increase considerably through the development of other forms of complex organization? To what extent can diverse pathways to complexity be discerned? Rather than taking centralization as a given in discussing complexity and then concentrating on how leaders maintain control through economic leverage or coercion, it is useful to ask what constitutes complexity and consider how social and ritual resources are mobilized and collective action made possible in the absence of significant economic control. Both approaches are of value, although the former has received the lion's share of the attention in the literature to date.

I begin by situating Africa within the critique of the neo-evolutionist narratives of complexity that have dominated (either explicitly or covertly) discussions of complexity, especially among American archaeologists, since the 1960s.

Complexity: narratives and dichotomies

Much of the difficulty with complexity as a subject of archaeological investigation arises from the powerful legacy of nineteenth-century social theorists. As Robert Netting (1990: 21) memorably observed, archaeologists carry large diachronic portmanteaus whose internal dividers still bear the labels of unreconstructed evolutionism. From the familiar dichotomous formulations of the nineteenth century – *societas/civitas*, mechanical/organic solidarity, collective/individual consciousness, kinship/territory, homogeneous/heterogeneous – archaeologists, as well as historians and sociologists, have crafted complex narratives of progressive change, in which various elements together form a coherent configuration. This functionally related complex of elements has been postulated to include agricultural intensification and surplus production; increasing population scale, density, and heterogeneity; development of private property/unequal access to land or other strategic resources; centralized, supracommunity political organization; vertical hierarchies of wealth, power, and status; functional specialization, commerce and intercommunication. It is a list with which Spencer, Marx, Durkheim, Morgan, and Weber would have been comfortable, as indeed they originally proposed many of its basic elements. Although archaeologists have, over time, varied the ordering of the elements, positing various ones as prime movers or many together as mutually reinforcing elements of multivariate models (summarized by Drennan 1996), the basic postulate of functional relationships among these elements has been very durable.

Sahlins' study of social stratification in Polynesia (1958) appeared to demonstrate the functional interrelations of a number of these different elements in societies far removed from the European societies (including the ancient Greeks and Romans) that had been the basis of nineteenth-century social theories. In Polynesia, different degrees of stratification (complexity) could be defined by the extent of co-occurrence within different societies of many of the functional elements listed above (Table 1.1). This supported the notion that the narrative tying all these elements together was of general applicability. Once incorporated within Service's (1962) formulation of chiefdom as a general stage of cultural evolution, Sahlins' work became enormously influential for archaeologists. Sahlins' (1963, 1968) elevation of Melanesian and Polynesian patterns to the status of generalized, ideal Big Man and Chiefdom types was instrumental in inaugurating what I refer to as the Oceanic hegemony in complex society archaeology.

Unpacking the evolutionary portmanteau

As research continued to accumulate in different areas of the world, however, dissonant notes were occasionally sounded. The identified elements of the narrative did not seem to correlate in some areas, and the slow work of unpacking the evolutionary portmanteau and of decou-

Table 1.1 *Social stratification in Polynesia*

Stratification criteria	Group I Hawaii, Tonga, Samoa, Tahiti	Group IIa Mangaia, Uvea, Mangareva	Group IIb Marquesas, Tikopia	Group III Pukapuka, Toketau
Status levels	3	2	2	2
Pre-eminent stewardship of land by chiefs	Yes	Yes	No (but rights of access to stategic resources usually held by elites)	No
Control of communal and craft production by persons of high rank	Yes	Yes	Usually	No
Direct supervision of household production	Yes	No	No	No
Legitimate use of force for infringement of chiefly decrees	Yes	Limited/No	No	No
Segregation of upper ranks from subsistence production	Yes	Highest chiefs only	No (except Marquesas)	No
Status markers (clothes, ornaments) elaborated	Yes	Yes, but less than in Group I	Few	None
High status endogamy	Yes	Not strictly enforced	Slight preference only	No
Sumptuary rules and obeissance behaviors	Yes	Not marked	Few to none	Few to none
Spectacular and unique life crisis rituals for high chiefs	Yes	Some	Differences of degree, not kind	Almost none

Source: Summarized from Sahlins 1958.

pling elements formerly believed to be functionally related began in earnest. McGuire (1983), on the basis of Near Eastern archaeological material, concluded that substantial vertical inequality preceded significant horizontal heterogeneity there, forcing a decoupling of inequality and heterogeneity, a finding that has been expanded by general discussions that recognize the existence of some inequality (by gender, age, ability, and temperament) in even the most egalitarian human social systems (Feinman 1995: 256; Flanagan 1989). With the documentation of institutionalized inequality among some hunter-gatherer populations, its emergence has been decoupled from agricultural production and intensification (Feinman 1995: 256). Gary Feinman and Jill Neitzel (1984) found no uni-

versal links between political ranking and agriculture, population, trade or surplus production in a comparison of New World middle-range societies. Hastorf (1990) in a study of the pre-Inca Sausa of Peru, separated the onset of political inequality and ranking from economic production, and by extension, decoupled political inequality from wealth inequality. Recently, Nelson (1995) suggested that scale and hierarchy must be considered as elements that do not necessarily covary, a theme that I also consider in my other contribution to this volume.

Looking at African case materials relevant to our baggage-sorting, we find that some of these critiques were anticipated in the African literature. In *Social Stratification in Africa*, a title whose similarity to that of

Sahlins' 1958 monograph is quite intentional, Tuden and Plotnicov (1970: 6) pointed out that "some of the prevalent assumptions regarding the nature and underlying factors of social stratification have failed to utilize comparative data sufficiently." Unfortunately, this message went largely unnoticed by archaeologists. Tuden and Plotnicov decoupled economic inequality from ranked social differentiation (social stratification):

> One of the most critical comparative problems in the study of stratification concerns the primacy and inter-relationship of the factors that produce and maintain hierarchical groupings. The view is commonly shared that a society becomes stratified when some groups are excluded from access to strategic economic resources . . . (Fried 1967). Economic power is postulated as having priority over political power in this process . . . African societies provide no clear correlation between economic power, control of the political system, and stratification. In a number of cases – Amhara, Galla, Marghi – the superior strata neither control economic power systematically nor consistently receive honor. Of all the societies included here, only two – Rwanda and South Africa – manifest clear economic, political and evaluative differences between strata. (Tuden and Plotnicov 1970: 8)

Lloyd Fallers (1973: 75) drew a similar conclusion: "Traditional African societies have characteristically exhibited a pattern of role differentiation in which political specialization has been more prominent than economic specialization . . . . While sharply 'peaked' systems of stratification have been created in the great traditional kingdoms, even in these cases, there has been relatively little cultural differentiation between elite and common folk and little concentration of the non-human means of production in elite hands." There is, on the other hand, a highly developed appreciation of and competition for status and prestige in African societies, with even tiny polities often richly accoutered with titles, offices, and insignia, as, for example, the Sukur polity described by David and Sterner in this volume. Bargatsky (1987: 27) has suggested that economic status has emerged from the enormous complexity of status systems in pre-industrial societies to become the one status criterion valued above all others in capitalist societies. This can blind us to the importance of status distinctions that lack a material, economic foundation, or even to the possibility that significant status differences can be thus constructed.

Goody (1971, 1976: 111–13) also noted the low incidence of economic stratification in African societies based on agriculture and argued that it was linked to abundant land, such that economic stratification based on access to and control over scarce land (the European model, also relevant to Polynesia [Goldman 1970]) rarely developed. Thus, theoretical formulations which stress the fundamental importance of rent extraction to the emergence of social complexity (e.g., Earle 1991b; Gilman 1991) may be inappropriate for Africa.

Instead, chiefship tends to be over people rather than land, and goods are dispersed more readily than accumulated, through bridewealth payments for as many wives as one can afford. Of great strategic significance in terms of building up a following is the power held by chiefs throughout Africa to allocate land to new settlers, a costless resource overlooked by narrowly materialist explanations for the emergence of chiefdoms (Kopytoff, this volume). The widespread emphasis on maximizing fertility through polygyny made generational conflict over access to women a more important historical dynamic than class conflict. For Goody (1976), the practice of royal–commoner marriage (open connubium) even in some of the most highly centralized African societies (e.g., Buganda) produced a centrifugal effect on wealth that was quite the opposite of the wealth sequestering effects of hypergamy and dowry in Europe. Iliffe (1995: 96) points out that the African board game known in West Africa as *mankala* makes an interesting contrast with chess, which is a game of a stratified society with unequal pieces and the objective of destroying the opposing forces. In *mankala*, all the pieces are of equal value and the aim is to capture the opposing pieces and add them to one's own. It is the game of an essentially classless society dedicated to building up its numbers. This puts the tremendous demographic advantage arising from cattle possession (Bantu East and southern Africa, the Nilotic and Great Lakes regions, and the West African Sahel) in perspective: no other scarce, storable, and reproducible form of wealth existed by which to gain political clients or to acquire wives without exchanging kinswomen (Iliffe 1995: 106; Kuper 1982).

This does not mean that there was no inequality in African societies, nor that control over material resources other than cattle did not play an important role in articulating power. As mentioned above, the pervasive emphasis on fertility and polygyny created significant inequalities in access to wives, inequalities that were mediated through control by elders and chiefs of the goods required for bridewealth (Douglas 1967; Meillassoux 1960). Jan Vansina (1990) has shown for Central Africa how political inequality is an extension of the elders/juniors model of inequality within domestic units ("houses"). However, widespread ideals of chiefly generosity, relative material equality among (not within) "houses" and lineages, plus the constant cycle of amassing then redistributing goods to expand one's prestige by enlarging the household unit (adding wives or slaves) or by purchasing titles and society memberships, meant that many (but by no means all) African hierarchical societies did not manifest the elements of economic stratification that archaeologists most often seek (e.g., Peebles and Kus 1977; Wason 1994). As Burton observed while on a mission to the king of Dahomey: "Truly it is said, while the poor man in the North is the son of a pauper, the poor man in the Tropics is the son of a prince" (cited in Goody 1976: 99).

Gwyn Prins (1980) provides insights into the value system underlying this common phenomenon in Africa as he describes the food redistribution system (*silyela*) common in the great Bulozi kingdom of the Zambezi floodplain in the 1900s. Within each village at dinner time, all villagers would gather at the headman's compound, bringing their cooked food, which would then be divided into the bowls of various groups, including slaves, at the headman's direction. Parallel to this was a similar system for allocating high status food (cattle, large game animals). Through *silyela*, the social hierarchy of headman, freemen, women, children, and slaves was restated daily, but within a framework that ensured adequate food to all groups. In this way, the effects of shortage could be generally shared and mitigated. As Prins observes:

> It [*silyela*] indicates a set of extra-economic priorities at work influencing the material base of the community. These priorities constituted the moral economy, in contrast to the material economy, which it embraced and directed . . . here again, it has to be stressed in order to stifle at birth a common reaction to such a statement – that of course this usage should not be taken to imply that Lozi villagers were insensible to the motivations of the market economy. Simply, the creation and manipulation of a surplus in the sense in which we generally take it was a lower priority than the dominant concern, which was to ensure the survival of the moral community with minimum risk of famine . . . Furthermore, *silyela* shows how uneven accumulation of surplus was not feasible. What was surplus to the "reproduction of necessary labour" was committed to the "reproduction of the community." (Prins 1980: 91)

The same "culture-specific rationality" governed the disposal of the produce of state gardens, which were scattered throughout the land, "owned" by the king and cultivated by labor tribute. But they were not "private estates." Their products were dispersed in three ways: they were placed in storehouses of the guardian to be released in time of need. The remainder was collected by emissary chiefs and taken to the capital as tribute, the bulk of which was taken to public storehouses to feed the public, while a smaller amount went to the royal storehouse to feed the court. The village-level *silyela* distribution was in all its essentials echoed at the top of the hierarchy (Prins 1980: 93). It is, of course, possible to contrast the Lozi kingdom with another equally extensive paramountcy, Ashanti, where wealth accumulation was assiduously pursued (McCaskie 1995; Wilks 1993), but all this is merely to demonstrate that wealth accumulation and manipulation of surplus by elites primarily to further personal political agendas is a highly variable aspect of political hierarchies. As Miller (1988: 47) observed with reference to West Central Africa: "What ambitious men struggled to achieve was . . . not direct supervision over others, and still less stocks of the physical products of their labour beyond immediate needs, since both people and their fabrications were all too perishable, but rather a general claim to unspecified future labor and its product at whatever moment need for them might arise."

Functionalist assumptions about the relationship of agricultural intensification, population density, and land tenure to political centralization and hierarchies of wealth, power, and status have also been seriously challenged in much of Africa (Netting 1990; Shipton 1984, 1994). Service (1971: 152) found Fortes and Evans-Pritchard's (1940) conclusion that there is no significant general relationship between high population density and political centralization in Africa "dangerously misleading" and "astonishing." We have already mentioned Stevenson's (1968) valiant but flawed attempt to restore order, prompting Marvin Harris (1968: 530), Stevenson's thesis chairman at Columbia, to extol his "brilliant defense" against the distortions of Fortes and Evans-Pritchard, which "threatened to reduce our understanding of state formation to a shambles." For Stevenson, the Igbo (Ibo) of southeastern Nigeria, acephalous populations with pre-colonial densities of 150–400 persons/km^2, posed a particularly intractable problem. He went to considerable lengths to contrive an "emergent Ibo state" out of a widespread Igbo oracle cult (the Arochukwu) that organized regional trade. While certain centralized pan-Igbo features emerged in the context of the Arochukwu, these did not constitute an integrated political hierarchy (Northrup 1978; Ottenberg 1970). The Arochukwu oracle traders are in fact much more relevant to discussions of alternate pathways to complexity, and we will return to them below.

In fact, Fortes and Evans-Pritchard's observation has proven to be remarkably robust (Netting 1990: 56–7; Shipton 1984, 1994; Taylor 1975: 34; Vengroff 1976). Hierarchical, statelike forms of political organization turn out, in much of agrarian eastern and southern Africa, to be just as likely to occur in the context of extensive agricultural systems and easy rural mobility, with population densities under four persons/km^2 in the case of the complex Lozi polity (Gluckman 1951). Leaders competed with each other to attract as subjects shifting cultivators who moved frequently and did not ordinarily establish heritable property rights. Descent-based lineage systems (e.g., the Tiv of Nigeria, the Nuer of Sudan) may occupy regions of high population pressure in which the segmentary lineage organization is well suited to expansion into the neighboring lands of non-kin (Sahlins 1961; Stone 1996: 188–94). Here, land was inherited from agnates and there were elaborate systems of land clientage for those who could not obtain adequate holdings.

As Netting (1990: 46, 56) has pointed out, this inverts common evolutionist assumptions (with a pedigree extending back to the publication of Morgan's *Ancient Society* in 1877) that link heritable property rights with political hierarchies and kin-based societies with free, communal access to resources. Heritable property rights emerge as resources become scarce through population increase and intensification, but occur at every political level from the autonomous village through states and empires (Netting 1990: 49). That these property rights do not generally or permanently become an instrument of class oppression appears to reflect an African ideal of "fairness in flexibility," according to which "access to land should go to those who need it and can use it, and no one should starve for want of it" (Shipton 1994: 350). Netting (1990: 59, 61) concludes that "political centralization, valuable as it may be for organizing territorial defense and promoting regional exchange, does not appear to be directly implicated in the efficient functioning of intensive agriculture under rural demographic pressure." In some cases, such as the Gamo of the south-central Ethiopia highlands, the logic of permanent intensive agriculture at high population densities (200–1000/km^2) appears to have militated against the emergence of the state. Here, although the basic political unit was a neighborhood (*guta*), vast federations were created by conquest, with a balance of power between priests (who would be kings) and citizens' assemblies successfully preventing the consolidation of hierarchy (Abélès 1981; Netting 1990: 58).

These African studies can thus contribute to the important archaeological critiques (e.g., Feinman 1995; Feinman and Neitzel 1984; McGuire 1983; Paynter 1989; Roscoe 1993; Saitta and Keene 1990; Yoffee 1979) of what Yoffee (1993) calls the "holistic" model of evolutionary change, in which economic inequality and control, heterogeneity and social stratification, hierarchy, power, centralized authority, and prestige are assumed in various combinations or all together to be systematically linked in an evolutionary lock-step. The complex narrative that was constructed out of nineteenth-century dichotomies is no longer acceptable as a general account of the development of human society. With the universal relevance of various elements derived from these dichotomies in question, mechanistic models identifying them as subsystems of homeostatic cultural systems have consequently been rejected. In their place, human actors, not reified systems, take pride of place as agents of culture change (Brumfiel 1992; Eisenstadt et al. 1988a). Chiefdoms, previously situated in passive functionalist/adaptationist theoretical mode, are now recast, with the emphasis on political leaders as agents and strategizers (Earle 1991a, 1991b).

Despite this welcome shift in emphasis, the dichotomizing polarities of the nineteenth century still shape research approaches and priorities. Among the most deeply embedded concepts is the notion of change from simple to complex social forms as successive differentiation from incoherent homogeneity to coherent heterogeneity involving the emergence of specialization and hierarchy (Crumley 1995; Rowlands 1989b; Spencer 1971). For Herbert Spencer, writing in 1857, the degree of hierarchical differentiation was the essence of political complexity. His political typology of simple (autonomous village), compound (chiefdom), doubly compound (state) and trebly compound (empire) societies was adopted by Carneiro (1981: 45) in his influential discussion of chiefdoms. Spencer's (1971) ideas on progress and evolution were shaped by an organic analogy of ontogenic unfolding, in which the elements of each succeeding evolutionary stage are present in earlier phases. In archaeology, this metaphor can easily lead to teleology in the quest for centralized hierarchy and control in non-state societies presumed to be the ancestors of future states, as Shennan (1993: 53) points out.

The pervasive metaphor of complexity as hierarchy continues to shape research priorities by privileging the search for vertical differentiation in the archaeological record, a point that Ann Stahl, Rod McIntosh and Raymond Asombang also explore in their contributions to this volume. In recent years, the unilineal shape of this quest for emergent verticality has attracted comment and criticism, accompanied by calls for exploration of models of horizontal complexity, of systems of diffuse, decentralized, consensus-based, or horizontally counterpoised power, and of the variety of pathways to complexity that can be detected in human history (e.g., Arnold 1996; Blanton et al. 1995; Crumley 1979, 1987, 1995; Drennan 1996; Ehrenreich et al. 1995; Feinman 1995; Morris 1997; Nelson 1994; Price and Feinman 1995; Stone 1997; Yoffee 1993). Africa has much to offer to this discussion, since critiques of narrowly construed hierarchical approaches to complexity in African political systems go back almost fifty years. These critiques open up issues of particular relevance to recent archaeological concerns with documenting variability in intermediate-level societies.

African perspectives

As we have seen, Fortes and Evans-Pritchard's (1940) influential classification of political systems in Africa, true to its intellectual roots in the Durkheimian enterprise and Maine's studies of ancient law, seriously considered only two major types: those with centralized authority, administrative machinery and judicial institutions, and those without, for which the structure of order was provided by kinship. Their approach provoked a deluge of negative commentary. Both Brown (1951) and Kaberry (1957) pointed out that lineage organization was not the only structural principle ordering acephalous societies: in numerous cases, horizontal, cross-cutting associations – such as age sets, secret societies, cult groups, and title societies – were important in creating complex political structures. Such associations also played significant political roles in some societies where central authority was also present, such as West Africa's Mende and Yoruba and virtually all of the Lakes kingdoms in East Africa. The diversity of acephalous organization forms in Africa has been wrestled into a variety of alternate classifications (e.g., Cohen 1965; Eisenstadt 1959), the most elaborate of which recognized four types and three subtypes (Middleton and Tait 1958). Horton (1971), in an important article too often overlooked by non-Africanists, recognized, in addition to Fortes and Evans-Pritchard's segmentary lineage systems, two other, more complex forms of organization found in acephalous societies: one is the dispersed, territorially defined community, consisting of a local confederation of lineages of mixed origin, (the result of disjunctive migrations into the area), integrated politico-ritually by cult organizations; the other is the large compact village, in which a substantial population aggregation (as high as 11,000 in the case of the Yakö of southeastern Nigeria [Forde 1964]) is horizontally integrated by a variety of associations, cults, and secret societies. Often, a conciliary body of title-holders or cult

priests holds moral, ritual and/or juridical authority. In both cases, considerable complexity has emerged in the absence of centralized authority. As Dillon (1990: 1) points out, although studies of elaborate non-centralized systems have a long tradition in Africa – including the Tallensi, Lowili, Anuak, some Igbo polities, and the Yakö – the literature reflects little agreement on how these systems are to be understood. Consequently, they tend to be overlooked in general accounts of cultural evolution (e.g., Johnson and Earle 1987), an example of the "winnowing of variability" to which Ann Stahl refers in her contribution to this volume. However, the study of complex, horizontally integrated societies is essential for understanding the extent to which – and under what circumstances – alternatives to the development of hierarchy are pursued.

Horizontal complexity: an Igbo example

The Igbo (formerly written as Ibo) provide a different configuration for non-centralized organization of populations numbering in the thousands. They are organized into over 200 separate, clustered village groups in southeastern Nigeria, each one with its own name, internal organization, and central market. Each group has its own characteristic rituals and other cultural features that distinguish it from its neighbors. There is, in fact, a great deal of variation among Igbo groups, reflecting differing patterns of contact and accommodation with other societies. The village groups range in size from several thousand to over 75,000 people. The Afikpo village group (Figure 1.1), with twenty-two villages and a population of 26,000, provides an example of the spatial organization of these entities (Ottenberg 1971). Each village group is organized on the basis of segmented patrilineal descent groupings and associations, particularly age sets and grades, secret societies, and title societies. Village governance is conducted by direct democracy (all adult males); at the level of the village group, which represents the largest unit of regular political action, a representative system is adopted. Although the present-day system of governance of sprawling village groups by consensus of elders is undoubtedly a product of the centralized power of the colonial and post-colonial state, it is not clear whether the Igbo were differently, perhaps more centrally, organized in the pre-colonial period (Ottenberg 1971: 312). What we can say is that the British who first entered the Igbo area reported finding no traditional rulers, in contrast to the situation they observed elsewhere, such as among the Igala to the north and the Yoruba to the west.

Researchers have long puzzled over why the Igbo, who were deeply involved in the oil palm and slave trade in the

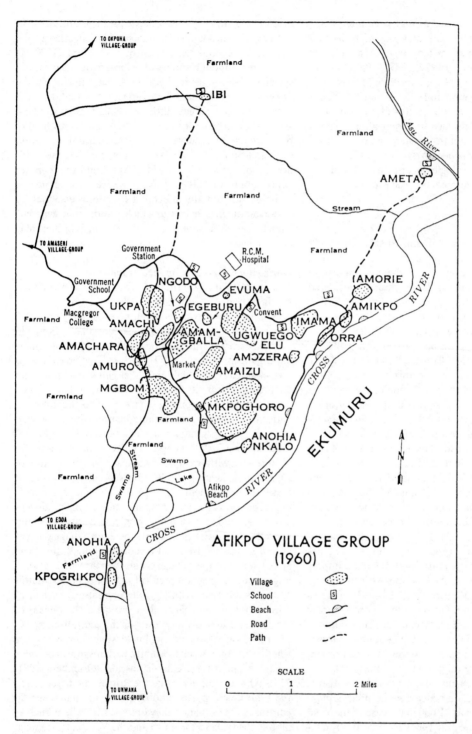

Figure 1.1   Afikpo village group (reproduced with permission from Leadership and Authority in an African Society *by Simon Ottenberg, © University of Washington Press 1971).*

eighteenth and nineteenth centuries, did not develop political structures comparable to Ashanti or Benin under seemingly comparable conditions. In *Trade Without Rulers*, Northrup (1978) showed how complex merchant networks expanded throughout Igbo country, not through regulation by central authority, but in the context of the religious institution of the local oracle of one Igbo village group, the Arochukwu. The oracle, the *Ibini Okpabe*, developed a reputation for its power in resolving disputes, settling warfare, ameliorating misfortunes due to sorcery, and advising on important undertakings. It was believed to kill anyone harming its agents, and under the oracle's protection, the Arochukwu traveled widely, and established colonies and trading alliances, bringing their oracle shrine and its services to all groups wishing it. The obstacles that consensus-based village governance posed to the need of traders to reach rapid decisions were solved by the growth of secret societies and title-taking associations among the trading communities. Through these organizations men could rise to positions of power as political leaders, judges, and peacemakers (Northrup 1978: 108). In some places, these societies replaced village councils of elders as the primary structure of governance. It was the centralizing nature of these developments that led Stevenson to see an "emergent Ibo state," as mentioned earlier. But Northrup makes it clear that the Arochukwu maintained a segmentary organization and never created a central structure of authority over multiple village groups.

The Igbo case material illustrates a number of important points. First of these is the significance of cross-cutting associations to the development of complexity. The Igbo have an especially intricate association system, incorporating age sets, age grades, secret societies, and title groups; for example, an adult male in the Afikpo village group may belong to over fifteen different descent, residence, and associational groups (Ottenberg 1971: 305). If we can, as Paynter (1989: 369) suggests, recast complexity as *the degree of internal differentiation (horizontal as well as vertical) and the intricacy of relations within a system*, the Igbo are complex. Furthermore, they used associations to engage effectively in regional trade on a large scale, a phenomenon that has also been described in Central Africa (Janzen 1982). In this case, the trading activities of the Arochukwu resulted in the development of a specialized decision-making apparatus that functioned simultaneously and in parallel with the normal, sequential hierarchy[1] of Igbo village groups. While a simultaneous hierarchy as defined by Johnson (involving permanent, ranked, decision-making structures, and leadership positions) has not emerged, local sequential hierarchies have been transcended, without undergoing structural change in most cases, by the emergence of specialized decision-making within regionally organized horizontal subgroups. This permits considerable increase in complexity without recourse to integrated vertical control hierarchies.

Elman Service (1962: 165) stressed the importance of sodalities (as he called horizontal associations) in integrating tribes, but postulated that at the level of chiefdom, sodalities largely disappeared, their integrative function being replaced by redistribution. In this, the presence of sodalities in some African states did not deter him (Service 1962: 165), perhaps because Polynesian chiefdoms were his primary model and, in them, associations are absent or of minor importance. For Sahlins (1968: 23) as well, associations were "more like fraternal orders with chapters established in different locales – so that for the price of a secret handshake one may be able to cadge a free lunch in another place," and of little relevance to higher levels of political organization. Never actively linked to complexity in any case, associations virtually disappeared from discussion with the demise of the concept of "tribe." It is time to recall them to active duty, this time identifying them as one potential modality of emergent complexity.

As a second and related point, associations such as secret societies and title-taking associations provide an arena, certainly for the Igbo as well as more broadly in Africa, for the elaboration of individualistic displays of prestige and wealth. These displays may be linked to political influence or power, but can also be used to channel wealth and ambition in such a way as to impede political consolidation. In some cases, such as Kongo and Ashanti, costly title-taking ceremonies are a key strategy to obtaining a position with the political hierarchy. But in the case of the Igbo, title-taking occurs in the absence of political centralization. Individuals gain prestige by taking progressively higher titles, each of which costs more than the previous one, and brings more influence. Access to titles is unrestricted. The Igbo *Ozo* title system, for example, involves a process of progressive ritual purification with the goal of bathing one's personal god in wealth and purity. Elaborate feasts and payments to the title society are required (Henderson 1972; Ottenberg 1971). Historical accounts of title-holder burials indicate that they can be extremely elaborate, involving sumptuous grave goods, slaves (in some places), and ostentatious public ceremonies (Shaw 1977: 98–9).

In this light, it is possible to consider the fabulous late first millennium burial and ritual bronze deposits of Igbo Ukwu, which, if discovered elsewhere in the world would likely be taken as evidence for chiefship and attached specialists, as products of a non-centralized society. Shaw (1977) suggests that the individual buried with elephant tusks, copper crown, pectoral, anklets and staff, and over 100,000 imported glass and carnelian beads (Figure 1.2) was a high status title-holder in a non-hierarchically organized society. The elaborate cast bronze vessels and regalia found in a repository (Figure 1.3) near the burial are thought to be the remains of the title-holder's *obu*, a kind of temple within his domestic compound in which are kept the ritual and ceremonial materials used in connection with the title system and in communicating with the spirits of the former members of the lineage in order to secure their favor (Shaw 1977: 99). It is, of course, possible that Igbo Ukwu represents a much more hierarchically organized society than existed historically in Igboland. Political devolution (from hierarchical systems in the past to non-hierarchical systems historically) on a significant scale has been suggested for Melanesia (Friedman 1981) as well as parts of Africa (e.g., Ekeh 1990; Ekholm Friedman 1991). Within the context of Yoruba–Igbo tensions since independence, the interpretation of Igbo Ukwu and the Igbo past has been, and remains, a highly charged issue (Afigbo 1996; Onwuejeogwu 1981). But for archaeologists, the challenge posed by the Igbo Ukwu material is the existence of a persuasive, non-hierarchical alternative interpretation, with many identifiable historical referents and correspondences.

How would we go about evaluating these two competing hypotheses? Were survey to reveal a settlement pattern of village groups, each comprising a cluster of villages, some large, some small, surrounded by an empty zone of farmland, would the possibility of non-hierarchical organization spring to mind? Or would we be tempted to see an embryonic chiefdom and its buffer zone? This is of course hypothetical, since no survey or other archaeological work has been done around Igbo Ukwu since the excavations of the burial and repositories. Ann Stahl's (1993) prescription for evaluating direct historical analogies provides some guidance. She recommends moving back through time from an early twentieth-century baseline, constructing a series of analogies from successively earlier time periods, using diverse, but temporally related sources for each time unit. Wherever possible, archaeological data should be incorporated, especially where contemporaneous archival, ethnohistoric, or ethnographic sources exist for an archaeological site. By focusing on successively earlier points in time, it discourages the practice of "time travel" that results from applying twentieth-century models to prehistoric sites without

reference to historic transformations (Stahl 1993: 249).

The rigorous methodology outlined by Stahl certainly points the way. Yet it is worth pondering how extensive the archaeological data requirements would have to be to allow us to distinguish a system of ascribed differences within a hierarchy of political control from a ranked, acephalous system of achieved differences such as that described for Igbo title associations. In this case, I am inclined to Steve Shennan's (1993: 54) suggestion that our aim should be to attend first and foremost to "reportage," describing our archaeological observations in terms that are as theory-neutral as possible (in much the manner that Thurstan Shaw [1970] in fact reported the Igbo Ukwu material). As archaeologists come increasingly to grapple with the issue of equifinality – i.e., that different conditions can produce similar archaeological patterns – the need to insure that our reports do not pre-empt particular interpretations or theoretical positions from the outset becomes crucial (Nelson 1994: 3; Shennan 1993: 54).

As a final point, the Igbo examples underscore the significance of ritual in understanding increasing complexity. Ritual reduces "scalar stress" (i.e., social strains engendered by increasing numbers of people) in large sequential hierarchies not primarily because of the opportunities that it provides for "passive stylistic signaling" – as Johnson (1982: 405) suggested – but because the combination of fear, belief, supernatural sanctions, and fines that typically accompany ritual is effective in securing compliant behavior and resolving disputes. Bargatsky (1988) has also noted that ritual ceremonies have important components for decision-making and integration in large groups. Africa offers many opportunities to apprehend ritual as something more than "generalized feather-waving" (Johnson 1982: 405). Cult associations and secret societies are, after all, ritual corporations that own property and control socially recognized resources (Apter 1992: 55). Through their control of ritual technology and ritual knowledge which allows members to harness ritual power and direct it to specific ends, they have potent political roles. They also mobilize labor and wealth through payment of membership and initiation fees, payments for ritual services, and fines for infractions. And, as we are reminded by Evans-Pritchard's (1940: 186, Plate XXV) account of a 50–60 foot (15–18 meter) high tumulus built last century by followers of the Nuer prophet Ngundeng of the cult of the Sky-god Deng, they can direct resources to collective projects of significant scale.

We have seen the importance of ritual potency (of the Arochukwu oracle) and purification (of the Ozo men) in enlarging the arena of potential political action and the political influence of those involved. The role of ritual

Figure 1.2   Reconstruction of the Igbo Ukwu burial. The corpse is seated on a stool, its arms supported by copper brackets. (Original painting by Caroline Sasson, reproduced with permission of Thurstan Shaw [see Shaw 1970])

Figure 1.3.   Reconstruction of ritual deposit at Igbo Ukwu. Many of these are lost wax bronze castings of great artistry. (Original painting by Caroline Sasson, reproduced with permission of Thurstan Shaw [see Shaw 1970])

and supernatural power in the emergence of power hierarchies has been hotly debated. Those who maintain that any power differential must lie in control over labor through control of subsistence remain skeptical of the idea that populations can be drawn into sociopolitical systems through the "smoke and mirrors" of religiously sanctioned centrality (Earle 1991a: 8). But the African data unambiguously support the idea, elegantly articulated by Netting (1972), that religious modes of focusing power are often primary in overcoming the critical structural weaknesses of non-centralized societies:

> To integrate a number of [localized, autonomous] units or to allow an existing unit to expand without fission, ways must be found to keep the peace while enlarging personal contacts beyond the range of kin group and locality . . . The overwhelming need is not to expand existing political mechanisms (they are in certain respects radically inelastic) but literally to transcend them. The new grouping must be united, not by

kinship or territory alone, but by belief, by the infinite extensibility of common symbols, shared cosmology, and the overarching unity of fears and hopes made visible in ritual. A leader who can mobilize these sentiments, who can lend concrete form to an amorphous moral community, is thereby freed from complete identification with his village or age group or lineage. (Netting 1972: 233)

Segmentary states and heterarchical formations

Netting cites the Jukun (Nigeria) and Alur (Uganda–Zaire border) as examples of the ritually centralized polities that can emerge as larger moral communities take shape. As described by Aidan Southall (1956) in a classic monograph, the Alur offer several insights to those interested in processes of centralization. First, the Alur represented the spread of a minimally centralized political system, in the absence of force or material inducements, among ethnically diverse groups who invited immigrant ritual leaders to come and rule over them. What they sought from the immigrant leaders was the ability to make rain and arbitrate disputes. In such systems of sacred kingship Southall (1989: 211–12), like Netting, sees the "pivot between egalitarian and hierarchical society, between the monopoly of the imaginary and the material means of production." Second, both lineage groups and central political administration were important in the organization of the resulting polities, in contradistinction to Fortes and Evans-Pritchard's (1940) lineage/centralized government dichotomy. Southall coined the term segmentary state to refer to polities in which ritual suzerainty extends beyond the central, core domain to which political sovereignty is confined (Southall 1956, 1988b, this volume).

The segmentary state concept has proven extremely useful in identifying a particular kind of polity that has its basis in ritual, personal, and charismatic authority rather than in effective coercion or control. The similarities of the segmentary state and Tambiah's "galactic polity" in Southeast Asia seem to indicate "the presence of a cluster of functionally related features: governance based primarily on personal ties of the ruler, and the concomitant absence of an effective and spatially dispersed bureaucracy" (Houston 1993: 144). The segmentary state has been "exported" from Africa to a wide variety of situations ranging from Late Classic Maya (Houston 1993: 142) and Post-Classic Maya (Fox 1987) to the vast Vijayanagara empire of India (Southall 1988; Stein 1977), raising some concerns about the utility of a concept that can cover situations so different in scale and complexity (Houston in press). Southall argues (this volume) that the segmentary states operating under different modes of production (domestic vs. tribute) will look very different, despite the similarity of underlying process.

It is quite common to find in African segmentary states a pattern of power counterpoised between a king and either associations (such as secret societies or cults with titled elders) and/or a council of lineage heads. This mother lode of African case material has not yet been mined by those interested in heterarchical political organization (e.g., Crumley 1987, 1995; Ehrenreich et al. 1995). In the case of the Yoruba, for example, the sacred king (*oba*) of a Yoruba city state has no power to coerce his subordinate chiefs, who control the kingdom's army. As one of several mechanisms for curbing the size and political power of the royal lineage, princes are excluded from holding political positions or inheriting the *oba*'s wealth, although they may hold administrative positions (Lloyd 1960). Even in the case of the sacred paramount, the *Alafin* of Oyo ("Lord of the World and of Life, Owner

of the Land, Companion of the Gods"), power was limited in practice by opposing it to certain strong corporations, of which the most important was the *Oyo Mesi*, or governing council of titled lineage heads. The *Oyo Mesi* can reject the *Alafin* and demand his suicide, while the *Alafin* in his turn has no power to collectively dismiss the *Oyo Mesi* from office. The conflicts created by the distribution of power between the *Alafin* and *Oyo Mesi* are mediated by a second corporation composed of titled priests of the secret *Ogboni* Cult of the Earth (Morton-Williams 1967). Here, the ascriptively oriented power of the town and lineage chiefs is counterbalanced by power centers based on achievement – the elected *Oyo Mesi* and the egalitarian *Ogboni* cult whose membership is open to all (Chazan and Abitbol 1988: 42).

Principles similar to but much more limiting than those of Yoruba structure the sacred kingship in the Igbo city state of Onitsha, where Henderson (1972) describes a king (an Ozo title holder) who is *primus inter pares* among eight other Ozo priests with sacred powers very similar to his own. The king is, however, ritually marked and sequestered with his wives for the entirety of his reign in a sacred grove outside the city, unable to participate in daily community life or to control the other chiefs in any way. Power is distributed among the king, chiefs, and an alliance of age sets and the "collective incarnate dead" (masked dancers representing the ancestors) without any structurally coherent hierarchical relations.

Another balance of power configuration is exemplified by the Mende of Sierra Leone, where the power of secular chiefs in polities of up to 20,000 people was counterbalanced by the political authority of a secret society, the *Poro* (Little 1967). It has been suggested that *Poro* is a remnant of a previously more widespread distribution of secret societies (also called power associations) in Mande societies, including the Sudanic empires of Ghana and Mali (Brooks 1993: 44–6). In Central Africa, the Luba empire and Songye kingdom are additional examples of polities in which power is counterpoised primarily between chiefs and secret societies (de Maret, this volume; Reefe 1981: 205). The small-scale Cameroonian Grasslands polities described by Kopytoff and Assombang in this volume are similarly structured.

These examples illustrate a common theme in African polities: complex and counterpoised articulation of ritual and secular power. In some cases, such as Onitsha (and also Nyakyusa [Wilson 1959], Shilluk [Evans-Pritchard 1948], and Jukun [Netting 1972]), sacred kings, who are highly differentiated ritually, reign over a central ritual domain but do not govern (MacGaffey 1987). This is not to suggest that ritual and political domains are either separate or separable, as they assuredly are not. Rather, it is to point out that multiple hierarchies – political, administrative, and ritual – each with certain political tasks, are a regularly observed feature in African complex societies. The result is a range of societies with relatively weak vertical political control and extremely complex horizontal integration. Far from being referable to a category of "primitive" chiefdom, however, which implies early and imperfect attempts at hierarchy, some of these systems have long developmental histories in which the evolution of increasingly complex configurations designed to decentralize or distribute power can be discerned (e.g., Apter 1992).

Fortes and Evans-Pritchard (1940: 16) made it clear that the main issue in sacred kingship was indigenous conceptions of power, legitimacy, and prosperity, which Europeans did not share. A number of recent discussions have elaborated this theme. Jane Guyer, for example, has explored the problematic of wealth in Africa, considering how the concept was configured differently in historic African cultures than either in Melanesia or "under any straightforward political-materialist notion of status and accumulation" (Guyer 1995: 88). The concept of wealth-in-people (as opposed to wealth-in-things) – embodying the idea that rights in people could be the basis of accumulation in Africa – was developed in the 1970s, mainly by Miers and Kopytoff (1977), but it was also fundamental to Goody's (1976) analysis of the relations among land, "class," kin, and marriage in Africa vs. Eurasia. The concept has resonated widely and is now "generally invoked as a shorthand for many syndromes of interpersonal dependency (including slavery) and social network-building in Africa that clearly involve strategizing, investing, and otherwise cultivating interpersonal ties at the expense of personal wealth in material things" (Guyer and Belinga 1995: 106). Guyer and Belinga critique the notion of accumulation in the context of wealth in people, suggesting that the dynamic of expanding social networks is not merely about adding labor, for example, but about mobilizing different types of knowledge – technological, ecological, agricultural, and ritual – that make possible a successful life in the uncertain environments of the forest and savanna. Leadership is the capacity to do this effectively. Guyer and Belinga (1995) call this dynamic *composition*, and differentiate it from accumulation. We can usefully consider the concept of power from a similar standpoint, suggesting that leadership in many African societies involves the composition of networks of social and ritual power. This permits us to expand our conceptual arena beyond the notions of control and competition that have tended to dominate discussions in the archaeological literature.

Concepts of power[2]

Archaeological studies of complex society have tended to construe power in very Western terms: individualistic, rational, and secular. Most social scientists, archaeologists included, have accepted and used Weber's (1964: 152) definition of power (*Macht*) as "the probability that one actor within a social relationship will be in the position to carry out his own will despite resistance." In this view, power has four key attributes: first, it arises from relationships between social actors in a mutually acknowledged competitive or cooperative context; secondly, power is exercised for the achievement of practical ends through mechanisms of domination and submission; thirdly, it focuses primarily on the pursuit of individual rather than collective goals, since power is considered to be the outcome and expression of dyadic relationships; and finally, it is deployed by rational human agents who calculate the costs and returns of using different means in the pursuit of accepted goals. It is rationality that differentiates power from authority, which is accepted without reflection (i.e., it is legitimate), in Weber's view. The view of power as rational calculation tends to produce accounts of the exercise of power and political relationships that are secularly based, even when religious activities are being described. African philosophers such as Mudimbe (1988) have decried the tendency towards a universalizing stance in these accounts, in which the source and application of power relationships is almost always secular and unvarying in time and space.

Lukes (1978: 26) has argued that particular views of power arise out of and operate within particular moral and political perspectives; that the act of definition implies a particular view of the nature of society, political institutions, the goals of action, and the means used to achieve them. By logical extension, "the semantic equivalents of 'power' in different languages and cultures embody as much a view of society and human action as they do in the Western social sciences" (Arens and Karp 1989: xii). Thus, models of power that emerge from a Western cultural context may obscure the beliefs and experiences of those the social scientist seeks to understand (Clastres 1987).

As an example of this, Arens and Karp (1989: xvii) critique, in the light of several African case studies, Foucault's (1978) argument that "power is tolerable only on condition that it mask a substantial part of itself. Its success is proportional to its ability to hide its own mechanisms."

. . . we believe that the African societies analyzed . . . do more than merely "mask" the exercise of power with a more emphatic concern for the relationship between this and the other world. Members of these societies assert that the source of power resides in the interaction between natural, social, and supernatural realms. This contrasts with the ideal image of Western political systems. Arrangements in the liberal social democratic tradition typically draw attention to the common good and the consent of the governed as paramount ideological features, in order to obfuscate the potential exercise of power for the achievement of the political ends of a particular segment of society. In many African social systems, however, the exercise of political influence derives from access to and work upon the natural and supernatural spheres, both as a source of power to control others and as the legitimization for actions. As a consequence, power itself has a different cultural foundation, since it involves several domains ordinarily separated in experience and practice. (Arens and Karp 1989: xvii)

Thus, Fortes and Evans-Pritchard (1940: 17) remarked some time ago that "an African ruler is not to his people merely a person who can enforce his will on them. He is the axis of their political relations, the symbol of their unity and exclusiveness, and the embodiment of their essential values."

In a classic study of Bashu chiefs, Packard (1981) looked beyond the conventional political activities (tribute collection, levying of fines, competition, and succession struggles) they engaged in to consider the Bashu's own view of chiefship as primarily mediating between the world of homestead (order) and bush (disorder) forces (see Newbury 1991 for a more historical, less synchronous treatment than Packard's). Through central, ritual chiefship, the ritual powers of a host of subordinate local ritual leaders were consolidated and collectively brought to bear on the most fundamental issue facing Bashu society: the control of polluting forces that, if unchecked, would result in famine. Bashu believe that ritually powerful individuals are tempted to use power destructively and for their own ends in order to make names for themselves; sorcerers, for example, are defined by the fact that they act alone, horde wealth and do not share, and are generally opposed to the communal interests of society. Ritual leadership thus involves the creation of alliances with other ritual leaders to ensure that power is always properly socialized, legitimate, and morally warranted. An important goal of leaders is to create a sphere of effective ritual control. These alliances are important instruments of political expansion. But a fundamental purpose of the alliances was the creation of spheres of

ritual control and knowledge, and the core of each network was composed of groups that possessed ritual influence.

In this example, a number of themes emerge that we encounter recurrently in different parts of Africa: (1) Political leaders and competitors for authority seek resources (special knowledge, medicines) and the support of other ritual leaders to bolster their ritual powers; (2) the political arena is one of collective action because of the belief that ritual power deployed for individual ends is dangerous and a potential threat to the interests of society; (3) the payments received for ritual services are often not stored, to become the basis of personal wealth, but are expended in alliance formation to expand the zone of effective, collective, ritual action (although, as Guyer [1995: 89] points out, not all wealth-in-things was converted to wealth-in-people, because we know of vast storehouses of cowries, gold, and other goods). Under these circumstances, Weber's coercive notion of *Macht* is more usefully replaced with M. G. Smith's (1975:175) notion of power as *the capacity for effective action*. As Eugenia Herbert (1993: 2, 237) observed, power, in order to be translated into authority, requires a cosmology – an understanding of the forces that effect outcomes in the world and the knowledge to influence them – and cosmologies cannot be created by force or coercion. The mobilization by leaders of appropriate specialist knowledge and ritual power is a key element of the capacity for effective action in many African societies.

The issues touched on here involving knowledge-based (in contrast to wealth-based) political economies, and power strategies that involve collective action (as opposed to individual, exclusionary strategies) have also emerged as a focal point in the archaeological literature. In a recent article, Blanton et al. (1995) propose a "dual processual theory" to explain the development of complexity in Mesoamerica, incorporating a number of ideas on individualizing vs. group oriented (or collective) chiefdoms (Feinman 1995; Kristiansen 1991; Renfrew 1974) and their putative associated modes of finance (wealth vs. staple [Brumfiel and Earle 1987; D'Altroy and Earle 1985]) that have been put forward in the two decades since Renfrew (1974) first proposed the distinction. Many of the points already raised in this introduction resonate fully with concerns voiced by Blanton et al.: the need to consider different sources of power; the existence of different types of political economy; the overemphasis in the literature on political centralization, exclusionary strategies, and the development of inequality; the lack of attention to and understanding of collective political strategies. Although African primary case material was

Table 1.2. *Major elements of the dual processual model*

	Network	Corporate
Power strategy	Exclusionary/power monopoly sought; centralized	Power shared among multiple loci; segmentary, diffuse
Source of power	Objective	Symbolic
Political economy	Wealth-based: prominence linked to individual prestige in network of extragroup, prestige goods exchange	Knowledge-based; political action primarily local; concerned with maintenance of local solidarity
Scale of action	Regional, subject to inability to control trade partners at a distance; vulnerable to prestational competitors	Local, but can grow in scale through development of staple finance systems; prestige goods unimportant
Ideological strategies	Patrimonial rhetoric; manipulation of prestige goods systems	Communal ritual, collective representations; fertility and renewal emphasized
Archaeological manifestations	Elaborate prestige goods in individual graves; expanded production and standardization of prestige goods	Communal monuments; collective graves without elaborate prestige goods

Source: Summarized from Blanton et al. 1996.

only minimally utilized by Blanton et al. in constructing their argument (the main illustrative material is from Melanesia), it would certainly seem that African materials can be of particular utility in evaluating and refining the "corporate" (collective) strategy they describe. Furthermore, since the "network" (individualizing) strategy they outline is tied to a prestige goods/wealth finance model originally described for Africa (Ekholm 1972; Coquery-Vidrovitch 1969), the rationale for examining dual processual theory in the light of the African material is even stronger.

I have attempted to summarize the functionally interrelated elements of the dual processual model in Table 1.2.

It is important to note that the two processes are on the one hand posited to involve dissimilar and mutually antagonistic political economies, but on the other to be present in one degree or another in many societies, so that they should not be thought of as mutually exclusive. This equivocality makes testing the theory a bit difficult; nevertheless, we can begin by noting that we have already made the case that "corporate" (shared, or distributed) power strategies are common in African polities. And others have noted that prestige goods systems operate throughout Africa within a competitive, "hierarchical" sphere that is linked to and exists simultaneously with an "egalitarian" sphere of agricultural production con-

cerned with basic maintenance. Coquery-Vidrovitch (1969) called this the "African mode of production," a concept she advanced to account for the wide diversity of political structures within Africa that were fashioned out of relatively unvarying circumstances of economy, technology, and self-sufficient agricultural production. She proposed that under circumstances of abundant land and low agricultural productivity, African "states" could not emerge by exploiting agricultural surplus. Rather, they emerged as minorities were able to manipulate long-distance exchange to extract revenues. It was Ekholm (1972) who worked this idea into a prestige-goods model for Kongo, which Friedman and Rowlands (1978) employed in their "epigenetic model" for the evolution of civilization.

So the question raised by the widespread co-occurrence of prestige goods systems and "corporate" power strategies in Africa is whether Blanton et al.'s proposal that these are relatively unlinked aspects of two different processes of political action can be sustained. The African material does not generally support the idea that wealth-based and knowledge-based political economies are "antagonistic" and thus "likely to be temporally or spatially separated" (Blanton et al. 1996: 7). As Jane Guyer's work, discussed above, indicates, the concept of wealth-in-people and the associated concept of composition, by which leaders operate at both local and regional scales to align themselves with the necessary specialist and ritual knowledge to enable effective action, applies broadly in Africa. Such knowledge-based strategies operate concomitantly with prestige goods systems in many, if not most, African societies. Nor does there seem to be support for dichotomizing patrimonial rhetoric and communal, collective representation as different ideological strategies. Kopytoff (this volume) points out with reference to the Aghem that patrimonialism and populism are two contradictory parts of one system, such that the strongly patrimonial ideology of the sacred kingship is also strongly corporate and communal in perspective.

In a manner very similar to the tiny Aghem polity, the vast Lozi polity employed explicitly patrimonial rhetoric for the kingship, construing the polity as the king's estate. But, as the discussion of *silyela* above suggests, its resources do not belong to him, although he has rights in them which he holds as trustee for his people (Gluckman 1951). Lozi, as one of the very few sub-Saharan polities to have established large-scale staple finance, is of great interest for testing Blanton et al.'s model. Although the model predicts that prestige goods should be relatively unimportant, they are very significant for the articulation of political position. [On the other hand, the Shambaai of Tanzania have staple finance on a much smaller scale and few prestige goods, thus apparently conforming to the model (Feierman 1974)]. And the major royal rituals in the Lozi kingdom revolve not around the communal rituals of fertility and renewal predicted by the model, but around the graves of individual royal ancestors (Prins 1980). However, since the power of kingly ancestors to assure fertility and renewal is an important aspect of these rituals, we see again that Blanton et al.'s attempt to separate these two strands is highly problematic in the African context.

As a further example, we can consider Ashanti, well known for the flamboyant wealth displays of its *henes* (chiefs). Historically, this wealth emanated from prestige goods exchange via participation in long-distance trade. Using the dual process model, we would predict a centralized paramountcy with considerable exclusionary power. However, Ashanti, like other Akan polities, was a loosely bound confederacy with a highly decentralized paramountcy. The paramount chief "was restricted by a whole series of injunctions . . . read to him publicly on his enstoolment" (Rattray 1929, quoted in Mamdani 1996: 47). Should a chief make the least attempt to act on his own initiative, it was considered legitimate cause for destoolment. Before embracing the "corporate or network" model and reifying it as a dichotomy (a development that its authors do not appear to have intended),

archaeologists would be well advised to evaluate it carefully. The African evidence supports the position of a number of the commentators on Blanton et al.'s (1996) article, namely, that it is more useful to conceive of the various elements of *both* the corporate and network model as existing together, in tension, rather than as systematically related parts of a dichotomy.

The African case material suggests that under conditions of land availability (making it easy for people to vote with their feet), where individual leadership offices emerge, they likely involved shared, distributed, corporate power systems designed to block effective consolidation of power with emerging wealth differentials, such as those produced by incipient prestige goods systems. The wide diversity of African political systems can be seen in one sense as the outcome of the various ways in which individuals seeking to consolidate or manipulate power (with prestige goods systems as one prominent mechanism) have been constrained to a greater or lesser degree by coalitions of other individuals operating within a variety of corporate frameworks (age sets, cults, secret societies, descent groups) and promoting rival interpretations of power. Thus, cults or title-taking societies might appropriate "kingly" prestige goods as part of initiation fees for titled positions that exist as a check on kingly power. Examples of the dynamics of these power competitions and the varieties of political forms they produce among the Yoruba have been provided by Lloyd (1960, 1968, 1971) and Apter (1992).

Eisenstadt et al. (1988) suggest that our error in trying to understand the institutional setting of power has been the tendency to view political structure as a distinct sphere with specialized roles and organization. In Africa, we see that the major characteristics and boundaries of the system are shaped by a wide variety of coalitions of elites and entrepreneurs in various settings and their modes of control (in regulating power, creating systems of meaning, and articulating ideologies, for example). The particular outcomes of coalitional negotiation and competition will depend on: (1) the level and distribution of resources available to different groups; (2) the entrepreneurs or elites available or competing for resources and the articulation of their various group interests; (3) the nature of the conceptions informing the activities of the elites and entrepreneurs (Eisenstadt et al. 1988:13). As David Schoenbrun emphasizes in his contribution to this volume, although the potential for concentrating power exists wherever humans have wants, the struggle for dominion follows more than one path because the resources and the forms of power also differ.

Pathways to complexity

In addition to providing examples of the diversity of forms that African political systems can take, many of the chapters in this volume also address the issue of different trajectories of development through time. Ann Stahl discusses how the variation in archaeological sequences that is currently of great interest in theoretical discussions has been obscured until recently in Africa (and certainly elsewhere as well) by site selection criteria defined in terms of the grand evolutionary narrative. In choosing iron-using sites in sub-Saharan Africa for investigation, she argues, archaeologists have privileged towns, monumental architecture, or Great Tradition art (e.g., Benin, Ife). By this process, variation is winnowed out, diverting attention from the coexistence of and relationships between societies at different scales, ultimately ensuring that the African past mirrored the Big Sequence defined elsewhere. It also obscures an understanding of the variable response of local populations to interregional developments, concerns that have also been articulated by Gailey and Patterson (1987).

James Denbow's contribution provides an example of what an archaeology more sensitive to interstitial communities can look like. He uses the ecological conditions of production and the political structures of distribution to explore the shifting organization and relationships through time of foragers, agro-pastoralists, and pastoro-foragers in the Kalahari. The result is a picture of widespread and systematic relationships between what had once been thought of as "separate" Stone Age and Iron Age peoples. The shifting connections among these groups has been a long-term feature in the regional dialogue through which ethnic identities have been fashioned and transformed. Peter Robertshaw also picks up this theme and presents an analysis of archaeological data from Bunyoro-Kitara in the East African Great Lakes region that is sensitive to detecting contemporaneous polities at different levels of scale and integration. He concludes that only discarding the notion of the state as the goal of political evolution will permit exploration of the diversity of non-state, rather than "pre-state," polities.

Raymond Asombang and Rod McIntosh also target the implicit evolutionary notions that underpin investigations of urban forms in Africa. Both comment on Western representations of civilization and urbanism that considered monumental architecture and accumulated wealth as the signatures of the despotic power at the heart of these developments. This conceptual tyranny of the monumental has long foreclosed any examination or understanding of urban centers lacking obvious large-scale architecture or public works. The 33-hectare occupation mound of Jenné-jeno (by no means the largest of the Middle Niger tell sites – Togola [1993, 1996] has recorded mounds in excess of 80 hectares), for example, was known to French administrators and amateur archaeologists, who failed to appreciate its potential significance. Constructed of unbaked mud brick, the structures and city wall had long since decayed. Africa's historically peripheral status within complex society archaeology is directly attributable to the general lack of monuments and preciosities in the archaeological record of sub-Saharan Africa (such that Great Zimbabwe, Ife, and Benin, as representatives of a generally small set of African archaeological occurrences have become its canonical exemplars). It also flows from the discourse on primitivism that anthropologists and archaeologists helped create, partially as a consequence of black Africa's non-monumentality. Primitive society was constructed as a mirror image of modern state society (Kuper 1988), where the power of the state found its most obvious expression in elite wealth and monumental public works.

R. McIntosh suggests that ideas rooted in nineteenth-century biblical exegesis influenced Weber, Spengler, and other early theorists on the sociology of the city, from which ultimately derive our archaeological expectations for early cities. In this volume, S. McIntosh, R. McIntosh, and Asombang decouple the development of urbanism from the emergence of the state. In my case study, I consider the rapid growth of population settled on tightly packed clusters of tells around Jenné-jeno in the first millennium AD and find little evidence to suggest that hierarchical political organization emerged. Yet both the density and the scale of nucleated settlement go well beyond the level that archaeologists have historically labeled as characteristic of emergent urbanism. R. McIntosh suggests that some of the hamlets in the Jenné-jeno cluster were occupied by specialist producers (blacksmiths, fisherfolk), who participated in a centralized economy but resisted any loss of political autonomy. Asombang explores how space is structured around a ritual center that grows to urban proportions by the addition of newcomers who seek to ally themselves with the ritual power of a *Fon* (chief) in the Grassfields. In each of these cases, traditional archaeological conceptions of early urbanism are challenged.

Several contributors find the model of the "internal African frontier" developed by Igor Kopytoff (1987) to be extremely useful for conceptualizing historical processes of political development. Of particular interest from the perspective of alternate pathways to complexity is the model's description of a process in which larger, more complex polities at the center give rise, through the fission and dispersal made possible by land availability, to smaller polities of pioneers at the frontier. Jan Vansina (1990, this volume) describes how these Big Men, with their retinues of family members and hangers-on, colonized new areas and organized their extended family compounds ("Houses") into villages composed of several Houses. Subsequent political development could take a number of different forms, depending initially on how sucessful individual Big Men were at attracting followers, either through marriage, other kinds of alliance, and immigration.

Two factors shaped the political culture of these new groups: the models for civic and political organization that the immigrants brought with them and the principle of precedence, of being first, that is a key to legitimate authority in African societies. Thus Kopytoff envisions a process of social construction in these immigrant communities that constantly recreated with variations the political culture of the source area. The variants were created in the course of interaction with pre-existing groups or later arriving groups, and the struggle of newcomers to co-opt the mystical powers of the earliest settlers in relation to the land. The political order does not, in this model, evolve *sui generis* due to internal parameters such as population growth and intensification of land use, and thus contrasts with Boserup's (1965, 1981) well-known hypothesis. It takes shape and changes as a direct outcome of the interactions of populations in constant flux, of the political and cultural relations between the source area and the frontier, of the organization and strength of the interacting societies at the frontier. Where acephalous societies are involved, a hierarchy can emerge through the simple process of adding new layers of immigrants under the kin groups that settled the area first. The nature of these hierarchies may differ, however, as Fardon (1988) showed in a study of Chamba chiefdoms in Cameroon. While indigene/immigrant (or ethnic) distinctions were important in all Chamba chiefdoms, two polar types could be distinguished: *consociating*, in which ethnic difference was the basis for ritual cooperation, and complimentary offices and ritual functions were distributed among sections of the community; and *adsociating*, in which ethnicity was the basis for exclusion from office and ritual functions, which a dominant alliance attempted to monopolize. Like Fardon, David and Sterner (this volume) are struck by the tendency of Cameroonian polities in similar historical and ecological circumstances to develop very different concepts of leadership.

Although Southall (this volume) sees nothing in the Alur case that resembles an African frontier, Schoenbrun and Robertshaw (this volume) find it a powerful tool for modeling political developments in the Lakes region. There, as elsewhere in Africa, the wide diversity of political formations that exist can be seen as emerging from a common substrate of basic forms and ideological elements. Kopytoff makes this point for the Grassfields societies of Cameroon, Vansina for the Bantu of the equatorial zone, Schoenbrun for the Great Lakes Bantu, and David and Sterner for the Mandara of northern Cameroon. Southall (1989) has made the point strongly for the Nilotic Sudan. Robertshaw (this volume) suggests that the "Bigo culture" in Uganda, characterized by earthworks and distinctive painted pottery, may be an archaeological example of this kind of local variation imposed on a widespread core tradition.

Schoenbrun and Vansina offer us, through linguistic reconstruction, a method for viewing the conceptual and semantic shifts at the level of local actors that underlay the production of diversity. As Schoenbrun points out, the crafting of polity involved material resources, but also invisible resources, such as the manipulation and invention of forms of meaning (as, for example, the ability to nominate others as equal or unequal) and abstract units of social organization. By means of comparative historical linguistics, it is possible to reconstruct semantic histories of shifting meanings, retentions, and innovations, suggesting changing configurations of instrumental and creative power through time in different areas. Importantly, Schoenbrun's analysis opens up the issue of the changes in gendered identities and domains of control, reflected in shifts in word meanings, and implicated in the development of social complexity and the creation of institutional locations for the deployment of creative and instrumental power. For example, the extension, from formerly female domains, of the terms for "hearth" and "house" to include patriclan and patrilineage probably reflects the outcome of a struggle over gendered control of material and cultural resources: children, productive lands, livestock, and jural process.

An important result of these reconstructions of sequences of change is that while in some cases they track the trajectory of increasing centralization expected by evolutionary theories, in other cases, they do not. Vansina suggests that alternative pathways for more efficient cooperation among groups for security and economic reasons emerged without centralization whenever there was effective resistance to loss of local autonomy.

Similarly, in those areas where archaeological sequences are beginning to become available, some conform to an evolutionary pathway of increasing scale, wealth differentials, labor mobilization, political hierarchy, and specialization. But again, some do not. The Upemba sequence described by de Maret (this volume) is unusual in sub-Saharan Africa in providing a stunning series of well-preserved burials, which show a steady increase over many centuries in status differentiation reflected in number and types of grave goods. The sequence is especially crucial for demonstrating the very early, indigenous emergence of a prestige goods system based on copper. Yet, interestingly, grave goods virtually disappear with the emergence of the historic Luba kingdom. Robertshaw sees a fluctuating landscape of variable-sized polities over several centuries in the Great Lakes region. My own work focuses on how to approach the question of political organization in a case such as Jenné-jeno, which has some of the familiar attributes of emergent complexity (nucleation, population growth, and increasing scale) but not others (subsistence intensification, highly visible ranking or stratification, imposing public monuments). I conclude that archaeological theory is at present ill-equipped to evaluate such instances because our current conceptual toolkit for investigating complexity has been fashioned with only a subset of complex sites and societies in mind. In societies where political action and coordination is achieved through assemblies, councils, and other forms of horizontally arrayed or democratic structures, and not through conspicuous vertical control hierarchies, we have relatively little idea how we might recognize the material manifestations of such an organization.

Conclusion

The reinsertion of sub-Saharan Africa into comparative theoretical discussions on the nature, origin, and development of complexity provides an empirical base that is particularly suited to addressing recent concerns with counterbalancing archaeology's long-standing focus on vertical hierarchies with an understanding of flexible hierarchies, multiple overlapping hierarchies, and horizontal differentiation as alternative modes of complex organization. While it is certainly possible to identify African societies that look and function in many ways like classic Polynesian chiefdoms – with conical clans, elite control of craft production, and differential access of elites to land and, especially, cattle – the real story of interest, I have argued, lies in the many complex African societies that are not so configured. In many African kingdoms, the chief's domestic unit (including wives and slaves) is directly involved in subsistence pursuits; attached craft specialists are rare or non-existent; and it is the king's job to ensure adequate access to land for all his subjects. Conical clans

and control of succession through primogeniture are more the exception than the rule, adding a significant element of achievement to ascribed kingship as dozens of princes or other eligible members of the royal lineage compete during often protracted interregna to establish alliances among the many significant loci of power within the society in order to secure the kingship, frequently through council election.

In looking at these cases, it emerges clearly that power relations do not conform to the elite/non-elite dichotomy found in so many archaeological discussions. Rather, power relations involve categories of age, gender, descent, and association, often simultaneously (Cobb 1993: 51 makes a similar point). The successful maintenance of multiple power loci and institutional strategies that act to constrain and counterbalance the political role of chieftaincy/kingship are recurring themes. Such shared, distributed, corporate power systems, often fueled more by social than material wealth, may tend to emerge among food-producing peoples where agricultural land is relatively abundant, a condition that persists in large parts of sub-Saharan Africa, although it is increasingly rare elsewhere in the world. Under circumstances of land availability, people are free to respond to attempts at coercion by moving to the unsettled frontier, where new settlements grow by attracting other settlers, resulting in considerable cultural heterogeneity.

Is it possible that these conditions have permitted the persistence and proliferation in sub-Saharan Africa of a wide range of social types that were formerly much more widespread in the world, as David and Sterner suggest in their contribution? In this case, the industrial production of iron by family-based units in Sukur described by David and the massive nucleated settlement clusters at Jenné-jeno would be exemplars of formerly wide-ranging phenomena. Was it only once the frontier was "frozen" (Schoenbrun, this volume) that economic stratification and the politics of control and coercion arose, paving the way for progressive reduction in societal variety, most notably by the development of two or more major types of hierarchically organized state? David and Sterner's point is an intriguing one: ". . . if disparity in societal plans did become suddenly greater in the period following . . . food production, then we may expect the bulk of Holocene archaeological cultures to represent societal types either extinct or existing as relics in the historical record and ethnographic present. Surely this is a more liberating approach than to expend great efforts on forcing recalcitrant archaeological entities – the Harappan is a prime example, the Chacoan phenomenon another – into 'state-jackets' that must be strained to bursting to contain them?"

The African data do not generally support approaches that seek to explain the origins of complexity by circumscription or to describe complexity primarily in terms of chiefdoms based on economic stratification or control. The initial establishment of supralocal organization in sub-Saharan Africa more likely took the form of a central ritual authority, lacking any significant political power or particular economic advantage. It is possible that the historical lack of interest in the potential of ritual for providing a supralocal organizational focus may be corrected by more serious examination of the African case material. Similarly, the role of associations (sodalities) in creating complex organizational structures has not been adequately examined. In some cases, such as the Arochukwu oracle cult, it may be that associations can develop specialized decision-making structures permitting them to transcend the limitations of sequential hierarchies without developing simultaneous hierarchies. Full appreciation of the salience of these examples to theories of emerging complexity requires that we rethink earlier emphases on the emergence of vertical hierarchies and focus attention on the degree of internal differentiation (horizontal as well as vertical), and the intricacy of relations within a system, as Paynter (1988) suggested a decade ago.

At a time when the "captains and kings" (recast as warriors and chiefs) approach to complexity is encountering growing dissatisfaction (despite its considerable successes) because of its relatively narrow focus, an African perspective promises to broaden the empirical base for complex society studies in various and indispensable ways. African case material introduces us to a variety of salient factors in the organization and variation in complex societies that archaeological theory has not considered seriously to date, among them, social wealth (wealth-in-people), mobilization of knowledge and ritual power as important elements in supralocal organization, the role of associations in constructing shared, distributed, corporate power systems, the importance of understanding how the forms of resistance to loss of autonomy influence the form and structure of emergent hierarchies, and variation in the resources and forms of power. These considerations will take us into new theoretical territory and offer the potential of a largely untapped vein of insights into the emergence and development of complexity.

Notes

1. Sequential hierarchy refers to the supra-household decision-making structure characteristic of small-scale, egalitarian societies, according to Johnson's (1982) widely used terminology. Task evaluation and leadership are *ad hoc*.
2. The discussion of power in the first three paragraphs of this section is drawn from Arens and Karp's (1989) excellent article.

References

Abélès, M.
  1981 In search of the monarch: introduction of the state among the Gamo of Ethiopia. In *Modes of Production in Africa: The Precolonial Era*, edited by D. Crummey and C. C. Stewart. Beverly Hills: Sage Publications: 35–67.

Afigbo, A. E.
  1996 Central-South Nigeria and Igbo-Ukwu. *History in Africa* 23: 1–15.

Apter, A.
  1992 *Black Critics & Kings: The Hermeneutics of Power in Yoruba Society.* Chicago: University of Chicago Press.

Arens, W. and I. Karp
  1989 Introduction. In *Creativity of Power*, edited by W. Arens and I. Karp, Bloomington: Indiana University Press: xi–xxvii.

Arnold, J.
  1996 (ed.) *Emergent Complexity: The Evolution of Intermediate Societies.* Ann Arbor: International Monographs in Prehistory. Archaeological Series 9.

Bargatsky, T.
  1987 Upward evolution, suprasystem dominance, and the Mature State. In *Early State Dynamics*, edited by H. J. M. Claessen and P. van de Velde. Leiden: E. J. Brill: 24–38.
  1988 Evolution, sequential hierarchy, and areal integration: the case of traditional Samoan society. In *State and Society: The Emergence of Social Hierarchy and Political Centralization*, edited by J. Gledhill, B. Bender, and M. T. Larsen. London: Unwin Hyman: 43–56.

Blanton, R., G. Feinman, S. Kowalewski, and P. Peregrine
  1996 A dual-processual theory for the evolution of Mesoamerican civilization. *Current Anthropology* 37(1): 1–14.

Boserup, E.
  1965 *The Conditions of Agricultural Growth.* Chicago: Aldine.
  1981 *Population and Technological Change: A Study of Long-Term Trends.* Chicago: University of Chicago Press.

Brooks, G.
1993 *Landlords and Strangers: Ecology, Society, and Trade in Western Africa, 1000–1630.* Boulder: Westview.

Brown, P.
1951 Patterns of authority in Africa. *Africa* 21: 262–78.

Brumfiel, E.
1992 Distinguished lecture in archaeology: Breaking and entering the ecosystem—gender, class and faction steal the show. *American Anthropologist* 94: 551–67.

Brumfiel, E. and T. Earle
1987 Specialization, exchange, and complex societies. In *Specialization, Exchange, and Complex Societies,* edited by E. Brumfiel and T. Earle. Cambridge: Cambridge University Press: 1–9.

Carneiro, R.
1981 The chiefdom: precursor of the state. In *Transition to Statehood in the New World*, edited by G. D. Jones and P. R. Krautz. Cambridge: Cambridge University Press.

Chazan, N. and M. Abitbol
1988 Myths and politics in precolonial Africa. In *The Early State in African Perspective*, edited by S. N. Eisenstadt, M. Abitbol, and N. Chazan. Leiden: E. J. Brill: 28–59.

Claessen, H. J. M.
1984 The internal dynamics of the early state. *Current Anthropology* 25(4): 365–79.

Claessen, H. J. M. and P. Skalník
1978 (eds.) *The Early State*. The Hague: Mouton.
1981 (eds.) *The Study of the State*. The Hague: Mouton.

Claessen, H. J. M. and P. van de Velde
1987 *Early State Dynamics*. Leiden: E.J. Brill.

Claessen, H. J. M. and J. G. Oosten
1996 *Ideology and the Formation of Early States.* Leiden: E.J. Brill.

Clastres, P.
1987 *Society Against the State*. New York: Zone Books.

Cobb, C.
1993 Archaeological approaches to the political economy of non-stratified societies. *Archaeological Method and Theory* 5: 43–100.

Cohen, R.
1965 Political anthropology: the future of a pioneer. *Anthropological Quarterly* 38: 117–31.

Cohen, R. and E. Service
1978 (eds.) *Origins of the State: The Anthropology of Political Evolution*. Philadelphia: ISHI Press.

Coquery-Vidrovitch, C.
1969 Recherches sur un mode de production africain. *La Pensée* 144 (avril): 61–78.
1976 The political economy of the African peasantry and modes of production. In *The Political Economy of Contemporary Africa*, edited by P. Gutkind and I. Wallerstein. London: Sage.

Crumley, C.
1979 Three locational models: an epistemological assessment of anthropology and archaeology. *Advances in Archaeological Method and Theory* 2: 141–73.
1987 A dialectical critique of hierarchy. In *Power Relations and State Formation,* edited by T. Patterson and C. Gailey. Washington D.C.: American Anthropological Association.
1995 Heterarchy and the analysis of complex societies. In *Heterarchy and the Analysis of Complex Societies*, edited by R. Ehrenreich, C. Crumley, and J. Levy. Washington, D.C.: Archaeological Papers of the American Anthropological Association 6: 1–6.

D'Altroy, T. and T. K. Earle
1985 State finance, wealth finance, and storage in the Inka political economy. *Current Anthropology* 26: 187–206.

Dillon, R.
1990 *Ranking and Resistance*. Stanford: Stanford University Press.

Douglas, M.
1967 Primitive rationing. In *Themes in Economic Anthropology*, edited by R. Firth. African Studies Association Monograph 6. London: Tavistock: 119–47.

Drennan, R.
1996 One for all and all for one: accounting for variability without losing sight of regularities in the development of complex society. In *Emergent Complexity: The Evolution of Intermediate Societies*, edited by J. E. Arnold. Ann Arbor: International Monographs in Prehistory. Archaeological Series 9: 25–34.

Drennan, R. and C. Uribe
1987 (eds.) *Archaeological Reconstructions and Chiefdoms in the Americas*. New York: University Press of America.

Earle, T.
1987 Chiefdoms in archaeological and ethnohistorical perspective. *Annual Review of Anthropology* 16: 279–308.
1991a The evolution of chiefdoms. In *Chiefdoms: Power, Economy, and Ideology*, edited by T. Earle. Cambridge: Cambridge University Press: 1–15.

1991b Property rights and the evolution of chiefdoms. In *Chiefdoms: Power, Economy, and Ideology*, edited by T. Earle. Cambridge: Cambridge University Press: 71–99.

1991c (ed.) *Chiefdoms: Power, Economy, and Ideology*. Cambridge: Cambridge University Press.

Ehrenreich, R., C. Crumley, and J. Levy
1995 (eds.) *Heterarchy and the Analysis of Complex Societies*. Washington, D.C.: Archaeological Papers of the American Anthropological Association 6.

Eisenstadt, S. N.
1959 Primitive political systems: a preliminary comparative analysis. *American Anthropologist* 61: 200–22.

Eisenstadt, S. N., M. Abitbol, and N. Chazan
1988a The origins of the state reconsidered. In *The Early State in African Perspective*, edited by S. N. Eisenstadt, M. Abitbol, and N. Chazan. Leiden: E. J. Brill: 1–27.

1988b (eds.) *The Early State in African Perspective*. Leiden: E. J. Brill.

Ekeh, P. P.
1990 Social anthropology and two contrasting uses of tribalism in Africa. *Comparative Studies in History and Society* 32(4): 660–700.

Ekholm, K.
1972 *Power and Prestige: the Rise and Fall of the Kongo Kingdom*. Uppsala: Skriv Service.

Ekholm Friedman, K.
1991 *Catastrophe and Creation: the Transformation of an African Culture*. Chur: Harwood Academic Publishers.

Evans-Pritchard, E. E.
1940 *The Nuer*. Oxford: Oxford University Press.

1948 *The Divine Kingship of the Shilluk of the Nilotic Sudan*. Cambridge: Cambridge University Press.

Fallers, L.
1964 (ed.) *The King's Men: Leadership and Status in Buganda on the Eve of Independence*. London: Oxford University Press.

1973 *Inequality*. Chicago: University of Chicago Press.

Fardon, R.
1988 *Raiders and Refugees*. Washington D.C.: Smithsonian.

Feinman, G.
1995 The emergence of inequality: A focus on strategies and processes. In *Foundations of Social Inequality*, edited by T. D. Price and G. Feinman. New York: Plenum: 255–79.

Feinman, G. and J. Neitzel
1984 Too many types; an overview of sedentary pre-state societies in the Americas. *Advances in Archaeological Method and Theory* 7: 39–102.

Feierman, S.
1974 *The Shambaai Kingdom*. Madison: University of Wisconsin Press.

Flanagan, J. G.
1989 Hierarchy in simple "egalitarian" societies. *Annual Review of Anthropology* 18: 245–66.

Forde, D.
1964 *Yakö Studies*. London: Oxford University Press.

Forde, D. and P. Kaberry
1967 (eds.) *West African Kingdoms in the Nineteenth Century*. London: International African Institute.

Fortes, M. and E. E. Evans-Pritchard
1940 *African Political Systems*. London: Oxford University Press.

Foucault, M.
1978 *The History of Sexuality*, vol 1. New York: Pantheon Books.

Fox, J. W.
1987 *Maya Postclassic State Formation*. Cambridge: Cambridge University Press.

Fried, M.
1967 *The Evolution of Political Society*. New York: Random House.

1975 *The Notion of Tribe*. Menlo Park: Cummings.

Friedman, J.
1981 Notes on Structure and History in Oceania. *Folk* 23: 275–95.

Friedman, J. and M. Rowlands
1978 Notes towards an epigenetic model of the evolution of "civilisation". In *The Evolution of Social Systems*, edited by J. Friedman and M. Rowlands. London: Duckworth: 201–76.

Gailey, C. and T. Patterson
1987 Power relations and state formation. In *Power Relations and State Formation*, edited by T. Patterson and C. Gailey. Washington D.C.: American Anthropological Association: 1–26.

Gilman, A.
1991 Trajectories towards social complexity in the later prehistory of the Mediterranean. In *Chiefdoms: Power, Economy, and Ideology*, edited by T. Earle. Cambridge: Cambridge University Press: 146–68.

Gluckman, M.
1951 The Lozi of Barotseland in northwestern Rhodesia. In *Seven Tribes of British Central Africa*, edited by E. Colson and M. Gluckman. Manchester: Manchester University Press: 1–93.

Goldman, I.
1970 *Ancient Polynesian Society*. Chicago: University of Chicago Press.

Goody, J.
1970 Review of *Population and Political Systems in Tropical Africa* by R. F. Stevenson. *Political Science Quarterly* 85: 671–3.
1971 *Technology, Tradition and the State in Africa*. Oxford: Oxford University Press.
1976 *Production and Reproduction*. Cambridge: Cambridge University Press.
1977 Population and polity in the Voltaic region. In *The Evolution of Social Systems*, edited by J. Friedman and M. J. Rowlands. London: Duckworth: 535–46.

Gregg, S.
1991 *Between Bands and States*. Occasional Paper no. 9, Center for Archaeological Investigations, Southern Illinois University.

Guyer, J.
1995 Wealth in people, wealth in things – introduction. *Journal of African History* 36: 83–90.

Guyer, J. and S. E. Belinga
1995 Wealth in people as wealth in knowledge: accumulation and composition in Equatorial Africa. *Journal of African History* 36: 91–120.

Haas, J.
1982 *The Evolution of the Prehistoric State*. New York: Columbia University Press.

Harms, R. W.
1981 *River of Wealth, River of Sorrow*. New Haven: Yale University Press.

Harris, M.
1968 *The Rise of Anthropological Theory*. New York: Crowell.

Hastorf, C.
1990 One path to the heights: negotiating political inequality in the Sausa of Peru. In *The Evolution of Political Systems*, edited by S. Upham. Cambridge: Cambridge University Press: 146–76.

Henderson, R. N.
1972 *The King in Every Man: Evolutionary Trends in Onitsha Ibo Society and Culture*. New Haven: Yale University Press.

Herbert, E.
1993 *Iron, Gender, and Power*. Bloomington: Indiana University Press.

Hobsbawm, E. and T. Ranger
1983 (eds.) *The Invention of Tradition*. Cambridge: Cambridge University Press.

Horton, R.
1971 Stateless societies in the history of Africa. In *History of West Africa: Volume I*, edited by J. F. A. Ajayi and M. Crowder. London: Longman: 78–119.

Houston, S.
1993 *Hieroglyphs and History at Dos Pilas: Dynastic Politics of the Classic Maya*. Austin: University of Texas Press.
in press Deciphering Maya politics: Archaeological and epigraphic perspectives on the segmentary state concept. In P. Dunham (ed.) *Segmentary States and the Maya*.

Iliffe, J.
1995 *Africans: The History of a Continent*. Cambridge: Cambridge University Press.

Inikori, J. E. and S. L. Engerman
1992 (eds.) *The Atlantic Slave Trade*. Durham: Duke University Press.

Janzen, J. M.
1982 *Lemba, 1650–1930: A Drum of Affliction in Africa and the New World*. New York: Garland.

Johnson, A. W. and T. Earle.
1987 *The Evolution of Human Societies*. Stanford: Stanford University Press.

Johnson, G.
1982 Organizational structure and scalar stress. In *Theory and Explanation in Archaeology: The Southampton Conference*, edited by C. Renfrew, M. Rowlands, and B. Segraves. New York: Academic Press: 389–422.

Kaberry, P.
1957 Primitive states. *British Journal of Sociology* 8: 224–34.

Karp, I.
1978 New Guinea models in the African savannah. *Africa* 48: 1–16.

Kopytoff, I.
1987 The internal African frontier. In *The African Frontier*, edited by I. Kopytoff. Bloomington: Indiana University Press: 3–84.

Kristiansen, K.
1991 Chiefdoms, states, and systems of social evolution. In *Chiefdoms: Power, Economy, and Ideology*, edited by T. Earle. Cambridge: Cambridge University Press: 16–43.

Kuper, A.
1982 *Wives for Cattle*. London: Routledge & Kegan Paul.
1988 *The Invention of Primitive Society*. London: Routledge.

Lemarchand, R.
1977 In search of the political kingdom. In *African Kingships in Perspective*, edited by R. Lemarchand. London: Frank Cass: 1–32.

Little, K.
1967 The Mende chiefdoms of Sierra Leone. In *West African Kingdoms in the Nineteenth Century*, edited by D. Forde and P. Kaberry. London: International African Institute: 239–59.

Lloyd, P.
1960 The political structure of African kingdoms: an explanatory model. In *Political Systems and the Distribution of Power*, edited by M. Banton. London: Tavistock: 63–112.
1968 Conflict theory and Yoruba kingdoms. In *History and Social Anthropology*, edited by I. M. Lewis. London: Tavistock.
1971 *The Political Development of Yoruba Kingdoms in the Eighteenth and Nineteenth Centuries*. London: Royal Anthropological Institute, Occasional Paper 31.

Lovejoy, Paul
1989 The impact of the slave trade on Africa in the eighteenth and nineteenth centuries. *Journal of African History* 30: 365–94.

Lukes, S.
1978 Power and Authority. In *A History of Sociological Analysis* edited by T. Bottomore and R. Nisbet. New York: Basic Books: 633–76.

MacGaffey, W.
1987 Kingship in Sub-Saharan Africa. In *The Encyclopedia of Religion*, edited by M. Eliade, vol. 8. New York: MacMillan: 322–5.

Mamdani, M.
1996 *Citizen and Subject: Contemporary Africa and the Legacy of Late Colonialism*. Princeton: Princeton University Press.

Manning, P.
1990 *Slavery and African Life: Occidental, Oriental and African Slave Trades*. Cambridge: Cambridge University Press.

McCaskie, T. C.
1995 *State and Society in Pre-Colonial Asante*. Cambridge: Cambridge University Press.

McGuire, R.
1983 Breaking down cultural complexity: inequality and heterogeneity. *Advances in Archaeological Method and Theory* 6: 91–142.

Meillassoux, C.
1960 Essai d'interprétation du phénomène économique dans les sociétés traditionelles d'auto-subsistance. *Cahiers d'Etudes Africaines* 4: 38–67.

Middleton, J. and D. Tait
1958 (eds.) *Tribes Without Rulers: Studies in African segmentary systems*. London: Routledge and Kegan Paul.

Miers, S. and I. Kopytoff
1977 (eds.) *Slavery in Africa: Historical and Anthropological Perspectives*. Madison: University of Wisconsin Press.

Miller, J.
1988 *Way of Death, Merchant Capitalism and the Angolan Slave Trade 1730–1830*. Madison: University of Wisconsin Press.

Moore, C. B.
1974 (ed.) *Reconstructing Complex Societies: an archaeological colloquium*. Supplement to the American Schools of Oriental Research, 20. Ann Arbor.

Morgan, L. H.
1964 [1877] *Ancient Society: or Researches in the Lines of Human Progress from Savagery through Barbarism to Civilization*. Edited by L. A. White. Cambridge: Harvard University Press.

Morris, I.
1997 An archaeology of equalities? The Greek city-states. In *The Archaeology of City-States*, edited by D. L. Nichols and T. H. Charlton. Washington D.C.: Smithsonian Institution Press: 91–106.

Morton-Williams, P.
1967 The Yoruba kingdom of Oyo. In *West African Kingdoms in the Nineteenth Century*, edited by D. Forde and P. Kaberry. London: International African Institute: 36–69.

Mudimbe, V.
1988 *The Invention of Africa: Gnosis, Philosophy, and the Order of Knowledge*. Bloomington: Indiana University Press.

Nelson, B.
1994 (ed.) *The Ancient Southwest Community*. Albuquerque: University of New Mexico Press.
1995 Complexity, hierarchy and scale: a controlled comparison between Chaco Canyon, New Mexico and La Quemada, Zacatecas. *American Antiquity* 60 (4): 597–618.

Netting, R.
1972 Sacred power and centralization. In *Population Growth: Anthropological Implications*, edited by B. Spooner. Cambridge: MIT Press.
1990 Population, permanent agriculture, and pol-

ities: unpacking the evolutionary portmanteau. In *The Evolution of Political Systems*, edited by S. Upham. Cambridge: Cambridge University Press: 21–61.

Newbury, D.
1991 *Kings and Clans*. Madison: University of Wisconsin Press.

Northrup, D.
1978 *Trade Without Rulers: Pre-colonial Economic Development in Southeastern Nigeria.* Oxford: Clarendon Press.

Oberg, K.
1955 Types of social structure among the lowland tribes of South and Central America. *American Anthropologist* 57: 472–88.

Onwuejeogwu, M. A.
1981 *An Igbo Civilization: Nri Kingdom and Hegemony.* London.

Ottenberg, S.
1970 Review of *Population and Political Systems in Tropical Africa* by R. F. Stevenson. *African Historical Studies* 3: 231–6.
1971 *Leadership and Authority in an African Society.* Washington D.C.: American Ethnological Society Monograph 52. Seattle: University of Washington Press.

Packard, R.
1981 *Chiefship and Cosmology.* Bloomington: Indiana University Press.

Parkin, D.
1990 Eastern Africa: The view from the office and the voice from the field. In *Localizing Strategies*, edited by R. Fardon. Washington D.C.: Smithsonian: 182–203.

Paynter, R.
1989 The archaeology of equality and inequality. *Annual Review of Anthropology* 18: 369–99.

Peebles, C. and S. Kus
1977 Some archaeological correlates of ranked societies. *American Antiquity* 42: 421–48.

Price, T. D. and G. Feinman
1995 (eds.) *Foundations of Social Inequality.* New York: Plenum.

Prins, G.
1980 *The Hidden Hippopotomus.* Cambridge: Cambridge University Press.

Rattray, R. S.
1929 *Ashanti Law and Constitution.* Oxford: Clarendon Press.

Reefe. T. Q.
1981 *The Rainbow and the Kings: a History of the Luba Empire to 1891.* Berkeley: University of California Press.

Renfrew, C.
1974 Beyond a subsistence economy: The evolution of social organization in prehistoric Europe. In *Reconstructing Complex Societies: an archaeological colloquium,* edited by C. Moore. Supplement to the American Schools of Oriental Research 20. Ann Arbor: 69–85.

Renfrew, C. and J. F. Cherry
1986 (eds.) *Peer-polity Interaction and Socio-political Change.* Cambridge: Cambridge University Press.

Rodney, Walter
1972 *How Europe Underdeveloped Africa.* [Reissued 1982.] Washington, D.C.: Howard University Press.

Roscoe, P.
1993 Practice and political centralization. *Current Anthropology* 34(2): 111–40.

Roseberry, W.
1989 *Anthropologies and Histories.* New Brunswick: Rutgers University Press.

Rowlands, M.
1989a The archaeology of colonialism and constituting the African peasantry. In *Domination and Resistance*, edited by D. Miller, M. Rowlands, and C. Tilley. London: Unwin Hyman: 261–83.
1989b A question of complexity. In *Domination and Resistance*, edited by D. Miller, M. Rowlands, and C. Tilley. London: Unwin Hyman: 29–40.

Sahlins, M.
1958 *Social Stratification in Polynesia.* Seattle: University of Washington.
1961 The segmentary lineage: an organization of predatory expansion. *American Anthropologist* 63: 322–45.
1963 Poor man, rich man, big man, chief: political types in Melanesia and Polynesia. *Comparative Studies in Society and History* 5: 285–303.
1968 *Tribesmen.* Englewood Cliffs: Prentice Hall.
1985 *Islands of History.* Chicago: University of Chicago Press.

Saitta, D. and A. Keene
1990 Polities and surplus flow in prehistoric communal societies. In *The Evolution of Political Systems*, edited by S. Upham. Cambridge: Cambridge University Press.

Service, E.
1962 *Primitive Social Organization.* New York: Random House.
1971 *Cultural Evolutionism: Theory in Practice.* New York: Holt Rinehart and Winston.

1975 *Origins of the State and Civilization.* New York: Norton.

Shaw, C. T.
1970 *Igbo-Ukwu: An Account of Archaeological Discoveries in Eastern Nigeria.* London: Faber.
1977 *Unearthing Igbo Ukwu.* Oxford: Oxford University Press.

Shaw, T., P. Sinclair, B. Andah, and A. Okpoko
1993 (eds.) *The Archaeology of Africa. Food, Metals, and Towns.* London: Routledge.

Shennan, S.
1993 After social evolution: a new archaeological agenda? In *Archaeological Theory: Who Sets the Agenda?* edited by N. Yoffee and A. Sherratt. Cambridge: Cambridge University Press: 53–9.

Shipton, P.
1984 Strips and patches: a demographic dimension in some African land-holding and political systems. *Man* 19: 613–34.
1994 Land and culture in tropical Africa. *Annual Review of Anthropology* 23: 347–77.

Smith, M.G.
1975 *Corporations and Society: The Social Anthropology of Collective Action.* Chicago: Aldine.

Southall, A.
1956 *Alur Society: A Study in Processes and Types of Domination.* Cambridge: W. Heffer and Sons.
1960 Typology of states and political systems. In *Political Systems and the Distribution of Power*, edited by M. Banton. London: Tavistock: 113–40.
1970 The illusion of tribe. *Journal of Asian and African Studies* 5: 28–50.
1988a On mode of production theory: the foraging mode of production and the kinship mode of production. *Dialectical Anthropology* 12: 165–92.
1988b The segmentary state in Africa and Asia. *Comparative Studies in Society and History* 30 (1): 52–82.
1989 Power, sancitity, and symbolism in the political economy of the Nilotes. In *Creativity of Power*, edited by W. Arens and I. Karp. Bloomington: Indiana University Press: 183–221.
1996 Tribes. In *Encyclopedia of Cultural Anthropology*, edited by D. Levinson and M. Ember. New York: Henry Holt: 1329–36.

Spencer, H.
1971 Progress: its law and cause. In *Herbert Spencer: The Evolution of a Sociologist*, edited by J. D. Peel. New York: Basic Books.

Spielmann, K.
1994 Clustered confederacies: sociopolitical organiza-

tion in the protohistoric Rio Grande. In *The Ancient Southwest Community*, edited by B. Nelson. Albuquerque: University of New Mexico Press: 45–54.

Stahl, A.
1993 Concepts of time and approaches to analogical reasoning in historical perspective. *American Antiquity* 58 (2): 235–60.

Stein, B.
1977 The segmentary state in South Indian history. In *Realm and Region in Traditional India*, edited by R. Fox. Durham: Duke University Press: 3–51.

Stevenson, R. F.
1968 *Population and Political Systems in Tropical Africa.* New York: Columbia University Press.

Stone, E. C.
1997 City-states and their centers: the Mesopotamian example. In *The Archaeology of City-States*, edited by D. L. Nichols and T. H. Charlton. Washington D.C.: Smithsonian Institution Press: 15–26.

Stone, G. D.
1996 *Settlement Ecology: The Social and Spatial Organization of Kofyar Agriculture.* Tucson: University of Arizona Press.

Strathern, M.
1990 Negative Strategies in Melanesia. In *Localizing Strategies*, edited by R. Fardon. Washington, D.C.: Smithsonian Institution Press: 204–16.

Taylor, D.
1975 Some locational aspects of middle-range hierarchical societies. Ph.D. dissertation, City University of New York. Ann Arbor: University Microfilms.

Togola, T.
1993 Archaeological investigations of Iron Age sites in the Méma region (Mali). Ph.D. dissertation, Rice University. Ann Arbor: University Microfilms.
1996 Iron Age occupation in the Méma region, Mali. *The African Archaeological Review.* 13 (2): 91–110.

Trigger, B.
1993 *Early Civilizations: Ancient Egypt in Context.* Cairo: American University in Cairo Press.

Tuden, A. and L. Plotnicov
1970 (eds.) *Social Stratification in Africa.* New York: Free Press.

Upham S.
1990 (ed.) *The Evolution of Political Systems.* Cambridge: Cambridge University Press.

Vansina, J.
1989 Deep-down time: political tradition in Central Africa. *History in Africa* 16: 341–62.

1990 *Paths in the Rainforests.* Madison: University of Wisconsin Press.

Vengroff, R.
1976 Population density and state formation in Africa. *African Studies Review* 19 (1): 67–74.

Wason, P.
1994 *The Archaeology of Rank.* Cambridge: Cambridge University Press.

Weber, M.
1964 *The Theory of Social and Economic Organization.* New York: Free Press.

Wilks, I.
1993 *Forests of Gold.* Athens: Ohio University Press.

Wilson, M.
1959 *Divine Kings and the 'Breath of Men'.* Cambridge: Cambridge University Press.

Wood, W. R.
1990 Ethnohistory and historical method. In *Archaeological Method and Theory* 2: 81–109.

Wolf, E. R.
1982 *Europe and the People Without History.* Berkeley: University of California Press.

Yoffee, N.
1979 The decline and rise of Mesopotamian civilization: an ethnoarchaeological perspective on the evolution of social complexity. *American Antiquity* 44: 1–35.
1993 Too many chiefs? (or, Safe texts for the '90s). In *Archaeological Theory: Who Sets the Agenda?,* edited by N. Yoffee and A. Sherratt. Cambridge: Cambridge University Press: 60–78.

2

The segmentary state and the ritual phase in political economy

AIDAN SOUTHALL

The ethnography of the Alur segmentary state

The Alur taught me the practice of the segmentary state, as well as their language. I had to make it theory in my language, the most stereotypical and intractable form of distancing the Other.[1] The segmentary state is one in which the spheres of ritual suzerainty and political sovereignty do not coincide. The former extends widely towards a flexible, changing periphery. The latter is confined to the central, core domain. A number of such partially overlapping entities with political cores at the center of wider ritually based zones may be related to one another pyramidally at several levels. The Other may be partially assuaged by exploring the origin of the Alur segmentary state. Alur society emerged as a distinct entity in the sixteenth and seventeenth centuries, when Lwo migrants from the north crossed the Nile and moved west (Crazzolara 1950/51). The segmentary state of Atyak[2] became the largest among the Alur (Southall 1956: 349), because its early leaders and their following moved into a part of the country where they were able to develop the most favorable combination of agriculture and pastoralism, while also remaining beyond the disturbing influence of Bunyoro (Southall 1956: 9, 16). As they moved up into the highlands, they were able to incorporate (Southall 1970) small groups of earlier settlers (Okebo, Lendu, Madi, Abira, etc.) who belonged to quite different ethnic groups and spoke mutually unintelligible languages (Southall 1956: 16–24). I have not found it possible to relate the concept of the internal frontier to this situation in any meaningful way.

My account represents the most plausible hypothesis based on Alur traditions and elders' statements. The Atyak say the greatness of the king was obvious to the earlier settlers as soon as he arrived among them, so it was natural for them to pay homage to him. He could make rain (Southall 1956: 376–9) and provide food, drink, and entertainment. Descendants of earlier settlers say "the Atyak beguiled us with food." Other peoples also accepted their overlordship because they knew how to rule. When the Atyak ancestors arrived, they must have been a small, relatively homogeneous group of members of various Lwo lineages. They recognized a ritual leader, credited with superior ability to make rain and ensure the fertility of plants, animals, and women, but having no coercive power. They brought cattle, a few sheep, goats, and chickens, with some millet, beans, and spinach. They were not migrating long distances, but settled down to productive cultivation and herding whenever they stopped.

The population of earlier settlers was very sparse and they had fewer domestic animals, especially cattle, than the Atyak. There was little difference in tools or weapons, but the Atyak were organized on a larger scale with their extensive agnatic lineages and respect for a superior leader. They entertained the earlier settlers with beer, food, music, and dancing, offering ritual services in general and arbitration in disputes. The encounter was not violent and the process of interaction was very gradual, as each side observed and became familiar with the other in the daily activities of material and supernatural production. There may have been threats of force, but neither side speaks of forceful conquest.

> For relations of domination and exploitation to have arisen and reproduced themselves durably in formerly classless society, such relations must have presented themselves as an exchange and as an exchange of services. This is how they managed to get themselves accepted . . . and to gain the consent – passive or active – of the dominated . . . The services rendered by the dominant individuals or group must have involved, in the first place, invisible realities and forces controlling (in the thought of these societies) the reproduction of the universe and of life . . . The monopoly of the means (to us imaginary) of reproduction of the universe and of life must have preceded the monopoly of the visible material means of production. (Godelier 1978: 767, quoted in Southall 1991)

Such processes occurred in many parts of the world, over and over again, even if forceful conquest attracts more attention. The peaceful acceptance of Brahmin superiority, influence, and moral authority by South Indian peasants, without the aid of any coercive political force, is a case in point (Stein 1977: 66, 123, 144). At the very simplest level it is illustrated by the Plateau Tonga (Colson 1948: 272–83).

The Atyak polity was actually created by this process of the incorporation of foreigners (Southall 1970) and did not exist before. A new political element intruded as the process of incorporation took place, for the Atyak who had been lineage mates in a kinship order were now acquiring subjects in an embryonic political order. Those who accepted food, drink, entertainment, ritual services, and mystical supernatural benefits were expected to reciprocate, either with labor in the fields or with gifts of produce needed by the Atyak. The Lendu seem to have had little with which to reciprocate except their labor, although the Alur did make important borrowings from them, of dance magic, herbal lore, and material culture. The Okebo were able to provide the vital service of iron-working. The Alur had not been without iron, but it was scarce. The Okebo were both smelters and forgers. Here the Atyak gained ascendancy by the most immaterial payment for very solid services. In Alurland the Okebo had free access to land like everyone else. They lived in their own localized descent groups, were paid in kind for their hoes, spears, knives, and arrowheads, also taking them as offerings to the rulers for their mystical and adjudicative services. The Lendu gave more direct labor service, for which they were fed. This was a mark of subordination in the sense of a material one-way flow. Although the Lendu received recompense in food, it was an asymmetrical, unequal relationship. Lendu worked for Atyak, but Atyak did not work for Lendu. But the same one-way flow occurred among the Atyak, when ordinary folk went to dig the ruler's field and received a feast of beer and food. Among themselves there was a two-way flow, as each family in turn summoned all its neighbors to dig and provided a feast of beer and food.

My hypothesis differs in one fundamental respect from the account given by some Atyak rulers, who insist that they have always been rulers. But nothing has always been so. I make a logical explanation of how their polity came into existence. Once the process of incorporation began, it was accompanied by a parallel process of ritual elaboration and legitimation. The Alur conceived of three social strata: *rwodhi*, commoners and non-Lwo. *Rwodhi* may be glossed as nobles. *Rwoth* (the singular form of *rwodhi*). means the king or any ruler of a segmentary component group. One can describe a whole group as *rwodhi* in status, but one cannot refer to any individual member of it as *rwoth* unless he is a ruler. The wealth and polygyny of the ruling Atyak lineage enabled it to grow faster than any other, so that there are enormous numbers of nominal

rwodhi. The more distant their genealogical connection with the central ruling line, the more their social status and daily life approximates to that of ordinary commoners. The non-Lwo groups of Lendu, Okebo, and others ranked lower. Others might look down on them or prefer not to marry them, but their material disabilities were few. Royal and general polygyny, combined with clan exogamy, meant frequent marriage of Atyak Lwo with non-Lwo and Alur commoners with non-Alur.

A group of special ritual clans surrounded the monarch: the Padere were fire-drillers who started the king's fire and renewed the fires of the whole kingdom at each accession; the Panyong'a were softeners of the skins of wild game for the king's robes; the Padwur gave the man on whom the king stepped, pointing his spear at him at his accession, a symbolic human sacrifice; and the Palei had the right to the tail of the bull slaughtered at royal ceremonies, because they had tracked a lost bull up the river bed into the highlands, thus discovering the blessed land that became the core domain of the Atyak rulers. These clans basked in the aura of these highly honored, if only occasionally performed, ritual duties. Some of them also provided an embryonic staff of royal confidants and envoys.

The segmentary polity developed in practice from the hiving off of kings' sons from the central line in successive generations (Southall 1956: 181–228). Some two dozen such hived off segments could be traced over the last twelve generations recorded in oral tradition. Some prospered more than others. The larger ones were those which, like the central core domain, developed in the highlands and were among the oldest offshoots founded eight or more generations ago (from 1950). Some stagnated politically and demographically or even reverted to virtual commoner status. Some were invigorated by further infusions of kingship in the form of new king's sons. Each established a new localized segment of the Atyak lineage. Each achieved at least a ritual supremacy over other Alur lineages, either already there or attracted to them, and over non-Alur groups which they proceeded to incorporate in their hegemony. Some of the larger and more successful gave rise to their own internal hiving-off process, so that there were several levels of political segmentation within the Atyak segmentary state, all above the level of the localized lineage segments that formed the basic local communities.

There were two emphases: the dispatching of kings' sons from the center and the efforts of some peripheral groups to obtain them. I call the first "banishment" (Southall 1956:186) and the second "kidnapping."[3] Considerations of political as well as religious and mystical power were involved. The life cycle of the large, royal, polygynous homestead generated many problems. Sons reared with a sense of pride in their potential capacity to rule could throw their weight about, causing trouble among the king's followers, stealing their goats and harassing their wives, or even misbehaving with the king's own young wives. Rather than imposing discipline, the king could send his son out to the periphery to fend for himself and make his fortune politically and mystically speaking. It was banishment but also setting up a successful new political and ritual ruler, if he had the qualities to cope with the opportunity. He could be sent off with a small entourage, herd of livestock and food supply, a wife or wives, and perhaps his mother. "Go!" said the king, "tame the country over there," pointing to some distant hill.

Outlying commoner groups felt the need to have a king's son living with them, for the benefits that would flow. With the king's blessing he could provide all the same services on a lesser scale, generating new flows of exchange, reciprocity, mystical protection and well being, rain making, political leadership, arbitration, and adjudication. Commoners said that a king's son, even if only a child, could protect them from the wrath and costly reprisals of the king himself, if he was threatening to come and plunder them for some serious offence. They would send envoys to the king begging him to send a son to live among them, promising to treat him with the respect his royalty deserved. The king would say "Look down there in the valley. My son is playing there with his mother. Go and catch them and take them both." The banishment was half serious, the kidnapping half play-acting a ritual drama. Either resulted in an increase in secondary units of segmentary kingship within the realm as a whole and to an increase in the extent and intensity of kingship operating in the region. The kidnapping theme also dramatized the reluctance to accept the mystically dangerous kingly role, which also required certain personality characteristics to make it a success. This phenomenon is widespread in Africa (e.g., Wilson 1959: 28).[4]

The combination of foot transport, hilly terrain, a highly localized economy, no markets, and quite limited exchange meant minimal communication between the different components of the segmentary polity, apart from those close to one another, so that a centralized, unitary political organization was out of the question. There was a definite recognition of the greatness and seniority of the rulers of the core domain, although a few of the larger offshoots tended to claim autonomy and equality, which probably reflects colonial influences, especially the Uganda/Zaire boundary.

The hived-off units were supposed to send prestations of elephant tusks, lion and leopard skins, and cattle to the core domain at the death and accession of kings. For the core domain this was tribute, but for the sender it was more like a gift, voluntary recognition of the shared heritage of mystical power. The sacral power of kingship, to make rain and ensure fertility was ultimately derived from the center. The core ruler sent royal apparel, regalia, and rain-making equipment (Southall 1956: 376–9) to each successive ruler of a peripheral domain on his accession, or special paraphernalia for making rain in a situation of great need.

Revered shrines mark the westward migration route up into the highlands, to which the ruler should send a deputation with a bull for sacrifice, in the presence of representatives of the other major component segments, symbolically representing the ritual unity of the segmentary state (Southall 1956: 370–5).

The Alur had the right of self-defense, and short-term fighting between neighboring groups was legitimate. But continued fighting brought down the wrath of the king as an affront to his stool. The king's only means of enforcement was to call upon other loyal local groups to join with him in plundering the recalcitrant groups. Such reprisals were greatly feared, for the king would establish himself in the disobedient group and eat up their substance of grain and livestock. This plunder mechanism is one of the most elemental and effective forms of political coercion, with the great advantage of freely harnessing the baser motives of rival groups in a cost-free state policing operation that brings its own reward. It is also the essential practice defining the political limits of the core domain and similarly the range of political sovereignty in peripheral domains, often minuscule, but no more so than those of medieval Irish kings (Byrne 1973). The plunder mechanism is worthy of wider study as a critical diagnostic.

Some examples of the segmentary state in Africa

The segmentary state as here defined, is extremely widespread in Africa. Many ethnographies are highly suggestive but fail to provide adequate information. The segmentary state is one hypothesis among others and commends itself to some and not others. The historical kingdom of Bunyoro-Kitara was a segmentary state. Beattie's (1960, 1970) studies of the Nyoro state concentrated, as functionalism demanded, on the colonial Nyoro state, reduced to a mere fragment of its former size. Beattie accepted the idea of Bunyoro-Kitara as a segmentary state (J. Beattie, personal communication), held together by ritual suzerainty, with a centralized core, but Weber's (1968) notions of sultanism and patrimonialism were his preferred formulations. Willis (1981: 13) calls Ufipa a "proto-state" and says that in its emergent form it was a segmentary state: "Its tenuous unity was focused on a paramount kingship centered on Milansi [an ancient center of ironworking] . . . the Mambwe possess an indigenous political system of this type. The ranking of Mambwe lesser chiefs with the dominant Sichula royal clan is determined by the putative descent status of their founding ancestors as junior patri-kin of the clan ancestor."

Although Vansina stresses centralization and the development of bureaucracy in the Kuba state, he contradicts himself, referring to it as among the less centralized African kingdoms: "all the chiefs are still descendants of the aboriginal rulers and the kingdom is little more than a protectorate from the nucleus over the outlying provinces" (Vansina 1962: 333). "The state consisted of a core with about 43% of the population and perhaps 40% of the land in the center, with satellite chiefdoms east and west . . . The Bushong dominated the state" (Vansina 1978b: 360). "The other ethnic units were not united at all and consequently formed a large cloud of satellite chiefdoms around the core" (Vansina 1978a: 6). This illustrates the fundamental characteristics of a segmentary state.

Kopytoff appears to describe the Suku polity as a segmentary state in every respect. The kingdom was divided into a dozen regions in a pyramidal structure. The position of regional chiefs duplicated that of the king, but on a smaller scale. There were no formal lines of communication between the king and subordinate chiefs, who had no representatives in the king's village. The king traveled around the kingdom every four years to collect tributes gathered by the regional chiefs. He had "no professional standing army, but his judgment could be swiftly enforced by his retinue, much of it consisting of hangers-on amassed during the trip and only too eager to burn and loot a designated village" (Kopytoff 1965: 465). This is the plunder mechanism described above. To say, as Kopytoff does, that Suku society possessed both the principal types proposed to classify African political systems (Fortes and Evans-Pritchard 1940) abolishes meaning. The same mechanism occurred over three millennia ago in Shang China (Southall 1993: 31–2). Supporting my own reading of the ethnography, Park (1988: 186) confirms that "both the Ngonde and the Kinga states were segmentary until nominally unified by European administrations."

Weissleder (1967: 10) studied the Amhara as a segmentary state. He concluded that it could never transform itself into a unitary state "because there will be no progression from any kind of segmentary to a fully realized unitary organization in any situation where the ideology

of domination in the superarching structure is precisely the same as that of the minimal units." But easily conceivable processes, such as increasing land scarcity, could lead to a change in ideology. No real system is wholly self contained and external jolts are inevitable. There were certainly plenty in Ethiopia, such as the Muslim invasion of the sixteenth century, or the Portuguese penetration.

The Kongo kingdom is uniquely fascinating because it is absolutely the first African state for which even minimal evidence is available, and because it demonstrates the essential fragility of African polities in face of the Western onslaught, even in the fifteenth century, not simply in a military sense, but essentially one of scale. When the Portuguese came upon it in the 1480s it was a very large but clearly a segmentary state, but within twenty-four years the pristine state of the Kongo had ceased to be (Ekholm 1972; Southall 1991: 83–7). It was never "despotic" in any meaningful sense, except that of the weight of the sovereign in the core domain where networks of kin, clients, and other sycophantic beneficiaries were concentrated.

Segmentary states, modes of production, and competing paradigms

The segmentary state hypothesis may be applied to many more societies in Africa than we have space to mention. It has been applied to major historical states in Asia and more recently to the classic Maya. According to Houston (1992: 3) "many scholars agree that the polities of the classical Maya conform to an unstable and weak political arrangement known as the segmentary state," but the Maya segmentary state "will remain a nebulous concept until scholars understand the articulation of its internal components, of how ruler related to the ruled" (Houston 1992: 3). Like Beattie, he notes that the segmentary state echoes Weber's (1968: 1040–1, 1051) formulations of patrimonial kingship and charismatic authority, where as in Alur, the assertion of rule "becomes less effective in the regions remote from the overlord's capital, where governors also rule in a patrimonial fashion and yield as little as possible to the king" (Houston 1992: 3). Houston goes on to observe:

> The galactic polity (Tambiah) differs little from the segmentary state: strong rulers irradiate political influence, weak rulers cannot prevent the disintegration of their polities . . . Segmentary states and galactic polities are difficult to distinguish from Webb's notion of a conditional state, which depends on the acceptance of the ruler by his subjects (1975: 163–4).

In the past decade, these models have exercised a seductive effect on archeologists and historical sociologists in Africa, southeast Asia, and beyond. Thomas Kiefer, for example, describes a Filipino sultanate in terms of a segmentary state; rule was highly personalized and charismatic, with little functional differentiation yet still capable of assembling large, intermittent armies through pyramidal alliances (1972: 28, 40) . . . Both segmentary state and galactic polity are invoked to explain the royal centre of Vijayanagara in India (Stein 1977; Fritz et al. 1984: 148; Fritz 1986: 46). Vijayanagara satisfies many of the requirements for the capital of a segmentary state: provincial polities were relatively autonomous, and Vijayanagara enjoyed little to no permanent bureaucratic organization, but rather served as a gigantic proscenium for the theatre of state (Fritz 1986: 46). Application of the model to archaic Greece is also noted (Runciman 1982: 353) . . . Arguably, the merit of the segmentary state model is that it bridges complex chiefdoms, which tend to have relatively small populations (Feinman and Neitzel 1984: 67, 69; Wilson 1959: 91–2, 135), and early states, which display a relatively high degree of stability and centralization. For all its advantages, particularly in contrasting sovereignty and suzerainty the segmentary state must be taken for what it is: a heuristic device that should not be asked to do too much – after all, a concept that likens polities of vastly different scale (such as those of Vijayanagara and Bali) is surely missing some important differences! (Houston 1992: 8)

I quite agree with these comments, and emphasize that the segmentary state refers primarily to processes and there is no a priori reason why processes should not be operative at very different scales. The model does not liken these polities of vastly different scale, it merely finds analogous processes operative in them. As Burton Stein has emphasized, the segmentary state is a formal notion.

The question of the impossibility of transformation raised by Weissleder, and the question of divergence of scale, demand careful consideration. The same issue arises in Richard Fox's doubts about the applicability of the model where the structure of the society is not uniform, as in the case of a segmentary lineage system, which is present in so many cases but not in the case of the Cola Empire analyzed by Stein.

Until the 1980s, the application of the model to Rajput polities within the Moghul Empire by Fox (1971, 1977) and to the Cola Empire by Stein were the major extensions of my original idea of the 1950s. The divergence in scale struck me as bizarre, to the point of threatening to strain credulity. The divergence had to be interpreted and justified in theoretical terms. The most fundamental gulf between the Alur and the Cola was that of political economy. The greater scale of the Cola was based upon higher productivity made possible by the plow, the wheel, the cart, draft oxen, horses, rice cultivation, massive irrigation, and above all writing, all unavailable to the Alur. The Cola and Rajput were part of the Indian Hindu world, with a vast and ancient heritage of written texts, combining literary excellence and powerful religious inspiration. Writing was one of the eminent forces of production, offering control of the calendar of work, supporting the numinous authority of the organizers of production, legitimizing and sanctifying the system of exploitation and the social relations of production embodied in it. Writing, like kinship, operated both among the forces and the relations of production. It tied together the whole political economy, regulating the seasons and their appropriate productive activities, facilitating trade, and making banking and finance possible. It recorded all important transactions increasing the area of state knowledge and control, as well as enshrining the whole religious system in sacred texts, giving a sense of confidence, faith, and place to ordinary folk, enabling them to glorify their superiors, who in turn glorified the rulers in glorifying themselves. No wonder the state could impose its hegemony over a vast area compared with the few hundred square miles of the Alur segmentary state.

The irrigation of a few river valleys arose within the agrarian economy as it became more specialized in adapting to the differential opportunities of particular ecological niches. It was not the result of large-scale state public works (as Wittfogel argued). Population and economy were markedly differentiated between the irrigated basins, with large numbers of landless laborers, the dry and swidden cultivation areas, and the pastoral and hunting and gathering zones, with very unequal shares of the product even within the peasant class having general access to the land. It is evident that the forces and relations of production were significantly different from those of the Alur. Both Cola and Rajput ruling classes had royal estates and control of the labor force from which they extracted direct income. They enjoyed a wide range of specialized crafts and prestige luxury goods. They lived in sumptuous courts and palaces which supported and enhanced the sacred mystique of their ritual dharmic status, which was empowered by the immensely influential services of the Brahmin caste and of the great temples under their care. They had bands of professional warriors and could indulge in constant raids and occasional wars of conquest. Yet, like the Alur, they extended their sway over people rather than territory, and what they gained was recognition of the magnificence of their symbolic rule rather than any secure system of central administration and taxation. It was the same with Sargon's ephemeral empire in the third millenium BC. The main material gain was momentary booty to help finance their extravagance. While kings and local rulers could control estates and labor, the vast proportion of the territory remained under the autonomous control of local kin groups, and the basic relationship between the center and peripheral units remained that of ritual suzerainty rather than political sovereignty.

The Cola and Rajput ruling classes were quite clearly separated from the mass of direct producers. The Alur rulers and their small entourages were not. All this amounted to demonstrating that the Alur and most other African peoples were practicing a mode of production quite different from that of the Cola and Rajput. The Alur remained within the kinship mode of production, while the Cola and Rajput practiced the Asiatic mode of production (Southall 1988a, 1988b). The meaningful difference between their polities does not lie in the elaboration of culture, or caste, or religion, or anything called civilization, but in the mode of production. It is this meaningful, theoretical interpretation of the divergence of scale which Weber's patrimonial formulations fail to catch. This is the missing difference referred to above by Houston. Despite the differences of scale they both remained segmentary states (Southall 1988b: 71).[5]

> There is a movement away from cultural evolutionary Marxist, or other kinds of typologies and more interest in political diversity, in political strategies versus structure . . . Southall's discussion of segmentary states is a good example of these widening interests in political anthropology. (de Montmollin 1989: 2)

At present there are several competing paradigms, which is all to the good unless they are mixed up together. This may be hard to avoid in composite edited volumes, but it is unfortunate. A group of distinguished archaeologists recently took a bold new turn, explaining techno-economic development and demographic change as consequences of factional competition. "Rather than being prime movers, technology, land, and labor are simply factors of production manipulated to promote factional interests" (Fox 1994: 3). But in attempting a concluding summation of that volume, which "argues that factional competition is implicated in developments as diverse as the spread of ceramic technology and maize

agriculture, the origins of permanent instituted leadership offices, the expansion and collapse of states" and so on (Brumfiel and Fox 1994: 3), Fox is faced with the difficulty that factional theory never provided any complete alternative theory of periodicity, so he is left with a mixture of the old concepts which clutter archaeology: chiefdoms, complex chiefdoms, ranked societies, segmentary and centralized or unitary states, without any clear distinctions. "The ranked societies (of Mesoamerica) were transitional between kin-ordered (segmental) and civil (stratified) society, with both kinship and tributary modes of production" (Fox 1994: 205). None of these concepts, piled like Pelion on Ossa, are defined. The mode of production model can hardly be adopted without re-theorizing. I made an initial attempt, but far more needs to be done. It is hardly passé (Southall 1988b).

> It is impossible at the present time to write history without using a whole range of concepts directly or indirectly linked to Marxist thought and situating oneself within a horizon of thought which has been defined and described by Marx. One might even wonder what difference there could be between being a Marxist and being a historian. (Foucault 1980: 52–3)

Notes

1 I recently received a proposal from an Alur in Paris to translate my book *Alur Society* into the Alur language. I hope it may happen.

2 It was I who named it Atyak, after the praise cry (*pak*) of its ruling clan. When I visited the unofficial ruler in 1992 I found that he had adopted the name, in order to submit a memorandum to the Uganda Constitutional Commission on behalf of the "Kingdom of Atyak."

3 They say *jubyele abyela* "they just carried him off."

4 Ritual kingship such as the Atyak is enhanced by the process of segmentation but when kingship or government comes to be defined and practiced in more political terms, then, of course, such segmentation becomes a dissipation and a weakness. Even in recent years African leadership has often followed the path of segmentation, but in the Westminster model which most independence leaders in Africa adopted, such segmentary forces were defined as tribalism, party organization being now the only legitimate form of pluralism. However, the segmentary process continued to operate, while political parties failed to take root, so governments had to maintain the fiction of party politics by forming one-party states and sup-

pressing segmentary movements. But some of the latter were too strong and went off into the bush like banished kings' sons, to make their own way and rival or even replace the regime from which they had fled. The modern African state has officially ignored (while privately practicing) this kind of segmentary activity.

As the first District Commissioner said when he reached the Alur in 1914, "among the Alur every petty chief wants to be independent. Among the Lugwari (Lugbara) every man wants to be independent" (Southall 1956: 28, 9).

5 To make sure of the relationship of incongruity between Alur and Cola, or Bali and Vijayanagara, an incongruity in which culture and history seem to be at cross-purposes, I found myself forced into a reformulated revisionist Marxist framework because after a century and a half of severe and critical testing, it remains the best thought out, most sophisticated, and most viable approach to periodicity in human affairs. Archaeology can only escape periodicity if it escapes from the past.

References

Beattie, J. H. M.
1960 *Bunyoro: An African Kingdom.* New York: Holt, Rinehart and Winston.
1970 *The Nyoro State.* Oxford: Clarendon.
Byrne, F. J.
1973 *Irish Kings and High Kings.* New York: St. Martin's Press.
Brumfiel, E. and J. Fox
1994 (eds.) *Factional Competition and Political Development in the New World.* Cambridge: Cambridge University Press.
Colson, E.
1948 Rain shrines of the Plateau Tonga of Northern Rhodesia. *Africa* 18 (3): 272–83.
Crazzolara, J. P.
1950/51 *The Lwoo*, 2 vols. Verona: Missioni Africane.
de Montmollin, O.
1989 *The Archaeology of Political Structure: Settlement Analysis in a Classic Maya Polity.* Cambridge: Cambridge University Press.
1992 Classic Maya settlement patterns and the segmentary state. Paper presented at the Conference on the Segmentary State and the Classic Lowland Maya, Cleveland State University.
Ekholm, K.
1972 *Power and Prestige: The Rise and Fall of the Kongo Kingdom*, Uppsala: Skriv Service AB.

Feinman, G. and J. Neitzel
1984 Too many types; an overview of sedentary pre-state societies in the Americas. In *Advances in Archaeological Method and Theory,* vol. 7, edited by M. Schiffer: 39–102.
Fortes, M. and E. E. Evans-Pritchard
1940 *African Political Systems.* Oxford: Oxford University Press.
Foucault, M.
1980 *Power and Knowledge: Select interviews and other writings 1972–77.* edited by Colin Gordon. New York: Pantheon.
Fox, J. W.
1994 Conclusions: Moietal opposition, segmentation, and factionalism in New World political arenas. In *Factional Competition and Political Development in the New World*, edited by E. Brumfiel and J. Fox. Cambridge: Cambridge University Press: 199–206.
Fox, R. G.
1971 *Kin, Clan, Raja and Rule: State-Hinterland Relations in Pre-industrial India.* Berkeley: University of California Press.
1977 *Realm and Region in Traditional India.* Durham: Duke University Press.
Fritz, J. M.
1986 Vijayanagara: authority and meaning of a South Indian imperial capital. *American Anthropologist* 88 (1): 44–55.
Fritz, J. M., G. Michell, and M. S. Nagaraja Rao
1984 *Where Kings and Gods Meet: The Royal Centre at Vijayanagara, India.* Tucson: University of Arizona Press.
Godelier, M.
1978 Infrastructures, society and history. *Current Anthropology* 19: 4.
Harvey, D.
1990 *The Condition of Postmodernity: An Inquiry into the Origins of Cultural Change.* Cambridge: Blackwell.
Houston, S. D.
1992 Weak states and segmentary structure: The internal organization of Classic Lowland Maya society. Paper presented at the Conference on the Segmentary State and the Classic Lowland Maya, Cleveland State University.
Kiefer, T. M.
1972 The Tausug polity and the Sultanate of Sulu: a segmentary state in the southern Philippines. In *Sulu Studies I*, edited by G. Risehoul. Jolo: Notre Dame of Jolo College.

Kopytoff, I.
    1965 The Suku of Southern Congo. In *Peoples of Africa,* edited by J. Gibbs, Jr. New York: Holt, Rinehart and Winston.
Park, G.
    1988 Evolution of a Regional Culture in East Africa. *Sprache und Geschichte in Africa.* Band 9. Hamburg: Helmut Buske Verlag.
Runciman, W. O.
    1982 Origins of states: the case of archaic Greece. *Comparative Studies in Society and History* 24 (3): 351–77.
Southall, A.
    1956 *Alur Society: A Study in Processes and Types of Domination.* Cambridge: Heffer.
    1970 Incorporation among the Alur. In *From Tribe to Nation in Africa,* edited by J. Middleton and R. Cohen. Scranton: Chandler: 71–92.
    1988a Mode of production theory: the foraging mode of production and the kinship mode of production. *Dialectical Anthropology* 12 (2): 165–92.
    1988b The segmentary state in Africa and Asia. *Comparative Studies in Society and History* 30 (1): 52–82.
    1991 The segmentary state: from the imaginary to the material means of production. In *Early State Economics,* edited by H. J. M. Claessen and P. van de Velde. New Brunswick: Transaction Publishers.
    1993 Urban theory and the Chinese city. In *Urban Anthropology in China,* edited by G. Guldin and A. Southall. Leiden: E. J. Brill.
Stein, B.
    1977 The segmentary state in South Indian history. In *Realm and Region in Traditional India,* edited by R. Fox. Durham: Duke University Press: 3–51.
Tambiah, S. J.
    1976 *World Conquerer and World Renouncer: A Study of*
Buddhism and Polity in Thailand against a Historical Background. Cambridge: Cambridge University Press.
    1977 The galactic polity: the structure of traditional kingdoms in Southeast Asia. *Annals of the New York Academy of Sciences* 293: 69–97.
Vansina, J.
    1962 A comparison of African kingdoms. *Africa* 22: 324–35.
    1978a *The Children of Woot: a History of the Kuba Peoples.* Madison: University of Wisconsin Press.
    1978b The Kuba State. In *The Early State,* edited by H. J. M. Claessen and P. Skalník. Mouton: The Hague: 359–80.
Webb, M. C.
    1975 The flag follows trade: an essay on the necessary interaction of military and commercial factors in state formation. In *Ancient Civilization and Trade,* edited by J. A. Sabloff and C. C. Lamberg-Karlovsky, School of American Research Advanced Seminar series. Albuquerque: University of New Mexico Press: 155–210.
Weber, M.
    1968 *Economy and Society* vols. 1 and 2. Edited by G. Roth and C. Wittich. New York: Bedminster.
Weissleder, W.
    1967 The Political Economy of Amhara Domination. Ph.D. dissertation, University of Chicago.
Willis, R.
    1981 *A State in the Making: Myth, History, and Social Transformation in Pre-colonial Ufipa.* Bloomington: Indiana University Press.
Wilson, M.
    1959 *Communal Rituals of the Nyakyusa.* London: Oxford University Press.

3

Perceiving variability in time and space: the evolutionary mapping of African societies

ANN B. STAHL

Archaeologists of my generation have experienced dramatic shifts in the ideas that orient our field – as students in the early 1970s we cut our teeth on the New Archaeology, and many embraced the neo-evolutionary models that informed a processual understanding of human development. The musty culture history of our instructors' elders seemed uninteresting, and our imaginations were fired by questions of origins and transitions: the origins of food production and the transition to sedentary village life; the origins of complex societies and the growth of cities. We were concerned with modeling, with cross-cultural comparison, and ultimately with processual questions of evolutionary change. During the 1980s we weathered another sea-change in theoretical currents with the upwelling of critical stances loosely grouped under the rubric of post-processual archaeology. Although this belies the diverse perspectives of archaeologists so-labeled – some marxist, some feminist, some post-structuralist (Kohl 1993) – they share a disdain for the evolutionary models that played a prominent role in processual archaeology. They criticize evolutionary models as universalizing, winnowing diversity by forcing an array of societies into rigid types; as hierarchical, ranking societies along dimensions of complexity and heterogeneity; as reductionist, implying a correlation between particular economic and social forms; and, as distancing simple societies in time by treating them as relics of earlier stages (Andah 1995; Shennan 1993; Thomas 1989; Upham 1990a, 1990b; Yoffee 1993). Others have examined the relationship of evolutionary ideas with imperialism, ethnocentrism, and inequalities of power (Bowler 1992; Fabian 1983; Gamble 1992a, 1992b; Rowlands 1989b, 1994; Schmidt and Patterson 1995;

Stocking 1987; Thomas 1994; Trigger 1989). Thus progressive evolutionary schemes map societies in ways that are ideologically charged.

Archaeologists have responded in several ways to these compelling critiques of evolutionary models. Some reject the criticisms out of hand (Binford 1987), but have turned sustained attention away from big questions of evolution toward "middle range" issues (Kohl 1993: 16); others continue to tinker with evolutionary ideas, trying to overcome problems of typology and reductionism, and developing models more sensitive to such issues as inequality and resistance (e.g., Earle 1991; Upham 1990c); still others reject evolutionary approaches altogether (e.g., Gardin and Peebles 1992; Tilley 1993). For the most part, however, our responses have focused on higher level questions: for example, on whether there are definable entities such as chieftaincies, what they imply, and how they relate, if at all to states (Yoffee 1993); whether there is a necessary link between particular economies and social forms (Netting 1990); or whether complex societies are best viewed as cooperative, consensual entities or characterized by contradictions, inequalities, and coercion. Others have begun to examine the epistemic roots of the categorical knowledge that shapes these inquiries (R. McIntosh, this volume; Rowlands 1994). Significantly, however, our efforts to develop alternative visions are based on the same archaeological data as before. What of the more fundamental legacy of evolutionary thought for the archaeological data with which we work?

What I argue is that an evolutionary model, whether implicit or explicit, has framed not just how we understand the relationship of excavated sites to one another – in terms of what Dennell (1990) calls the "Big Sequence" – but more fundamentally our choice of *which* sites to excavate. In short, an evolutionary agenda determined (1) the kinds of sites deemed important, and therefore generated an archaeological record constructed in the image of evolution; and (2) how we conceptualize similarity and difference between sites, and thus how a site relates to the developmental sequence of a region. I consider these issues in the context of sub-Saharan African archaeology; however, they are equally important in other world areas. If we want to examine the structuring effect of evolutionary models, we must go back in time and consider the time–space systematics that so bored us in our youths.

Sources of evolutionary models

American anthropologists have viewed nineteenth-century evolutionary thought as a homogeneous set of ideas largely rejected by the beginning of this century. In an early essay Stocking (1974) characterized this view as superficial, and traced its origins to Boas' critique of evolutionary thought. Boas, in framing his objections and laying out an alternative vision of anthropology, painted nineteenth-century evolutionary ideas with a broad brush, glossing the variegated strands of thought subsequently detailed by Stocking (1987). Critiques of evolutionary thought in archaeology also suffer from a short memory and caricatured representations, focusing on the legacy of White and Steward whose ideas were introduced into archaeology by Binford and others (e.g., Yoffee 1993). While this may go far in explaining the character and excesses of evolutionary ideas in world areas where American archaeologists have worked over the last thirty-five years, it does not account for the pervasive influence of evolutionary thinking on "Old World" archaeology. Long after Boas' campaign swept evolutionary concerns from American archaeology, British anthropologists and archaeologists continued to address issues of progressive development (Childe 1936; Clark 1946; Dennell 1990; Kuklick 1991b). Moreover the typological categories that structure Old World archaeology are rooted contingently in nineteenth-century evolutionism and, more remotely, in Enlightenment universal histories (Trigger 1989: 73–86).

Shallow histories of evolutionary archaeology do not go very far in explaining why issues of origins and progress have been a central feature of world prehistory since its invention in the nineteenth century. Nor do they explain the continued influence of progressive development on diffusionist archaeology early in this century (e.g., Smith 1929; Sollas 1915; see Bowler 1992: 727–8). Gamble (1993: 40–1), following biogeographers, refers to this combination of evolution and diffusion as the *imperial tradition*. The goal was to identify centers of origin, perceived as active in relation to peripheral areas where innovations subsequently diffused. This concern with origins was given a distinctively progressive twist as it became linked to a linear progressive view of time that was characteristic of the late Victorian writings of Lyell, Lubbock, and others (Gamble 1993: 44).

Thus, if we want to examine how a progressive evolutionary model structured African archaeological data, we must look to the context in which African archaeology developed. I turn now to a brief history of African archaeology, looking at the roots of African time–space systematics in European palaeolithic schemes. Africanist archaeologists eschewed theory, and thought of themselves as constructing culture history that was theory-neutral. However, I argue that, even when an evolutionary model did not explicitly orient the study of African

archaeology, a progressivist stance was implied in the time–space systematics that provided the foundation for African culture history. A progressive evolutionary model became more explicit with African independence, when archaeologists worked to counter colonial images of Africa societies as backward by documenting their dynamic qualities. Special interest focused on sites that might provide evidence of early agriculture or early complex societies, considered hallmarks of progress. Here I focus on sites that were considered relevant to the study of complexity. In a concluding section I argue that, because archaeologists have trained their sights on particular kinds of sites deemed important within a progressive evolutionary model, reorienting our thinking to account for recent critiques of evolutionary thought involves more than just a reinterpretation of existing sites. Rather, it requires that we reorient our time–space systematics and investigative strategies.

Sources of time–space systematics in African archaeology

The first Pan-African Congress on Prehistory (held in Nairobi in 1947) was attended by some fifty archaeologists, physical anthropologists, and geologists, all of whom fit comfortably on the steps of a modest-sized building for a conference photograph (reproduced in Robertshaw 1990a: 9). The archaeologists in that photo included the majority of practitioners at the time (Robertshaw 1990a: 8), most of whom worked in relative isolation. The Congress provided the opportunity to discuss typology and compare regional sequences in areas as far apart as the Cape and the Maghreb. The conference photograph tells much about the character of African archaeology in the immediate post-war period. The participants were virtually all European, and predominately male (indeed the photograph could just as easily have been taken in Brussels or London as in Nairobi). Most practitioners had gained their initial archaeological experience in Europe (see Robertshaw 1990c), and a number had studied prehistory at Cambridge under Miles Burkitt and Grahame Clark, or were influenced by the Abbé Henri Breuil.

Breuil (1877–1961) was a Catholic cleric and the archaeology correspondent for *l'Anthropologie*, who had immense influence on palaeolithic archaeology in the first half of this century. Although Breuil subscribed to a developmentalist vision of the past, he viewed change as incremental and gradual – a view compatible with his Catholicism (Dennell 1990: 553). Dennell (1990) suggests that Breuil and members of the conservative Institut de

Paléontologie Humaine were influential in infusing palae-olithic studies with a gradualist progressivist stance. But Breuil's influence extended beyond theory – his 1912 and 1931 publications set new standards for typology, and replaced de Mortillet's scheme that had framed Palaeolithic studies to that point (see Trigger 1989: 95–101).

Burkitt and Breuil shared with other archaeologists of their day an interest in constructing chronology, but they were distinguished by their concern to correlate regional sequences. Burkitt co-authored with Childe a chart that attempted to correlate European prehistoric sequences (Childe and Burkitt 1932; Trigger 1989: 170), and this, together with Breuil's publications on the French palae-olithic sequence, provided a model for Leakey's (1934) attempt to correlate the African Stone Age sequence with the Palaeolithic sequences of other world areas (Dennell 1990).

The first generation of Africanist archaeologists thus saw systematics as their first task (Shaw 1990: 209–10), and, understandably, drew on their knowledge of European sequences in forging a typological framework (Kleindienst 1967: 823). In francophone northern and western Africa this resulted in a fairly direct mapping of French palaeolithic terminology onto African contexts using *fossiles directeurs* (de Barros 1990; Gowlett 1990; Sheppard 1990). Terminology in anglophone Africa was shaped by investigations in South Africa, which had a high density of practitioners compared to other regions (twenty-two of the approximately fifty participants at the First Pan-African Congress were from South Africa; Deacon 1990: 48). A. J. H. Goodwin, a former student of Burkitt who took up an appointment at the University of Cape Town in 1923, felt the need to develop ". . . an entirely new cultural terminology for southern Africa" because of the vast distance between it and Europe (Goodwin, quoted in Deacon 1990: 43). He worked jointly with C. Van Riet Lowe, an engineer who had undertaken archaeological investigations in the northern provinces of South Africa, and their *Stone Age Cultures of South Africa* (Goodwin and Van Riet Lowe 1929) introduced the scheme of an Earlier, Middle and Later Stone Age that was later adopted by archaeologists throughout anglophone Africa (Deacon 1990: 43–5). The concept of an Iron Age, which encompassed the pre-historic remains of contemporary cultures, was intro-duced in the post-war period, and again, initially in southern Africa. This technological category, borrowed from the European three-age system, was preferable to the idea of a "Bantu period" which invited controversy over the links between archaeological sites and the increasingly marginalized Africans in the settler colonies of Rhodesia and South Africa (Hall 1990: 64; see also Kuklick 1991a). The term "Iron Age" was also considered preferable to the concept of a "Protohistoric" period which had come into currency but ". . . implies links with historic themes which in most cases cannot be demonstrated" (Posnansky 1967: 630).

Early researchers were also interested in standardizing terminology (Kleindienst 1967). A Standing Committee on Nomenclature in Prehistory was created at the First Pan-African Congress, which was to approve any new names that researchers wished to introduce. Resolution 13 of the Fourth Pan-African Congress (1959) reaffirmed the importance of this process (Mortelmans and Nenquin 1962: 49–50). These resolutions seem to have had little effect, for by 1965, the state of terminological confusion in Africa was a primary focus of a four-week Wenner-Gren symposium at Burg Wartenstein, Austria (Bishop and Clark 1967).

The six years between the Fourth Pan-African and the Wenner-Gren symposium coincided with decolonization and the founding of independent African nation-states. The period witnessed a significant increase in the level of archaeological research. The growing body of archaeological data, combined with the possibility of independently dating sites using radiometric techniques, pointed to significant problems with the Big Sequence adopted/adapted from Europe. Prior to the advent of radiocarbon chronology, the sequence of Early/Middle/Late Stone Age followed by a Neolithic and an Iron Age which graded into the ethnographic present, provided both a *technological* and a *chronological* framework for establishing the relationship of sites both within and between regions. Radiometric dating provided an inde-pendent means by which to establish chronology (Clark 1962), and began to point to anomalies in the Big Sequence. Technologically defined ages were not neces-sarily synchronous in all areas (i.e., the "Middle Stone Age" in one area might be contemporaneous with the "Later Stone Age" in another). Participants in the Wenner-Gren symposium were particularly concerned with the potential muddling of what Clark (1967a: 415) termed the cultural-stratigraphic (essentially technolog-ical) implications of the age/stage terminology and their time-stratigraphic (or chronological) implications. Because the terms were imprecise, participants agreed that archaeologists should discontinue using "Earlier," "Middle," and "Later Stone Age" as formal terms (Clark 1967a: 415; see Bishop and Clark 1967: 866–72). They also recommended that the term "neolithic" be aban-doned because African sites did not fit the European model of a neolithic culture (Clark 1967b: 621; see Sinclair et al. 1993: 3–8 for a revisitation).

What was the impact of these resolutions? The two major syntheses of African prehistory published in English since the Burg Wartenstein conference eschewed the terms because they masked the complexities of the archaeological record (Clark 1970: 25–6; Phillipson 1985: 5). However, a glance through any recent issue of the *African Archaeological Review* shows the terms to have remarkable tenacity, and they are commonly used as a structuring narrative in reviews of African prehistory (e.g., Clark 1982; Stahl 1994b). Indeed, even those synthetic volumes that have deliberately avoided the terminology of the Big Sequence are still organized according to its logic (see table of contents in Clark 1970 and Phillipson 1985, 1993). Hence, the narrative structure of the Big Sequence, implicitly one of progressive development (Sinclair, et al. 1993a: 2–3), remains intact.

Progressive underpinnings of the "Big Sequence"

Those who debated the age/stage problem at Burg Wartenstein were concerned primarily with systematics. They did not question the relationship of the Big Sequence with a progressive evolutionary interpretation of prehistory. In other words, despite their concerns about how the *details* of the Big Sequence varied from region to region – especially with respect to chronology – archaeologists working in Africa continued to subscribe implicitly to the progressive model that had underwritten the earlier typology. Thus, the more fundamental legacy of Breuil and Burkitt remained intact.

Recent authors have explored the ideological character of nineteenth-century progressive evolution (e.g., Rowlands 1989b; Shennan 1993; Stocking 1987; Trigger 1989: 110–47). It provided a universalizing narrative structure for the story of human development by stressing that societies developed along a similar trajectory from simple to complex, from homogeneous to heterogenous, in what Gamble (1993: 49) has described as a "salute to civilization." Emphasis was on *shared* characteristics of societies in a similar stage of development, and Europe occupied the pinnacle of the progressive trajectory. That these views were compatible with an imperial agenda is well established in the literature. What is less explicitly discussed is that a progressivist perspective continued to hold sway even after archaeologists became less optimistic about the ubiquity of human creativity, and turned to diffusion as a means of explaining change. Significantly, diffusionism offered a convenient mechanism for dating in the period before

radiometric techniques; however, Trigger (1989: 150–1) describes the turn to diffusionism as a reaction *against* progress associated with a belief that human capabilities were biologically determined: "If the insecurity of the middle classes of Western Europe in the 1860s had led Lubbock and other Darwinians to abandon the doctrine of psychic unity and view native peoples as biologically inferior to Europeans, the still greater insecurity of the 1880s led intellectuals to jettison the doctrine of progress and regard human beings as far more resistant to change than they had been since before the Enlightenment."

Although there may have been growing pessimism about progress, it is important to recognize that a progressivist assumption was implicit in the archaeology of diffusionist scholars. This is perhaps most apparent in the writings of V. Gordon Childe, who organized his popular overviews of archaeology in terms of a cumulative, progressive narrative of human development (see chapter headings in Childe 1936, 1942). One might attribute this to the influence of a marxist perspective; however, the writings of other, clearly non-marxist scholars, belie a continued belief that human societies could be understood as differentially positioned along a single trajectory of progressive development (Clark 1946). The primary difference seems to have been their conviction that people were differentially endowed with the ability to innovate, and that some marginal groups were in essence "trapped" in earlier stages (see Bowler 1992 on Sollas). Now there were *few* active centers of innovation from which change emanated (Gamble 1993: 40–1).

Africans in particular were viewed as unprogressive, and scholars sought external sources for innovations like agriculture, metallurgy, cities, and states (Sinclair et al. 1993a: 16–31). Progress did occur, but only by imitation, and not universally. Thus the relevance of societies – both prehistoric and living – was defined in terms of the grand narrative. Groups, living or dead, were relevant only insofar as they shed light on the universal story of human development. For example, San hunter-gatherers were relevant for what they could tell us about the early reaches of the Palaeolithic. So-called simple agricultural societies became irrelevant as the narrative turned to the emergence of complex societies, because their importance was as precursors of complex societies (and see Sharpe [1986] for a fascinating analysis of how this affected colonial perceptions of relationships between contemporary "tribes" and "states" in northern Nigeria). In essence then, diversity in African prehistory was winnowed out in an effort to accommodate the African archaeological record with the grand narrative of the Big Sequence. And ultimately, African prehistory was winnowed out of world prehistory after hominids radiated to the Near East and Europe, which then took center stage in the grand narrative of human development (Stahl 1994b: 51–2, 103–4).

It is a fair generalization that the archaeologists who gathered for the First Pan-African Congress believed that, although Africa's Stone Age past was characterized by innovation and progress, the period following the close of the Pleistocene was one of stagnation (e.g., Cole 1954) or at best imitation (Clark 1962: 309), rather than invention (Hall 1990; Holl 1990; Robertshaw 1990a, 1990b; Trigger 1990: 313). The primary markers of progress – agriculture, metallurgy, and cities – all appeared to be late developments, and were assumed therefore to have been introduced from outside the continent (see Stahl 1984 on agriculture; McIntosh and McIntosh 1988: 102–10 and Okafor 1993 on metallurgy; and McIntosh and McIntosh 1984, 1993a on cities). This was a view that was to come under serious question in the period of early independence.

Independence and the decolonization of Africa's past

Decolonization became a reality in the aftermath of World War II as African states gained independence, beginning with Ghana in 1957. New states required new histories that demonstrated the achievements of African peoples, and the intellectual capacity of Africans to make their own history (Temu and Swai 1981: 2–22). This reached its most extreme expression in the writings of scholars such as Diop and Obenga (Holl 1990: 302; 1995).

Compared to historians, archaeologists have been unreflective about how our understanding of the African past was recast in the period of early independence (cf. Hall 1990; Holl 1990, 1995; Rowlands 1994). Part of the explanation may lie in the fact that historians who wished to create a history independent of European documents were forced to pioneer new sources, and hence new methodologies (Vansina 1965). Archaeologists continued to work with the same materials and methodologies, but turned their efforts to two new ends: (1) forging of national histories for newly emerging nation states, which translated into a growing interest in the archaeology of the "Iron Age"; and (2) countering the image of Africa as an unprogressive cultural backwater. We must also take into account the impact of a new generation of scholars, a number of whom were influenced by the processual, evolutionary approaches of the New Archeology (Andah 1995; de Barros 1990: 167–70; Deacon 1990: 53–4; Trigger 1990: 314–16; Vansina 1995; cf. Robertshaw 1990b: 85–6).

The new focus on Iron Age studies rapidly produced a wealth of information (Shinnie 1971). What issues were defined as pressing by Iron Age archaeologists, and how did that agenda influence the choice of sites targeted for investigation? I focus my attention on anglophone West Africa; however, the trends I describe are borne out in other areas as well. I think we can discern three predominant themes in Iron Age studies over the past forty years: (1) tracing the history of contemporary ethnic groups, often for purposes of nation-building; (2) establishing the antiquity of metallurgy in Africa; and (3) documenting the existence and antiquity of cities and complex societies. These last two themes were defined as important by the grand narrative of evolution – the perception of Africa as a backward continent could only be countered by demonstrating that Africa was active in the story of recent human development. Thus, it was important to establish that metallurgy and cities were early, and preferably independent, developments (McIntosh and McIntosh 1984; Okafor 1993; Stahl 1984). These concerns had implications for the kinds of sites that were targeted for investigation. For purposes of brevity, I focus my comments here on efforts to document complex societies.

Cities were considered a primary marker of civilizations by nineteenth-century scholars (although the idea has deeper roots; R. McIntosh, this volume). Sub-Saharan Africa seemed notable for its lack of cities and other attributes associated with European images of civilization (writing, the wheel, and so on; McIntosh and McIntosh 1993a: 622–5). This contributed to an image of the "Dark Continent" as unprogressive, and to the self-assured belief that any evidence of civil society must be the result of outside influence. The most extreme example was the controversy that surrounded Great Zimbabwe (Kuklick 1991a); however, the assumption similarly affected the interpretation of cities in West Africa (McIntosh and McIntosh 1984, 1993a) and elsewhere (Connah 1987).

Hence the revision of African history and prehistory that took place in the wake of independence placed the issue of cities and civilizations high on the research agenda. Many historians and archaeologists were anxious to demonstrate that cities and civilizations existed in Africa prior to European contact, and that they had substantial antiquity. Oral historians devoted considerable energy to collecting the histories of indigenous states, and worked to extract chronology from king lists and genealogies. Archaeologists attempted to verify traditions by excavating sites associated with former states (e.g., Mauny 1971; Willett 1971; and see Schmidt 1990 for a critical history of attempts to link the Bacwezi with the site of

Bigo in Uganda). In Nigeria, archaeology was driven by interest in the spectacular brass and bronze sculptures of Ife and Benin, which were taken to signal the presence of court artisans associated with complex societies. Survey was dominated by efforts to locate former capitals, and excavation with identifying royal residences (Connah 1975, 1987: 130–7; Willett 1960). In Ghana, attention initially focused on Iron Age sites near the coast which had the potential for yielding datable artifacts that could be used to cross-date locally made tobacco pipes (Ozanne 1962). However, attention soon turned inland in an effort to identify early centers involved in the trans-Saharan trade (Posnansky 1973) and the early capitals of historic states (e.g., Effah-Gyamfi 1985; Shinnie and Ozanne 1962). The preoccupations of archaeologists working on these sites reveals concerns set by a progressive developmentalist model. Interest focused on evidence of complexity – craft specialization and trade – and its antiquity. Other questions, deemed relevant to the study of earlier periods (i.e. subsistence as a "neolithic" issue), were largely ignored (cf. Voigt 1983).

This burgeoning interest in Iron Age studies contributed much to our understanding of African societies over the past 2,000 years. But that understanding is heavily skewed by a progressive developmental framework. Our knowledge is based primarily on sites selected for investigation because they were deemed important for their ability to shed light on the development of complexity. Neale (1985, 1986) has examined this problem in African historiography, arguing that revision of African history in the early post-colonial period was shaped by many of the same assumptions as earlier colonial history. The newly revised history was intended to create African self-respect by demonstrating that "Africans, too, had participated in and contributed to this development. Where colonial writing had tried to show that Africans stood outside of the 'mainstream' of progress, post-independence writing sought to portray them as active within it; the mainstream, however, is a Western idea, and one which scarcely anyone thought to question" (Neale 1985: 3–4). In other words, while post-colonial historians questioned the characterization of Africa as stagnant, they did not question the notion of progress that informed this characterization (Neale 1985: 9). Thus, Africa's historical development was constructed in the image of Europe's, and aspects of Africa's past that did not conform to expectations of a developmental model were treated as peripheral to history (Neale 1985: 15). "The defenders of African civilisation never challenged the definition of civilization, the values of the conquerors, but conducted the defense in terms of these values" (Neale 1985: 26), so

creating what Fuglestad (1992) has termed the "Trevor-Roper trap."[1]

Early post-colonial African history thus became the study of kingdoms (Neale 1985: 38; Ajayi and Crowder 1976; Davidson 1959; Vansina 1966). History shared with archaeology a preoccupation with complex societies, considering stateless, so-called acephalous societies important only insofar as they represented precursors of more complex forms (Neale 1985: 117). Indeed, the prominent historian, Ali Mazrui, expressed concern that more documentation of simple groups might perpetuate the image of Africa as unprogressive (Neale 1985: 15).

Winnowing variability

Thus even as archaeologists and historians of the post-colonial period worked to revise their understanding of Africa's past, they continued to work within a model of progressive development. This had the effect of winnowing variability from Africa's past. Where earlier scholars judged Africa harshly – as a passive recipient of cultural developments from outside – post-colonial writers emphasized the agency of Africans in independently achieving the markers of progress. But, as Neale (1985, 1986) and Fuglestad (1992) have stressed, scholars continued to work within the confines of an evolutionary model, introducing significant distortions into how we understood Africa's past. The history of certain communities (those perceived as "simple") was marginalized, and an evolutionary model trained our focus on particular issues and problems, obscuring others (Neale 1985: 14–15). Attention was diverted away from relationships between neighboring societies/sites that had been mentally mapped as representatives of different evolutionary stages (Sharpe 1986). So too was attention diverted away from questions of subsistence – deemed an appropriate problem for "neolithic" studies, but considered less pressing in the study of complex societies which, by definition, had crossed the threshold of agriculture.

Some might charge that I overestimate the structuring influence and homogenizing effect of a progressive evolutionary model on our understanding of Africa's past, pointing to numerous examples in recent literature that describe how African sites depart from the expectations of this model (McIntosh 1994b). Trigger (1990: 318), for example, stresses the role that archaeological data have played in debunking the negative stereotypes of the colonial period and the well-intentioned claims of the Negritude movement. Francophone researchers were more influenced by historical than evolutionary models (Olivier and Coudart 1995). Many contributors to the recently published compendium, *The Archaeology of Africa* (Shaw et al. 1993), examined variability and explored how individual case studies departed from the expectations of a simplistic evolutionary model. Several authors stressed the complex nature of the shift to agriculture (Andah 1993) and the continued importance of foraging for African agriculturalists (Robertshaw 1993; Stahl 1993b; Wetterstrom 1993; see also Posnansky 1984). Chapters on complex societies stressed how African sequences departed from the expectations of evolutionary models drawn from the Near East and Europe (Fletcher 1993; McIntosh and McIntosh 1993a; Sinclair et al. 1993). Yet if we take a closer look, the *themes* that dominate investigations of sites in particular time-periods continue to be framed by an evolutionary agenda. Despite the influence of history and an *Annales* focus on rural life in France, archaeologists of francophone Africa showed more interest in cities and stone circles than in rural agricultural villages. The editors of *The Archaeology of Africa* identified five themes that unified the forty-four contributions to the volume: (1) terminology; (2) innovation and diffusion; (3) environmental relations; (4) food production; and (5) urbanism (Sinclair et al. 1993a). Virtually all the articles that dealt with food production focused on the *transition* to food production; the articles that focused on more recent times paid little attention to subsistence (cf. Horton and Mudida 1993). Metallurgy, trade, urbanism, and state formation dominated chapters on the "Iron Age." Similarly, in a recent review article on African metallurgy, Childs and Killick (1993: 322) identified the "most significant developments in sub-Saharan Africa during the first and early second millennia AD [as] 1. the collapse of the Nubian and Ethiopian civilizations, 2. the Islamization of North Africa, 3. the establishment of long-distance trade routes, and 4. the rise of towns and states in West and Southeast Africa." The emphasis on trade, towns, and states is consistent with a progressive developmentalist perspective that is alive and well in African archaeology.

We can only speculate on the sociology of why a progressivist framework has persisted despite strident critiques of it. First, the need to reclaim a role for Africa and Africans in the story of human development remains. This is a significant item on the agenda of multiculturalists and Afrocentrists alike (e.g., Clarke 1990; Takaki 1993). Despite the perception that the postmodern era is witness to the death of the grand narrative, Africa continues to occupy a marginal space in world history and prehistory. While our recent attention to variability may thus help us avoid the trap of trying to demonstrate that Africa's development was " . . . just as good as Europe's

because it was the same" (Neale 1986: 114), we continue to train our attention on aspects of the past that will elevate respect for Africa – towns, kingdoms, and complex crafts. Afrocentric scholars take a different tack – their focus is on *unity* among African cultures (inclusive of ancient Egypt), for they believe that the emphasis on diversity was a tactic adopted by Europeans to divide and rule African peoples (Asante 1990). Hence, they seek universals among African cultures; but again, this search for universals is underwritten by a progressive developmentalist model (Blakey 1995; Holl 1995: 204–8). For example Yansane (1990: 39) emphasizes the contributions of African civilization to general knowledge in "mathematics, mechanics, commerce, law, art, medicine, writing and religion." His discussion of universals in West Africa focuses on kingdoms and empires, and he concludes that "[t]he empires of Ghana, Mali, Songhay, Kanem-Bornu, the Hausa states, the coast kingdoms, and the Nok culture show that the African way of life has a very long, famous, and distinctive history and culture, but is still similar to other world people's experiences. These civilizations may have been exceptional diamonds; but yet they were and are diamonds, which illuminate the unfortunate epithet 'dark' applied by Stanley to the African continent." (Yansane 1990: 63–4)

Agencies that assess site significance and mete out research funds also play a role in perpetuating a progressive evolutionary framework. Despite the critical stance toward progress in a *Unesco Courier* forum (Banuri 1993; Boorstin 1993; Debray 1993; Ki-Zerbo 1993; Lewis 1993; Touraine 1993), the United Nations Convention concerning the Protection of the World Cultural and Natural Heritage emphasizes universality and the category "civilization" in its criteria for assessing site significance. World Heritage designation requires that sites be associated with "ideas or beliefs of universal significance," provide "evidence of a civilization that has disappeared," or have "exercised considerable influence at a certain period" (Beschaouch 1990: 44). A glance at the World Heritage list reveals a preoccupation with cities and monumental architecture – the handful of cultural sites in Africa are towns or European ruins (Bolla and Batisse 1980; *Unesco Courier* 1990: 48).

Funding is also prioritized by "significance," which often means judging the significance of a site to world prehistory. "Significant" problems associated with particular time periods are pegged to a progressive developmental model. A gulf thus remains between theoretical critiques of progressive evolutionary models and the practical realities of defining site significance. These inconsistencies are revealed in Drewal's (1996) essay on "Empowering

Africa's cultural institutions." Opening sections call for greater reflexivity and a reorientation of the power centers that shape cultural heritage (Drewal 1996: 111). Later sections discuss taking action, and reproduce parts of a proposal to establish a Foundation for African Archaeology/Fonds pour l'Archéologie Africaine (FAA) directed at stemming the destruction of archaeological sites by

> providing financial, material, and personnel support for emergency, in-progress, and long-term archaeological projects, especially (but not exclusively) those focused on the last two to three millennia – a period in which the processes of urbanization and nation-state formation produced rich, sophisticated artistic traditions comparable to any created anywhere in the world – and which, as a result, are in the highest demand in the illegal international art market.

Further,

> It is precisely during this era of the last two millennia that we have growing evidence of major cultural developments – animal husbandry, sedentary agricultural technologies and practices, metalworking technologies, trading networks, urbanization, craft specialization, centralized governments and city-state, nation and empire formation in Africa – and rich attendant material cultural production, including some of the world's finest artistic achievements. (Drewal 1996: 116)

The funding priorities of the FAA thus reproduce an emphasis on aspects of the past deemed important by a progressive developmental model. In a footnote Drewal (1996, note 2) addresses the inconsistency between his call for reflexivity and reshaping of power relations, and the FAA call for action by observing that it is a "shift that reflects in part the geopolitical and economic realities of grantsmanship. The proposal is a document of specifics meant to persuade funding agencies in the so-called First World . . . the rhetoric of the proposal attempts to bridge worlds in order to achieve results." My intent is not to single Drewal out – indeed the FAA proposal was drafted by a group of prominent African and Africanist scholars. If asked to identify the most significant developments in recent African prehistory, most of us would probably generate a list that looked very similar to that of the FAA working group or to that of Childs and Killick (1993). What we must ask in addition, however, is *what such a list obscures*, and how it perpetuates models we think we have rejected.

Similarly we need to ask how our continued use – however informal – of the age/stage terminology introduced early in this century shapes our narratives about the African past. In the introduction to the most recent synthesis of African archaeology published in English, Phillipson (1993: 4) characterizes his focus on "economic development and general life-style, correspondingly less attention being paid to the definition, succession and inter-relationship of named industries." Further,

> Since more plentiful data relating to absolute chronology are now available than could be employed by the writers of previous syntheses, and in view of the . . . disparate rates of development in different areas, this book does not employ the conventional terminology based upon broad technological/chronological subdivisions such as Late Stone Age, "Neolithic" or "Iron Age." It has long been recognised that such terms cannot be precisely defined, but their informal use has continued, often at the expense of clarity; they are avoided in this book. (Phillipson 1993: 5)

Yet a glance at the contents of the chapter on the second millennium AD (Phillipson 1993: 208–40) reveals a preoccupation with trade, towns, and empires, with little mention of those interstitial "simple" societies in which perhaps the majority of people lived (Fuglestad 1992). This preoccupation is probably a more accurate reflection of the concerns of archaeologists working within a progressive developmentalist framework than it is of the daily lives of the majority of African peoples during the second millennium AD (Stahl 1994b: 99).

What are the alternatives?

It is always easier to diagnose a problem than to solve it. But there are examples in the recent literature that depart from the preoccupations of a progressive developmentalist model and offer insights into different research strategies. I briefly consider these in relation to the following problems: (1) distancing of non-complex societies in time; (2) focus on particular types of sites during particular ages/stages; and (3) the related problem of focusing on particular dimensions of the past during particular time periods. I will illustrate alternative approaches by reference to selected published works, and conclude with some recommendations for research strategies that can help us rethink how we perceive variability in time and space.

Recent concern with the effects of an expanding global system have generated new interest in relationships between societies formerly conceived as occupying different rungs of an evolutionary ladder (e.g., Wolf 1982). While there is debate over the applicability of different models (core-periphery, peer-polity), they share an interest in the relationships between societies of different scales. A political economy perspective (Roseberry 1988) further trains our attention on the local effects of global developments (Denbow, this volume). By examining relationships between societies, archaeologists and historians have been able to document changes in a variety of directions. Contrary to diffusionist models, which posit that systematic contact will result in a spread of attributes we associate with complexity, there is evidence that many societies experienced a decrease in complexity through incorporation into global networks (Holl 1990: 307; Rowlands 1989a). Thus, a political economic perspective is attentive to: (1) the contemporaneity of societies that an evolutionary model would tease apart and order hierarchically; (2) their interrelationships; and (3) the variable responses of local populations to inter-regional developments. In the study of Iron Age contexts then, the study of small hamlets would, in theory, be as significant as the study of a large town. It would also treat as significant those cases that did not fit easily into an evolutionary model; for example, cases where town sites were abandoned and polities seemingly dissolved. This perspective also draws attention to societies formed on the fringes of metropoles in what Kopytoff (1987, this volume) terms the internal African frontier.

Neither the political economic nor recent historical literature focused on interstitial societies is free of evolutionary overtones. The marxist framework from which political economy derives is inherently evolutionary (Neale 1985: 154–7), and Kopytoff's (1987) distillation of the social dynamic in ethnically ambiguous marginal societies has evolutionary overtones:

> The new immigrant compound becomes the nucleus of a hamlet. In time, the hamlet grows into a village as it attracts relatives from back home and other settlers that have been similarly ejected from the surrounding societies onto the frontier. Sometimes the new settlement solidifies, joins with other settlements or establishes a hegemony over them, and finally crystallizes into a new polity and eventually a society. (Kopytoff 1987: 6)

Despite the persistence of progressive developmentalist elements, however, they diverge from more conventional evolutionary models in their attention to the diverse array of societies characteristic of an area at a given point in time, and to their systematic interrelationships.

An agenda for archaeologists

What should archaeologists concerned about the persistent and distorting effect of a progressive developmental model on our understanding of Africa's past do? I share a few thoughts, although I do not pretend to provide a comprehensive solution.

The first item on our agenda needs to be a concerted effort to abandon, once and for all, the age/stage terminology that has permeated our efforts to write about Africa's past with progressive overtones. But avoiding the terms is not enough, as illustrated by the continued emphasis on cities and civilizations in recent overviews that eschew the terms (Connah 1987; Phillipson 1993). This will require that we rethink the narrative structure of our overviews – this is easier said than done, and I abandoned myself to the standard narrative in an overview of the archaeology of Ghana (Stahl 1994b). But to some extent, overviews reflect the preoccupations of the archaeologists whose work is being reviewed. Thus, we need to be attentive to the ways in which the research questions that we define as priorities – both in our own work and in the work of others through peer review – perpetuate a progressive developmental model.

The archaeologists who gathered at the First Pan-African Congress recognized the need for a chronological framework on which to base their emerging understanding of African prehistory. Without radiometric techniques at their disposal, they employed typological criteria to provide a relative ordering to their assemblages. While this resulted in widespread use of the age/stage terminology that I have critiqued, it also resulted in detailed analyses of artifact assemblages with chronological questions in mind (e.g., Ozanne 1962; Shaw 1961). This required a focus on deeply stratified sites or sites that overlapped in time. Growing reliance on radiocarbon dating seemingly freed us from the task of carefully constructing local sequences – we were able to focus on sites of particular ages and generate chronology independent of what preceded or followed the site. We were free to follow the research priorities associated with particular time frames, which, as we have seen, were determined by an evolutionary agenda. Today we are less sanguine about the accuracy of radiocarbon dating (McIntosh and McIntosh 1986b: 413–17) and are recommitted to building local chronologies based on combinations of typological and physical methods. These frameworks are a prerequisite for understanding variability both within and between regions, and for avoiding the problems associated with the age/stage approach.

A second item on our agenda needs to be a regional approach that is sensitive to variability within regions through time. Rather than focusing exclusively on town sites during the past millennium, we need to extend analyses to other contemporary sites. This requires programs of comprehensive survey which should be linked to the development of national and international databases (McIntosh 1994a). While regional studies have been common in other world areas for some time, they have been less so in Africa, which probably reflects limited resources. Nevertheless, there are outstanding exceptions in southern Africa (Denbow 1990, this volume; Hall 1981; Sinclair et al. 1993b), central Africa (David and Sterner 1989, this volume; MacEachern 1993), and western Africa (Connah 1981; McIntosh and McIntosh 1986a; 1993b), and more recently in East Africa (Robertshaw 1994). Systematic regional surveys do not in and of themselves overcome the structuring effects of a progressive developmentalist framework; however, careful attention to variability and chronology associated with careful surveys are a first step.

Regional surveys need to be combined with excavation programs that target different types of sites in a region both through time and in particular temporal contexts (e.g., Denbow, this volume; Robertshaw, this volume). Thus, our efforts to understand the nature of towns should be augmented by attention to associated hamlets or villages. However, it is equally important to examine sites through time. I, for example, am pursuing a variant of the direct historical approach examining adjacent village sites occupied at different points over the last 600–700 years (Stahl 1994a). Ongoing investigations document the variable character of daily life in the Banda area through time. Sites occupied from *c.* AD 1300 to AD 1600 are large, characterized by durable structures that are periodically refurbished, and have deep midden deposits (to 4 meters). Sites dating to the late eighteenth and early nineteenth century cover a considerable area, are similarly characterized by periodically refurbished structures, but exhibit far less substantial midden deposits. Late nineteenth- and early twentieth-century sites suggest a relatively ephemeral occupation – structures are less substantial and the midden takes the form of a thin sheet deposit. These changes in settlement correspond to shifts in broader political economic relations, including waxing and waning involvement in sub-continental trade, differential reliance on hunted vs. domestic animals, and changing patterns of craft production (Caton 1997; Cruz 1996; Stahl and Cruz 1998). Few if any of the patterns emerging from our Banda Research Project investigations are accommodated by the progressive developmental model that has underwritten African archaeology. To label these sites "Iron Age"

would create an impression of sameness, divert attention from change, and isolate them from a broader political economic context.

Finally, we need to be attentive to how our methodologies maintain a progressive evolutionary framework. Elsewhere (Stahl 1993a) I have discussed the role of evolutionary criteria in framing our choice of analogical models (and see David and Sterner, this volume). Archaeologists have long felt most comfortable using ethnographic analogues drawn from the same "evolutionary stage" as the site to which the analogue is applied. Thus, evolutionary mapping of sites meshed with an evolutionary mapping of contemporary societies. This facilitated mapping on of ethnographic detail to archaeological sites, perpetuating an evolutionary vision of human development. Greater awareness of the criteria that guide our choice of analogues, combined with rigorous source-criticism and a comparative approach to their application, may help us to circumvent this problem (Stahl 1993a: 246–53; Wylie 1985). Source criticism is equally important when we use oral history. Historians and archaeologists recognized the importance of oral history early in the post-colonial period, and have become increasingly sophisticated in gleaning historical evidence from these sources. Yet we need to examine how oral histories have been affected by feedback from the grand narrative of progressive development, whether through the interpretations of historians and archaeologists, or by the producers of those traditions (e.g., Ranger 1979; Schmidt 1990).

Concluding comments

One way to counter the homogenizing effects of a progressive developmental model is to stress variability and diversity, using Africa's past as a source of alternative models (S. McIntosh, this volume; Schmidt and Patterson 1995). But while we struggle to recognize and counter the ideological implications of a progressive evolutionary model for our understanding of Africa's past, we must recognize that our solutions may equally be ideologically charged and have unintended implications. Rowlands (1989b: 38) questions the relationship between an ideology of local difference and the needs of the dominant order to pursue "an ideology of localized identity and nationalist difference" in the face of an emerging international working class in the industrializing Third World (see also Handsman and Richmond 1995: 115). Afrocentric scholars are equally suspicious of an emphasis on localized diversity within Africa, seeing it as just one more attempt to denigrate the role of Africans in world history (Asante 1990).

Although the ideological underpinnings of emerging alternatives are less immediately obvious, it is clear that a progressive evolutionary model has led us to map variability among African societies in hierarchical fashion. As the narrative proceeds, many societies, both past and present, are deemed irrelevant to the story of human development. Further, we have trained our attention on particular dimensions of life in particular time periods – for example, on aspects of complexity in the "Iron Age." As a result, we have learned little of how rural agriculturalists coped with seasonal and annual variability, of the rich symbolic life of villagers, of gender in the past, or of how hamlets and towns interrelated (cf. David and Sterner, this volume; Denbow this volume; Kent 1998). Granted, some of these are difficult issues to address archaeologically, but to date we've not tried because they were questions that were not relevant to a progressive vision of human history.

As with any generalization, there are of course exceptions, and the exceptions provide cause for optimism that we may escape the limits of an evolutionary model that winnows variability from Africa's past and from world prehistory. Recent discussions of symbolic reservoirs provide one example (David 1992; MacEachern 1994; McIntosh 1989; Sterner 1992). In addition, practitioners are becoming more reflective about the context in which they work (e.g., Ellison et al. 1996; Schmidt and McIntosh 1996; Schmidt and Patterson 1995). Although commentators draw attention to the crisis of training on the continent, there are more African archaeologists than ever (e.g., Segobye 1995), and they are positioned to move beyond early independence efforts that sought to establish that Africa had a past of which it could be proud because it was the same as Europe's.

The predecessors of my generation laid the foundation for African archaeology – they undertook pioneering surveys, forged sequences that are the framework for African culture history, and worked to create respect for the African past at a time when Africa was widely regarded as a stagnant backwater. While I have great regard for their efforts, I have argued that the progressivist framework within which they labored has left us in the "Trevor-Roper trap" to borrow Fuglestad's (1992) phrase. A new generation has critiqued the progressivist model that framed Trevor-Roper's characterization of Africa, but the hard work of examining the implications of that legacy for our data and our day-to-day procedures lies ahead. The challenge is to recognize the distinctive qualities of an African past without further marginalizing the continent and its peoples.

Notes

1 Hugh Trevor-Roper, an Oxford historian, proclaimed to his BBC listeners in the early 1960s that Africa had no history, that its past was the endless gyrations of barbarous tribes. He became a foil for a generation of post-colonial historians who worked to counter his claim by documenting the dynamism of African societies. Yet, as Fuglestad (1992) describes, they never questioned Trevor-Roper's framework (one of progressive development), and continued to write history in a "Trevor-Roperian" way (Fuglestad 1992: 310).

References

Ajayi, J. F. A. and M. Crowder
1976 (eds.) *History of West Africa*. London: Longman.
Andah, B. W.
1993 Identifying early farming traditions of West Africa. In *The Archaeology of Africa. Food, Metals and Towns*, edited by T. Shaw, P. Sinclair, B. Andah, and A. Okpoko. London: Routledge: 240–53.
1995 Studying African societies in cultural context. In *Making Alternative Histories. The Practice of Archaeology and History in Non-Western Settings*, edited by P. R. Schmidt and T. C. Patterson. Sante Fe: School of American Research Press: 149–81.
Asante, M. K.
1990 Afrocentricity and culture. In *African Culture. The Rhythms of Unity*, edited by M. K. Asante and K. W. Asante. Trenton: Africa World Press: 3–12.
Banuri, T.
1993 The shadow of oppression. *The Unesco Courier*, November: 23–4.
Barros, P. de
1990 Changing paradigms, goals and methods in the archaeology of francophone West Africa. In *A History of African Archaeology*, edited by P. Robertshaw. London: James Currey: 155–72.
Beschaouch, A.
1990 The World Heritage Convention: a new idea takes shape. *The Unesco Courier* October: 44–5.
Binford, L. R.
1987 Data, relativism and archaeological science. *Man* 22: 391–404.
Bishop, W. W. and J. D. Clark
1967 (eds.) *Background to Evolution in Africa*. Chicago: University of Chicago Press.
Blakey, M. L.
1995 Race, nationalism, and the Afrocentric past. In *Making Alternative Histories. The Practice of*

Archaeology and History in Non-Western Settings, edited by P. R. Schmidt and T. C. Patterson. Sante Fe: School of American Research Press: 213–28.

Bolla, G. and M. Batisse
1980 Nature and culture. The human heritage. *The Unesco Courier*, August: 4–32.

Boorstin, D. J.
1993 Metaphors should be made at home. *The Unesco Courier*, November: 13–14.

Bowler, P. J.
1992 From "savage" to "primitive": Victorian evolutionism and the interpretation of marginalized people. *Antiquity* 66: 721–9.

Caton, A. S.
1997 Beads and bodies: embodying change in bead practices in Banda, Ghana. Unpublished M.A. Thesis, Department of Anthropology, State University of New York at Binghamton.

Childe, V. G.
1936. *Man Makes Himself*. London: Watts.
1942 *What Happened in History*. Hammondsworth: Penguin.

Childe, V. G. and M. C. Burkitt
1932 A chronological table of prehistory. *Antiquity* 6: 185–205.

Childs, S. T. and D. Killick
1993 Indigenous African metallurgy: nature and culture. *Annual Review of Anthropology* 22: 317–37.

Clark, J. D.
1962 Carbon 14 chronology in Africa south of the Sahara. In *Actes du IVᵉ Congres Panafricain de Préhistoire et de l'Etude du Quaternaire*, edited by G. Mortelmans and J. Nenquin. Tervuren: Musée Royal de l'Afrique Centrale: 303–11.
1967a Introduction to Part III. B. Sub-Saharan Africa. Archaeological considerations. In *Background to Evolution in Africa*, edited by W. W. Bishop and J. D. Clark. Chicago: University of Chicago Press: 413–16.
1967b The Problem of neolithic culture in Subsaharan Africa. In *Background to Evolution in Africa*, edited by W. W. Bishop and J. D. Clark. Chicago: University of Chicago Press: 601–27.
1970 *The Prehistory of Africa*. New York: Praeger.

Clark, J. D.
1982 (ed.) *The Cambridge History of Africa*. Volume 1. *From the Earliest Times to c. 500 BC*. Cambridge: Cambridge University Press.

Clark, J. G. D.
1946 *From Savagery to Civilization*. London: Cobbett.

Clarke, J. H.
1990 African–American historians and the reclaiming

of African history. In *African Culture. The Rhythms of Unity*, edited by M. K. Asante and K. W. Asante. Trenton: Africa World Press: 157–71.

Cole, S.
1954 *The Prehistory of East Africa*. Harmondsworth: Penguin.

Connah, G.
1975 *The Archaeology of Benin*. Oxford: Oxford University Press.
1981 *Three Thousand Years in Africa. Man and his Environment in the Lake Chad Region of Nigeria*. Cambridge: Cambridge University Press.
1987 *African Civilizations. Precolonial Cities and States in Tropical Africa: An Archaeological Perspective*. Cambridge: Cambridge University Press.

Cruz, M. D.
1996 Ceramic production in the Banda area (west central Ghana): an ethnoarchaeological approach. *Nyame Akuma* 45: 30–7.

David, N.
1992 The archaeology of ideology: mortuary practices in the Central Mandara Highlands, Northern Cameroon. In *An African Commitment: Papers in honour of Peter Lewis Shinnie*, edited by J. Sterner and N. David. Calgary: University of Calgary Press: 181–210.

David, N. and J. Sterner
1989 Mandara Archaeological Project, 1988–89. *Nyame Akuma* 32: 5–9.

Davidson, B.
1959 *Old Africa Rediscovered*. London: Victor Gollancz.

Deacon, J.
1990 Weaving the fabric of Stone Age research in Southern Africa. In *A History of African Archaeology*, edited by P. Robertshaw. London: James Currey: 39–58.

Debray, R.
1993 A Western myth. *The Unesco Courier*, November: 9–12.

Denbow, J.
1990 Congo to Kalahari: data and hypotheses about the political economy of the western stream of the Early Iron Age. *The African Archaeological Review* 8: 139–76.

Dennell, R.
1990 Progressive gradualism, imperialism and academic fashion: Lower Palaeolithic archaeology in the 20th century. *Antiquity* 64: 549–58.

Drewal, H. J.
1996 Past as prologues. Empowering Africa's cultural institutions. In *Plundering Africa's Past*, edited by

P. R. Schmidt and R. J. McIntosh. Bloomington: Indiana University Press: 110–24.

Earle, T.
1991 (ed.) *Chiefdoms: Power, Economy and Ideology.* Cambridge: Cambridge University Press.

Effah-Gyamfi, K.
1985 *Bono Manso: An Archaeological Investigation into Early Akan Urbanism.* African Occasional Papers no. 2. Calgary: University of Calgary Press.

Ellison, J., P. Robertshaw, D. Gifford-Gonzalez, R. J. McIntosh, A. B. Stahl, C. R. DeCorse, L. H. Robbins, S. Kent, A. Nagaba-Waye, M. Sahnouni, and A. K. Segobye
1996 The future of African archaeology. *African Archaeological Review* 13: 5–34.

Fabian, J.
1983 *Time and the Other: How Anthropology Makes its Object.* New York: Columbia University Press.

Fletcher, R.
1993 Settlement area and communication in African towns and cities. In *The Archaeology of Africa. Food, Metals and Towns,* edited by T. Shaw, P. Sinclair, B. Andah, and A. Okpoko. London: Routledge: 732–49.

Fuglestad, F.
1992 The Trevor-Roper trap or the imperialism of history. An essay. *History in Africa* 19: 309–26.

Gamble, C.
1992a Archaeology, history and the uttermost ends of the earth – Tasmania, Tierra del Fuego and the Cape. *Antiquity* 66: 712–20.
1992b Uttermost ends of the earth. *Antiquity* 66: 710–11.
1993 Ancestors and agendas. In *Archaeological Theory: Who Sets the Agenda?,* edited by N. Yoffee and A. Sherratt. Cambridge: Cambridge University Press: 39–52.

Gardin, J-C. and C. S. Peebles
1992 (eds.) *Representations in Archaeology.* Bloomington: Indiana University Press.

Goodwin, A. J. H., and C. Van Riet Lowe
1929 *The Stone Age Cultures of South Africa.* Annals of the South African Museum, no. 27, Cape Town.

Gowlett, J. A. J.
1990 Archaeological studies of human origins and early prehistory in Africa. In *A History of African Archaeology,* edited by P. Robertshaw. London: James Currey: 13–38.

Hall, M.
1981 *Settlement Patterns in the Iron Age of Zululand.* Oxford: British Archaeological Reports.
1990 "Hidden history:" Iron Age archaeology in Southern Africa. In *A History of African Archaeology,* edited by P. Robertshaw. London: James Currey: 59–77.

Handsman, R. G. and T. L. Richmond
1995 Confronting colonialism. The Mahican and Schaghticoke peoples and us. In *Making Alternative Histories. The Practice of Archaeology and History in Non-Western Settings,* edited by P. R. Schmidt and T. C. Patterson. Sante Fe: School of American Research Press: 87–117.

Holl, A. F. C.
1990 West African archaeology: colonialism and nationalism. In *A History of African Archaeology,* edited by P. Robertshaw. London: James Currey: 296–308.
1995 African history: past, present and future. The unending quest for alternatives. In *Making Alternative Histories. The Practice of Archaeology and History in Non-Western Settings,* edited by P. R. Schmidt and T. C. Patterson. Sante Fe: School of American Research Press: 183–211.

Horton, M. and N. Mudida
1993 Exploitation of marine resources: evidence for the origin of the Swahili communities of East Africa. In *The Archaeology of Africa. Food, Metals and Towns,* edited by T. Shaw, P. Sinclair, B. Andah, and A. Okpoko. London: Routledge: 673–83.

Kent, S.
1998 (ed.) *Gender in African Prehistory.* Walnut Creek, CA: Altamira Press.

Ki-Zerbo, J.
1993 North–South: Beyond the Great Divide. The universal and the particular. *The Unesco Courier,* November: 18–20.

Kleindienst, M. R.
1967 Questions of terminology in regard to the study of Stone Age industries in Eastern Africa: "Cultural Stratigraphic Units." In *Background to Evolution in Africa,* edited by W. W. Bishop and J. D. Clark. Chicago: University of Chicago: 821–59.

Kohl, P. L.
1993 Limits to a post-processual archaeology (or, The dangers of a new scholasticism). In *Archaeological Theory: Who Sets the Agenda?,* edited by N. Yoffee and A. Sherratt. Cambridge: Cambridge University Press: 13–19.

Kopytoff, I.
1987 The internal African frontier: the making of African political culture. In *The African Frontier. The Reproduction of Traditional African Societies,* edited by I. Kopytoff. Bloomington: Indiana University Press: 3–84.

Kuklick, H.

1991a Contested monuments. The politics of archeology in southern Africa. In *Colonial Situations. Essays on the Contextualization of Ethnographic Knowledge*, edited by G. W. Stocking, Jr. Madison: University of Wisconsin Press: 135–69.

1991b *The Savage Within. The Social History of British Anthropology*, 1885–1945. Cambridge: Cambridge University Press.

Leakey, L. S. B.

1934 *Adam's Ancestors*. London: Methuen.

Lewis, F.

1993 Relative values. *The Unesco Courier*, November: 15–17.

MacEachern, S.

1993 Archaeological research in northern Cameroon, 1992 – the Projet Maya-Wandala. *Nyame Akuma* 39: 7–13.

1994 "Symbolic Reservoirs" and inter-group relations: West African examples. *The African Archaeological Review* 12: 205–24.

McIntosh, R. J.

1989 Middle Niger terracottas before the Symplegades Gateway. *African Arts* 22 (2): 74–83.

McIntosh, S. K.

1994a Archaeological heritage management and site inventory systems in Africa: The role of development. In *Culture and Development in Africa*, edited by I. Serageldin and J. Taboroff. Washington, D. C.: The World Bank: 387–409.

1994b Changing perceptions of West Africa's past: archaeological research since 1988. *Journal of Archaeological Research* 2 (2): 165–98.

McIntosh, S. K. and R. J. McIntosh

1984 The early city in West Africa: towards an understanding. *The African Archaeological Review* 2: 73–98.

1986a Archaeological reconnaissance in the region of Timbuktu, Mali. *National Geographic Research* 2: 302–19.

1986b Recent archaeological research and dates from West Africa. *Journal of African History* 27: 413–42.

1988 From stone to metal: new perspectives on the later prehistory of West Africa. In *Journal of World Prehistory*, vol 2, edited by F. Wendorf and A. Close. New York: Plenum: 89–133.

1993a Cities without citadels: understanding urban origins along the middle Niger. In *The Archaeology of Africa. Food, Metals and Towns*, edited by T. Shaw, P. Sinclair, B. Andah, and A. Okpoko. London: Routledge: 622–41.

1993b Field survey in the Tumulus Zone of Senegal. *The African Archaeological Review* 11: 73–107.

Mauny, R.

1971 The western Sudan. In *The African Iron Age*, edited by P. L. Shinnie. Oxford: Clarendon: 66–87.

Mortelmans, G. and J. Nenquin

1962 (eds.) *Actes du IVᵉ Congres Panafricain de Préhistoire et de l'Etude du Quaternaire*. Tervuren: Musée Royal de l'Afrique Centrale.

Neale, C.

1985 *Writing "Independent" History. African Historiography, 1960–1980*. Westport: Greenwood Press.

1986 The idea of progress in the revision of African history, 1960–1970. In *African Historiographies. What History for Which Africa?*, edited by B. Jewsiewicki and D. Newbury. Beverly Hills: Sage Publications: 112–22.

Netting, R. Mc.

1990 Population, permanent agriculture, and politics: unpacking the evolutionary portmanteau. In *The Evolution of Political Systems. Sociopolitics in Small-Scale Sedentary Societies*, edited by S. Upham. Cambridge: Cambridge University Press: 21–61.

Okafor, E. E.

1993 New evidence on early iron-smelting from southeastern Nigeria. In *The Archaeology of Africa. Food, Metals and Towns*, edited by T. Shaw, P. Sinclair, B. Andah, and A. Okpoko. London: Routledge: 432–48.

Oliver, L. and A. Coudart

1995 French tradition and the central place of history in the human sciences. In *Theory in Archaeology. A World Perspective*, edited by P. J. Ucko. London: Routledge: 363–81.

Ozanne, P.

1962 Notes on the early historic archaeology of Accra. *Transactions of the Historical Society of Ghana* 6: 51–70.

Phillipson, D. W.

1985 *African Archaeology*. Cambridge: Cambridge University Press.

1993 *African Archaeology*. Second edition. Cambridge: Cambridge University Press.

Posnansky, M.

1967 The Iron Age in East Africa. In *Background to Evolution in Africa*, edited by W. W. Bishop and J. D. Clark. Chicago: University of Chicago Press: 629–49.

1973 Aspects of early West African trade. *World Archaeology* 5: 149–62.

1984 Early agricultural societies in Ghana. In *From*

Hunters to Farmers. The Causes and Consequences of Food Production in Africa, edited by J. D. Clark and S. A. Brandt. Berkeley: University of California Press: 147–51.

Ranger, T.
1979 The mobilization of labour and the production of knowledge: the antiquarian tradition in Rhodesia. *Journal of African History* 20: 507–24.

Robertshaw, P.
1990a A history of African archaeology: an introduction. In *A History of African Archaeology*, edited by P. Robertshaw. London: James Currey: 3–12.
1990b The development of archaeology in East Africa. In *A History of African Archaeology*, edited by P. Robertshaw. London: James Currey: 78–94.
1990c (ed.) *A History of African Archaeology*. London: James Currey.
1993 The beginnings of food production in southwestern Kenya. In *The Archaeology of Africa. Food, Metals and Towns*, edited by T. Shaw, P. Sinclair, B. Andah, and A. Okpoko. London: Routledge: 358–72.
1994 Archaeological survey, ceramic analysis, and state formation in western Uganda. *The African Archaeological Review* 12: 105–31.

Roseberry, W.
1988 Political economy. *Annual Review of Anthropology* 17: 161–85.

Rowlands, M.
1989a The archaeology of colonialism and constituting the African peasantry. In *Domination and Resistance*, edited by D. Miller, M. Rowlands, and C. Tilley. London: Unwin Hyman: 261–83.
1989b A question of complexity. In *Domination and Resistance* edited by D. Miller, M. Rowlands, and C. Tilley. London: Unwin Hyman: 29–40.
1994 The politics of identity in archaeology. In *Social Construction of the Past. Representation as Power*, edited by G. C. Bond and A. Gilliam. London: Routledge: 129–43.

Schmidt, P. R.
1990 Oral traditions, archaeology and history: a short reflective history. In *A History of African Archaeology*, edited by P. Robertshaw. London: James Currey: 252–70.

Schmidt, P. R. and R. J. McIntosh.
1996 (eds.) *Plundering Africa's Past*. Bloomington: Indiana University Press.

Schmidt, P. R. and T. C. Patterson
1995 From constructing to making alternative histories. In *Making Alternative Histories. The Practice of Archaeology and History in Non-Western Settings*, edited by P. R. Schmidt and T. C. Patterson. Sante Fe: School of American Research Press: 1–24.

Segobye, A. K.
1995 Revisiting the past in the present: a personal note on doing archaeology in Botswana. *Anthropology Newsletter* 36 (2): 11–12.

Sharpe, B.
1986 Ethnography and a regional system: mental maps and the myth of states and tribes in north-central Nigeria. *Critique of Anthropology* 6 (3): 33–65.

Shaw, T.
1961 *Excavation at Dawu*. Edinburgh: Thomas Nelson and Sons.
1990 A personal memoir. In *A History of African Archaeology*, edited by P. Robertshaw. London: James Currey: 205–20.

Shaw, T., P. Sinclair, B. Andah, and A. Okpoko
1993 (eds.) *The Archaeology of Africa. Food, Metals and Towns*. London: Routledge.

Shennan, S.
1993 After social evolution: a new archaeological agenda? In *Archaeological Theory: Who Sets the Agenda?*, edited by N. Yoffee and A. Sherratt. Cambridge: Cambridge University Press: 53–9.

Sheppard, P. J.
1990 Soldier and bureaucrats: the early history of prehistoric archaeology in the Maghreb. In *A History of African Archaeology*, edited by P. Robertshaw. London: James Currey: 173–88.

Shinnie, P. L. (ed.)
1971 *The African Iron Age*. Oxford: Clarendon.

Shinnie, P. L. and P. Ozanne
1962 Excavations at Yendi Dabari. *Transactions of the Historical Society of Ghana* 6: 87–118.

Sinclair, P. J. J., T. Shaw, and B. Andah
1993a Introduction. In *The Archaeology of Africa. Food, Metals and Towns*, edited by T. Shaw, P. Sinclair, B. Andah, and A. Okpoko. London: Routledge: 1–31.

Sinclair, P. J. J., Pikirayi, I., Pwiti, G., and Soper, R.
1993b Urban trajectories on the Zimbabwean plateau. In *The Archaeology of Africa. Food, Metals and Towns*, edited by T. Shaw, P. Sinclair, B. Andah, and A. Okpoko. London: Routledge: 705–31.

Smith, G. E.
1929 *The Migrations of Early Culture*. Manchester: Manchester University Press.

Sollas, W. J.
1915 *Ancient Hunters and their Modern Representatives*. Second edition. London: MacMillan.

Stahl, A. B.
1984 A history and critique of the investigations into early African agriculture. In *From Hunters to Farmers: Causes and Consequences of Food Production in Africa*, edited by J. D. Clark and S. Brandt. Berkeley: University of California Press: 9–21.
1993a Concepts of time and approaches to analogical reasoning in historical perspective. *American Antiquity* 58: 235–60.
1993b Intensification in the West African Late Stone Age: a view from central Ghana. In *The Archaeology of Africa. Food, Metals and Towns*, edited by T. Shaw, P. Sinclair, B. Andah, and A. Okpoko. London: Routledge: 261–74.
1994a Continuity and change in the Banda area, Ghana: the direct historical approach. *Journal of Field Archaeology* 21: 181–203.
1994b Innovation, diffusion, and culture contact: the Holocene archaeology of Ghana. *Journal of World Prehistory* vol. 8, edited by F. Wendorf and A. Close. New York: Plenum Press: 51–112.
Stahl, A. B. and M. D. Cruz
1998 Men and women in a market economy: gender and craft production in West Central Ghana *c.* 1700–1995. In *Gender in African Prehistory*, edited by Susan Kent. Walnut Creek, CA: Altamira Press: 205–26.
Sterner, J.
1992 Sacred pots and "symbolic reservoirs" in the Mandara Highlands of northern Cameroon. In *An African Commitment: Papers in Honour of Peter Lewis Shinnie*, edited by J. Sterner and N. David. Calgary: University of Calgary Press: 171–9.
Stocking, G. W., Jr.
1974 Some problems in the understanding of nineteenth century cultural evolutionism. In *Readings in the History of Anthropology*, edited by R. Darnell. New York: Harper and Row: 407–25.
1987 *Victorian Anthropology*. Madison: University of Wisconsin Press.
Takaki, R.
1993 *A Different Mirror. A History of Multicultural America*. Madison: Little, Brown and Co.
Temu, A. and B. Swai
1981 *Historians and Africanist History: A Critique*. London: ZED Press.
Thomas, N.
1989 *Out of Time. History and Evolution in Anthropological Discourse*. Cambridge: Cambridge University Press.

1994 *Colonialism's Culture. Anthropology, Travel and Government*. Princeton: Princeton University Press.
Tilley, C. (ed.)
1993 *Interpretative Archaeology*. Providence: Berg.
Touraine, A.
1993 One world. *The Unesco Courier*, November: 21–2.
Trigger, B. G.
1989 *A History of Archaeological Thought*. Cambridge: Cambridge University Press.
1990 The history of African archaeology in world perspective. In *A History of African Archaeology*, edited by P. Robertshaw. London: James Currey: 309–19.
Unesco Courier
1990 The World Heritage List. *The Unesco Courier*, October: 48.
Upham, S.
1990a Analog or digital? Toward a generic framework for explaining the development of emergent political systems. In *The Evolution of Political Systems. Sociopolitics in Small-Scale Sedentary Societies*, edited by S. Upham. Cambridge: Cambridge University Press: 87–117.
1990b Decoupling the processes of political evolution. In *The Evolution of Political Systems. Sociopolitics in Small-Scale Sedentary Societies*, edited by S. Upham. Cambridge: Cambridge University Press: 1–17.
1990c (ed.) *The Evolution of Political Systems. Sociopolitics in Small-Scale Sedentary Societies*. Cambridge: Cambridge University Press.
Vansina, J.
1965 *Oral Tradition: A Study in Historical Methodology*. Chicago: Aldine.
1966 *Kingdoms of the Savanna*. Madison: University of Wisconsin Press.
1995 Historians, are archeologists your siblings? *History in Africa* 22: 369–408.
Voigt, E. A.
1983 *Mapungubwe: An Archaeozoological Interpretation of an Iron Age Community*. Transvaal Museum Monograph, no. 1.
Wetterstrom, W.
1993 Foraging and farming in Egypt: The transition from hunting and gathering to horticulture in the Nile valley. In *The Archaeology of Africa. Food, Metals and Towns*, edited by T. Shaw, P. Sinclair, B. Andah, and A. Okpoko. London: Routledge: 165–226.
Willett, F.
1960 Ife and its archaeology. *Journal of African History* 1: 231–48.

1971 Nigeria. In *The African Iron Age*, edited by P. L. Shinnie. Oxford: Clarendon: 1–35.

Wolf, E. R.
1982 *Europe and the People without History*. Berkeley: University of California Press.

Wylie, A.
1985 The reaction against analogy. *Advances in Archaeological Method and Theory*, vol. 8, edited by M. B. Schiffer. New York: Academic Press: 63–111.

Yansane, A. Y.
1990 Cultural, political, and economic universals in West Africa. In *African Culture. The Rhythms of Unity*, edited by M. K. Asante and K. W. Asante. Trenton: Africa World Press: 39–68.

Yoffee, N.
1993 Too many chiefs? (or, Safe text for the '90s). In *Archaeological Theory: Who Sets the Agenda?*, edited by N. Yoffee and A. Sherratt. Cambridge: Cambridge University Press: 60–78.

4

Western representations of urbanism and invisible African towns

RODERICK J. MCINTOSH

The problem of archaeological invisibility

This chapter examines certain aspects of the history of thought about the origins of pre-industrial cities in an attempt to better understand why African urban expressions in the archaeological record remained unrecognized and unexamined for so long. In some cases, such as that of the Inland Niger Delta (also discussed in this volume by S. K. McIntosh), these include massive *tells* that are, on the face of it, difficult to overlook. How could such distinguished observers of the ground as Raymond Mauny (1961: 101–2) or Théodore Monod (1955), for example, walk over the massive site of Jenné-jeno, yet dismiss it with barely a mention? And these are only the most distinguished of the cohorts of prehistorians and natural scientists who, during perhaps a century, have yawned their way over the high and extensive *tell* remains of many early Middle Niger towns. I contend that they lacked the intellectual toolkit to recognize and process the evidence under their feet. They failed to recognize the town they trod upon because they did not find the *expected signs of pre-industrial urbanism*, namely, encircling wall and citadel (or palace or temple) reflecting coercive political organization, elite tombs or residences or other accoutrements as monuments to economic social stratification, and monumentality of architecture as monument to state ideology (R. McIntosh 1991: 203).

I argue here that our deeply rooted view of the non-Western city as despotic, depraved, and a place of bondage comes out of the tradition of Bible exegesis called Yahwism (or Jahwism)[1]. Few of the greats who formulated our canon of historical sociology of the early Oriental city in the nineteenth century would have been unaware of Yahwist thought, which influenced, I contend, the earliest debates about the conditions of emerging cities. In these debates, the ancient city could connote highly positive values if considered within the confines of the Greco-Roman world. However, there was a divergence of opinion about ancient Near Eastern cities. For some, there was a continuous evolution of positive morality from the earliest Mesopotamian towns, through the Semite cities of the southern Levant, to Greece and Rome, and finally to modern Europe and America. Others looked at those same Sumerian, Babylonian, and even Palestinian cities as morally discontinuous with the Western experience. It is the intellectual origin of this second, "Orientalizing," and negatively judgmental view of the early city that is most pertinent to understanding the archaeologists' neglect of urbanism in Africa as well as in other parts of the world.

To one degree or another, a number of influential social thinkers concerned with the early city (e.g., Weber, Wittfogel, Engels, Spengler), whose conception of primitive urbanism resonated with a larger audience, reproduced in their writings a shared representation of all but a restricted sub-set of towns as dark moral exemplar. What are the hidden values of this view of pre-industrial urban despotism? At root, those values create a terrifying cityscape, a newly invented space of asymmetrical power (R. McIntosh 1991: 203; see Lefebvre 1991: 235–53). Divorced from the freedom and piety of the country and of the soil, city life is bondage, rootlessness, namelessness, and depravity. The city creates a new order of human nature forever dedicated to the control of the many by the few – to hierarchy – and to a control that robs one of essential freedoms and of essential connectedness of (kinship-based) community and of the covenantal relationship with God that is the very core of Yahwism. This control is reflected in the monumental constructions that came to be viewed as the signature of the city, whether they be the positively viewed Greek or Roman polis or the contrasting Oriental seats of despotism. Sites without large-scale construction could not, in this view, be candidates for urban status.

These pervasive yet implicit representations of urbanism are profoundly implicated in the archaeologist's choice of urban models and data. Only a deeper exercise in disciplinary self-reflection can open our eyes to alternative forms and trajectories of early urban process. The process of understanding why some early cities have remained hidden from archaeological discovery, whether in West Africa, northern China, or Southeast Asia, is just another route to understanding alternative and non-hierarchical courses towards complex society (R. McIntosh

1997). That is why I argue that we must step back and look at the process by which expectations of hierarchy and coercive power came to have such a defining role in the search for cities. Therefore, we must take excursions to the realm of epistemology (specifically to the linkage of values and systems of knowledge) and, ultimately, to nineteenth-century biblical exegesis.

Power and place of representations

Archaeology is in a period of rethinking itself. Most archaeologists are moving to distance themselves from the most intolerant logical positivist and overly functionalist "New Archaeology" positions (Trigger 1989a: 289–369). Likewise, they shun the radical "post-processualist" view that material remains are a text subject to multiple, unverifiable interpretations and that all archaeological inference and interpretation is just story-telling with a nasty, hegemonic moral (Kohl 1993: 15–16; Renfrew and Zubrow 1994; Trigger 1989b; Yoffee and Sherratt 1993: 6). Rather, there is a general recognition that self-reflexivity about archaeologists' models and research priorities leads to explorations of prehistoric motivations and intentionality – and not just to navel-gazing paralysis.

Self-reflexivity is the midwife attending the birthing room of archaeological theory. Self-reflexive archaeologists employ two concepts of representation. One definition of the word focuses upon the language used in the description of archaeological materials in systems of categories, classifications, databases – i.e., in the arguments and words that link the empirical data to the more speculative level of hypotheses and interpretations (Gardin and Peebles 1992a: 1–4). The purpose of this first, more semiotic definition of representations is to make explicit the language and cognitive structure of archaeological reasoning.

A second definition of representation gives us the title of this present chapter. Here I am interested in those historically grounded models of causation in the world *held by the researcher* that mold and create the ways in which that observer reconstructs past peoples' culturally generated view of the world (Gardin and Peebles 1992b: 386; see Gregory 1994: 6–9, 34–7). An investigation of this second aspect of representation helps us to understand how inference is biased by the observer's fundamental, and often unarticulated, views of the world.

Representations are the work-a-day foundations of self-reflexivity, where the prehistorian makes explicit and subjects to historical analysis the hithertofore implicit web of values behind certain key archaeological cate-

gories, theory or model choices, or interpretive constructs. The archaeological category of interest here, the early town, is simultaneously an interpretive construct *and* an embodiment of social motivations. To understand why that should be so requires a brief digression into the role of values in theory building.

Historical or archaeological representations are analytical superstructures built upon their own preselected foundation of theory-mediated facts. Representations serve a portmanteau role. The term is inclusive enough to subsume all the functions of Hayden White's (1973: ix) metahistories ("deep structural narrative rules . . . precritically accepted paradigms of what explanations should be"). In archaeology, representations as used here would best be described conceptually as metamodels. Representations are larger abstractions about the place of humans in their world that conceptually link and make sense of models, defined by David Clarke (1972: 1–2) as ". . . pieces of machinery that relate observations to theoretical ideas . . . [that] isolate the essential factors and interrelationships which together largely account for the variability of interest in the observations."

There must be a higher order conceptual structure organizing the task of explanation. Representations are the executive metamodels setting the work schedule, overseeing, structuring – and not infrequently stifling the productive curiosity – of our work-a-day, shopfloor explanatory models. What makes representations so forceful, so omnipresent in the workings of our interpretive tools is the fact that they remain stubbornly implicit. In fact, if examined too closely and under too critical a light, their weaknesses (logical and factual) often become all too apparent. The purpose of this paper is to turn just such a light upon one tradition of Western representation of the early town.

The reasons why representations must remain stubbornly hidden from the researchers whose work they permeate are critical to our understanding of the link between values and theory. In his highly influential *Naturalism and Social Science*, David Thomas (1979: 141) argues that every social science (and I would argue, every historical discipline) is steeped in its own metaphysic. Thomas uses the term "metaphysic" in a less structured way than I will use the term "representations" here. But he is moving in a parallel direction when he argues that the underlying metaphysic structures and validates the knowledge base of every interpretive theory. This, Thomas argues, is accomplished by grounding all aspects of knowledge production in deeper (implicit) assumptions about human nature. Theory develops in terms of those features of fundamental human values and of people's history that the researcher holds as basic or immutable. These values are the counterparts of fundamental (largely unexamined) views of space, time, and matter in the physical sciences. Conformity to values and to fundamental views of human nature (originating in the investigator's own web of belief) adds a moral theme to our theories and narratives. I will argue shortly that the views of human nature that permeate the historical Western representation of non-Greco-Roman early towns derive from the nineteenth-century, Yahwist value of Covenantal Piety.

What is the purpose of excavating values and the moral components of theories or models? It is decidedly not to assert that, because values permeate the data we select for recording as facts and the theories or models that we weave together into our causal chain of explanation, we can know nothing about the motivations of past peoples. Indeed, some of the most articulate theory-relativists, such as D. Thomas (1979: 138) and P. Roth (1987), argue that, only by being self-reflective can the social sciences and historical disciplines pursue the objectives of science. One of the most important of those objectives is self-correcting skepticism (Converse 1996; D'Andrade 1995). Thomas and Roth would also contend that the common objective of science is the accumulation of a class of knowledge about the world that reveals chains of causation and that allow a statistical degree of prediction. Archaeology as a discipline has a particular history of raucous internal debate about the proposition that the "facts speak for themselves." The majority view would now, I think, incline to Trigger's view (1989b: 770) that "most historical facts are not self-evident but acquire meaning within the context of stereotypes and belief about human behavior that are held by individual historians." That statement, in and of itself, is not remarkable. However, Trigger goes on to argue that self-reflective archaeology does not need inevitably to lead to dogmatic hyperrelativism or to a sullen and defensive positivism:

> What is needed is a limited, and carefully nuanced, commitment to empiricism. Seen from this perspective, the main role of relativism is to sensitize archaeologists to the subjective influences that have shaped the beliefs and actions of the people whose remains they study and that additionally influence their own interpretations, both as individuals and as members of a profession. Neither empiricism nor relativism ensures objectivity, but when utilized together they promote a more informed and self-reflective analysis of human behavior. (Trigger 1989b: 788)

This, indeed, is the point of all self-reflective archaeology that has as its purpose something other than "structural oppositions to their constructed category of 'processualists'" (Yoffee and Sherratt 1993: 5). We use an historical analysis of representations – their intellectual genealogies and their internal logical structure – in order to identify the implicit social values that encourage disciplinary adherence to those representations: only then may we understand how the (often unspoken) expectations grounded in those values intrude in a major way upon the nitty-gritty decisions of fieldwork.

I hope to show here that major classes of West African cities long remained invisible to archaeologists because of the heavy mask of a mainstream Western representation of the early city. In so doing, I hope further to show that brand new data fields become available once the underlying social values (e.g., Covenantal Piety) are made apparent. In order to do this, we need to visit the contrasting historical scholarship about the social world of the Greco-Roman and Biblical lands.

Pastoral vs. urban, piety vs. ideology: The dichotomy of Yahwist values

What were the assumptions about the moral life of the pre-industrial city that drove the writings of social thinkers and resonated with their scholarly and educated lay readership? I contend that an historical criticism of a dominant tradition of Bible exegesis, Yahwism, shows clearly why the primitive town was represented as dark moral exemplar. Yahwism was subscribed to by several generations of biblical scholars and, most importantly, by many social theorists of the origins of cities beyond the Greco-Roman world. The positive value attributed to an idealized, pastoral piety – and the condemnation heaped upon the impious lifestyles of non-White, oriental urban dwellers – are dichotomies that underlie much of this Old Testament biblical scholarship.

Not all ancient cities were equal. It will help us to understand what the Yahwist city was understood to be by looking at the counter-tradition of what those oriental cities were not. For the classically educated scholar or layperson of the last century and, for that matter, of more recent decades, the Greco-Roman cities were the birthplace of enduring Western political and moral forms. In this sense, the divide between them and oriental cities (of all lands east and south of Europe) was absolute. Let us look first at the attributes that made the ancient Mediterranean *polis* so attractive.

From the beginning, the *polis* was graced by the monumental: "a fortified place," that included the community's sanctuaries, cult places (temples) of increasing splendor (Seaford 1994: 1, 197). These monumental manifestations will be important to classical archaeologists' definition of what elements of the city are important priorities for excavations and restoration (e.g., Camp 1986). However, in the Western intellectual tradition, the defining and unique glory of the Greco-Roman city was its role in a fundamental mode shift of authority and rule of law that will lead in an evolutionary straight line to modern European and American civilization. As early as 1864, in Fustel de Coulanges' influential and much-quoted *The Ancient City*, the nostalgic urban panegyrics of Livy, Sallust, Tacitus, and Ammianus Marcellinius were interpreted in the light of social evolutionist metanarratives of progressive human advances as the exclusive preserve of this unilinear path of civilization (Mazzolani 1967: 25–6; Kuklick 1996: 184).

The circumstances of the mode shift may be obscure, but all scholars promulgating a privileged view of Greco-Roman cities would subscribe to some variation of this fundamental narrative. For most of the (non-Western) world, in which cities arose spontaneously or because of contact with "superior" cultures, the process of urbanism was coincident with a shift from small-scale, egalitarian and non-centralized forms of authority and economy to control over the many by a single leader and eventually to the despotic, monarchical state. The eastern Mediterranean was on this very same path in Homeric/Dark Age times, as represented by the growing power, for example, of the Mycenaean chiefdoms. Then came a unique (if mysterious) historical process linked to the 8th to 6th century rise of cities such as Athens. The power of the hereditary chief/king wanes with the emergence of a confederation of the ruling class and (especially) with the invention of authorities invested in new judicial institutions such as law courts (Seaford 1994: 191–7, 220; Vernant 1982). The essential contrast was between the oriental city as seat of ever tightening despotism, versus the *polis* as locus first of an aristocratic council of family heads to resist the king, leading then to expanding political rights based upon property, then to the enfranchisement of the poor according to military service, and finally to a democratic ideal of equal political and legal rights to all free men (Fustel de Coulanges 1864: 314–20).

The idea of the classical city, then, was embodied in two parallel metanarratives. The first was the civilizing role of Greco-Roman urban culture: the city as a design for a heterogeneous society in which local gods and loyalties would be assimilated to citizenship and to a national pantheon. All persons living under the rule of reason, law,

and republican morality would be a part of the expanding *oikoumene*, the Great City (City of Mankind, City of Justice), irrespective of their birthplace (Mazzolani 1967: 11, 36–7, 188–91; see Tarn 1948, and Tarn and Griffith 1952). The Victorian vision of Greece (Jenkyns 1980) and Rome (Mazzolani 1967) implied a continuity from the (imperial) classical Great City through the medieval City of God (still physically centered in Rome) to the civilizing burdens of imperial England, Germany, and France. Only "lunatic barbarians" (Mazzolani 1967: 19) would destroy order and set back civilization by sacking the City, as did the Visigoths in AD 410.

The second genius of the Hellenic and Roman *polis* was expansive inventiveness – progress. This was entirely consistent with the Victorians' vision of their own role in history (and of what defined them as uniquely contrasted to all other peoples of the earth). Fustel de Coulanges (1864) gives us a catalogue of the moral and material benefits springing from the classical city: acceptance and hospitality towards strangers (potential fellow citizens) (pp. 117–18), a new "natural" religion allowing the absorption of family and local gods (pp. 118–19, 123), a confederated government that, at the same time, ensures each constituent unit non-interference in its own sectional affairs and cults (pp. 119–20), shift from passion to reason as authority shifts from family to the community (p. 124), hereditary leaders consigned to ritual and sacerdotal roles while real power passes to the people (pp. 134–71), and especially the aforementioned rise of republican morality and the rule of law. In this narrative, the one critical element of Western civilization not authored by the classical world was monotheism – and in this omission resided a central intellectual quandary for theoreticians of the early city.

If the evolutionary line between the *polis* and the nineteenth-century West could be traced easily, it was considerably more difficult to link Judeo-Christian civilization (including life in the cities of the southern Levant and Mesopotamia) to the Greco-Roman world. In his very useful *Puritans in Babylon*, Bruce Kuklick (1996) provides a detailed analysis of the moral and Scriptural motivations of the pioneering American (and German) excavators and patrons of those expeditions to Mesopotamia. Kuklick argues that these excavators linked the prestige of scientific investigation to a profound wish to confirm the literal truth of the Bible and to relate Judeo-Christian morality, from its origins in the ancient cultures of Mesopotamia, to the rise of the (God-fearing) West.

The problem became one of evidentiary and prejudicial contradictions: opposed to the continuity of Greco-Roman (urban) morality, laws and rules of governance (interrupted only by barbarian incursions), the story from the urban dirt of Mesopotamia and Palestine was one of impermanence, decay, and waste, and of great states and cities stricken down because of impiety and oriental despotism (Kuklick 1996: 8, 38). Just how the monotheism of the Hebrews and the transcendent spirituality of early Christianity emerged from all this was not entirely clear!

The German "pan-Babylonians" attempted to get around this problem by the invention of an *ur-Semitic* (for some, "Aryan"), Sumerian homeland of a (non-Israelite) race responsible for the first flickerings of monotheism. This was rejected as rank invention by influential synthesizers of the newly uncovered Mesopotamian and Egyptian evidence, especially James Henry Breasted of Chicago, Albert Clay of Yale, and Hermann Hilprecht of Penn. Each argued, in his own way, for a Greco-Roman distillation of the best elements of earlier or adjacent Egyptian, southern Levantine, and Mesopotamian civilizations. As influential as these secular, compromise interpretations were, they were ultimately unconvincing to the majority of scholar-excavators of the Biblical lands (such as William Foxwell Albright) and world civilization synthesizers (such as Arnold Toynbee). For these scholars, profoundly immersed as they were in Old Testament sentiments, there was a fundamental discontinuity between ancient Near Eastern religions and morality and Hebrew belief in the absolute transcendence of God (Kuklick 1996: 185–7).

Kuklick's one failing, in my opinion, is not to have explored further Albright's thesis of the Israelites' "evolutionary mutation" and "abrupt break" (Albright 1957; quoted in Kuklick 1996: 187) with earlier oriental civilization. The focus of these scholars' attention (in excavation and exegesis) was the southern Levant, Syrian, Egyptian, and Mesopotamian cities of the Bible. Unlike the republican moral and political trajectory that took place *within* the Greco-Roman city, an influential current of Biblical exegesis developed that argued that the monotheistic mode shift (Albright's "evolutionary mutation") took place *physically exterior to* and *morally in contrast to* the impious, despotic oriental city. This is the tradition of Yahwist exegesis that will occupy us for the rest of this chapter. The contrast of the Yahwists' vision of the rise of oriental cities with the classicists' vision of the Hellenic and Roman city could not be greater, even though both thought in terms of historically revolutionary mode shifts in morality.

In the Yahwist tradition, the clearest commandments of Judeo-Christian piety are etched onto the lenses that scholars held up to the continuing revolt of early Israelites

against the iniquitous and impious cities of the Mediterranean coast. Israel is founded in that revolt. In the period of roughly 1800 to 1200 BC (and especially after *c.* 1550 BC), the southern Levant coast Bronze Age ends in a jumble of famine, political turmoil, and plague stories (Gottwald 1979; Matthews and Benjamin 1993: 3–5; Mazar 1990: 191–300). Yahwist scholars interpreted this chaos not as the result of climate change, outside interference by Hittites, Hurrians, Hyksos, and Egyptians, or of random local political adjustments but as an expression of divine retribution (Albright 1957).

Yahweh was signaling not only his extreme displeasure with Canaanite urban culture. He was also offering a covenant to those willing to leave the material security of a centralized urban existence for the spiritual fulfilment of a life on the margins, in Yahweh's care.

Those who elected to pioneer this new relationship with Yahweh would sacrifice much. They would sacrifice the security of life behind thick city walls. They would sacrifice the surplus harvests and abundant pastures of the coastal plain. They would sacrifice the potential to work their way into the higher citadel or temple bureaucracies. But, this is precisely the Yahwist lesson: only by sacrificing these *apparent* advantages would the pioneers of a new way of life and a new piety be in a position to become the chosen of an all-powerful God. The early city was the physical seat and the metaphor of all the surpluses, riches, and the iniquities that would be sacrificed by the move to the marginal existence at the Judean hills. Thus, by fleeing the material security of their former homes in the coastal cities, the early Israelites fled the values that have persistently characterized the Western representation of the primitive oriental city. These same values gave rise to archaeologists' expectations of what they should expect to find at the earliest cities of the southern Levant, or Mesopotamia – and beyond.

In Yahwist exegesis, the values of the urban dweller are the values of the unfree. Only those relatively few with kinship ties to the monarch are free; all others were the king's bondspersons. The king's power rested upon a centralized, surplus economy supporting the standing army needed both to protect the city from covetous neighbors and to maintain a degree of state terrorism within the city walls. The surplus economy depended upon the administratively directed labor of an unfree populace, be they *de jure* slaves or the *de facto* servile urban peasantry.

Despotic power reinforced the urban kings' distinctive form of authority that so enraged Yahweh. The unfree craftsmen and laborers built security in the form of the city wall. And they built monumental public structures, secular palaces and cultic temples that glorified the ideology of monarchy and idols of the god(s) from whom the monarch derived his authority to rule.

Thus, according to the Yahwist interpretation, the state-based authority prevailing at the earliest cities is based upon the exclusive, personal relationship of the despot monarch with the city's god. This is Weber's (1968: 241–3) "anointed" right to rule at the dawn of *Gottesgnadentum* (divine right of kings). The right to head a brutal, exploitative social structure derives from what Weber labels "charismatic authority . . . by virtue of which he [the monarch] is considered extraordinary and treated as endowed with supernatural, superhuman, or at least specifically exceptional powers or qualities" (Weber 1968: 241). The state (and all corollary institutions, such as the city – seat of the king) exists as an expression of the exclusive relationship of a god and monarch. All relationships of power in the social structure are reckoned by distance from that essential axis. Piety is equated with absolute submission, absolute loyalty to the monarch's person. Because of the exclusive, anointed relationship of monarch to his god, there can be no higher check to the power of the state. Power is celebrated in the absolute. Cults elaborate their affronts to the austere Yahwists' God – and the town way of life sinks "to extremely sordid depths of social degradation" (Albright 1953: 77).

Historical exegesis uses this representation of the city as its springboard to exhortation to piety. Dichotomous with primitive urban despotism and degradation is the Yahwists' free-will covenant with God and the harsh strictures of the pastoral life on the Judean hills. The city must appear before the Israelites can reject its temptations for true Covenantal Piety. Here, it is not our purpose to critique the history of this idea of piety as a personal covenant with God. Rather, we are concerned with how archaeologists' expectations for the kinds of artifacts and features that would serve as signatures for the earliest cities may derive from this Yahwist moralizing upon impious urban life. Interestingly, the Yahwists concentrate on the Prophets' criticisms of urban life, but tend to ignore the theocratic urbanism central to the evolution of Judaism with David and Jerusalem (M. Maas, pers. comm.). All metanarratives treat evidence selectively in this manner.

This perspective casts the early city's role mechanistically (R. McIntosh 1991: 203). A complex, surplus economy is made possible by and is massaged by a hierarchical, centralized administration. The first demand of that administration is that everyone affirm their allegiance, vertically, to the hierarchically flowing font of authority. Everyone must accept the sacred, charismatic

nature of that authority. In time, and with evolving control of the economy and material/monumental props of ideology, the hierarchy becomes ever more elaborated, ever more rigid. Perceived threats to its authority are dealt with ever more brutality. Centralized state administration necessarily precedes or emerges simultaneously with urbanism.

In plan and in monumentality, the city is a unity focused on the temple-palatial center of the monarch and his font of authority. Its encircling wall exists as much to keep in the subject population as to keep out threats from rival powers. Plan and monumentality reinforce state ideology in their implied statement that the social condition is eternal, inevitable, and without recourse. All are locked into their condition. Just as physical freedom is just a dream for most of the population, so too is piety expressed (under pain of torture, formal enslavement, or death) in terms of the relationship of the individual to monarchy. To flee this requires much more than slipping away from the city's walls. To flee, in Yahwist terms, means to have the ability to make the free-will choice to enter into a covenantal relationship of piety with Yahweh. The formerly oppressed voluntarily marginalize themselves in order to eschew charismatic authority.

The city as dark moral exemplar (and the underlying unspoken values of Covenantal Piety) are such integral parts of the Western intellectual tradition that we must acknowledge and analyze their influence if we are to understand the history of archaeological investigations of cities, whether in Africa or in the Near East. Few of the founding scholars who formulated our canon of historical sociology of the early city could have escaped the endless scriptural descriptions of bondage, despotic rule, and urban impiety that came out of Yahwist exegesis. Weber's conception of early city economy (the "city-house"), for example, and political authority ("patrimonial kingship") as articulated in his classic essay, *The City* (1921), reflect the legacy of nineteenth-century Yahwism (Weber 1956: 1282–90; 1958). Wittfogel's (1957) focus on hydraulic methods of social control (permanent surrender of their labor and essential freedoms by the many to a few), and monuments as the physical expression of the despotic ideology similarly echoes Yahwist themes. Engels (1942), too, shared a view of the town as the product and the instrument of a new order of society, based not upon consensual rule of the tribe, but upon plunder, oppression of neighbors, and the domination and oppression of the people by an aberrant hereditary (and charismatic) monarchy of the rich, bellicose, and slave-owning. His vision of the city as the locus of Decline, was shared by those of contrasting political persuasion, such as the right-wing, mystical agrarianist Oswald Spengler:

> The stone Colossus "Cosmopolis" stands at the end of the life's course of every great Culture. The Culture-man whom the land has spiritually formed is seized and possessed by his own creation, the City, and is made into its creature, its executive organ, and finally its victim. (Spengler 1928: 98–9).

Small wonder that the first urban archaeologists were fully convinced that cities contained only the material expression of primal state despotism (see R. McIntosh 1991: 202). Layard (1853: 639–40), preparing to dig Nineveh, could scarcely imagine finding anything of importance that did not reflect this: "It is very doubtful whether these fortified enclosures contained many buildings besides the royal palaces, and such temples and public edifices as were attached to them."

Hierarchy and heterarchy

The extent to which reassessment and critique of this kind of monolithic representation of the earliest cities is gathering steam is illustrated by a recent collection of essays on *The Archaeology of City States* (Nichols and Charlton 1997). Morris (1997) offers a pointed critique of the model of the "agro-literate state" (Gellner 1983) towards which, he claims, virtually all archaeologists envision social evolution as leading. In the agro-literate state, the ruling classes consist of stratified elites, who use writing and religion to underwrite social structure, rigidly separating themselves from the great majority of the direct producers, or peasants (Gellner 1983, cited in Morris 1997: 92). This "controlling model" of the state is radically undercut by the example of the city-state of Athens in the 5th century BC, which "was not dominated by a small wealthy elite lording it over peasant subjects" (Morris 1997: 98). Partly because of this failure of city-states to conform to archaeological expectation, Morris (1997: 91) argues, archaeologists have not paid much attention to them. Morris concludes with a call for a broader range of ideas and concepts, an idea endorsed by Small (1997: 114): "Future analytical paradigms will have to develop scales of social complexity beyond current measures of hierarchy."

The development of new paradigms needs to move in two directions, one concerned with rethinking how we infer social organization from monumental remains, the other focused on assumptions we make about social organization in the absence of such vestiges. In her work at the early second millennium late Sumerian and early

Babylonian site of Mashkan-Shapir (north of Nippur), Elizabeth Stone's work (1997; Stone and Zimansky 1995) exemplifies developments in the first direction, suggesting that even in architecturally potent Mesopotamia, concensual political arrangements, power sharing, and strongly egalitarian ideologies may have characterized city-state organization. Stone and Zimansky (1995: 119) contend that earlier theorists reconstructing the social structure behind Sumerian city plans were unduly influenced by their excavation focus on ziggurats, palaces, and other monuments to *apparent* control of the many by the few. In other words, the circular logic of excavation of control structures, driven by expectations and a value-assessment of what were the really important elements of an early city, led archaeologists to underappreciate the organizational potential of consultation rather than of coercion.

My own work, and that of S. McIntosh (1995, this volume) has been concerned with the second focus: cities that have been invisible to archaeologists because they lack monumental construction (R. McIntosh 1991, 1993, 1997; S. and R. McIntosh 1993).

I believe the West African examples of clustered cities require us to drop the outdated Yahwist moralizing that lodged in the writing of many contemporary thinkers about the origins of complex society. Once recognized for what it is, it is much easier to jettison. Better, perhaps, that we adopt Spiro Kostof's (1989: 117) "spontaneous" versus "planned" processes of town birth, as a way to deal not just with the infinity of local city histories but, more importantly, with the infinity of authority relations with which early town dwellers experimented. Indeed, some early cities will have been the legacy of a despotic, highly centralized state structure. These will be laboratories for the archaeological elucidation of vertical hierarchy and the material expression of the control of one over many. However, I suspect that once we look, the similarities of non-hierarchical Mashkan-Shapir or the similarities of Jenné-jeno with the clustered "network of specialized parts" (Chang 1986: 363) of Erh-li-t'ou or even An-yang will not be too remarkable.

I suspect that, instead, we will have to be increasingly on our guard against making *too much* of the surface similarities of Kostof's "spontaneous" settlements, of which the Middle Niger towns will surely be prime examples. Surely very different conceptions of authority and traditions of resistance to consolidation or monopolies of (coercive) power could result in superficially similar settlement plans. We need a way to guard against the lure of false cognate settlement pattern evolution and, equally, a way to get at the underlying, quite distinct, cultural codes of authority distribution. Kostof may point in the right direction with his insistence upon the Aristotelian notion of synoecism: the administrative merging of several proximate villages to form a town in a process by which the eventual settlement retains much of the original villagescape (Kostof 1989: 120; see Cavanagh 1991: 105–10).

As archaeology matures we will look more inclusively at the full range of processes by which complex society emerged. Other comparative studies of early settlement aggregation, far from emphasizing the centrality of centralization, show that equals need not surrender their status or autonomy when they aggregate (e.g., Hays 1993). Then, today's neo-evolutionist near-obsession with hierarchy will give way to equal investigations of heterarchy, "connection of many to many, rather than the control of one over many" (Barnett 1994: 52; see Crumley 1995). Weber was supremely skeptical that "municipal associations" could rival (or keep in check) the princes' administrative apparatus. Archaeology unshackled by Yahwist values may prove him wrong on a global scale. For us all, making explicit the hidden values behind our representations of cultural processes is the first thing that must be done as we slip off outmoded intellectual blinders.

Notes

1 Yahwism is the term I apply both to this historical biblical commentary tradition and to the description of a way of life of the pastoral, pious Israelites. Therefore, Yahwist assumptions flowed naturally from the Yahwist representation of the Israelites' conscious rejection of life in cities. See Gottwald (1979), Matthews and Benjamin (1993), and Benjamin (1983). The core concept is the covenant ("*berîth*") between the tribal Israelites and their God = Covenantal Piety (see Albright 1957: 271).

References

Albright, W. F.
    1953 *Archaeology and the Religion of Israel*. Baltimore: The Johns Hopkins University Press.
    1957 *From the Stone Age to Christianity; Archaeology and the Religion of Israel*. 2nd edition [1st edn 1940]. Baltimore: The Johns Hopkins University Press.
Barnett, S.
    1994 Futures: probable and plausible. *Anthropology Newsletter* 37 (7): 52.
Benjamin, D. C.
    1983 *Deuteronomy and City Life*. Lanham: University Press of America.
Camp, J. M.
    1986 *The Athenian Agora. Excavations in the Heart of Classical Athens*. Rev. edn. London: Thames & Hudson.
Cavanagh, W. G.
    1991 Surveys, cities and synoecism. In *City and Country in the Ancient World*, edited by J. Rich and A. Wallace-Hadrill. London: Routledge: 97–118.
Chang, K. C.
    1986 *The Archaeology of Ancient China*. 4th edn. New Haven: Yale University Press.
Clarke, David L.
    1972 *Models in Archaeology*. London: Methuen & Co.
Converse, P. E.
    1996 The ultimate cross-cultural convergence. *Anthropology Newsletter* 37 (5): 1, 4.
Crumley, C. L.
    1995 Heterarchy and the analysis of complex societies. In *Heterarchy and the Analysis of Complex Societies*, edited by R. Ehrenreich, C. Crumley, and J. Levy. Washington, D.C.: Archaeological Papers of the American Anthropological Association, no. 6: 1–6.
D'Andrade, R. G.
    1995 What *do* you think you're doing? *Anthropology Newsletter* 36 (7): 1, 4.
Engels, F.
    1942 *The Origin of the Family, Private Property and the State*. Reprint of the 1884 edn. London: Lawrence and Wishart, Ltd.
Fustel de Coulanges, N. D.
    1864 *The Ancient City*. [1980 edn.] Baltimore: The Johns Hopkins University Press.
Gardin, J.-C. and C. S. Peebles
    1992a Introduction. In *Representations in Archaeology*, edited by J.-C. Gardin and C. S. Peebles. Bloomington: Indiana University Press: 1–11.
    1992b Epilogue. In *Representations in Archaeology*, edited by J.-C. Gardin and C. S. Peebles. Bloomington: Indiana University Press: 385–91.
Gellner, E.
    1983 *Nations and Nationalism*. Oxford: Blackwell.
Gottwald, N. K.
    1979 *The Tribes of Yahweh. A Sociology of the Religion of Liberated Israel. 1250–1050 BCE*. Maryknoll: Orbis Books.
Gregory, D.
    1994 *Geographical Imaginations* Oxford: Blackwell Publishers.
Hays, K. A.
    1993 When is a symbol archaeologically meaningful? Meaning, function and prehistoric visual arts. In

Archaeological Theory: Who Sets the Agenda? edited by N. Yoffee and A. Sherratt. Cambridge: Cambridge University Press: 81–92.

Jenkyns, R.
  1980 *The Victorians and Ancient Greece.* Cambridge: Harvard University Press.

Kohl, P. L.
  1993 Limits to a post-processual archaeology (or, The dangers of a new scholasticism). In *Archaeological Theory: Who Sets the Agenda?* edited by N. Yoffee and A. Sherratt. Cambridge: Cambridge University Press: 13–19.

Kostof, S.
  1989 Junctions of town and country. In *Dwellings, Settlements and Tradition*, edited by J.-P. Bourdier and N. Alsayyad. Lanham: University Press of America: 107–33.

Kuklick, B.
  1996 *Puritans in Babylon. The Ancient Near East and American Intellectual Life, 1880–1930.* Princeton: Princeton University Press.

Layard, A. H.
  1853 *Discoveries in the Ruins of Nineveh and Babylon.* London: John Murray.

Lefebvre, H.
  1991 *The Production of Space.* Oxford: Blackwell Publishers.

McIntosh, R. J.
  1991 Early urban clusters in China and Africa: the arbitration of social ambiguity. *Journal of Field Archaeology* 18: 199–212.
  1993 The pulse theory: genesis and accommodation of specialization in the Middle Niger. *Journal of African History* 34: 181–220.
  1999 Clustered cities and alternative courses to authority in prehistory. *Journal of East Asian Archaeology.*

McIntosh, S. K.
  1995 (ed.) *Excavations at Jenné-jeno, Hambarketolo, and Kaniana (Inland Niger Delta, Mali), the 1981 Season.* Berkeley: University of California Press.

McIntosh, S. K. and R. McIntosh
  1993 Cities without citadels: understanding urban origins along the Middle Niger. In *The Archaeology of Africa. Foods, Metals, and Towns,* edited by T. Shaw, P. Sinclair, B. Andah, and A. Okpoko. London: Routledge: 622–41.

Matthews, V. H. and D. C. Benjamin
  1993 *Social World of Ancient Israel, 1250–587 BCE.* Peabody: Hendrickson Press.

Mauny, R.
  1961 *Tableau géographique de l'Ouest Africain au*

Moyen Age. D'après les sources ecrites, la tradition, et l'archéologie. Dakar: Mémoire no. 61 de l'Institute Fondamental d'Afrique Noire.

Mazar, A.
  1990 *Archaeology of the Land of the Bible, 10,000–586 BCE.* New York: Doubleday.

Mazzolani, L.S.
  1967 *The Idea of the City in Roman Thought. From Walled City to Spiritual Commonwealth.* Trans. S. O'Donnell. Bloomington: Indiana University Press.

Monod, T.
  1955 A propos des jarres-cercueils de l'Afrique occidentale. *Africanischen Studieren* 26: 30–44.

Morris, I.
  1997 An archaeology of equalities? The Greek city-states. In *The Archaeology of City-States*, edited by D. L. Nichols and T. H. Charlton. Washington D.C.: Smithsonian Institution Press: 91–106.

Nichols, D. L. and T. H. Charlton
  1997 (eds.) *The Archaeology of City-States.* Washington D.C.: Smithsonian Institution Press.

Renfrew, C. and E. B. W. Zubrow
  1994 *The Ancient Mind. Elements of Cognitive Archaeology.* Cambridge: Cambridge University Press.

Roth, P. A.
  1987 *Meaning and Method in the Social Sciences.* Ithaca: Cornell University Press.

Seaford, R.
  1994 *Reciprocity and Ritual. Homer and Tragedy in the Developing City-State.* Oxford: Clarendon Press.

Small, D.
  1997 City-state dynamics through a Greek lens. In *The Archaeology of City-States*, edited by D. L. Nichols and T. H. Charlton. Washington D.C.: Smithsonian Institution Press: 107–18.

Spengler, O.
  1928 *The Decline of the West. Perspectives of World-History.* Vol. II. Translated by C. F. Atkinson. New York: Alfred A. Knopf.

Stone, E. C.
  1997 City-states and their centers: the Mesopotamian example. In *The Archaeology of City-States*, edited by D. L. Nichols and T. H. Charlton. Washington D.C.: Smithsonian Institution Press: 15–26.

Stone, E. C. and P. Zimansky
  1995 The tapestry of power in a Mesopotamian city. *Scientific American* 272 (4): 118–23.

Tarn, W. W.
  1948 *Alexander the Great.* Cambridge: Cambridge University Press.

Tarn, W. W. and G. T. Griffith
  1952 *Hellenistic Civilisation.* 3rd edn. London: Edward Arnold & Co.
Thomas, D.
  1979 *Naturalism and Social Science: A Post-empiricist Philosophy of Social Science.* Cambridge: Cambridge University Press.
Trigger, B.
  1989a *A History of Archaeological Thought.* Cambridge: Cambridge University Press.
  1989b Hyperrelativism, responsibility and the social sciences. *Canadian Review of Sociology and Anthropology* 26: 776–97.
Vernant, J. P.
  1982 *The Origins of Greek Thought.* [Trans. of 1962 edition] Ithaca: Cornell University Press.
Weber, M.
  1956 *Economy and Society.* 4th edn. New York: Bedminster.
  1958 *The City.* Trans. and ed. by D. Martindale and G. Neuwirth. [1st edn 1921] Glencoe: The Free Press.
  1968 *Economy and Society.* 3 vols. 4th edn. New York: Bedminster.
White, H.
  1973 *Metahistories: The Historical Imagination in Nineteenth-Century Europe.* Baltimore: The Johns Hopkins University Press.
Wittfogel, K.
  1957 *Oriental Despotism. A Comparative Study of Total Power.* New Haven: Yale University Press.
Yoffee, N. and A. Sherratt
  1993 Introduction: the sources of archaeological theory. In *Archaeological Theory: Who Sets the Agenda?* edited by N. Yoffee and A. Sherratt. Cambridge: Cambridge University Press: 1–9.

5
Modeling political organization in large-scale settlement clusters: a case study from the Inland Niger Delta

SUSAN KEECH MCINTOSH

In the Western popular imagination, sub-Saharan Africa has long been the domain of small-scale, dispersed, mobile, swidden agriculturalists. Yet within the Inland Niger Delta in the Sudanic zone of West Africa, some of the earliest documented agricultural communities display quite the opposite pattern: rapid population growth over the course of centuries-long occupation of high density settlement clusters. Commonly, a cluster comprises a large, central settlement mound of up to 10 meters in height and 20–80 hectares in area, surrounded by inter- mediate and smaller mounds at distances of 200 meters or less. In the vicinity of Jenné-jeno, where multiple clusters are present and there is evidence from survey and excava- tion for the extent of occupational contemporaneity among the various mounds, the total occupied mound surface exceeded 100 hectares within a millennium of the initial pioneering settlement c. 250 BC. From a compar- ative perspective, the lengthy occupation sequences and the pattern and scale of population nucleation docu- mented in the Inland Delta are relevant to a number of long-standing theoretical discussions in archaeology, among them the relation of population growth and the evolution of agricultural systems, and the relation of population size and political hierarchy. In this case study, both the lack of evidence for agricultural intensification and the distinctive pattern of nucleated settlement clus- ters are considered essential elements for understanding the particular trajectory that developing complexity assumed in the region.

Colonization and settlement clustering in the Inland Niger Delta

The Inland Niger Delta (IND), as its name implies, is an area of false deltaic hydrology located in the heart of the modern state of Mali over 1,500 km inland from any sea coast. It is an area of extraordinary productivity and importance in the prehistory and history of the sahelian zone (Figure 5.1). Every year in August and September, an area of over 50,000 km^2 is inundated by floodwaters; this zone supports a teeming succession of marsh, swamp, and grassland vegetation as waters recede. Annual rainfall ranges from 600 mm in the southern (Upper) IND to 200 mm annually in the northernmost sector near the Niger Bend, and is concentrated in a brief rainy season. Vegetation is richest in the deepest basins which retain water the longest, but these are not the areas of highest population density. Low basins support primarily fisherfolk for much of the year, because basins flood too deeply for flood cultivation of rice, which is the dominant agricultural pursuit on the Upper IND floodplain. The dry season grasslands in the deep basins, however, support a vast number of cattle brought in by transhu- mant Peul herders in April and May (Gallais 1967, 1984). Stock herding, fishing, and rice cultivation, all rendered highly productive by the natural flood regime of the IND, have sustained human populations since they first settled permanently in the IND c. 250 BC.

Research directed by R. J. McIntosh and myself between 1977 and 1987 indicates that the floodplain opened up for permanent settlement in the third or second century BC, due to a widespread dry episode (S. McIntosh 1995; S. McIntosh and R. McIntosh 1980). At that time, the high floods, perennially marshy conditions, and active hydrology present in the Middle Niger in prior millennia subsided dramatically. This movement into the well-watered valley of the Niger was the final act in an attenuated drama involving southward movement along drainage systems of mixed agriculturalists no longer able to water their cattle or successfully grow crops in the higher latitudes of their ancestors, which were progressively turning to desert. The Sahara, which had perennially flowing streams as recently as 3000 BC, had declined to arid conditions approximating those of the present by the first century AD.

Currently, it is not known where and when the African rice (*Oryza glaberrima*) grown by the pioneer farmers in the IND was first domesticated. Most researchers accept Portères' (1976) hypothesis, based on the distribution of the wild progenitor (*Oryza barthii*) and variability in *O. glaberrima*, that domestication occurred somewhere

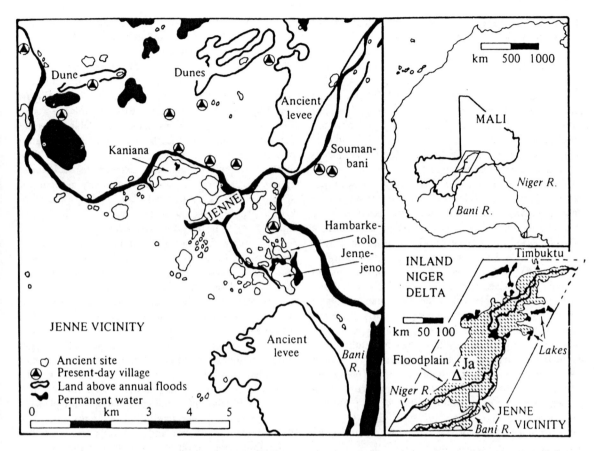

Figure 5.1   The Inland Niger Delta of West Africa: the Jenné region, the sites clustered around Jenné-jeno, and the location of Ja.

along the Middle Niger, probably around 1500 BC. The most likely source areas lie to the west and north of the IND regions such as the Méma, which had seasonally flowing channels, backswamps, and marshy depressions that were exploited by Late Stone Age peoples. The Upper IND, by contrast, has thus far revealed no hint of occupation by stone-using peoples. Whatever the actual date of rice domestication, there can be no question that the colonization of the IND by rice growers in the first millennium BC was the initial phase of a phenomenal expansion marked by dramatic population increase and both linear and leapfrog migration throughout the first millennium AD that are recorded both in oral traditions of the Soninké peoples of the IND and in the archaeological record. The availability of iron technology after *c.* 500 BC is clearly implicated as an important factor, since the use of iron hoes to break up the heavy soils of the IND

floodplain would have facilitated expansion throughout this zone.

Excavations at the mounds of Ja and Jenné-jeno at the westernmost and easternmost extremity, respectively, of the Upper IND have revealed virtually identical ceramic and iron assemblages in the earliest levels dating to 250–0 BC, produced by groups with a similar subsistence economy based on domestic cattle, sheep and goat, fish, wild bovid and waterfowl exploitation, and domestic rice in conjunction with extensive wild cereal collection (R. McIntosh and S. McIntosh 1987; S. McIntosh 1995). According to oral traditions, migrants from Ja founded Jenné-jeno (Monteil 1971). In both areas, settlement mound clustering and density is unusually high. Few other sectors of the IND have a similar number, density, and scale of settlements. Few other sectors of the IND have produced evidence of occupation at this early date.

While research coverage of the IND is admittedly sparse, with much of the basic outline of occupation yet to be documented, I have suggested that the available evidence is consistent with pioneering settlement in narrow zones of maximum productivity (S. McIntosh in press b). For the mixed agriculturalists colonizing the IND, this meant zones where good rice growing soils (not too shallowly or too deeply inundated) were present, as well as non-inundated areas (primarily levees or areas beyond the floodplain) for pasturing livestock in flood season, plus deep basins for dry-season pasture.

The distribution of levees and deep basins is extremely patchy (Figure 5.2). Ja is located at the southern end of a linear zone where these two landforms occur in close proximity to good rice soils. Jenné-jeno represents a highly localized occurrence of all three at the southeastern tip of the IND. Additionally, the location of Ja and Jenné-jeno at the margins of the floodplain would have facilitated access to raw materials, such as iron ore, that were not available within the floodplain. I suggest that colonists during this initial phase of settlement preferentially sought out such limited, maximally productive zones, which supported rapidly increasing numbers of people. If this is true, future archaeological survey should reveal an abundance of late first millennium BC/early first millennium AD sites throughout this optimal zone along the western margin of the IND. Certainly, this pattern is characteristic of the region surveyed around Ja (R. McIntosh and S. McIntosh 1987). Around Jenné-jeno, however, the optimal zone is limited and there is little evidence so far for first millennium BC settlement other than at Jenné-jeno itself. While populations in the Ja area had many opportunities for linear expansion into optimal adjacent areas, the highly localized nature of the maximally productive zone at Jenné-jeno resulted in population expansion within a central, 12 km^2 area.

A similar pattern of nodal population growth has been documented in the Méma by Togola (1993, 1996). There, the pattern of tightly packed site clusters centered on a large mound (up to 80 ha in area) was strongly developed during the first millennium AD, with considerable evidence for clustering extending back into the first millennium BC or earlier among stone-using peoples in the region. Food-producing economies with domestic sheep/goats and a small breed of domestic cattle similar to the modern, tsetse resistant N'Dama and West Africa dwarf shorthorn breeds are present in the Méma from the second millennium BC (MacDonald 1994). Flotation samples are currently being analyzed to determine the plant species exploited. For the moment, we can only note that the Méma mounds are well situated for rice cultiva-tion. Ceramic elements from Méma Late Stone Age sites dating to the late second and early first millennium BC show strong similarities to the earliest ceramic assemblage of iron-using colonists in the IND. It is tempting to think, and plausible to hypothesize, that mixed agriculturalists from the Méma expanded into maximally productive zones for rice cultivation and stock-keeping within the IND once drier conditions made it available for settlement in the final centuries BC. If evidence from future research supports this hypothesis, then we will have another example of an early, expansionist cultivation system based not on swidden, as early agricultural systems are often portrayed, but on horticulture on hydromorphic soils, consistent with a pattern that Sherratt (1980) proposed for temperate western Eurasia.

According to Sherratt, the initial phase of agriculture was localized fixed-plot horticulture in a narrow range of alluvial and lake-margin habitats, using simple broadcast methods and requiring little or no tree clearance. The rapid expansion of these early systems was due not to shifting cultivation necessitated by long fallow, but to the restricted and often linear pattern of suitable habitats. In the next phase of Sherratt's developmental scheme, agricultural systems expanded and differentiated in succeeding millennia by diverting surface water to reach a wider area (irrigation) and by adaptation to dry conditions by a better use of rainfall (including adoption of the plow).

The pattern of Sherratt's initial phase appears to be documented in the Méma and the IND, characterized by continuing colonization of new sectors of the alluvium, rapid population growth, and notable concentration of population in optimal zones. But there is no evidence to suggest that water control or irrigation techniques were subsequently developed in either zone. There is no evidence visible in aerial photographs or on the ground of abandoned canal or bund systems. In the mid-twentieth century, as the French colonial government struggled to implement irrigation-based agriculture along the Middle Niger, they lamented the "primitive" state of indigenous floating rice agriculture in the IND: weeding was rare, broadcast sowing haphazard and wasteful, transplanting, manuring, and plowing non-existent. Wild rice grew alongside domesticated varieties, and in some fields, reseeding occurred entirely from grains that had fallen to the ground during harvest. Bemused, the French wondered whether this was really agriculture or simply gathering (Gallais 1967: 218–19).

The apparent lack of intensification through two millennia of occupation in the Djenné area is both interesting from a comparative perspective and informative with regard to the kind of political organization we might

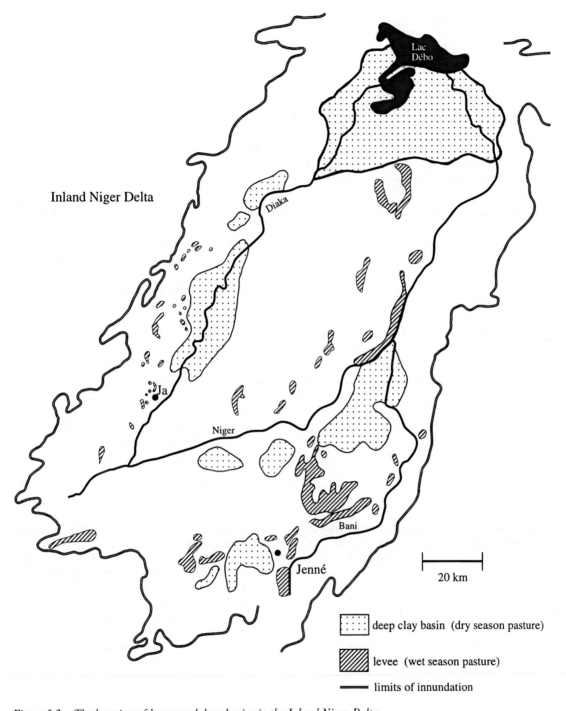

Figure 5.2 The location of levees and deep basins in the Inland Niger Delta.

Table 5.1. *Sequence of development at Jenné-jeno, reconstructed from excavation*

Jenné-jeno	Phase I/II 250 BC–AD 400	Phase III AD 400–900	Phase IV AD 900–1400
SITE AREA	12 ha–AD 100 25 ha–AD 400	33 ha (maximum extent) by AD 800	gradual contraction after AD 1100 abandoned by AD 1400
SUBSISTENCE ECONOMY	domestic rice, wild Brachiaria, rare domestic sorghum & millet; cattle, dwarf ovicaprids, antelope, fishing water fowl	antelope decline, dwarf ovicaprids increase; large and small cattle breeds present; all other elements remain constant	same as Phase III, but only small cattle present
ARCHITECTURE	daub-smeared pole-and-mat huts	banco huts *c.* 3 m diam.	cylindrical mud brick round huts *c.* 3 m. diam *c.* AD 900 city wall *c.* AD 1000 rectilinear mud brick houses appear
EXCHANGE/ TRADE	iron, stone from up to 50 km distant; rare glass beads from Mediterranean sphere	copper appears AD 500 (nearest source 300 km); gold present by AD 900 (nearest source 600 km); geometric painted ware distributed from Jenné-jeno to Lakes Region	from AD 1000, North African brass, glass, spindle whorls
BURIAL	single flexed inhumation; no grave goods	large funerary urns in cemetary precincts; inhumation also practiced;no grave goods	funerary urns in cemeteries or associated with residences; no grave goods
SYMBOLIC		potsherd pavements	terracotta statuettes; warrior styles appear *c.* AD 1200

expect at a large settlement complex such as Jenné-jeno. In the next section, I turn to a brief overview of the available evidence we have for the growth and development of this site complex, and I then consider the dynamics of the subsistence system that supported such a high local concentration of population under conditions of considerable production risk and uncertainty.

The archaeological sequence at Jenné-Jeno

Based on controlled excavations at the 33 hectare tell of Jenné-jeno, the adjacent 8 hectare tell of Hambarketolo and the 41 hectare site of Kaniana some 3 kilometers away, we have been able to establish a four-phase ceramic and cultural sequence for Iron Age occupation, which extended from 250 BC to AD 1400 at the long-lived sites of Jenné-jeno and Hambarketolo (S. McIntosh 1995; S. McIntosh and R. McIntosh 1980). The essential features of site expansion, economy, trade, and symbolic behavior are

summarized in Table 5.1. Of particular significance is the fact that, although material culture, building technology, exchange relations, and symbolic behavior underwent significant change through time, the subsistence economy changed relatively little. Flotation and faunal samples show a mixed economy with heavy exploitation of domestic rice, wild *Brachiaria* millet, rare domestic millet and sorghum, hunting of wild antelope and waterfowl, herding of domestic cattle and sheep/goats, and a significant fishing component. This economy is broadly similar to that in the Upper IND today, although hunting is only occasionally possible now, owing to overhunting in the recent past. Within the agrarian sector, rice is the primary domesticate, but wild cereals constitute the dominant component throughout the sequence. This is of considerable interest, in view of the rapid growth of the mound. By AD 100, it measured at least 12 hectares; by the end of Phase I/II at AD 400, it had expanded to 25 hectares. Jenné-jeno had reached its maximum size of 33 hectares by AD 900.

Other important elements of the sequence include the development of long-distance exchange involving copper and gold, apparently on a very limited scale, between AD 400 and AD 900, and the lack of any evidence from residential or burial contexts for elites during this period. The first defensive structure, a city wall 3 meters wide and 2 kilometers long constructed of mud brick, was built shortly after AD 900, at about the same time that North African goods and influence, in the form of brass, glass beads, spindle whorls, and rectilinear house form, first appear in the sequence. Within a century of North African contact, Jenné-jeno and neighboring Hambarketolo are in decline. The last vestiges of occupation at Jenné-jeno date no later than AD 1400.

Site cluster chronology and population

Survey was conducted within a study area covering 1100 km² to the north and west of Jenné-jeno, focusing on areas above flood level, including tell sites, levees, and dunes, where permanent settlement could be supported. In this region, only a handful of sites were known prior to 1977. In 1977, 404 sites were discovered in the course of fieldwalking and from aerial photographs. Of these, sixty-five were clustered within 4 kilometers of Djenné. Of the forty-two sites randomly selected for surface investigation during survey (focusing particularly on the area within 4 km of Jenné-jeno, where thirty-two of the sixty-five tells present were investigated) three-quarters of the sites had no surface material later than Phase IV, indicating abandonment during that phase. The fact that most of these were tells over 2 meters high suggests an occupation that spanned several centuries, given the slow rates of deposition documented by excavation at Jenné-jeno and its neighboring mound, Hambarketolo. Nearly all these sites were located on intermediate-depth floodplain soils favored for rice cultivation. Figure 5.3 shows the clear association of sites with areas such as marigot channels and borders of low floodplain basins. Levees and dunes were apparently not favored for permanent occupation until the arrival after the thirteenth century of the Bambara, who practice rain-fed millet cultivation on these soils. The sites that we encountered during survey of these landforms had Phase V (post-1400) abandonment assemblages.

Surface remains on several of the largest sites in the vicinity of Jenné-jeno indicate maximally extensive occupation during Phase III/early Phase IV, and a reduction in the area of more recent deposits before final abandonment. These results imply that site density and population reached a peak in late Phase III/early Phase IV, at the same time that Jenné-jeno reached its maximum areal extent.

Estimating population size for this period of maximum expansion is difficult, since we do not have enough information on floor area or numbers of compounds and must use site size as a proxy measure (for a discussion of these problems, see S. McIntosh and R. McIntosh 1993). An IND town such as Djenné has 9,000 people living on 44.8 hectares, giving a density of 221 people per hectare, which is lower than the density factor for non-market towns in the hinterland that lack large public spaces. One such town near Djenné, for example, packs 2,750 people onto a 7.07 hectare mound (389 people per hectare). Other villages around Djenné have a mean density of 237 people per hectare (for fifteen villages within 8 kilometers of Djenné).

Still, these density factors cannot be uncritically projected back to the first millennium because the adoption of two-story architecture in the area sometime after the beginning of the second millennium presumably allowed greater residential densities. If we turn to a village further afield (but inhabited by the same linguistic group, the Soninké) where single story construction is still the norm, however, we still find a high residential density. The 9 hectare village of Yaguiné had 1,750 inhabitants early this century, giving a population density of 195 people per hectare (Brasseur 1968: 198–9). Nucleation with extremely tight residential spacing seems to be a characteristic of Soninké settlements.

Whether we can safely project that characteristic back in time over a millennium is open to question. One major factor to consider is the penning of livestock. Herds are kept pastured outside Soninké villages today, although individual homes may keep one or two sheep tethered in or beside the house. It is primarily this factor that accounts for the high settlement densities in the IND. The intensive use of residential space in Djenné and other towns in the IND today contrasts with low densities in villages along the Middle Senegal Valley, for example, where cattle and sheep are penned in the villages at night. Excavations in the Middle Senegal Valley revealed characteristic "fumier" (manure) layers in first millennium AD occupation deposits, demonstrating that the practice is of considerable antiquity there (R. McIntosh et al. in prep.) No such evidence has been detected at Jenné-jeno. Rather, all evidence suggests that the Phase III and IV components of the mound are substantially composed of mud wall-melt, indicating intensive occupation. I believe that it is reasonable, therefore, to use the figure of 195 people per hectare as a density factor that may be applicable to Jenné-jeno. Interestingly, this is very close to the density of 200 people per hectare that Adams and Nissan (1972: 29) used in discussing the Warka

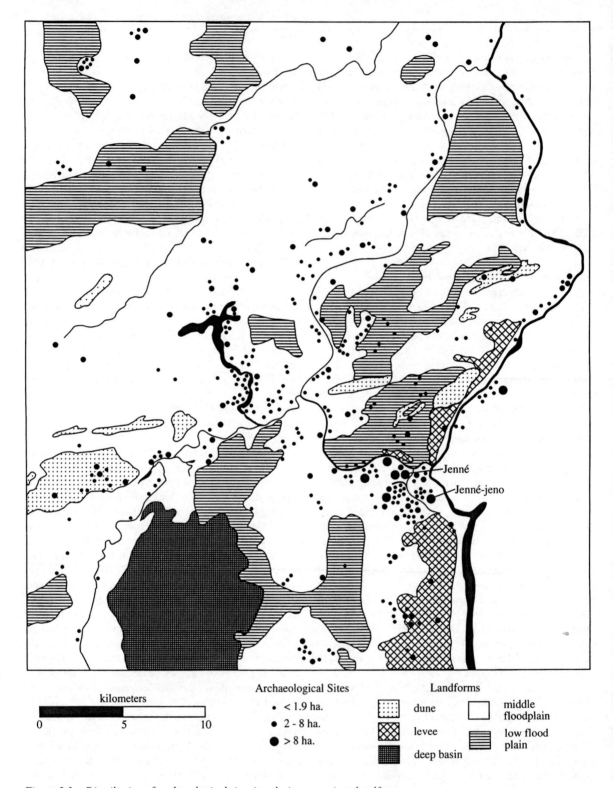

Jenné

Jenné-jeno

Archaeological Sites	Landforms

Archaeological Sites
- • < 1.9 ha.
- ● 2 - 8 ha.
- ⬤ > 8 ha.

Landforms
- dune
- levee
- deep basin
- middle floodplain
- low flood plain

kilometers

0   5   10

Figure 5.3   Distribution of archaeological sites in relation to various landforms.

Table 5.2 *Possible range of population at Jenné-jeno, AD 800–1000*

Area	Estimated population	
	97 persons/ha	195 persons/ha
Jenné-jeno (33 ha)	3,200	6,400
Jenné-jeno and Hambarketolo (33 + 8.8 = 41.8 ha)	4,100	8,200
Jenné-jeno cluster (includes satellite sites within 1 km) (33 + 35.7 = 68.7 ha)	6,700	13,400
Maximal cluster (includes all Phase IV sites within 5 km) (68.7 + 68 = 136.7 ha)	11,000	22,000

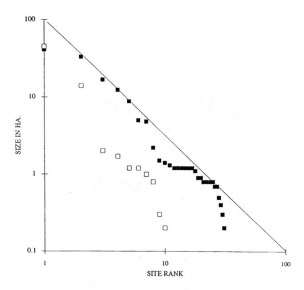

Figure 5.4 Rank–size distributions of archaeological sites occupied in AD 1000 within 4 km of Jenné-jeno and the present-day settlements (open squares) of the same area.

Survey, extrapolating from a study of fifty-three Khuzestan villages, although the variance was high in that case, just as it is for the IND villages. Adams and Nissan (1972: 29–31) prudently settled for 50 percent of that figure as a reasonable approximation, taking into account early spatial fragmentation of sites and the probability that not all areas of settlements were contemporaneously occupied in any period. The same approach is reflected in Table 5.2 which estimates the possible range of population at Jenné-jeno and its immediate vicinity *c.* AD 800–1000.

The integrated nature of this site complex is indicated by the close approximation of site sizes and ranks to the classic rank–size distribution characterizing urban systems (Figure 5.4). Moreover, this distribution can be mapped to show that a two- or three-tier settlement hierarchy had emerged by late Phase III, with two very large sites (>20 ha), several medium sites (between 8 and 19 ha), and a large number of smaller sites (Figure 5.5). This pattern of clustered settlement had disappeared by AD 1400, as three-quarters of the mounds in the Jenné-jeno maximal cluster, including Jenné-jeno itself, were abandoned. Population was reorganized onto a single large mound (the existing town of Djenné) and a handful of small, dispersed villages. This is the pattern that characterizes settlement in the area today.

The evidence for rapid population growth and settlement nucleation through both site expansion and close-packed clustering of settlement mounds is, I believe,

indisputable. This raises questions about the subsistence system that supported this dense population.

Subsistence intensification and risk

Nucleation on the scale found at Jenné-jeno is often assumed to have involved considerable subsistence intensification. To Plog, for example, the relationship between "intensified production and increased settlement size (nucleation) should be obvious . . . Intensification involves large coordinated projects . . . Nucleated settlements are not essential for such projects but they help, since it is much easier to mobilize people" (Jolly and Plog 1987: 439, cited in Stone 1996: 48). How did Jenné-jeno's occupants avoid the growth/intensification spiral? To a very limited extent, they did not, since there is reason to think that cultivation/fallow ratios increased. But for the most part, they maximized production through the development of specialized subsistence niches linked by exchange and interdependence, maintaining wild resources as a significant element of diversification within otherwise specialized economies. For flood rice cultivation, part of this diversification-within-specialization strategy was avoidance of increased labor inputs to single, fixed plots. Elsewhere (S. McIntosh, in press a), I have detailed how production has historically been specialized

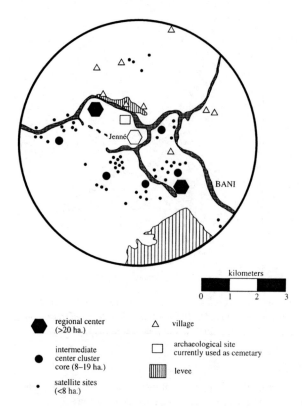

regional center
(>20 ha.)

△ village

intermediate
center cluster
core (8–19 ha.)

☐ archaeological site
currently used as cemetary

· satellite sites
(<8 ha.)

▨ levee

*Figure 5.5   Dividing sites into three size categories
reveals a settlement hierarchy in the maximal site cluster
around Jenné-jeno, c. AD 1000.*

by ethnic groups linked by exchange and tradition to form a vast network joining together different productive sectors within the IND and beyond. And I argue that the first elements of subsistence specialization in the IND, involving rice farmers and fisherfolk, were established soon after initial colonization.

The paradox is the maintenance of diversity, involving continued heavy reliance on wild plant and animal resources, despite the growth of subsistence specialization. There is no increase in commitment to domestic rice over wild cereals; nor is there evidence for increasingly labor-intensive technologies for rice farming, such as development of swamp (paddy) rice cultivars requiring bunded fields and irrigation, or for hydraulic interventions of any magnitude. Some idea of population/arable land constraints locally can be obtained by calculating the number of hectares that must be farmed to support a population of 11,000–22,000, using the historical average of 0.6 hectares farmed per person under hoe cultivation

of flood rice in the region (Gallais 1967: 204, 239). We find that the population of the Jenné-jeno maximal cluster (all Phase IV sites within 5 km of Jenné-jeno) would have needed to cultivate 6,500–13,000 hectares annually. Within the irregular oval that is described by drawing arcs of a 5 km radius circle outward from all the settlements in the maximal cluster, approximately 13,000 hectares of potential rice-growing soils are available. Today, a quarter of these soils are left fallow in any given year (the ratio of cultivation period to fallow period is 10:3.5 years on average in the densely populated Djenné region, but 3:3 elsewhere; Viguier 1937). These figures suggest that if, at any point in the past, more than three-quarters (10,000 ha) of the available soils were under cultivation annually, additional labor inputs beyond the level documented historically were likely to have been necessary to increase production. These could have included field labor intensification (additional time spent on agricultural tasks such as weeding, fertilizing, sowing, transplanting), locational intensification (expansion onto more distant rice growing soils), and/or infrastructural intensification (landscape modified by dikes or canals to enhance production; terminology from Stone 1996: 31, 52).

Much more research will be necessary to ascertain how large the population actually was at and around Jenné-jeno between AD 800 and AD 1100 and whether intensification took place. Nevertheless, I argue that for a variety of reasons related to buffering risk, Jenné-jeno rice farmers almost certainly eschewed any approach that required them to increase labor inputs to particular plots (S. McIntosh, in press a). Instead, dense, nucleated populations and an extensive exchange system based on reliable surplus production have been maintained by an agricultural system characterized by low inputs to labor across a diversified portfolio of agricultural investments. Labor inputs averaging 380–450 hours per hectare in the IND can be compared with 1000 hours per hectare for the small-scale, acephalous Kofyar in the Benue Valley of Nigeria (Gallais 1967: 216; Stone 1996: 107, 121).

Historically, IND rice farmers have coped with chaotic inter-annual variation in the arrival, duration, and magnitude of rains and floods by farming in several different locations, keeping field locations mobile, rather than fixed, from year to year, and diversifying production. Not only do they cultivate several different fields with different topographic characteristics, but they plant them with a mixture of rice varieties, including varieties maturing early/late, tolerant of shallow/deep water, and resistant to rizophagous fish (Gallais 1967; Viguier 1937). French agronomists disdained the IND farmers' habit of letting weeds, including wild rice (*O. barthii*), grow in the rice fields, but more recent research suggests that this is part of the diversification strategy, since seed-type diversity in *O. glaberrima* is highest in fields where weeds comprise 40–50 percent of the biomass (Oka 1988: 117). This permissive attitude towards weeds also ensures harvestable amounts of wild cereals from fields when losses in the domestic crop are considerable. The presence of predominantly wild cereals in nearly all the 150 flotation samples from throughout the 1600–year Jenné-jeno occupation sequence prompted research by ICRISAT (Institute for Cereal Research in the Semi-Arid Tropics) in Mali on wild cereal use today in the IND. The result was the unexpected discovery of a continuing exploitation of wild cereals at all times, not just as a famine food. Indeed, a number of these cereals are cultivated and actively traded (Boré 1983; Harlan 1989).

The portfolio strategy of the IND rice farmers has several important consequences. First, it confers resistance to moves towards a fixed field system. IND rice farmers often relocate one or more of their fields in response to the previous year's conditions. Second, labor inputs such as manuring or transplanting are subject to a negative double whammy: in bad years, they will be wasted on those fields where crop losses are high and in good years they will produce increased yields that cannot be harvested unless additional sources of labor are available. A worker can harvest only 100 kg/day (Gallais 1967: 241), so when high floods promote rice yields of 1,300 kg/ha or more (compared to an average yield of 700 kg/ha), the labor necessary to harvest the crop within the small time window (7–10 days) at maturity before birds devour the crop is often lacking. With seed yields of wild rice relatively high (Oka 1988: 90), it makes good sense to delay additional labor inputs until the need for them is clear and then expend them on wild cereal collection.

These points help us understand why infrastructural intensification, such as water management projects, appear to have been limited to the building of small-scale barrages and dikes to prevent floodwaters and fish from reaching seedlings too early (a dual purpose strategy, since it facilitates fishing) and floodwaters from departing too soon. Larger scale projects, such as canal digging to irrigate nursery seedlings or to breach levees, were apparently not attempted, even during the last 600 years when Djenné was successively incorporated into a number of states and empires variously concerned to organize, enhance, and tax agricultural production in the IND. This is a good example of a system in which gradual intensification in the manner posited by Boserup (1965) can go only so far before encountering a threshold requiring not just a jump in the quantity of inputs, but new *kinds*

of inputs and major organizational changes (Stone 1996: 37). All these elements together help us understand the apparent failure of the IND agricultural system in the first millennium AD to develop along lines predicted by standard neo-evolutionary accounts.

Modeling polity organization

In considering how the population of the Jenné-jeno settlement cluster might have been organized politically, it is hard to deny that a nucleated settlement complex of this scale must have been organized in a complex manner. But what was the nature of this complexity?

In the past, political centralization would have been routinely invoked due to the scale of the population involved (e.g., Baker and Sanders 1972: "a population of 10,000–12,000 would require a chiefdom-type organization to maintain it as a stable society"). The presence of large, medium, and small sites could easily be seen as evidence of a settlement hierarchy that reflected the structure of administrative/managerial organization. The assumption that hierarchization represents the only effective response to increases in social scale emerges clearly in the threshold theories that try to identify critical points in population size when new organizational structures emerge, due to stresses or limitations in information processing (Johnson 1982; Flannery 1972; Braun 1990), long-term memory structures of the human brain (Kosse 1990), or other, unidentified factors (Upham 1990, citing Mayhew and Levinger 1976). Feinman (1995:261) identifies the "magic number" for this threshold as 2,500 ± 500. While it is quite true that hierarchy constitutes an efficient way to organize large sets of many diverse kinds, we have seen elsewhere that it is not the *only* kind of organization possible, even if it is the complex organizational form that we are predisposed to find (Keller 1985: 154). Kowalewski et al. (1983: 36) opened up the terms of the discussion by asking in what ways large systems are more complex than small ones. They identified disagreements among systems theorists over whether, given an increase in size, central control per se is selected for, or merely increased integration. Crumley (1987, 1995) and others (Ehrenreich et al. 1995) expanded the debate by considering the heterarchical aspects of complex societies, in which different sources of power, rather than being centralized and consolidated, are counterpoised among different segments of society. There are good reasons to suggest that the Jenné-jeno settlement complex was integrated in this manner, without effective central control.

First, the distribution of settlements in tight clusters is

of considerable interest. Largely ignored in the archaeological literature, one finds this pattern elsewhere along the Middle Niger, in Shang China (R. McIntosh 1991), at Harappa (Kenoyer 1997) and to a lesser extent, in the Late Uruk period in Mesopotamia (Adams and Nissan 1972: 24–8). It is also characteristic of Igbo village groups (Ottenberg 1971). In geography, clustering of agrarian settlement is seen to be a result of fission and the creation of settlement clones by kin in locations that balance social propinquity with field proximity (Hudson 1969). But the settlements within the Jenné-jeno cluster in most cases have little or no agricultural land between them. Indeed, most of the potential agricultural land in the choice 1 kilometer belt around Jenné-jeno is taken up by settlement mounds. These seem to represent, rather, an interesting variation on nucleation. And since the scale of these nucleated clusters was so considerable, the cost of living in them, in terms of increased distance to fields, must also have been considerable. What advantages did this pattern have that counterbalanced the cost?

There is a tradition within archaeology (discussed by Stone 1996: 48) of linking nucleation (increased settlement size) with agricultural intensification (following Boserup 1965) and the organization of labor for large cooperative agricultural projects. However, Stone's work on Kofyar agriculture and settlement supports the notion that field labor intensification places a premium on field/residence propinquity and the establishment of individualized land tenure, thus promoting settlement dispersal (Stone 1996: 50). In the IND, the relatively extensive nature of the agricultural system is likely to have lessened the pull towards dispersal, such that it was more easily counterbalanced by other factors promoting nucleation. Among these, one can propose economic factors related to the early emergence of subsistence specialization and local exchange and the subsequent development of craft specialization (metalworking). In addition, social and religious factors associated with the powerful juxtaposition at Jenné-jeno of the founding families who controlled the spirits of both the land and the water must not be underestimated.

Still, this gets us no closer to thinking about the particular form that nucleation took at Jenné-jeno. Why multiple, tightly clustered settlements rather than nucleation within a single site? R. McIntosh (1991, 1993) has suggested that in an early phase of nucleation, clusters represented the desire of heterogenous groups of people to be near the center, but not of it; to function as part of an urban entity without being subsumed by it. The physical boundaries of satellite settlements are the insignia of identity. For McIntosh, the different groups were occupa-

tional specialists, an interpretation developed on the basis of data collected from surface investigations during survey. Recently, Mary Clark, a graduate student at Southern Methodist University, has resurveyed all the sites in the maximal cluster and undertaken subsurface excavations to evaluate the chronology of various features used by R. McIntosh in developing his hypothesis of specialist producers. Her analysis will tell us much more about the likelihood that these sites represent contemporaneous settlement by occupational specialists. They might equally well be the settlements of newcomers attracted to the cultural safety of this domesticated corner of the vast IND grasslands.

Whoever these groups may have been and whatever their function within the complex of settlements around Jenné-jeno, the most salient point of the clustered pattern is the maintenance of spatial boundaries in the face of cheek-by-jowl proximity. Proximity suggests that serious conflict and hostilities among mound settlements were not factors driving the spatial dynamic. The maintenance of settlement boundaries seems to reflect a degree of autonomy and resistance to the center, the spatial manifestations of which disappear with the great settlement reorganization that took place between AD 1200 and AD 1400, coincident with the conversion of local leaders to Islam and the expansion of the Empire of Mali. At this time, the settlement pattern takes on the more familiar characteristics of a city-state (Gallais 1984: 150). Yet Gallais (1984: 144) notes that, historically, the towns and villages of the Djenné region, united politically in loose federations, maintained a certain autonomy in the face of the urban power of nearby Djenné. The basis for these federations was the fundamental authority over the spirits of the land of the clans who arrived first in those settlements. Perhaps the polity represented by the Jenné-jeno cluster was organized in a similar manner.

Federations are a common form of supralocal organization in West Africa. To the extent that a central leader was recognized, it was likely that he had much ritual authority but relatively little power, since power was effectively distributed among the heads of the founding lineage in each settlement. This power was seated in the belief that survival on the land depended on the maintenance of a lasting accord between the divinities of the bush (the true owners of the land) and humans (mere holders of usufruct rights). The founding lineage in a settlement, by virtue of the pact it had originally made with the divinities, continued to claim a privileged link with the supernatural world (Raynaut 1997: 237). Newcomers had to seek authorization from the "land chief" (a senior member of the founding lineage); his mediation was essential for anyone wishing to work the land without danger and with any chance of success. Raynaut (1997: 239) suggests, following Meillassoux, that the purpose of these alliances under circumstances of land abundance "was not, despite appearances, the preservation of rights to land but the exercise of control over human beings . . . . In granting or refusing permission to a newcomer to settle, and in assimilating a newcomer into a network of alliances from the beginning, they ensured the regulation of a process by which a local community was constituted." Alliance was the touchstone of the land system, uniting land users with the land chief, just as it united the founding lineage with the deities. The difficulty for a central leader aspiring to the consolidation of power lay in the need to either weaken or re-negotiate these fundamental lines of lineage power, or trump them with a new source of power (which is essentially what happened with the arrival of Islam and the development of a prestige goods economy). R. McIntosh and I agree that the continued settlement and occupation of spatially discrete mounds in the immediate orbit of the eponymous settlement at Jenné-jeno indicates that any drive towards effective political centralization was successfully resisted for centuries prior to the arrival of Islam.

While a weak central structure within a federated system is one possible model for political organization at Jenné-jeno, and a ritual chieftaincy over functionally specialized components as suggested by R.McIntosh is another, there is a third model to consider, in which hierarchical features are completely absent. The analogy here is to the Yakö, in southeastern Nigeria, 11,000 of whom resided in the town of Umor at the time Darryl Forde studied them in the 1930s. Forde (1964) describes how social integration and cohesion in large Yakö settlements of neighboring territorial patriclans was achieved by the functioning of numerous associations exercising ritual or secular authority over part or all of the population with respect to major spheres of social life. Here, governmental powers are "widely distributed among a number of independent and overlapping agencies. Wider political relations resolve themselves into modes of cooperation with and competition between such associations. Coordination of political action . . . is achieved to the extent that there is mutual adjustment of their distinct competencies by the several associations which may include some form of conciliary organization of their respective leaders" (Forde 1964: 166). The large compact villages of the Yakö are also found in neighboring Igboland, clustered into village groups whose total population reaches into the tens of thousands.

Conclusion

Jenné-jeno does not fit the standard outline of a case study in emerging complexity; it has some of the familiar attributes (nucleation, population growth, and increasing scale) but not others (subsistence intensification, highly visible ranking or stratification, and imposing public monuments). For a long time, archaeology has preferred conformity, its preoccupation with elites, their monuments, and their power being best served by case studies that offered material remains of obvious relevance. As one Mayanist asked me (in a tone that was a perfect blend of patient condescension and strained credulity) in the question period after a lengthy seminar on Jenné-jeno some years ago: "So why, exactly, do you think this was a complex society?" While there can be no doubt that the study of elites and the struggle to consolidate power has produced important results, it is the non-conforming case studies (the ones we have been perhaps the least likely to select for study in the first place) that reveal the gaps in this theoretical framework. Jenné-jeno challenges us to make room in our explanatory schemata for a population of over 11,000 packed onto more than 130 hectares of tell surface within a 12 km^2 area that apparently did *not* do any of the following: increase reliance on domesticated at the expense of wild cereals; intensify agricultural production through large collaborative projects; display obvious wealth differentials; develop a settlement pattern reflecting increasingly centralized organization; or develop a settlement pattern consistent with high levels of intersite conflict.

The fact that we have so little in our theoretical portmanteaus to apply to the evaluation of such a case study reveals archaeology's increasingly problematic secret: our current conceptual and investigative toolkit for investigating complexity is applicable to only a subset of complex sites and societies. This is, as Morris (1997: 104) points out, a legacy of the narrow comparative foundations of neo-evolutionism, which neglected the diversity of social arrangements documented historically. In societies where political action and coordination is achieved through assemblies, councils, and other forms of horizontally arrayed structures, and not through vertical control hierarchies, we have relatively little idea how we might recognize the material manifestations of such an organization. We have not considered, for example, how the material signature of title-takers in a secret society might resemble or differ from that of an hereditary elite marked by the use of certain sacred symbols. All of our successes in identifying elites and their consolidation of power in the archaeological record can tell us nothing about trajectories of political development in societies where resistance to such consolidation was effective. Let us hope that we stand on the brink of a period that will offer theoretical insights into such societies that are on a par with the rich contribution made by studies of chiefly elites over the past decade.

References

Adams, R. M. and H. Nissan
  1972 *The Uruk Countryside: The Natural Setting Of Urban Societies*. Chicago: University of Chicago Press.
Baker, P. and W. Sanders
  1972 Demographic studies in anthropology. *Annual Review of Demography* 1: 151–78.
Boré, Y.
  1983 *Recensement des graminées sauvages alimentaires (ceréales mineures) utilisées en 5ᵉ, 6ᵉ, et 7ᶜ régions*. Mémoire de Fin d'Etudes, Ecole Normale Supérieure, Bamako.
Boserup, E.
  1965 *The Conditions of Agricultural Growth*. New York: Aldine.
Brasseur, G.
  1968 *Les établissements humains au Mali*. Dakar: IFAN.
Braun, D.
  1990 Selection and evolution in non-hierarchical organization. In *The Evolution of Political Systems*, edited by S. Upham. Cambridge: Cambridge University Press: 62–86.
Crumley, C.
  1987 A dialectical critique of hierarchy. In *Power Relations and State Formation*, edited by T. Patterson and C. Gailey. Washington D.C.: American Anthropologecal Association: 155–69.
  1995 Heterarchy and the analysis of complex societies. In *Heterarchy and the Analysis of Complex Societies*, edited by R. Ehrenreich, C. Crumley, and J. Levy. Washington, D.C.: Archaeological Papers of the American Anthropological Association, no. 6: 1–6.
Ehrenreich, R. M., C. L. Crumley, and J. E. Levy
  1995 (eds.) *Heterarchy and the Analysis of Complex Societies*. Washington D.C.: Archaeological Papers of the American Anthropological Association, no.6.
Feinman, G.
  1995 The emergence of inequality. In *Foundations of Social Inequality*, edited by T. D. Price and G. M. Feinman. New York: Plenum: 255–79.

Flannery, K.
  1972 The cultural evolution of civilization. *Annual Review of Ecology and Systematics* 3: 399–426.
Forde, D.
  1964 *Yakö Studies*. London: Oxford University Press.
Gallais, J.
  1967 *Le delta intérieur du Niger*. Mémoire No. 79 de l'Institut Fondamental d'Afrique Noire. Dakar.
  1984 *Hommes du Sahel*. Paris: Flammarion.
Harlan, J.
  1989 Wild grass seed harvesting in the Sahara and sub-Sahara of Africa. In *Foraging and Farming: The Evolution of Plant Exploitation*, edited by D. R. Harris and G. C. Hillman. London: Unwin Hyman: 79–98.
Hudson, J.
  1969 A locational theory for rural settlement. *Annals of the Association of American Geographers* 59: 365–81.
Johnson, G.
  1982 Organization structure and scalar stress. In *Theory and Explanation in Archaeology: the Southhampton Conference*, edited by C. Renfrew, M. J. Rowlands, and B. Segraves. New York: Academic: 89–121.
Jolly, C. and F. Plog
  1987 *Physical Anthropology and Archaeology*. 4th edn. New York: Alfred A. Knopf.
Keller, E. F.
  1985 *Reflections on Gender and Science*. New Haven: Yale University Press.
Kenoyer, J.
  1997 Early city-states in South Asia: comparing the Harappan Phase and early historic period. In *The Archaeology of City-States: Cross-Cultural Approaches*, edited by D. L. Nichols and T. H. Charlton. Washington: Smithsonian Press: 51–70.
Kosse, K.
  1990 Group size and societal complexity: thresholds in the long-term memory. *Journal of Anthropological Archaeology* 9: 275–303.
Kowalewski, S. A., R. E. Blanton, G. Feinman, and L. Finsten
  1983 Boundaries, scale and internal organization. *Journal of Anthropological Archaeology* 2: 32–56.
MacDonald, K.
  1994 Socio-economic diversity and the origins of cultural complexity along the Middle Niger (2000 BC to AD 300). Ph.D. Dissertation, Cambridge University.
Mayhew, B. and R. Levinger
  1976 On the emergence of oligarchy in human interaction. *American Journal of Sociology* 81: 1017–49.

McIntosh, R. J.
1991 Early urban clusters in China and Africa: the arbitration of social ambiguity. *Journal of Field Archaeology* 18: 199–212.
1993 The pulse theory: Genesis and accommodation of specialization in the Middle Niger. *Journal of African History* 34: 181–220.

McIntosh, R. J. and S. K. McIntosh
1987 Prospection archéologique aux alentours de Dia, Mali: 1986–1987. *Nyame Akuma* no. 29: 42–5.

McIntosh, R., S. McIntosh, and H. Bocoum (eds.)
in prep. *The Middle Senegal Valley Project: Excavations and Survey 1990–1993.*

McIntosh, S. K.
1995 (ed.) *Excavations at Jenné-jeno, Hambarketolo, and Kaniana: the 1981 Season.* University of California Monographs in Anthropology. Berkeley: University of California Press.
in press a Floodplains and the development of complex society: comparative perspectives from the West African semi-arid tropics. In *The Origins and Development of Complexity in the Tropics*, edited by E. Bacus and L. Lucero. Archaeological Papers of the American Anthropological Association, no. 9.
in press b A tale of two floodplains: comparative perspectives on the emergence of complex societies and urbanism in the Middle Niger and Senegal Valleys. In *East African Urban Origins in World Perspective: Proceedings of the Second WAC Intercongress*, edited by P. Sinclair.

McIntosh, S. K. and R. J. McIntosh
1980 *Prehistoric Investigations at Jenné, Mali.* 2 vols. Oxford: British Archaeological Reports.
1993 Cities without citadels: understanding urban origins along the Middle Niger. In *The Archaeology of Africa. Food, Metals and Towns*, edited by C. T. Shaw, P. Sinclair, B. Andah, and A. Okpoko. London: Routledge.

Monteil, C.
1971 *Une cité soudanaise: Djenné.* 2nd edn. Paris: Editions Anthropos.

Morris, I.
1997 An archaeology of equalities? The Greek city-states. In *The Archaeology of City-States: Cross-Cultural Approaches*, edited by D. L. Nichols and T. H. Charlton, Washington: Smithsonian Press: 91–106.

Oka, H. I.
1988 *Origin of Cultivated Rice.* Amsterdam: Elsevier.

Ottenberg, S.
1971 *Leadership and Authority in an African Society.* Washington D.C.: American Ethnological Society monograph no. 52. Seattle: University of Washington Press.

Portères, R.
1976 African cereals: eleusine, fonio, black fonio, teff, brachiaria, paspalum, pennisetum, and African rice. In *Origins of African Plant Domestication*, edited by J. R. Harlan, J. M. J. de Wet, and A. B. Stemler. The Hague: Mouton: 409–52.

Raynaut, C.
1997 Sahelian social systems: variety and variability. In *Societies and Nature in the Sahel*, edited by C. Raynaut. London: Routledge: 214–34.

Sherratt, A.
1980 Water, soil and seasonality in early cereal cultivation. *World Archaeology* 11(3): 313–30.

Stone, G. D.
1996 *Settlement Ecology: The Social and Spatial Organization of Kofyar Agriculture.* Tucson: University of Arizona Press.

Togola, T.
1993 Archaeological investigations of Iron Age sites in the Méma, Mali. Ph.D. thesis, Rice University.
1996 Iron Age occupation in the Méma region, Mali. *African Archaeological Review* 13 (2): 91–110.

Upham, S.
1990 Analog or digital? Toward a generic framework for explaining the development of emergent political systems. In *The Evolution of Political Systems*, edited by S. Upham. Cambridge: Cambridge University Press: 87–118.

Viguier, P.
1937 La riziculture indigène au Soudan Français. *Annales Agricoles de l'Afrique Occidentale Française et Etrangère* 1 (3–4): 287–326.

6

Sacred centers and urbanization in West Central Africa

RAYMOND N. ASOMBANG

Introduction

The concept of civilization was for a long time defined in terms of the presence or absence of what was considered to be key elements, such as writing. It is now generally accepted that civilization can exist without the presence of writing, which Gordon Childe had taken for the one ingredient that usually marked the turning point (Childe 1950, quoted in Connah 1987: 7). Many scholars have made the point that these definitions were based on a limited knowledge of other parts of the world, especially Africa.

Like civilization, the concept of urbanization has for a long time been pervaded by Western representations. Common to most of the early theories about the nature of a town or city is the belief that the existence of an agricultural population, a mercantile class, and writing were a prerequisite. Also considered as necessary was the idea that the settlement had to perform the functions of a religious and an administrative center, capable of mobilizing a massive labor force for monumental architecture and the accumulation of wealth (Hassan 1993; R. McIntosh, this volume; O'Connor 1993).

Long-distance trade and religion have indeed influenced the growth of towns in some parts of the world. The rise of the mercantile towns of East Africa, for example, was influenced by Portuguese and Arab trade during the sixteenth and seventeenth centuries. Similarly, the Islamic towns of North Africa, with their sultanates, mosques, Islamic schools, and wall enclosures, testify to strong Islamic influence in this part of the continent prior to European colonization. In our two examples, long-distance trade and religion are foreign impulses, but it is important to note that these are not always the causes of urbanization, nor indeed, are the causes of African urbanization always exotic.

In his book *Urbanization in Nigeria* (1968), Akin Mabogunje defined urbanism simply as "the process whereby human beings congregate in relatively large numbers at a particular spot of the earth's surface" (quoted in Connah 1987: 12). Mabogunje rejects the use of notions such as writing, agricultural workers, a mercantile class, etc., to distinguish between urbanized and non-urbanized communities. Many people will agree that Mabogunje's definition can be applied to the development of towns in any part of the world besides West Africa. My aim in this article is to pursue this line of argument, and using a specific case study, I will argue that earlier but still pervasive representations of urbanism are not very helpful in understanding the nature of early towns in the forest region of West Africa. As far as this region is concerned, it is yet to be demonstrated historically or archaeologically that colonial cities like Ife and Benin were military or administrative centers more than they were sacred centers. Sacred centers usually surround palaces and they incorporate people. Their sacredness acts as a focus of population accumulation.

In the Western Grassfields region of Cameroon, there are several examples of such sacred centers that have acted as the foci of population accumulation. Our case study comes from the kingdom of Bafut which is situated in the northwestern part of this region. (The term "kingdom" as used here refers to a polity centered on a spiritual and political leader with the title *Mfor*.) The settlement pattern here is very distinct. It is based on lineages surrounding the palace. The palace is the focus of all religious life because the king is also the chief priest of the cults. Therefore it can also be considered to be a sacred center. A cosmology radiating from the center includes populations living around it. I intend to argue here that the origin of towns in this part of Africa can be traced to this type of settlement pattern.

Background

The Grassfields is the name given to the highland savanna region of Cameroon. The Grassfields correspond approximately to the West and Northwest Provinces and lie immediately north of the tropical forest zone, between the Cross and Benue Rivers on the border with Nigeria. Bamenda, the provincial headquarters of the Northwest Province, is situated on a plateau almost in the center of the region. A number of kingdoms of differing sizes, origin and complexity crystallized on this plateau at the end of the nineteenth century. Kaberry (1962) speculated that the political nuclei of some of these kingdoms may have been established as early as the seventeenth century. Many of the big kingdoms were conquest states which likely boasted populations of a few thousand inhabitants at the end of the nineteenth century. Thanks to the British colonial policy of indirect rule, these kingdoms have been preserved until today. They have been the subject of intensive ethnographic survey (Chilver and Kaberry 1968; Dillon 1973; Engard 1986; Nkwi and Warnier 1982; Warnier 1975). Unfortunately, the history of archaeological research in the region only goes back a little over a decade and the results so far available are still exploratory and inconclusive. The few archaeological data available suggest strongly that the area has been occupied for several thousand years by people not too dissimilar from the present inhabitants (Asombang 1988; Warnier 1984).

However, many kingdoms of the Western Grassfields claim an origin from the east in the Upper Mbam River area where the present-day Tikar people live. As if to give credibility to their claim, their political institutions, spatial organization, and religious practices show very strong similarities: they are generally regional polities with centralized authority; kingship is sacred; populations are divided into commoners, royals, and notables; there is an elaborate system of ranked titles and powerful, closed, regulatory, secret societies and princes' fraternities, etc. (Chilver and Kaberry 1971). The palace is both the focal point of political, religious and ceremonial life and the headquarters of the principal secret societies. As Kaberry (1962: 269) rightly points out, this combination of sacred kingship with palace associations having governmental duties is quite unique to this region. But the palace is also the cosmological center and focal point around which larger than usual populations congregate. One may say it is a sacred city. The argument therefore, is that the origins of urbanization in this part of Africa are to be found in sacred centers or palaces. It was around these centers that the earliest known population concentrations in West Central Africa were formed even before the first contacts with Europeans.

The Bafut kingdom

The Myth

The Bafut kingdom is situated about 22 kilometers northwest of Bamenda (Figure 6.1). Oral traditions bring the people of Bafut, like many others on the plateau (Nso, Kom, Nkwen, etc.) from the Upper Mbam River area in the East. There are several conflicting versions of the myth

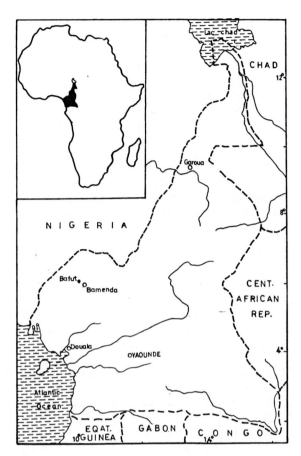

Figure 6.1   Cameroon, showing location of Bafut.

of origin, but there seems to be a near consensus on certain details. One of these is that when the immigrants, led by *Agha'anjo*, arrived at their present site, they found other groups already settled there. These were the *Alante* (Bawum) and *Mbebeli*, who were settled on a southern ridge and the *Buwe-Bukari* who were settled on a northern ridge. The central depression separating the two ridges was not settled at this time. The second point of agreement is that only the *Mbebeli*, whose leader was called *Nebachi*, claimed aboriginal status. Finally, there is also agreement that the immigrants from the Tikar plain preferred the southern ridge, so they obtained permission from *Nebachi* and settled there. A loose confederation appears to have been formed between the groups on this southern ridge with *Nebachi* as *primus inter pares* (Engard 1988: 56). In a palace *coup d'état* hatched by the notables of *Nebachi* (who was described as selfish and not at all entertaining),

Agha'anjo stepped on *Nebachi*'s foot during the latter's annual dance, thereby deposing him. *Agha'anjo* then ruled the confederation from *Nebachi*'s palace for several generations. One version of Bafut oral tradition claims that two kings were buried at *Mbebeli*. Whatever the case, it is clear that the palace (*Nto'o* – the residence of the leader and the headquarters of the kingdom) continued to be at *Mbebeli* for several generations before being relocated to its present site in the central depression.

Through a process that is still poorly understood, the relocation of the palace coincided with the disappearance of the segmentary protostate system, in favour of the development of a superstructure or state system with centralized political, religious, and social institutions. This was an important turning point in the building of the Bafut State. It marked the beginning of economic prosperity through involvement in local and long-distance trade and a subsequent monopoly of certain trade routes. It also marked the beginning of rapid expansion through warfare, conquest, and natural growth. Expansion was so rapid that at the time of first contact with Europeans (1889–1901), Bafut was considered militarily formidable by its neighbors. Its range of attack probably had a radius of between forty to fifty kilometers. Hans Glauning, who led one of Pavel's expeditionary forces against Bafut in 1901, estimated its population at 25,000 inhabitants, composed of a number of small groups of voluntary adherents of an immigrant dynasty, conquered peoples, refugees, and war captives (Chilver and Kaberry 1963: 4, 8).

Political institutions

Bafut is equipped with several institutions that maintain law and order at different structural levels. But perhaps one should begin by emphasizing that the kingship is sacred, meaning that the political organization is centerd on the king (*Mfor*), better known locally as *Fon*. He is titular leader with political as well as ritual powers associated with the fertility of the land and the people. The *Fon* is a member and head of all secret societies and chief priest of the cults. He is the dispenser of honors. Because he is ritually installed, it is believed that he takes on immortal attributes: he is never ill, it is the palace that is cold; he never dies, he disappears or is lost, etc. Therefore, the *Fon* means more than just a leader to his people. He is in fact seen as a living god, and hence he is feared, respected, and honored.

It is also worth noting that a general characteristic of Bafut society is its distinction between royals, commoners, and notables. This elaborate system of ranked titles is inextricably tied to the numerous powerful secret societies

which constitute the core of the political structure. The most important secret society is *Kwifor*, whose membership is open only to commoners and people of distant royal descent. *Kwifor* is the executive arm of government with wide-ranging powers, including the power to depose an ineffective or malfeasant king. In pre-colonial times, *Kwifor* also had the power to inflict capital punishment. Since its authority is impersonal, its agents could not be held to account. With the advent of the modern state of Cameroon, the government alone is empowered to administer capital punishment. This is the most significant change that *Kwifor* has witnessed since the segmentary protostate.

The next most important society is the closed male princes' fraternity – *Euchong*. This society is only indirectly political and has no executive powers. However, *Takumbeng*, one of its inner houses, plays a more active (regulatory) role at some cults; e.g. pollution removal, purification, and fertility rites. There are many other societies which one is expected to join on becoming a member of *Kwifor* or *Euchong*, and all of them, including *Kwifor*, *Euchong*, and *Takumbeng*, have their headquarters in the palace. This centralization consolidates the power base of the palace and the asymmetrical position, relative to one another, of the *Fon* and *Kwifor*, who execute that power. In a society where wealth and success in life are expressed in terms of the number of secret societies to which one belongs and the titles purchased in them, it is understandable that the palace represents such a powerful magnet pulling people to itself and holding them together.

The relationship between the *Fon* and *Kwifor* is rather intricate and on the face of it, conflictual. In practice, however, it is a relationship of mutual respect and cooperation. Even with its wide-ranging powers, *Kwifor* sometimes appears to play only an advisory role or is seen as supporting the *Fon*. Similarly, the *Fon* is quite often referred to as the son of *Kwifor*. So the two articulate very well in practice, and it is this institutionalization of the sacred and the judicial that constitutes the power base of the kingdom.

Spatial organization

For the purpose of effective government, Bafut is divided into villages (*nekuru*). The latter are further divided into wards (*Ayeunda*). Settlement is by lineage in a unit of space called a compound. A village which has the status of a sub-chiefdom is governed by a sub-chief (*Atangcho*), but generally, villages are governed by a council of elders or village heads (*Butabunekuru*). Decisions of the council are collective and its authority is impersonal. A network of seasonal roads and footpaths, which connect villages,

Figure 6.2   The neubah *monolith at the* nsani *of the Njibujang village.*

Figure 6.3   The Takumbang shrine (ndere) *in the dance plaza outside the palace.*

wards, and compounds all converge on the palace. The central nature of the palace is enforced by the location of the main weekly market very near to it. The villages around the palace are more densely settled than outlying villages since most people prefer to settle close to the central authority. New villages are situated in relation to the palace.

The system of villages and wards therefore comprises territorial or administrative units. Building the kingdom by peaceful expansion entails the creation of new villages. The latest example was in 1982 when the Nsem ward was raised to the status of a sub-chiefdom. Engard (1989: 143) reports that before the formal installation of the sub-chief designate, ritual activities to constitute the ward into a

sub-chiefdom and transform the compound of the sub-chief designate were performed. The rituals had to do with the planting of a monolith (*neubah*, Figure 6.2) by *Kwifor* members (*Bukum*) and the building of a *Takumbeng* shrine (*ndere*), a replica of the main *Takumbeng* shrine in the dance plaza outside the *Fon*'s palace (Figure 6.3) by princes. "Medicines" i.e., mixed herbs and specially medicated ropes were buried under the *neubah* and the *ndere* respectively (Rowlands 1985: 208). The creation of an ordinary new village entails the performance of these same rituals at a road junction. After the initial rituals, that road junction serves from thenceforward as the *nsani* of the new village. *Nsanis* are therefore the ritual and political foci of villages in the same way as the palace is the political and ritual focus of Bafut. The *neubah* and *ndere* are the insignia of independence as well as the umbilical cord linking the baby (village) to the mother (palace). The medicines planted under these insignia constitute the spiritual dimension of this link. It is by these twin insignia that fully constituted villages are identified. Quite often, the *nsani* is not necessarily the geographical center of the village, but being the focus of religious and ceremonial life, it is essentially the center or heart of the village. Thus the palace of Bafut, even though it is off the geographical center, leaves no doubt even in a visitor's mind that it is what R. and P. Ritzenthaler (1962: 17) call "the operational center and heart of Bafut." All rituals begin in the palace before they are extended to the *nsanis* of the different villages and sub-chiefdoms.

The beginning of the dry season (mid-November) is the start of the ritual cycle in Bafut. It is during this time (i.e., the third week of December) that the *Fon's* annual dance (*abin*) is held. In Bafut cosmology, waterfalls are the lodges of the spirits of deceased kings, whereas those of other deceased personalities, such as lineage heads, reside at road junctions. Therefore, prior to staging the *abin*, these places are visited and presented with gifts of palm wine and *camwood*. This cult of the ancestors is called *m'ma'abunwi* (worship the gods).

M'ma'abunwi is explicitly placatory, the intention being to ensure that no resentment that could be felt by the spirits of the ancestors will mar the *abin* festival. It starts from the palace where the *Bukum* assemble and, after chorus incantations and blessing of the gifts of palm wine and *camwood*, they are despatched in small groups in all directions. Each group is given a calabash of wine and a raffia bag containing *camwood*. At every *neubah* and waterfall where the spirit of a particular deceased king is believed to dwell, a little *camwood* would be placed and some wine poured on it. This is done amid requests that the *abin* be a success, that the coming year be more prosperous, and that crops may grow and women bear more children. This culminates in the sacrifice of a black ram at two "sacred" posts in the dance plaza outside the palace. This is the *mbaw-abin* (build the dance) ritual and it signals the official start of the *abin* festival which lasts for four days.

Another important ritual is the protection rite (*mundeughe*), which consists of laying specially "medicated" ropes across the junctions of roads linking Bafut to other kingdoms, village dance grounds, entrances to the compounds of "big men," and in and around the palace itself (Figure 6.4). The ropes are first gathered in the palace where they are specially "medicated" and

Figure 6.4   A fetish placed across the road to block witches and other evil spirits.

blessed. After those in the palace are laid, the *Bukum* are despatched in all directions with instructions to lay them at specific points. These ropes are believed to close Bafut from all evil influences or witchcraft which may be perpetrated by enemy kingdoms. To place a rope across the road symbolically locks the road; any evil influence will stop at it or be destroyed if it crosses.

Finally, there is the *Takumbeng* pollution removal rite (*mfee'nu*). This entails the assembly of the *Takumbeng* from all the villages at the main shrine outside the palace. Here they prepare and bless "medicines." A bundle of wood ashes taken from *Kwifor* lodge is untied and distributed to all participants. In unison they blow it into the air. Then they disperse to their respective villages with some of the medicines and the same rite is repeated at the village shrines in the village dance grounds (*nsanis*).

These rituals show clearly to what extent the spatial organization of Bafut is guided by very symbolic relationships. The forms planted, buried, or built at certain places within the kingdom more or less define it, inasmuch as they constitute a link between the center and the periphery. They are the ones that give that sense of belonging, and therefore serve to unite all the facets of the kingdom. Whatever physical distance exists between the palace and the villages or wards is reduced to zero by the symbolic links which are continually reactivated through the yearly rituals performed at the shrines. No matter its size, the entire kingdom constitutes a single agglomeration with the palace as the nucleus. Since the institution of the palace in the Western Grassfields region of Cameroon serves as the nucleus around which people have to congregate, it seems reasonable to argue that it gave the initial impulse for people to congregate in large numbers at a particular spot. Because it is the focus of religious life, the palace was and still is a sacred place. No one can take "bad medicine" into the palace in the hope of using it to settle personal scores. If they did, they would be destroyed. Therefore the palace epitomizes the kingdom. If it were to be burnt or destroyed, this would be tantamount to burning the kingdom. The settlement pattern described above can be observed with only minor differences throughout the Cameroon Grassfields region.

Bafut as well as many other Grassfields kingdoms may well have attained a status comparable to a city-state long before colonization. This is suggested in many Grassfields kingdoms by what appears to have been defense works, which would have served to keep out enemies. An example of such defensive works in Bafut is the remains of what appears to have been a moat (about 5 meters deep and more than 1 kilometer long) on its boundary with Nkwen in the southeast. It is thought that Bafut constructed it for defensive purposes, but no one is quite certain about this, nor do we know for sure when it was constructed. However, it is clear that it would have required extensive labor and organization to build such earthworks. It is the presence of such evidence that suggests that Bafut was a symbolic city long before colonization. A centralized authority controlling a large population and labor resources would have facilitated the construction of these defenses. Such a central authority is not to be equated with a coercive, centrally planned Western state, for as will be argued below, the concept of power and authority in Bafut, as elsewhere in Africa, has more to do with the ability to engage or contain occult forces than with military force, administrative authority, or economic control.

We showed earlier that once the turning point of a centralized political and religious authority was attained, the Bafut population grew rapidly. With a large population, it was possible to build earthworks, such as the moat mentioned above. It would also have been possible to build up a strong army, which would further accelerate expansion through warfare and conquest. Involvement in local and long-distance trade would have increased to the point where some people would specialize as traders. The more the state expanded demographically, territorially, and economically, the more important the nucleus (palace) would become. Along the lines of Mabogunje's definition, therefore, it seems to me that one can argue and rightly too, that Bafut was an urban center long before the arrival of the first Europeans at the end of the nineteenth century.

The concept of power in Bafut

The concept of power is complex, but archaeologists have tended to privilege definitions of power that emphasize the ability to compel obedience by the use of might or coercion. In Bafut, power is complex, but more often than not, it has nothing to do with coercion or might. Not only is it rooted in religion and ritual, but it is also associated with generosity and the ability to feed people. As we saw earlier, *Agha'anjo* was preferred to *Nebachi* because he was more generous and entertaining. Generosity in this case is directly linked to power. The Bafut myth, like that of other Grassfields kingdoms (Nso, Bamum, Nkwen, Kom, etc.), also associates the concept of power with "the one who comes from outside," i.e., a foreigner. *Agha'anjo* came from "outside" but he ended up subjugating *Nebachi,* the indigenous *Fon.* The concept of power in Bafut can best be understood through its spatial organization, institutions, and material culture. "Power" actually refers to different kinds of influences – for example, the power of a medicine man, the power of a fortune teller, and the power of the drinking horn activated by words to cause damage or bring good luck and fortune. Power is therefore not unified in any one person. This is clearly demonstrated by the division of roles between *Kwifor, Euchong,* and *Takumbeng.* Whereas *Kwifor* is in charge of the politics and administration, *Takumbeng* is in charge of pollution removal, purification, and fertility rites. The spatial organization of the kingdom, as we saw earlier, allows lineage heads, ward heads, village heads, and *Atangchos* to all share in the administration of the kingdom. Their "power" (authority), like that of *Kwifor* on whose behalf they govern, is also impersonal, so they too cannot be held to account.

It is worth stressing here that respect for the *Fon*'s authority is not so much the application of coercive force as the knowledge that he alone can intercede between the living and the dead. Because of this, it is believed that some of the *Fon*'s powers come from the gods, so to disobey him is tantamount to disobeying the gods whose judgment is irrevocable. All those who share in governing the kingdom do so on behalf of the *Fon.* To disobey any of them is tantamount to disobeying the *Fon.*

Finally, it is important also to mention that in Bafut cosmology there is the belief that certain members of one's family – the lineage head (*tacheu*), uncle, or aunt – possess the power to cause harm or bring good luck and fortune. If, for instance, an uncle were angry and threw away palm wine from his drinking horn, a niece or a nephew could become ill or even die if the angry uncle were not placated. In a majority of the cases, the victim does not have to be the one who caused the uncle's anger. If, on the other hand, good words are said as the wine is thrown from the drinking horn, it is seen as a blessing. So the symbolism of material objects like the drinking horn is very powerful. Speech (the power of words) activates some power in the drinking horn. Good words produce good effects and bad words produce bad effects. Therefore objects like these are not inert. They are active elements of material culture. They can destroy people if they are wrongly used. Clearly therefore, we cannot talk of power here in terms of coercion. It is rather the ability to control occult forces.

Conclusion

I have tried in these pages to describe a distinct settlement pattern of the Western Grassfields region of Cameroon whose foundations go back to the seventeenth or the eighteenth century, as an alternative to classic Western representations of intermediate-level societies. It is a settlement pattern based on kin groups called lineages and territorial units known as villages. The nucleus of the system is the palace which is at the same time the center of religious, political, social, and economic life of the polity. Because of the paramountcy of its religious function, the palace also qualifies as a sacred center.

In the above presentation, I have focused on only one of several cultural principles that underlie the emergence and formation of African polities – the role of ritual in shaping spatial hierarchies – to underscore the argument that intermediate-level polities vary in many aspects. Thus, to classify them into types is both difficult and of limited utility (Kopytoff this volume; S. McIntosh this volume). It seems to me that by multiplying the number of diachronic and contextual studies as this volume attempts to do, we stand a better chance of understanding the different causal processes involved in the development of intermediate-level societies. The Bafut example presented here is fairly representative of polities at this level of development in the Western Grassfields region of Cameroon. As we saw earlier, Bafut attained the level of a state with centralized authority and a population estimated at more than 25,000 people prior to European contact.

It has been argued that centralized authority grew from long-distance trade (Garlake 1978, quoted in Connah 1987: 16). Rowlands (1979: 2) believes that long-distance trade in the West African context is the mechanism by which goods were acquired that were necessary for the expansion of the political structure and for reproducing the conditions by which the production of commodities given in return could be controlled. As Engard (1988: 6) contends, it would appear that in the Bafut myth, the relocation of the palace gave Bafut an advantage for greater involvement in local and long-distance trade. Greater involvement in and possible monopoly of this trade would have given birth to a superstructure with centralized authority as we notice in the myth. In an investigative account of the regional trade on the Bamenda plateau in the nineteenth century, Chilver and Kaberry (1963) describe Bafut's involvement as consisting of exchange and trade between *Fons*. Palm oil and locally made iron hoes were exchanged for ivory armlets, stenciled cloth and brass pipes. As far as long-distance trade was concerned, slave labor was supplied to the coastal region in exchange for European imports such as brass rods, guns, and gun powder (Rowlands 1979). The wealth thus accumulated was redistributed as presents to notables, princes, and sub-chiefs who in return made regular gifts in kind to maintain the institution. In addition to these offerings, certain resources were allocated to the *Fon*. These included royal farms cultivated by the population, royal raffia bushes allocated to the *Fon*'s palm wine tappers, and a small garden plot maintained and cultivated by each village in order to supply the palace in emergency (Chilver and Kaberry 1963: 9). The emergence of a hierarchical society as early as the seventeenth century and prior to contact with external influence, is clearly an indigenous development which possibly resulted from one or a combination of ecological, economic, cultural, and historical factors. That this is the case certainly means that the urban phenomenon in Africa has so far been underestimated, owing to a limited knowledge of the continent and to conceptual bias.

Acknowledgements

I am grateful to the people whose works I have consulted and more especially to Michael Rowlands for discussions which helped to shape many of the ideas expressed in this paper.

References

Asombang, R. N.
    1988 Bamenda in prehistory: the evidence from Fiye Nkwi, Mbi Crater and Shum Laka rock shelters. Ph.D. thesis, University of London.
Chilver, E. M. and P. M. Kaberry.
    1963 Traditional government in Bafut, West Cameroon. *The Nigerian Field* 28: 4–30.
    1968 *Traditional Bamenda: The Pre-Colonial History and Ethnography of the Bamenda Grassfields*, vol. 1. Buea: Government Printing Press.
    1971 The Tikar problem: a non problem. *Journal of African Languages* 10: 2.

Connah, G.
1987 *African Civilizations: Pre-colonial Cities and States in Tropical Africa – An Archaeological Perspective.* Cambridge: Cambridge University Press.

Dillon, R. G.
1973 Notes on the pre-colonial history and ethnography of the Meta. In *Contribution of Ethnological Research to the History of Cameroon Civilizations*, edited by C. Tardits. Paris: International Colloquium of CNRS. No. 551: 361–70.

Engard, R.K.
1986 Bringing the outside in: commensuality and incorporation in Bafut myth, ritual, art and social organization. Ph.D. thesis, Bloomington: Indiana University.
1988 Myth and political economy in Bafut (Cameroon): the structural history of an African kingdom. *Paideuma* 34: 21–89.
1989 Dance and power in Bafut (Cameroon). In *The Creativity of Power: Essays in Ritual and Authority in African Societies*, edited by W. Arens and I. Karp. Washington: Smithsonian Institution Press.

Hassan, F. A.
1993 Town and village in Ancient Egypt: ecology, society and urbanization. In *The Archaeology of Africa: Food, Metals and Towns*, edited by T. Shaw, P. Sinclair, B. Andah, and A. Okpoko. London: Routledge: 551–69.

Kaberry, P. M.
1962 Retainers and royal households in the Cameroon Grassfields. *Cahiers d'Etudes Africaines* 2 (10) 282–98.

Mabogunje, A.
1968 *Urbanization in Nigeria.* London: University of London Press.

Nkwi, P. N. and J. P. Warnier.
1982 *Elements for a History of the Western Grassfields.* Publication of the Department of Sociology, University of Yaounde.

O'Connor, D.
1993 Urbanism in Bronze Age Egypt and northeast Africa. In *The Archaeology of Africa: Food, Metals and Towns*, edited by T. Shaw, P. Sinclair, B. Andah, and A. Okpoko. London: Routledge: 570–86.

Ritzenthaler, R. and P. Rithzenthaler.
1962 *Cameroon's Village: An Ethnography of the Bafut.* Milwaukee Public Museum Publication in Anthropology 8. Milwaukee: North American Press.

Rowlands, M.J.
1979 Local and long-distance trade and incipient state formation on the Bamenda plateau in the late 19th century. *Paideuma* 25: 1–19.
1985 Notes on the material symbolism of Grassfields palaces. *Paideuma* 31: 203–14.

Warnier, J. F.
1975 Pre-colonial Mankon: the development of a Cameroon chiefdom in its regional setting. Ph.D. thesis, University of Pennsylvania, Philadelphia, Ann Arbor: University Microfilms.
1984 Histoire du peuplement et genèse des paysages dans l'ouest Cameroun. *Journal of African History* 25 (4): 395–410.

7

Permutations in patrimonialism and populism: The Aghem chiefdoms of western Cameroon

IGOR KOPYTOFF

There is an evolutionary bias in the anthropological view of political development, a bias that makes it seem obvious that political forms should have moved from the simple to the complex. Thus, "chiefdoms" necessarily arose out of acephalous structures such as "bands," usually in response to similar economic conjunctures, such as a rise in trade. And the chiefdom, unless mired in evolutionary stagnation, necessarily moved in the direction of the "state." This view of political complexification is perhaps not unrealistic in the very long term, but it becomes misleading when we extend it to the formation of actual middle-range polities in a particular ethnographic area. If the grand evolutionary scheme had indeed been working itself out uniformly over the centuries, there should have been very few small-scale polities in the world by, say, the nineteenth century, and they should all have been of very ancient vintage. Yet, when we look, for example, at Africa in recent times, we find it full of small-scale polities whose formation usually dates back but a few centuries and often less.

I have argued elsewhere (Kopytoff 1987) that most of the African polities we know did not evolve out of simpler forms. To the contrary, they sprang out of more complex polities, having grown out of settlements of immigrants from chiefdoms and kingdoms, immigrants who had moved into the "internal frontiers" that lay at the fringes of fully formed polities. To these settlers, the frontier represented an institutional vacuum – an area that was out of the reach of established polities, or was entirely empty, or was under the uncertain sway of weak local hegemonies. These conditions allowed the frontiersmen to construct new autonomous mini-polities. Most of

them eventually faded away, but a few crystallized into the middle-range polities that are the stuff of much of African ethnography.

But the frontier only provided a stage; for the model of the polity the frontiersmen were constructing, they drew upon a political culture that they had brought with them, with the rest of their cultural baggage, from the mature local metropoles. The idea of a proper polity, the principles of its organization and growth, the notions of legitimacy, the accepted ways of attracting and dominating followers, the image of political success – all these were not invented on the spot but came ready-made. Each region of Africa possessed a common fund of such notions, as did in more general terms sub-Saharan Africa as whole.

I shall examine in this light the emergence of the Aghem polity in the Grassfields area of western Cameroon.[1] I shall focus on several themes:

(1) That the principles of political formation that shaped the growth of the Aghem polity were widely shared in the Grassfields, and, more broadly speaking, throughout Africa.
(2) That the Aghem chiefdoms emerged as the result of a gradual process of what I shall call "layered growth." Chiefly rulers did not so much "rise" above their neighbors as they were, so to speak, "levitated" upwards as more immigrants arrived and inserted more layers at the bottom of the hierarchy.
(3) That the existing cultural principles of political formation were capable of generating a certain range of kindred forms, any one of which could change into any other with relative ease.
(4) That these principles had two important ideological strands: populism and despotic patrimonialism – seemingly contradictory notions that co-existed within the same political culture.
(5) And finally, as a matter of general theoretical interest, that any given cultural universe (say, that of sub-Saharan Africa in contrast to medieval Europe or Central America) dictates the specific parameters within which political forms are created and recreated.

A word of warning. I shall use the term "chiefdom" pragmatically, in its plain English meaning, and not as a theoretical or analytical concept, and I shall use "chieftaincy" for the institution that governs a chiefdom.

Aghem origins

The Grassfields of western Cameroon is a region of rolling and mountainous savannas, some 160 by 210 kilo-

meters (100 by 130 miles). The area has, historically, constituted an ecumene, that is, a mosaic of closely interacting cultural and linguistic groups and polities
(Kopytoff 1977). The regional studies and syntheses
(Chilver and Kaberry 1968; Kaberry 1952; Nkwi and
Warnier 1982; Tardits 1981; Warnier 1985) suggest that
the mosaic was in constant motion. Lineages, sub-lin-
eages, families, and individuals moved among "ethnic"
groups whose boundaries were extremely porous; they left
one settlement cluster to join another, or set up new settlements subordinated to existing polities, or founded new
embryonic polities in the frontier areas between established ones, laying the foundations of future new societies
and "ethnic" groups. Migration and regrouping, the rise
and fall of polities, assimilation and conquest, trade and
tribute, acculturation and diffusion, institutional imitation and cultural resynthesis – all these shaped and
reshaped the ethnographic and political map of the
Grassfields over the centuries. This was the setting in
which, shortly before the mid-nineteenth century, arose
Aghem – a term now used for people, language, and
polity, while Wum (a German linguistic misrendering of
Aghəm) has become the accepted term for the settlement.

The Aghem polity began with a group of six neighboring hamlets, dispersed over several miles and composed of
settlers from different places in the Grassfields and
beyond. The locality was under the hegemony of a people
named U'pwa. The Aghem rose against them, defeated
them, expelled most of them, and intermarried with some.
The six small settlements, each of which was led by its
founding lineage, came to be called ZongƏKu, KƏSu,
WaeNdu, WaanaNgwƏn, ChereGha, and ZongƏFƏ. They
organized themselves into a federation; the head of
ZongƏKu, the oldest settlement, hosted the meetings of
hamlet heads, and he became a *primus inter pares* charged
with certain ritual responsibilities to the community as a
whole.

This scenario, in which community origins are placed
in a short-distance migration, occurs in the histories of
polities throughout the Grassfields (Tardits 1981a), and it
conforms to a widespread African tradition of "ethnic"
origins. That this tradition should be so common is
understandable: African social and political systems contained a variety of mechanisms that resulted in a continuous stream of people leaving their communities and
creating for themselves a new life elsewhere (Kopytoff
1987: 17–23). These movements were spurred on systemically by widespread repetitive events in African social
life: the tendency of kin groups to segment as they
expanded; the readiness to attribute misfortunes to the
witchcraft and sorcery of one's neighbors, leading to the
expulsion of the accused or the flight of the victims; and
the frequent quarrels over ambiguous rules of political
succession. The resulting scattering and creation of new
communities were in turn facilitated by the sparseness of
population in most of sub-Saharan Africa, so that land
for new settlement was seldom a scarce resource.

The politics of firstcomer primacy

A widely held African principle in organizing communities is that of the primacy of the firstcomer: the earliest
occupants establish a ritual relationship to the land to
which later settlers must defer. The principle raised a perennial problem: what was one to do, as an immigrant,
with these "owners of the land" that one encountered and
to whom one owed their political and ritual due?
Sometimes, the newcomers gave them a special (usually
ritual) niche in the new society being constructed. With
the U'pwa, the Aghem followed the other widespread
usage: they claimed that they had defeated them, that the
U'pwa thereby ceased to exist as a corporate entity, and
that they had departed and presented no further problem
(although in fact some Aghem lineages are known to be
of U'pwa origin).

The other problem raised by the notion of firstcomer
primacy is internal to the emerging immigrant community: the notion gives a political edge to some of the
founders of the polity – the very earliest newcomers – over
the others. Thus, the head of the ZongƏKu hamlet became
the natural *primus inter pares* because ZongƏKu was the
earliest settlement. But this arrangement soon ran into
difficulties. About the mid-nineteenth century, the region
was briefly devastated by some slave-raiding Chamba
horsemen from the north. After the raiders left, the
Aghem regrouped the six villages more tightly on a hill-
side some 3 kilometers across. Soon after (and, in one not
undisputed version, following the lynching of the *primus*
for his ritual failure to protect the community against the
raid), what may be regarded as a *coup d'état* took place.
Upon the death of the next head of ZongƏKu, the council
of village chiefs installed his son rather than a uterine
nephew as his successor. This meant changing for
ZongƏKu the rule of matrilineal succession, which was
(and is) the Aghem norm. The change had profound
political implications. From then on, the succeeding son
of each *primus* would belong to one or another matrilineage (his mother's) but the position would never permanently reside in any one of them. Moreover, an incumbent
was specifically prohibited from marrying a woman from
any one of the six chiefly (and competing) matrilineages,
so that his heir would never belong to one of them.

It would have been ritually dangerous simply to abolish outright the firstcomer primacy of the head of ZongƏKu, for he was needed to perform the necessary community rituals. Following the *coup d'état*, his ritual role was further elaborated while his political role was increasingly reduced. The result was an emphatically "sacred" chieftaincy, one bereft of secular power and held within a weak patriline by men who came from various powerless and often poor matrilineages. As to the matrilineage that had been expelled from the position, it formed a new settlement, MaaGha, thus giving rise to the seventh constituent chieftaincy in the federation, with a head who became the ritual scapegoat in the annual cycle of public rituals. My choice of the term *coup d'état* for this reorganization is fitting: present-day Aghem see these events as having been a deliberate move by the chiefs to prevent political centralization and to preserve a power balance among themselves.

While the Aghem action in blocking the emergence of centralized power was historically unique, the conundrum it dealt with was a cultural given, arising from widespread Grassfields and pan-African ideas about firstcomer primacy. Similar conundrums, though with varying outcomes, appear in the histories of Aghem neighbors (e.g., Geary 1976, 1981). The struggle was, to be sure, about power, but power as specifically embedded in a set of cultural notions that allowed only a certain limited range of actions.

The Aghem solution to the conundrum also drew on another regional pattern. In matters of descent, the western Grassfields is dually oriented. Matrilineality and patrilineality are both recognized as group-structuring principles, but different communities have attached to them different political, economic, and ritual functions (Nkwi and Warnier 1982: 54–6). The patrilineage *qua* structure was and is familiar to the Aghem, who limit it to rather minor and primarily ritual purposes, reserving the crucial functions to the matrilineage. By contrast, in most neighboring communities, patrilineal descent plays the central organizing role. Thus, when the Aghem created a fully-fledged corporate patrilineage specifically and exclusively for the ZongƏKu ritual paramountcy, they were being ingenious but not greatly inventive. Nor was the clever idea of enhancing the ZongƏKu chief's ritual functions while peeling away his political functions entirely original. African chieftaincies are always bundles of both political and ritual powers. The Aghem chiefs were merely shifting functions within an established cultural complex.

Lineage structure and chieftaincy

As institutions, the chieftaincies of Wum were not created *ex nihilo* by enterprising or ambitious individuals who then conferred their achievements on their successors. Rather, each of the village headships existed from the beginning of settlement, vested in the corporate kin group of first settlers. An individual chief's position derived from his membership in his kin group; he held the chieftaincy in its name and in trust for it, the chieftaincy being part of its estate together with all its other wealth, such as rights in women, or raffia groves, or hunting tribute.

The chieftaincies were thus completely enmeshed in the structures of their respective lineages. Consequently, they were responsive to a major characteristic of African lineage structure – that of periodic segmentation, in which a junior segment hives off from a growing lineage and becomes, in time, a replica of its parent. The segmentation of a lineage leads to the segmentation of its estate – in the case of a chiefly lineage, to the segmentation of the chieftaincy and the creation of a new chiefdom. Throughout Aghem history, the number of chiefdoms continued to increase in response to their own growth and the growth of their population, and the process continued into the colonial era. Thus, WaeNdu gave birth to ZongƏTrha, and WaanaNgwƏn to WaAtwiya. WaeNdu and WaanaNgwƏn then each split into two chiefdoms. As late as the 1940s, NaeKom detached itself from KƏSu (and by the 1960s, one of KƏSu's large wards was acting with increasing autonomy). In sum, after a little more than a century, the six original chiefdoms had grown to twelve.

Wum also grew into a regional power. In the later nineteenth century, three ambitious and energetic chiefs promoted the expansion of local Aghem hegemony by subordinating several neighboring palmoil-producing groups in the forest. Under the pressure of what is best described as institutionalized bullying, the forest settlements were required to furnish an annual tribute of palm oil to four Aghem chieftaincies. The oil, together with oil bartered by individual Aghem, was traded on to savanna communities where it was in great demand, and this allowed the Aghem to link themselves profitably into a large regional trading network (see Kopytoff 1981: 374–81; Nkwi and Warnier 1982: 38–54; Warnier 1985).

Layered growth

The structural growth of Wum went hand in hand with the expansion of its population. The process was gradual: the hamlets grew into what we, as outsiders, would with increasing assurance call villages; and these were ruled over by heads who increasingly conform to our image of chiefs. The community as a whole became more compact. At present, Wum looks to the outsider like a single continuous settlement; in fact, it is composed of several clearly defined sections corresponding to the chieftaincies. One might be tempted to call these sections "wards," but the term could mislead by implying a subdivision of an initially unified structure. From the Aghem point of view, the present map of Wum derives from the original clearly separated villages that have physically grown together over time. Where subdivision did take place was within the villages: as each grew, it kept producing new *ukon*, which may properly be called wards.

The population of Wum expanded as the Aghem brought in relatives, wives, and slaves from the surrounding region. Wum also continued to take in immigrants – people who were disgruntled with their kinsmen or chiefs; who lost out in disputes over succession; who had been accused of witchcraft or were fleeing the witchcraft of others; or who had been expelled for misconduct. This human traffic, of course, worked both ways: it also took people out of Wum. But on balance, as Wum became a regional political and trading power, the net population flow was in its favor; thus, neighboring polities (such as Kuk, We, or Isu) from which Wum drew heavily, are smaller. At the turn of the twentieth century, when the first German colonial agents appeared on the scene, Wum had attained a population of some 5,000. By the post-colonial period, in the 1960s, its population was approaching 10,000.

That the growth of Wum fed on the surrounding population is evident from Aghem genealogies. Except for chiefly lineages and a core of "true" Aghem, the genealogies are usually quite shallow. One usually arrives within a very few generations to the local beginnings of the lineage in the person of the woman-founder who arrived as a wife (sometimes a slave-wife) or as a new settler's sister. (With patrilineal groups, such foreign input of women is usually masked by the institutional focus on the local continuity of the patriline of husbands/fathers.)

In pre-colonial times, these outside links provided individual Aghem a refuge from dynastic quarrels and witch hunts. Many Aghem continue to recognize kinsmen in other Grassfields communities (for example, by frequent visits to funerals) and they use this network when they move out of Wum. Within Wum, certain minor variations in customs and linguistic usage among lineages are attributed to their different foreign origins.

I use the term "foreign" to refer to polities rather than ethnicities. In the western Grassfields ecumene, the con-

stant reshuffling of the population over the centuries made for a relatively continuous cultural landscape, but a landscape dotted with many separate polities. Around these polities would crystallize in time distinct customs and dialects and languages. The Aghem and their neighbors recognize that an Aghem language and Aghem customs exist, but they see their existence as a pragmatic historical product and not as a reflection of an essentialist "ethnicity."

When immigrants arrived in a Wum chiefdom, the village chief "showed them the place" where they could build their compound. He formally told them of their obligations to him and of the rules of village life; it was made clear that transgressions (above all, witchcraft) could lead to expulsion. Recent newcomers (especially those from the forest) were placed at the bottom of the chiefdom hierarchy – in effect, on probation. The longer they stayed, the more weighty became their claim to Aghemhood, with its right to participate in local affairs. But their Aghemhood continued to be a matter of hierarchical gradation. At the top stood, unchallenged, the "true" Aghem – the chiefly lineages and just below them their long-standing adherents who claimed to have been there at the founding of the settlement. Next were the entirely assimilated Aghem of remembered foreign origin but long resident in Wum and with extensive local kin connections. Below them were the recent and weakly integrated immigrants. And at the very bottom stood the most recent immigrants, usually poor strangers and slaves acquired within living memory, and their immediate descendants. In private and unguarded moments, anyone could lump together oneself and those above one as Aghem and all those below as "strangers," "slaves," and "outsiders."

The process of emergent political stratification that I have described does not fit the picture implied by the common metaphor in which chiefs appear by "rising" above their neighbors by using some newly available resource. For the Aghem, a more appropriate metaphor is that of "levitation": passively, the founding-lineage head finds himself to be a "chief" by simply remaining at the top of a pyramid that grows at the bottom.

Patrimonialism

Since the chiefdom was the patrimonial estate of the ruling lineage, every inhabitant who was not a member of the chiefly lineage was, formally speaking, a squatter, living in the village at the sufferance of the chief. The ground that the settlers built on was the chief's. Since the building materials came from the chief's forest, the houses belonged to the chief. Because the food came from the chief's soil, it was the chief who fed the people. If an inhabitant misbehaved or earned the chief's displeasure, he could be expelled and allowed to carry away with him only his personal belongings. At the same time, however, the chief had reciprocal responsibilities to the people: a good chief was supposed to "herd" the villagers and nurture them. In brief, the system was patrimonial – to use Max Weber's term for what he regarded as an early political form in which the polity is a private estate inherited by successive rulers. For the Aghem, as for Africa in general, one should stress the corporate element: the patrimony belonged not to the chief personally but to his corporate lineage.

A theorist of political development is likely to see the beginnings of an Aghem chiefdom at the point when its size and resources had sufficiently expanded to (for want of a more precise phrase) "make a difference" in terms of its physical character. But in a patrimonial corporate perspective, there is no such difference, no quantum step that ushers in a new political formation. The lineage with its estate (which includes the chieftaincy) existed as a single corporate entity from the start and regardless of the size of the estate. The beginnings of any corporation correspond to its first signs of life (the fast-food giant, McDonald's, sees itself beginning when its first hamburger stand opened and not when its shares were first traded on Wall Street). Similarly, an African chief dates the founding of his chiefdom to the time when his immigrant ancestor built his first hut. Such a perspective emphasizes continuity rather than radical change in the chiefs' transformation from hamlet head to village head, to village chief, to regional chief, to paramount chief, to king – and back again when the kingdom shrinks. The terminology of chieftaincy usually reflects this continuum by making little or no differentiation between these various positions (much as in French medieval terminology, *seigneur* could apply to the lord of a small manor no less than to the lord of a duchy).

The constitutional balance between chief and subjects

A patrimonial ideology harbors, of course, possibilities of despotism. And indeed, Aghem chiefs could be harsh and arbitrary. But the harshness was systemically mitigated by the chiefs' need to have subjects, the more the better. There is a saying common in African societies, that one cannot be a chief and be alone; and so Aghem chiefs had magical devices to help them attract and retain subjects. A chief's dependence on subjects was stressed in his installation rituals: at one point, the people hurled insults at the new chief to make it clear to him that without them

he was nothing. And at a chief's funeral, people would stand before the sitting corpse and loudly remind it how far he had fallen, now that he could command no subjects. There was thus, in the Aghem political culture, what we might call a "populist" strand side by side with the despotic strand. The coexistence of these seemingly contradictory sources of legitimacy, evident in African ethnography, has been extensively examined by Bradbury (1969) in his discussion of Benin political culture. (Bradbury uses the term gerontocracy where I use "populism;" in societies dominated by kin groups, gerontocratic lineage elders are of course the appropriate carriers of populism.)

It must be stressed that rather than being irreconcilable, patrimonialism and populism in Wum, as indeed generally in African polities, normally remain in balance. The Aghem see the two as parts of the same system. Both chiefs and ordinary Aghem agree that the chief "owns everything" in the chiefdom, including the people, as they also agree that the "people make the chief" – in the same way that it is wealth that "makes" its owner wealthy. Pragmatically, however, the divide between the claims of patrimonialism and those of populism is often fuzzy, and much of Aghem political history was shaped by this fuzziness.

Aghem political history

The more energetic Aghem chiefs tried periodically to institutionalize new exactions from their subjects. They would claim that control of all raffia bushes (the source of the much prized raffia wine) was ultimately a chiefly prerogative. They would try to extend the chiefs' existing rights to certain large animals – such as the leopard (a widely recognized symbol of chieftaincy in Africa) – to other large and even not so large animals. They would try to assert a monopoly of all meat resources. Several chiefs tried to extrapolate their normal ritually sanctioned right to first fruits into rights to a larger harvest tribute. Some redefined existing communal hunts in a way to make them benefit the chiefs directly; and some instituted special grass-cutting days to provide fresh material for their houses. In this drive for power, Aghem chiefs adapted certain elements of the regional culture. In many polities of the western Grassfields, a secret society (*kweifon*) acted as a popular check on chiefly power, with chiefs and their families being barred from membership. Several Aghem chiefs imported the institution with all its ritual paraphernalia, but made it into an instrument of the chieftaincy (for a richly textured view of Grassfields chiefly politics, see Ritzenthaler 1966).

The most dramatic instance of the enlargement of chiefly power followed the arrival of the first German officer in 1902. A chief of WaeNdu, MvϑNsi, secured the patronage of the German authorities and maintained for over a decade a murderous despotism that included the killing of several chiefs. MvϑNsi's use of colonial intrusion to transmute patrimonialism into outright despotism is not without precedent in Africa; and Brown (1963) has shown it to have been a widespread systemic feature of the early stages of colonial rule in general.

While the chiefs promoted the logic of patrimonialism, their subjects argued for the populist principle by pointing out that the chiefs often abused their judicial authority, that they were all too often greedy, and that they did not live up to the paternalism that was part of their patrimonial responsibilities. Shortly before the turn of the century, a populist movement erupted: the people instituted a community-wide popular tribunal called KangKϑm. Though Kangkϑm never questioned the legitimacy of chieftaincy per se, it bypassed the chiefs by resolving disputes on its own. How may Kangkϑm be characterized? Gluckman (among others) made a differentiation between "revolutions" (which make a fundamental change in the system) and "rebellions" (which change the personnel and preserve the system). KangKϑm was neither of these. It is best seen, perhaps, as a "constitutional initiative" – a failed one, for it eventually vanished in the morass of community politics. But it stayed long in Aghem memory: in the later 1940s, the name was revived when a faction attempted, though with little success, to curtail drastically the legal powers of the chiefs.

The source and currency of chiefly power

The main ingredient in the rise of an Aghem chiefdom was the acquisition by the chief of control over more and more people – people being simultaneously the origin, the substance, the goal, and the currency of chiefly authority. This acquisition of adherents was made possible not by wealth but by a costless resource – the chief's ability to grant or not to grant permission to reside to immigrants who were too weak to risk settlement in the open countryside; and the chief's position was further maintained by his power to evict. This authority was a given from the very beginning of the polity, whatever the polity's scope at the time; it was held by hamlet heads and embryonic chiefs no less than by those whom we would regard as fully-fledged chiefs. There is little place for such costless resources in theories that explain the emergence of chieftaincy by focusing on material advantages, such as control of trade or the redis-

tribution of goods. The problem is not that such theories are too materialistic but that their materialism is too narrow – one is tempted to say too consumerist. They ignore other resources more subtle than solid goods that lend themselves to political ends – resources such as provision of shelter and safety, of sociability, of psychic satisfactions in their various cultural guises.

Another problem lies in the assumptions one makes about the ends of power, for power is a contentless term. In African societies, not the least important of political goals is status in and of itself. Being a chief means such things as being a visibly important man, one who can claim precedence in seating at public functions, who can wear exclusive insignia, who has a title. These are not merely "symbols" of something more "concrete," such as power; they are valued goals in their own right, a part of "power" rather than a representation of it. Contemporary Westerners (unlike, say, their medieval ancestors) have little experience of or respect for an ethos that values hierarchical display for its own sake. This may make it difficult to conceive of impalpable prerogatives as being more than merely means toward some tangible ends.

Variations among Aghem chiefdoms

At a very general level, and for understandable historical reasons (Kopytoff 1987: 9–11), the societies of sub-Saharan Africa shared a political culture whose particular expressions varied by region. Similarly, societies within a region produced unique local configurations that were variants of the regional culture. Thus, in the Grassfields region, the political form of specific societies (as they appear, for example, in Chilver and Kaberry 1967; Dillon 1973; Geary 1976, 1981; Masquelier 1978, 1979; Nkwi 1976; Ritzenthaler and Ritzenthaler 1962; Tardits 1980; Warnier 1975, 1981) are clearly variants of regional patterns (as presented in such regional studies as Chilver and Kaberry 1968; Kaberry 1952, 1962; Nkwi and Warnier 1982). A similar situation prevails at the yet more local level of Wum: each of its constituent chiefdoms represents a unique historical version of a common Aghem model.

A major source of variation among the Wum chiefdoms came from their different approaches to the shared desire for adherents. Each chiefdom pursued quite consciously a distinct population policy. The result was variation in the size of the chiefdoms. At the turn of this century, after the original hamlets had been growing for over fifty years, the largest chiefdom, KϑSu, had a population approaching 2,000; the smallest chiefdom, ChereGha, had one of under 200.

K∂Su favored what might be called an open immigration policy. Its chiefs willingly took in immigrants but lorded it over them and maintained a strong hierarchy. K∂Su also produced chiefs who were aggressive both in asserting their chiefly prerogatives within the village and in extending Aghem hegemony over the neighboring forest communities. By contrast, the small ChereGha chiefdom had a reputation for mild and nurturing chiefs who admitted a few immigrants selectively and treated them paternalistically. Other chiefdoms developed other political personalities. The medium-size WaeNdu cultivated a lean-and-mean image. It preferred to integrate immigrants by way of an extensive marriage network. And its reputation was that of a united but quarrelsome family, headed by flamboyant and aggressive chiefs. WaanaNgw∂n, on the other hand, maintained from early times a segmentary type of system, but one with an oligarchic cast. Its founding lineages controlled rather loosely small immigrant lineages. It had a weak *primus inter pares* who represented the village at the council of Wum chiefs but had little power inside the village. With its quasi acephalous structure, the chiefdom was regarded in Wum as the repository of the populist tradition and it had furnished some of the leadership in both of the antichiefly outbursts I have mentioned.

Conclusion

For all this variety of designs, the Aghem political tapestry is strikingly seamless. The structural differences among the chiefdoms do not negate a uniformity of political substance. In this respect, Aghem is a microcosm of Africa. After Fortes and Evans-Pritchard (1940) drew their two sharply distinct types of African political systems – the centralized and the acephalous – Africanists began to see continuities between the types. Early on, Southall's (1956) study of the Alur confounded the distinction structurally, by presenting a political system that fit neither of the two types. Later, Horton's (1971) notable analysis of West African stateless societies confounded the typology processually, by showing how relatively simple was the transition from statelessness to the state. The data from Aghem reiterate these points.

Had the different Aghem chiefdoms been separate societies, they might be easily arranged in an evolutionary progression showing three particularly salient types. At the simplest end, WaanaNgw∂n would represent a nearly acephalous, lineage-based structure, but one showing signs of oligarchic differentiation. In the middle would be WaeNdu, an emergent chiefdom dominated by a single lineage but holding on to kinship mechanisms in

controlling its immigrant subjects. At the other end would stand K∂Su, which could pose as an embryonic kingdom were it not for its rather unimpressive population of a couple of thousand. And if we changed analytical levels and looked at Wum as a whole, we could perceive in its history a progression of different types: segmentary structure at its inception, then a segmentary mini-state (held together by an apolitical ritual head), and finally, a centralized and despotic chiefdom, the one created in the German period and abolished by the succeeding British administration.

The structural types we find in Wum appear elsewhere in the Grassfields, often with differences in scale. For example, K∂Su was not structured very differently from the kingdom of Bamum (Tardits 1980). The latter had, at its core, a royal lineage standing at the top of a hierarchy of vassal aristocratic lineages and, below them, commoner subject lineages and slaves. Many of the Aghem political processes similarly had their counterparts in other Grassfield polities – for example, the struggles over the distribution of power between chiefs and subjects, the chiefs' usurpation of control of the secret societies, the contention between centralization and federation, and the emergence of despots during early colonial occupation.

The easy transition of Aghem and Grassfields polities from one form to another suggests an underlying generative structure producing the variation in forms. The common principles governing this structure have cropped up in the course of my discussion – the frontier setting at the origin; the primacy of the firstcomer; the corporateness of the founding lineage; the notion of a lineage estate that, in addition to material resources, could include such symbolic political resources as the chieftaincy; the coexistence of patrimonialism and populism, once the original frontier settlement outgrew the capacities of the familial lineage model of organization; the application to chiefly lineages of the principles of lineage segmentation and replication; the recognition of both patrilineages and matrilineages as alternative structures for the allocation of social functions; and the integration of the ritual and the secular functions of the chieftaincy.

This common generative structure permitted a Grassfields polity to shift, at different points in its history, from one form to another – from acephalous communities, to federations of lineages, to lineage oligarchies, to despotic chieftaincies – as particular events and personalities came into play. At any given time, each polity exhibited what Gearing (1958) has called a "structural pose" – one out of the several possible poses inherent in the underlying structure. The historical sequencing of these variant Grassfields forms does not reveal any particular evolutionary trajectory. Nor is there an obvious theoretical logic that would allow one to arrange them into some convincing progressive sequence – unless one postulates a "strain-toward-monarchy" as a principle of political evolution.

When we turn our attention from the Grassfields to the larger stage of sub-Saharan Africa, we must recognize that most of the principles of organization that operated in the Grassfields are also pan-African, albeit in a more abstract form. And in a long-term historical, proto-historical, and prehistorical perspective on Africa, we must consider the possibility that some of these principles, long embedded in a shared and continuous political culture, already existed in the early and simple prehistoric societies, only awaiting appropriate conditions to generate more complex but specifically African forms.

This suggests that in our search for evolutionary models, we might adopt a truly Darwinian model and jettison the various versions of the Spencerian unilineal model. Darwinian evolution unfolds phylogenetically: the historical accidents of mutation and environmental change that transform a species transform it within the given parameters of its particular evolutionary corridor. Simply put, some of the crucial biological givens that have shaped the evolutionary trajectory of cats and dogs were distinctly different. There are analogies to this in ethnological processes: the systemic developments of what we choose to call "chiefdoms" and "kingdoms" were different in the different culture-historical corridors of, say, Africa, Polynesia, and Mesoamerica. My emphasis on the specificity of these corridors raises, of course, the issue of the hoary distinction between the nomothetic (scientific) and the idiographic (historical) approaches. But the choices this distinction seems to impose are far too stark. Just as Darwinian evolution incorporates – quite unselfconsciously – both approaches, so should the study of the evolution of political forms. Before we can deal with the nomothetic challenge of universal processes, we must allow for the characteristics of the cultural "phylogenetic" corridors whose impact on the development of political forms is singular in worldwide perspective and yet systemic in the local context.

Note

1 The fieldwork among the Aghem in 1969 and 1971 was conducted under a grant from the National Science Foundation. I must give, at the outset, a warning to the linguistic purist: since "Aghem" is now the established term in Cameroon and in the literature, I use it instead of the more phonetically correct "Aghəm," on the same principle that we say "French" instead of "français." On the other hand, the names of the Aghem chiefdoms have been rendered in the literature and documents in a number of different ways, and I have consequently felt free to resort to a relatively faithful phonetic spelling.

References

Bradbury, R. E.
1969. Patrimonialism and gerontocracy in Benin political culture. In *Man in Africa*, edited by M. Douglas and P. M. Kaberry. London: Tavistock 17–37.

Brown, P.
1963 From anarchy to satrapy. *American Anthropologist* 65: 1–15.

Chilver, E. M. and P. M. Kaberry
1967 The Kingdom of Kom in West Cameroon. In *West African Kingdoms in the Nineteenth Century*, edited by D. Forde and P. M. Kaberry. London: Oxford University Press: 123–51.

1968 *Traditional Bamenda: The Pre-colonial History and Ethnography of the Bamenda Grassfields*. Buea: Ministry of Primary Education and Social Welfare and West Cameroon Antiquities Commission.

Dillon, R. G.
1973 Ideology, process and change in pre-colonial Meta's political organization (United Republic of Cameroon). Ph.D. Dissertation, Department of Anthropology, University of Pennsylvania.

Fortes, M. and E. E. Evans-Pritchard
1940 Introduction. In *African Political Systems*, edited by M. Fortes and E. E. Evans-Pritchard. London: Oxford University Press: 1–23.

Gearing, F.
1958 The structural poses of 18th century Cherokee villages. *American Anthropologist* 60: 1148–57.

Geary, C.
1976 *We, die Genese eines Hauptlingtums im Grasland von Kamerun*. Wiesbaden: Franz Steiner.

1981 The historical development of the chiefdom of We (southern Fungom). In *Contribution de la recherche ethnologique à l'histoire des civilisations du Cameroun*, vol. 2, edited by C. Tardits (Colloques Internationaux du CNRS no. 551). Paris: Editions du CNRS: 383–92.

Horton, R.
1971 Stateless societies in the history of West Africa. In *History of West Africa*, vol. 1 edited by J. F. A. Ajayi and M. Crowder. New York: Columbia University Press: 78–119.

Kaberry, P. M.
   1952 *Women of the Grassfields*. London: Her Majesty's Stationery Office.
   1962 Retainers and royal households in the Cameroon Grassfields. *Cahiers d'Etudes Africaines*, 3–1 (10): 282–98.
Kopytoff, I.
   1977 Speculations about the internal African frontier. African Studies Association Papers. 8 pp.
   1981 Aghem ethnogenesis and the Grassfields ecumene. In *Contribution de la recherche ethnologique à l'histoire des civilisations du Cameroun*, vol. 2, edited by C. Tardits (Colloques Internationaux du CNRS no. 551). Paris: Editions du CNRS: 371–82
   1987 The internal African frontier: the making of African political culture. In *The African Frontier: The Reproduction of Traditional African Societies*, edited by I. Kopytoff. Bloomington: Indiana University Press: 3–84.
Masquelier, B. M.
   1978 *Structure and process of political identity: Ide, a polity of the Metchum Valley (Cameroon)*. Ph.D. Dissertation. Department of Anthropology, University of Pennsylvania.
   1979 Ide as a polity: ideology, morality and political identity. *Paideuma* 25: 41–52.
Nkwi, P. N.
   1976 *Traditional Government and Social Change: A Study of the Political Institutions among the Kom of the Cameroon Grassfields*. Fribourg: The University Press.
Nkwi, P. N. and J.-P. Warnier
   1982 *Elements for a History of the Western Grassfields*. Department of Sociology, University of Yaounde, Yaounde.

Ritzenthaler, P.
   1966 *The Fon of Bafut*. New York: Thomas Y. Crowell.
Ritzenthaler, R. and P. Ritzenthaler
   1962 *Cameroons Village: An Ethnography of the Bafut*. Milwaukee: Milwaukee Public Museum.
Southall, A. W.
   1956 *Alur Society: A Study in Processes and Types of Domination*. Cambridge: W. Heffer and Sons.
Tardits, C.
   1980 *Le Royaume Bamoum*. Paris: Armand Colin.
   1981a L'implantation des populations dans l'ouest Cameroun. In *Contribution de la recherche ethnologique à l'histoire des civilisations du Cameroun*, vol. 2, edited by C. Tardits (Colloques Internationaux du CNRS no. 551). Paris: Editions du CNRS: 475–84
   1981b (ed.) *Contribution de la recherche ethnologique à l'histoire des civilisations du Cameroun*, vol. 2, (Colloques Internationaux du CNRS no. 551). Paris: Editions du CNRS.
Warnier, J.-P.
   1975 Pre-colonial Mankon: the development of a Cameroon chiefdom in its regional setting. Ph.D. Dissertation. Department of Anthropology, University of Pennsylvania.
   1981 L'histoire pré-coloniale de la chefferie de Mankon (Departement de la Mezam). In *Contribution de la recherche ethnologique à l'histoire des civilisations du Cameroun*, vol. 2, edited by C. Tardits (Colloques Internationaux du CNRS no. 551). Paris: Editions du CNRS.: 421–36.
   1985 *Echanges, developpement et hierarchies dans le Bamenda pré-colonial (Cameroun)*. Wiesbaden: Franz Steiner.

8

Wonderful society: the Burgess shale creatures, Mandara polities, and the nature of prehistory

NICHOLAS DAVID AND JUDY STERNER

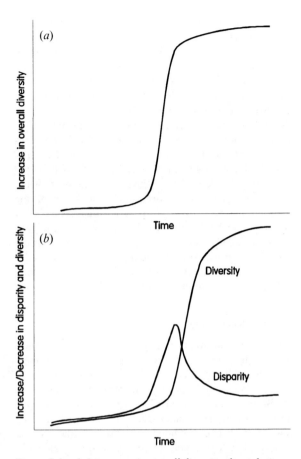

Figure 8.1 (a) increase in overall diversity through time; (b) contrasting increase and decrease in disparity and diversity through time.

The organic analogy

High in the Canadian Rockies of Yoho National Park lie outcrops of early Cambrian shale that contain the fossils of creatures as exotically named – *Ayesheaia, Wiwaxia, Anomalocaris, Hallucigenia* – as they are themselves fantastic and, indeed, out of this world. They have, as Stephen J. Gould (1989) proclaims in the book from which our title is derived, changed our view of life, for, despite the small numbers of species represented, they are more disparate – more varied at the level of phylum and class – than the "entire spectrum of invertebrate life in today's oceans" (p. 25), a spectrum now characterized by profligate diversification of a restricted number of classes.

This disparate, but not diverse, early Cambrian fauna appears to have arisen explosively in what must be the type specimen of punctuated evolution. There is, for the majority of these creatures, no lengthy preceding record of gradual change. Rather, some 600 million years ago, new patterns of life suddenly radiate through the Cambrian oceans. Elsewhere, Gould argues that this steep rise in organic diversity in the first 10 to 20 million years of the Cambrian, "was merely the predictable outcome of a process inexorably set in motion by an earlier Pre-Cambrian event . . . that initiated the evolution of complex life." The event, or rather complex of events, was the development of eukaryotic cells and of sexual reproduction. Once these were in place "[t]he pattern of the Cambrian explosion seems to follow a general law of growth" (Gould 1979: 127), the sigmoid curve that classically characterizes the career of a colony of bacteria on a Petri dish (Figure 8.1a).

But if we break down overall diversity into its two parts, higher-order disparity in basic plan versus lower-order diversity, the elaboration of basic plans, the graph changes (Figure 8.1b). After the long lag phase, there is a rapid initial rise in disparity, the log phase, followed by a decrease in phyla, during which time diversity, though progressively limited to fewer and fewer phyla and classes, nevertheless continues to increase. This contrasting patterning may also follow if not a general law then a common pattern of diversification seen, for example, in our own lineage at the *Australopithecus* stage – or in computer operating systems. May it not also apply to types of human societies?

The analogy that we are drawing runs as follows. A lag phase lasting from the origins of *Homo* two and a half million years ago to the end of the Pleistocene is characterized by human societies that, constrained by ecology and technology, could take only a limited number of simple forms. Then, in distant parts of the earth and in a few thousand years, the development of food production and concomitant increases in population densities, sedentism, storage and division of labor call forth a range of disparate societal types. This is the log phase. Thereafter, progressively and to us apparently inexorably, societal variety is reduced, most notably by the development of two or more major types of the hierarchically organized state (Lamberg-Karlovsky 1985) that for the past five millennia have been expanding and diversifying. They have long since incorporated a majority of the earth's population – and all its publishing academics. And before you make the obvious challenge to our inference that early food-producing societies in fact show much less disparity than we are retrodicting, we should consider why the story of the Burgess shale creatures was for long untold and is still so little appreciated.

The intellectual analogy

The second, and equally important, *Leitmotiv* of Gould's book deals with the scientific response to the Burgess shale fauna. We must greatly condense his exploitation of this rich intellectual seam. Charles Walcott, discoverer of the Burgess shale fauna in 1909, "premier paleontologist and most powerful administrator in American science" (Gould 1989: 13), was blinded by his scientific training and religious upbringing to its extraordinary richness, which might have been taken to imply a less than omniscient deity. Walcott consequently "shoehorned" its bounteous variety into the restrictive confines of the then current classificatory system. Others followed his lead. It was not until the late 1960s that Henry Whittington, armed with time to interrogate the fossils and the insight that they were three dimensional and micro-excavatable, initiated the modern reassessment. In the meantime, and still today, most renderings of the course of evolution emphasize the inevitability of progress from prokaryotic cell to *Homo* rather than the contingent nature and the historicity of evolutionary change and its many blind alleys. Gould uses representations of evolutionary trees to demonstrate how the long-prevailing anthropocentric paradigm consistently plays down "lower" organisms and their diversity while emphasizing that amongst the mammals and especially those closest to ourselves. *Paranthropus, Plesianthropus, Zinjanthropus, Pithecanthropus, Sinanthropus,* and many other genera once graced the hominid line.

Similarly, archaeologists and many anthropologists have long tended to view intermediate (i.e., between forager and state) level societies not in their own terms but in those of their evolutionary status and potential, the extent to which they have supposedly climbed a ladder of social evolution towards the state – from which viewpoint they are inevitably observed. Sahlins and Service's (1960: 37) band > tribe > chiefdom > state, and Fried's (1967) egalitarian > ranked > stratified > state society sequences have become classics in this regard.[1] Edited volumes such as Claessen and Skalník's (1978) *The Early State* and (1981) *The Study of the State* chart a supposed progression from chiefdoms to inchoate, typical, and transitional forms of the early state and on to later types. Despite much sophisticated work on the roles of ecology, modes of production, and ideology as dynamics of change in such societies, we would argue that, even where the emphasis has been on understanding the nature and workings of particular societies, evolutionary perspective distorts the disciplinary landscape. And, just as Haeckel (1866, [in Gould 1989: 264]) tucks away the highly disparate class of fishes into the basement of his diagram of the vertebrates in order to reserve a penthouse for *Gorilla* and *Homo* in the top right, so the cultural evolutionary literature virtually ignores those historically or ethnographically known peoples whose societies cannot comfortably be accommodated on the trajectory. This is especially true of that written by archaeologists, too busy seeking and too often finding evidence of institutions – redistribution is the classic example – interpreted as indices of developing hierarchy and centralization. The shoehorn is everywhere apparent, and alternative developmental scenarios are never seriously sought, far less tested against data.

Much of our research strategy has been misconceived. Instead of ignoring the not-so-rare societies that present what we judge to be atypical off-trajectory features, we should rather consider that they may be the latest – and last – representatives of societal types once common in the past, and thus in the archaeological record. Rather than attempting to insert societies known through archaeology into the straitjacket of Friedian or derivative evolutionary sequences, we should be actively looking for evidence that might indicate that they belong to separate evolutionary lines. For if our Gouldian evolutionary analogy is even approximately right, and if disparity in societal plans did become suddenly greater in the period following largely independent developments of food production on several continents, then we may expect the bulk of Holocene archaeological cultures to represent societal types either extinct or existing only as relicts in the historical record and ethnographic present. Surely this is a more liberating approach than to expend great efforts on forcing recalcitrant archaeological entities – the Harappan is a prime example, the Chacoan phenomenon another – into "statejackets," state-trajectory moulds that must be strained to bursting to contain them?

Perhaps we find this liberating because we are neither theorists nor have we worked with particularly complex societies. Others are both, and are indeed breaking the stranglehold on archaeological attention, prestige, and funding so long held by the evolutionary paradigm. Norman Yoffee's influential paper "Too many chiefs?" posits that "many evolutionary trajectories can exist and that not all known human societies fall on the progressive steps of a social evolutionary ladder" (Yoffee 1993: 72). As an approach to the analysis of socio-political transformations and stasis, he proposes "new social evolutionary theory." Here it is the extent and distribution in space and time of a variety of powers that constitute socio-political complexity. Economic power is the conversion of surplus production and of wealth acquired through mercantile activity into social dependencies. Societal power is the power to define social entities and their relations with other such entities, including territorial interactions. Political power is the ability physically to coerce and to enforce decisions. Yoffee conflates social and ideological power whereas we would rather regard them as analytically separate, with ideology in a dialectical relationship reflecting and legitimating as authority other sources of power. Ideological power thus consists of control over the symbols that define and interrelate institutions in the other three realms. As to a procedure and methodology, Yoffee proposes the analysis of institutions in tight historical context.

While cumulative accretion of powers may result in the formation of a state, there is no presumption that this will occur; on the contrary, the potential for and the constraints on the growth of power must be inferred from the evidence in each case. The errors of projecting onto archaeological data characteristics inferred for some metaphysical social stage, or of fitting prehistoric materials to ethnographic models drawn from societies that may well lie on different trajectories, are to be equally and rigorously avoided. Yoffee's new social evolutionary theory, neatly if briefly exemplified in his case study of state formation in Mesopotamia, is a near-perfect complement to our Gouldian thesis. We would however take issue with his deep distrust of ethnographic and ethnoarchaeological analogy. The task of the ethnoarchaeologist is to reveal the dynamic structures that generate patterning in culture and especially material culture. For each structure revealed, different values of its interacting components can result in differing material culture

outputs. Thus, by increasing our stock of ethnographic models and our understanding of the dynamics underlying their archaeological signatures, we may escape the tyranny of the ethnographic record of which Wobst (1978) wrote.

It is indeed a relief to have a theoretical excuse to revel in the particular, in the historicity of certain societies and cultures, with results (one may hope) as potentially rewarding as those of Whittington's co-worker, Simon Conway Morris, who by immersing himself in the details of the "laterally compressed ribbon-shaped creature" (Gould 1989: 321) *Pikaia gracilens* was finally able to demonstrate that it was not, as Walcott had thought, an annelid worm but the first recorded member of the Chordata, our own phylum.

We should privilege work on society's oddities, its *Wiwaxias* and *Anomalocarises*, the disparate social formations least likely to lie on a trajectory leading to statehood. And, as Susan McIntosh reminds us in her introduction, there are many of them in Africa and especially in West Africa where not a few appear to have achieved some measure of success in developing sustainable, alternative solutions to the problems and opportunities resulting from technological development beyond the forager level.

This then is our justification for presenting aspects of three societies of the Mandara highlands of north Cameroon and northeastern Nigeria from a new social evolutionary theoretical perspective.

Mandara polities

The Mandara highlands, located in the Central African savanna zone 250 kilometers south of Lake Chad, are occupied by small-scale, traditionally stateless societies (Figure 8.2). We refer to all these societies as "montagnard." Their pre-colonial economies were mainly based on subsistence agriculture (now complemented by cash-cropping and labor migration), and they practiced local religions (Islam and Christianity are now making inroads). In the pre-colonial era the plains below the mountains were occupied by Muslim state societies, who possessed in their cavalry a powerful technology of destruction – though one ill-adapted to a boulder-strewn mountain landscape.[2] Most immediately there were the Wandala state and various Fulbe lamidates or baronies, the latter deriving their *de jure* authority though not their *de facto* power from the Sokoto Caliphate founded in the early nineteenth century. In recent centuries and into the early years of the colonial episode, the highlands were treated by the plains states as a reservoir of slaves, live-

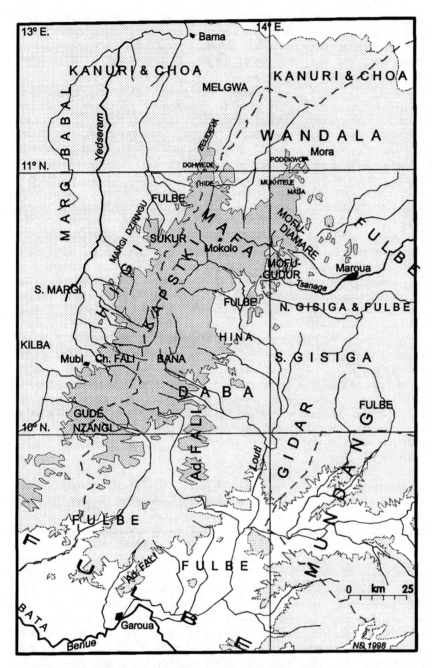

Figure 8.2   The Mandara highlands and surrounding plains, with larger towns and main ethno-linguistic groupings. (Ch. Fali = Chadic-speaking Fali; Ad. Fali = Adamawa-speaking Fali.) Contours at 1,000 and 2,000 feet.

stock, and iron, to be obtained by raiding or by trade with those montagnards willing or pressured to act as middlemen. Not only Muslim-montagnard but also intra-montagnard relationships were characteristically ambiguous. Competition for farmland and wives among hill communities often contributed to tension, erupting at times into hostilities, but nonetheless not precluding much peaceful economic and social interaction, often amounting to interdependence. For, while some languages are spoken over relatively large areas – and in the northern highlands Mandara polities may embrace thousands at population densities generally upwards of 100 people/km^2 – no single montagnard polity extended over even 100 km^2.

Montagnards are typically regarded as classically patriarchal and egalitarian. This characterization is misleading. Even the smallest social formation, a single settlement of subsistence farmers perched on a rocky massif, is a hierarchy in waiting, and has developed what we may describe, choosing the term precisely for its vacuity, as a chiefdom.[3] We seek to underline the commonalities between egalitarian, ranked, and stratified societies that extended over the Mandara region in precolonial times and together constituted a system in disequilibrium that had achieved stasis in opposition to surrounding states, but would itself never have developed into a state or states. Why this should be so is a question that can be asked and answered at several levels. We must admit that we do not find the answers particularly interesting. Far more informative about the human condition are the protean expressions of the underlying Mandara tradition, which we may conceive of as a subset of a social phylum represented over a considerable portion of Central Africa. Members of this grouping, which transcends the boundaries of linguistic phyla, are recognizable as transforms of the generative structure defined by Kopytoff (this volume, pp. 93–4). They include the Grassfields societies discussed elsewhere in this volume by Asombang and Kopytoff. Very similar processes are evident among the Alur (Southall 1954, and this volume), though different principles appear to operate amongst other Lakes polities (Schoenbrun, this volume; Robertshaw (this volume), and the equatorial Bantu are a phylum apart (Vansina, this volume).

The tradition is carried by speakers of over twenty-five languages of the Tera-Dzδpaw sub-branch of the central branch of the Chadic family. This is estimated to have been evolving in the Mandara highlands and surrounding plains for some 3,600 years (Barreteau and Jungraithmayr 1993: 126). The limited archaeological evidence (see David and MacEachern 1988; MacEachern 1993, 1994) and in particular continuities in ceramics (David et al.

1988; Walde et al. 1994) suggest that the conceptual reservoir underlying the tradition has been developing in this region for at least two millennia (Sterner 1992).

Many Mandara groups, including two of our cases, Sirak and Sukur, are casted, i.e., their societies are divided into farmers, who constitute the vast majority of the community, and the smith-potters (males typically work metal, divine and bury, while women pot) who make up the remaining 2.5–9 percent (the latter figure being the case in Sukur). The castes are endogamous (Sterner and David 1991). The Mofu-Diamaré, our third case, are not casted but share many attitudes with their casted neighbors (Vincent 1991).

Sirak – the petty priest-chief

Sirak is located just south of Mokolo in an area that came under Fulbe pressure only in the nineteenth century (Figure 8.3). However, exploitation and raiding by state societies and accompanying political unrest and fission were indirectly implicated in the formation of this small polity by the coming together from different directions of a small number of clans (exogamous agnatic descent groups). Its present population is about 2,000. The land to the south is unsettled though exploited for wood and used by Fulbe pastoralists, so its population density is hard to estimate though somewhat below the regional mean.

For administrative purposes the Cameroonian state has bypassed the traditional chief and named a "canton chief." A Muslim Fulbe, he is regarded as little more than a messenger of the administration by a community that continues to practice its religion and in which any substantive acculturation to Cameroonian national society is accompanied by physical and social alienation from the community.

In this little hierarchized society, economic, societal, and coercive powers are minimal and widely dispersed, usually being regarded as held by household heads and clan elders – whence perhaps the need for mystification and the ideological power, that legitimates the authority held by these same senior men, six of whom are dignified by titles that gain them no special privileges, and in particular by the traditional chief, the *buway*. The latter's primary role is to oversee the ceremonial cycle, offerings, and sacrifices on behalf of the community to a distant god, and to the main spirit of the place, that of the mountain around which the settlement clusters. Unlike the god, this spirit plays an immanent role in human affairs, in particular regarding the land, and must be honored and placated by humans. Privileged access to the spirit constitutes the basis of the chief's authority. While he has

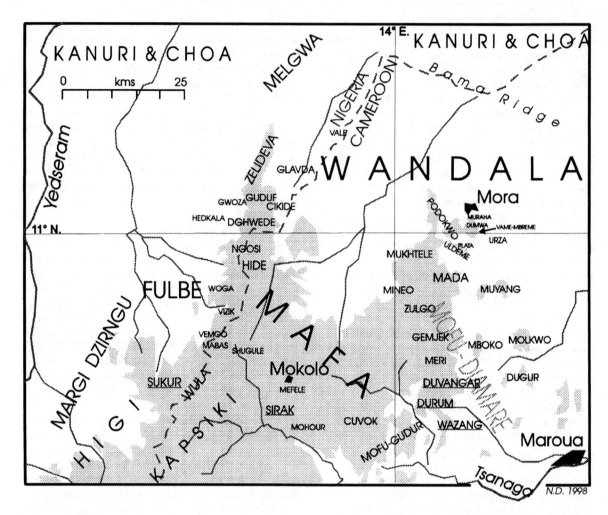

Figure 8.3   The northern Mandara highlands: larger towns, ethno-linguistic groupings, and selected pre-colonial polities. The names of Sirak, Sukur, and the three principal Mofu-Diamaré princedoms of Duvangar, Durum, and Wazang, are underlined. Contour at 2,000 feet.

sacred responsibility for the land, he does not own or control it. He could not himself divest another of farmland, although he might be called upon to pronounce a sentence of banishment. In such matters he acts not on his own initiative but rather as spokesman for the ill-defined grouping of clan elders that act as his counselors – though it must be realized that he and they listen also to younger men and to women. Rather than exercising power, the elders articulate the views of the community, and the primary task of title-holders is to undertake ritual responsibilities on its behalf.

If land is a primary force of production, rain is another

– and far less predictable. In the company of clan elders and the chief of the smiths, the Sirak chief makes offerings for rain but does not control it. In order to pay for a rainmaker's services he therefore has to solicit contributions from the community. (The prestige of rainmakers among the neighboring Mafa is expressed in the designation *bi yam* – chief or lord of the rains, but, unlike that of a Mafa chief, whose full title is *bi dza*, chief of the mountain, such authority is limited to one area of expertise.) In times of plague and famine, the chief used to send representatives to Gudur, a southern Mofu polity some 40 kilometers to the east from which some Sirak clans claim origin, and where until recently there lived a chief renowned for his magical powers over locusts, leopards and other natural forces (Jouaux 1989).

The chief of Sirak has no authority to raise taxes and might indeed be poor – we have known a widower Mafa chief who lacked even a decent mat to sit on. His jural authority is limited and depends upon the articulation of consent, perhaps also on others' fear of his sorcery. Neither does he monopolize the use of force, whether against outsiders or within the community. In case of serious disputes, he has two types of recourse. He can refuse to carry out his ritual duties, thus mobilizing the community's moral pressure against those responsible for the rift, or – at least in theory – he can call on the members of his own clan, affines, and others to provide physical force. But his clan is not large, and on one occasion a former chief and his clan members are said to have been driven out, though they were later recalled.

It is apparent that we are here dealing with a priest-chief, of the kind described by Netting (1972: 221) as an "essentially powerless figure . . . his authority is circumscribed; he *is* something, but he *does* very little." His main task is to represent the community to itself. For this he receives respect, materialized in his position at the apex of community rites and in minor gifts, especially of beer, which he can neither bank nor consume on his own. His primarily sacral authority is modeled on that of household heads, and is expressed in similar rites that differ essentially in their inclusiveness, his extending over the community as a whole. There is little competition for the chieftaincy, and its inheritance within one clan conforms to jural norms.

Mofu-Diamaré – the uxorious princes

The Mofu-Diamaré are a complex ethnological construct, and we are concerned here only with the chiefdoms that their ethnographer, Jeanne-Françoise Vincent (1991), has termed "princedoms," and not with smaller entities, some of which are as little hierarchized as Sirak. Durum, the largest princedom, is 90 km^2 in area with a population of 10,100 (giving a population density of 112 km^2). Its prince (*bi*) is culturally very like his Sirak counterpart but far more powerful. His power has been sustained in and after the colonial period by governmental recognition.

While the refuge character of the Mandara highlands has been overemphasized, small-scale migrations of culturally and linguistically related groups from eastern inselbergs to the mountains contributed to the development of princedoms. Critical in this process was achievement of control over the cult of the spirit of the mountain and acquisition of magical stones that can bring or halt the rain. Indeed, it is the combination, unusual in the Mandara, of chiefly roles as "lord of the mountain" and "lord of the rain" that lies at the core of the concentration of power in the hands of the Mofu prince.

While it would be easy to underestimate the extent to which economic and societal powers are distributed, as at Sirak, among households and clans, the prince is their focus, and there are fewer titles and title-holders. The prince greatly benefits from corvée labor, most notably of male initiates. He has some control over production and consumption of the staple millet, and has ultimate rights – though these are normally devolved to chiefs of villages and quarters – over the territory of the princedom, apportioning land to immigrants. The dispensing of justice is another princely duty, carried out with, but not subject to, the advice of respected elders. In former times the prince held power over life and death. He was also strategist and chief diplomat vis-à-vis the plains states and in the endemic, stylized, fratricidal conflicts between polities in this densely populated, land-hungry region, (never engaging in fighting himself but overseeing the battlefield). Above all the prince controls the rain, manipulating stones to call it, and another, more frightful, to stop it. This stone, kept buried much as a nuclear reactor is insulated from the world, is the chief's ultimate sanction against those whom he wishes to punish within and beyond his princedom.

Exterior signs of power include the prince's "castle" located on a summit above the houses of his subjects, and his remarkable polygamy, undertaken not to cement alliances but rather, sustained by a meat and beer diet, to celebrate his life force and to increase the numbers of his clan. A prince of Duvangar who died in 1988 begat 209 children on his forty-four wives.

The prince, no ordinary mortal, "is" the land, the rain, the leopard. Hedged about by taboos and clothed in symbols, he represents permanence, never really dies, and is said to climb unaided into his tomb. Yet he is no divine king, Vincent insists. When he sneezes, the grain does not wither.

Mofu-Diamaré princedoms constitute ranked societies in that "positions of valued status are . . . limited so that not all those of sufficient talent to occupy such statuses actually achieve them" (Fried 1967: 109), and they are also stratified. Members of the chiefly clan, the prince's people, lord it over the nobodies, members of other clans. This stratification is expressed in differential access to the supernatural, and to land, and in a range of jural and other differences. The nobodies can be pressed into service as gravediggers, bullied, or have their goats, girls, and even land appropriated by the prince's people. As initiates they work for the chief for eight years instead of four. They are docile and "like women."

Vincent sees the development of political power as the consequence of migrations that resulted in a quantum increase in clan heterogeneity within settlements, but at the same time one that introduced new politico-religious ideas for coping with such situations. The emergence of princedoms was a process – in which chiefly charisma was not inconsequential – of accretion of economic, societal, and political powers to a clan and its successive princes. The most critical and original element in the process was, as already noted, the fusion of privileged access to the supernatural with magical control over rainfall. A consequence was a progressive, though always limited, secularization of political authority. This is disguised and re-presented by the negotiation of symbols that constitutes the main Mofu-Diamaré discourse on the nature of power.

Sukur – the diplomat who represents himself as priest-chief

We now move to Sukur, on the Nigerian side of the border. Our description reconstructs the situation as it existed in the nineteenth century. At that time Sukur was a community located beyond the range of Wandala predation and, it seems, little if at all subject to Fulbe raiding. It had a relatively dense population of about 5,000, and it specialized in the production of iron that was exported in large quantities to the area around Lake Chad. A net importer of food, its economy was thus vastly different from that of Sirak and the Mofu-Diamaré princedoms.

In smelting, the critical force of production was neither capital nor labor but rather raw materials. Given access to a large enough area, both ore and charcoal could be obtained by familial production teams composed of small groups of kin and neighbors. The only managerial expertise required was that of the chief, the *xidi*, who negotiated access with neighboring chiefs. Men's and women's contributions were complementary; there was no institution of wage labor, nor, unlike on the plains, any significant slavery. There was therefore no development of a class of capitalists, nor of a proletariat. The making of iron and the associated export trade were major factors in shaping a Sukur polity that, uniquely in Africa and perhaps the world, can be categorized as a classless industrial society (David 1996). Nonetheless Sukur's cultural similarities and links to other montagnard social formations were and remain very close.

Unlike the chief of Sirak and the Mofu-Diamaré prince, whose authority emerges from politically neutral, cosmological origins, the powers of the chief of Sukur had constantly to be negotiated. While he resembled other Mandara chiefs in being hedged about with taboos, he was not responsible for sacrifices to a mountain spirit. Rather a number of titled part-time priests of several clans carried out sacrifices to local spirits on behalf of the community. Another, not of the ruling clan, acted as his chaplain. Neither did he control the rain, but mediated on behalf of the community with a rainmaker from among the neighboring Wula. Although the Yawal ceremony, organized by the chief at irregular intervals, can be interpreted in part as a claim to supremacy, power was in fact quite widely distributed. In comparison with other Mandara chiefs, *xidi* Sukur lacked legitimating authority (Smith and David 1995).

Thus while through his role in the iron industry and export trade the chief had greater access to wealth than the richest Mofu-Diamaré prince, this accrued to him personally and was converted into social dependencies only to a limited extent. He did, it is true, benefit from corvée labor, and we suspect that male initiates were largely responsible for building the famous paved ways and his impressive residence.

The Yawal ceremony, mentioned above, celebrates the chief as ruler and the preeminence of his clan, the Dur. However, other of its aspects represent the integration of Sukur and in particular the reconciliation of previous dynasties. Industrial Sukur, less dependent on land for agriculture than other Mandara polities, welcomed the immigration that would increase the size and reputation of its iron market. As a result it accumulated twenty-two clans, more than any other Mandara polity. A charter for societal integration existed in acknowledgment of the claim of each and every clan to an origin in Gudur, the prestigious magico-religious center with which so many Mandara communities including Sirak claimed links. Integration was assisted through elaboration of the institution of title holding. Titles, several of which carried economic benefits, were distributed among all the clans anciently installed. Since there are never more than four titles beside that of the ruler in Mofu-Diamaré princedoms, it would seem that Sukur has gone out of its way to create and distribute them. Sukur's economic interests and the organization of industrial production worked to limit the accretion of internal societal power in the hands of the chief, while his role vis-à-vis the exterior can be characterized as primarily diplomatic.

Justice links societal and political power. *Xidi*s are remembered for their delivery of justice, and one variant of the legend of the establishment of the Dur dynasty emphasizes this aspect of the chief's authority. Legal decisions against individuals were certainly enforced, but at a

Table 8.1 *Traditional dimensions of chiefly power in Sirak, Mofu-Diamaré princedoms, and Sukur*

Attribute	Sirak Priest-Chief	Mofu-Diamaré Prince	Sukur Chief
Ideological			
Sacifices to mountain spirit	Yes	Yes	No
Controls rain	No	Yes	No
Initiates community ceremonies	Yes	Yes	Yes
Initiates agricultural cycle	Yes	Yes	Yes
Economic			
Benefits from corveé labour	No	Yes	Yes
Mobilizes initiates	No	Yes	Yes
Receives taxes	No	Yes	Yes
Societal			
May have chiefs under him	No	Yes	No
Is hyper-polygamist	No	Yes	No
Holds personal feast	No	Annually	Sometimes
Titles of elders (including chief)	About 6	Up to 5	21
Political			
Dispenses justice, ordeals, oaths	No	Yes	Yes
Presides over inter-polity warfare	No	Yes	No

societal scale his political power was limited and fragile. Unlike the Mofu-Diamaré prince he was not a hyper-polygamist concerned to procreate political support. Dur, the chiefly clan, was and remains the largest, but although the chief could call for armed support on its members, on affines, and on those title-holders whom he had appointed and their followers, the response was situational rather than assured. Indeed, any tendency of a chief towards despotism was severely held in check by competition between Dur factions and by coup attempts that appear to have been frequent and often successful. Such coups are quite atypical of the Mofu-Diamaré princedoms.

In short, the power of *Xidi* Sukur flowed from many sources which he had constantly to negotiate and reinforce, including his positions of power in ritual, economy, justice, and politics. The privileges established were legitimated in reference to common Mandara themes and to social relations of the household, including a metaphorical representation of the chief as "wife" of the community that would have been anathema to the Mofu-Diamaré and quite foreign to the Sirak (Smith and David 1995).

The institutions of the chieftaincy and other titles certainly constitute complexity, but here this is not to be construed as implying the existence of classes or even a notable degree of ranking. The *xidi*ship apart, complexity is rather a facade, a veil thrown over a society in which the hierarchic principles of seniority of age and of the male gender operated very much as they did in the simplest Mandara societies, and in which the theoretical seniority of first settlers over later comers was a principle as frequently set aside or overtaken by political events.

Conclusions

Let us review the similarities and differences between the three polities and chiefs discussed (Table 8.1). Among the Sirak, economic power, such as it was, was widely distributed among household and clan heads, corresponding to a situation of limitations in the technology of production and the absence of surplus. Societal power was similarly distributed, and a cosmology that linked supernatural power with place militated against the formation of larger political groupings. Neither the demands of defense against raiders nor any other factor was sufficient to integrate neighboring communities into a larger whole even when they spoke the same language. As land was relatively abundant, immigration could be permitted, and new arrivals easily assimilated in part through participation in a cycle of ceremonies celebrating common Mandara themes. Segregation of the polity boundary was a community responsibility. The political power of the chief was negligible and his authority largely dependent upon his inherited relationship with the spirit of the mountain. Even with regard to his prerogative of scheduling community-wide ceremonies, his freedom of action was restricted by the need to consult diviners, of whom the most influential was the "chief" of the smith-potters.

In a context of sustained pressure from plains states, Mofu-Diamaré princes emerged through a combination of factors underpinned by their acquisition through generosity, trickery, or main force of privileged access to supernatural and magical powers. Their accretion of power over subsistence came about in part from corvée labor on their estates, a ritual as much as an economic duty undertaken to celebrate the prince's intimate relationship with the land. A significant portion of any surplus in foodstuffs was converted into hoes and other tribute paid to the plains states that required a human, princely, channel for its delivery. Mercantile enterprise scarcely existed. While considerable societal power was here in the hands of the prince, who strove to prevent fission within his territory, a byproduct of an ideology that stressed the fecundity of the chief was the breeding of surplus relatives who became factional competitors for power and had on occasion to be expelled. Princes could not prevent the voluntary relocation of families to neighboring polities where they might for a time suffer reduced access to resources but certainly no culture shock. Thus there were contradictions limiting the prince's control over maintenance and segregation of the polity. He could mobilize considerable coercive force, and, unlike at Sukur, his authority militated against its constraint or his overthrow by factions within the princely clan. However, we should not ignore evidence of resistance. Other categories of power holders considered by Vincent include the diviners and smiths, and assemblies of elders at both quarter and village level who might in times of drought organize marches on the prince to demand rain, vandalizing his castle and beating up members of his family.

Further accumulation of authority in the hands of the princes was inhibited by the absence of a technology of production capable of wresting a regular and substantial surplus from their toilsome land or of a technology of destruction permitting dominance of larger areas. Lacking also was an ideology that could break the legiti-

mating links between power and local spirits, and magical control over the uncontrollable.

Sukur took another route. Located beyond the limits of predation of plains states until the twentieth century, and benefiting from superior access to raw materials for iron making in its own territory, Sukur was able to take advantage of an apparently insatiable demand for iron from the inhabitants of the oreless plains to the north. While its chief was in a position to accumulate considerable wealth from the iron trade – no doubt a factor in the competition for his office – the familial organization of iron production ensured that its benefits were widely shared. Societal power was to a great extent still in the hands of the clans, though the chief managed the more important interactions with outsiders. Similarly, the community's economic stance restricted options with regard to community boundary maintenance. Factionalism within the chiefly clan and the solidarity of other large clans limited the chief's powers of coercion. Nor could he effectively mobilize the supernatural since, although partaking of the sacred, he was explicitly detached from the exercise of supernatural and magical power. The division of ritual labor was intermediate between that of the Sirak, where despite sacrifices made on behalf of the community by the chief and other title-holders, household heads are to a great extent ritually self-sufficient, and of the Mofu-Diamaré with their papal princes.

Ethnographies of the Mandara are replete with examples of individuals, families and clan sections moving between polities that can, in the terminology of cultural evolution, be characterized as egalitarian, ranked, and stratified. Whatever their reasons, their participation in the Mandara tradition ensured that they were quickly absorbed by the host society, and that even when montagnard outsiders came in force they did not replace but assimilated with previous occupants and learned their languages. This movement through space and polities has clearly been going on for a very long time and continues today.

As several contributors to this volume have noted, polities similarly move both up and down in the gymnasium of political complexity. While Sirak would seem to constitute a basal level of socio-political integration, Vincent's historical work makes it apparent that not so long ago the Mofu-Diamaré were remarkably similar. Some still are. There has certainly been a tendency for those societies most subject to sustained pressure from the exterior either to establish a *modus vivendi* with their oppressors, as for example the Sirak-like Muraha with their Wandala neighbors, or to consolidation of power in the hands of chiefs, as appears to have occurred among the little known northern Mafa of Vreke. Yet development has not always been in the direction of centralization. We lack historical evidence before the twentieth century, but the as yet unexcavated ruins of Kova-Mendossa are suggestive of the former presence there of a polity more hierarchized than that of its present Mafa inhabitants. Similarly the chiefdom of Gudur, famed throughout the area for the magical powers of a chief whose secular power once extended over a cluster of massifs, has under colonial and subsequent Cameroonian rule reverted to a political condition scarcely more hierarchized than Sirak.[4] The *xidi* of Sukur has lost many of his former powers as a result of the collapse of the smelting industry and the appropriation of his functions by the Nigerian state. And yet he remains, clothed in a sanctity entirely typical of the region, the simulacrum rather than the model of a Mandara priest-chief – and now, more and more, a civil servant.

The importance of the Mandara tradition

What strikes us about these movements of people in space and time and of societies up and down the scale of political centralization, is how easily and quickly they do it, with so little fundamental disruption in the lives of the people. We are indeed in the presence of a system in disequilibrium not unlike that found by Leach (1954) in the polyglot Kachin Hills, where individuals and communities can shift back and forth among *gumlao* segmentary republican anarchy, *gumsa* feudality, and Buddhist Shan statehood. Leach argued for the importance of shared ritual in facilitating such movements and in managing interactions between polities. In the Mandara also a conceptual reservoir – developing *in situ* for two millennia or more, and consisting of shared cosmological ideas, attitudes and values, symbols and rituals – underlies the socio-political and cultural diversity of the region. Mandara exists as Mesopotamia existed before Sargon, as a tradition not as a political entity.

Were these societies then on a trajectory different to those that led to the formation of states in other parts of the world. Surely, yes. Since they existed as functioning entities in the early ethnographic present there can be no analogy with *Hallucigenia*; are they then social coelacanths, relics of societal plans that are now largely extinct? Probably. But they are far from being fossils. Such is the "emergent Lamarkian feature [in social evolution] in which collectivities of actors can decide to choose a direction" (Cohen 1981: 89) – or in this case have a direction thrust upon them – that they are presently in process

of transferring from their former trajectory to that of the nation-state.

Here, of course, the organic analogy breaks down. But it has done its work, and we shall end where we began, high in the Rockies among the Burgess shale creatures. It is Gould's contention that the differential survival of these organisms was a lottery; that there is no obvious superiority of anatomy that enables us to explain the survival of rare *Sanctacaris*, "the first known member of a line that eventually led to horseshoe crabs, spiders, scorpions and mites" (Gould 1989: 187) or *Aysheaia*, probably a member of the Onychophoran group that links arthropods to annelid worms, rather than "the sleek and common *Marrella*, with sweeping spines on its head shield" (Gould 1989: 238) or a host of equally strange others. Can this be true also of society? Is the inevitability of the radiation of states an illusion, or has it been determined by organizational or other constraints? Is Gould's "lottery" an appropriate analogy, or merely an admission of our ignorance of natural/cultural selection in Cambrian/societal seas?

A final note: since we wrote the first draft of this paper, geological colleagues have advised us that the Burgess shale is to be placed perhaps 50 million years later, in the middle rather than the early Cambrian (see Ludvigsen 1990). If so, the rate of phyletic innovation was less explosive than Gould would have had us believe. Organic analogies applied to cultural evolution have proved illusory in the past; is ours equally misleading? Whatever the facts of the matter, the questions raised by this paper are real and surely deserving of archaeological debate.

Acknowledgments

Fieldwork in Cameroon and Nigeria was supported by grants from the Social Science and Humanities Research Council of Canada and the University of London, and authorized by the Ministry of Higher Education, Computing and Scientific Research of Cameroon, the National Commission for Museums and Monuments of Nigeria, and by Adamawa State and local government authorities, to all of which institutions and persons, and to Xidi Gezik Kanakakaw of Sukur, assistants Kodje Dadai and Isa E. Kawalde (Sirak and Mafa) and John T. Habga, Philip E. Sukur, Markus E. Makarma and Isnga D. Sukur (Sukur) we wish to express our gratitude. We also thank James and Marta Wade for base-camp and intellectual support in Maiduguri and Peter Robertshaw for inviting Nic David to the Complex Societies Group Conference, held at California State University, San Bernardino, in October 1995, at which a draft of this paper was presented and discussed. Charles Henderson and Ronald Spencer of the Department of Geology and Geophysics, University of Calgary, gave us valued advice on the geology of the Burgess shale.

Notes

1 The band-to-state sequence has several contributing developers including Julian Steward. The reference cited in the text offers epigrammatic descriptions of the stages and distinguishes "archaic" and "nation" states. It should properly be attributed to Thomas G. Harding and David Kaplan who were joint authors with Marshall D. Sahlins and Elman R. Service of the book edited by the latter two.
2 The dynamics of such states are well described in S. P. Reyna's (1990) study of the east-central Sudanic state of Bagirmi.
3 We entirely agree with Stephen Shennan (1994: 466–7) that "the term chiefdom has now become virtually devoid of conceptual content . . . and hardly provides analytical leverage." We apply it to a variety of Mandara polities for this reason, and because the obvious alternatives, "acephalous society" and "tribe", are actively misleading, while "ethnic group" is noncommittal regarding the nature of the polity. By Earle's (1991: 1) definition of a chiefdom as "a polity that organizes centrally a regional population in the thousands," none of our examples qualifies.
4 Gudur, and to a lesser extent Sukur, are instances of the non-coincidence of the spheres of ritual suzerainty and political sovereignty which Southall (this volume) considers characteristic of the "segmentary state," a term we find doubly misleading.

References

Barreteau, D. and H. Jungraithmayr
  1993. Calculs lexicostatistiques et glottochronologiques sur les langues tchadiques. In *Datation et chronologie dans le bassin du Lac Tchad (Actes du Séminaire du Réseau Méga-Tchad, ORSTOM-Bondy, 11–12 septembre 1989)*, edited by D. Barreteau and C. von Graffenried, Paris: Editions ORSTOM: 103–40.
Claessen, H. J. M. and P. Skalník
  1978 (eds.) *The Early State*. New York: Mouton Publishers.
  1981 (eds.) *The Study of the State*. New York: Mouton Publishers.

David, N.
  1996 A new political form? The classless industrial society of Sukur (Nigeria). In *Proceedings of the 10th Pan-African Congress on Prehistory and Related Studies (Harare, June 1995)*, edited by G. Pwiti and R. Soper. Harare: University of Zimbabwe Press: 593–600.
David, N. and A. S. MacEachern
  1988 The Mandara Archaeological Project: preliminary results of the 1984 season. In *Recherches comparatives et historiques dans le bassin du Lac Tchad*, edited by D. Barreteau and H. Tourneux. Paris: ORSTOM: 51–80.
David, N., J. Sterner, and K. Gavua.
  1988 Why pots are decorated. *Current Anthropology* 29 (3): 365–89.
Earle, T.
  1991 (ed.) *Chiefdoms: Power, Economy and Ideology*. Cambridge: Cambridge University Press.
Fried, M.
  1967 *The Evolution of Political Society*. New York: Random House.
Gould, S. J.
  1979 Is the Cambrian explosion a sigmoid fraud? In *Ever Since Darwin*, New York: W. W. Norton: 126–33.
  1989 *Wonderful Life: The Burgess Shale and the Nature of history*. New York: W. W. Norton and Company.
Haeckel, E.
  1866 *Generelle Morphologie der Organismen*, 2 vols. Berlin: Georg Reimer.
Jouaux, C.
  1989 Gudur: chefferie ou royaume? *Cahiers d'Etudes africaines*, 114: 259–88.
Lamberg-Karlovsky, K.
  1985 The Near Eastern "breakout" and the Mesopotamian social contract. *Symbols* (Spring): 8–11, 23–4.
Leach, E. R.
  1954 *Political Systems of Highland Burma*. London: Athlone Press.
Ludvigsen, R.
  1990 The Burgess shale: not in the shadow of the Cathedral escarpment. *Geo-Science Canada* 16 (2): 51–9.
MacEachern, A. S.
  1993 The Projet Maya-Wandala: preliminary results of the 1992 field season. *Nyame Akuma* 39: 7–13.
  1994 The Projet Maya-Wandala: preliminary results of the 1993 field season. *Nyame Akuma* 41: 48–55.

Netting, R. McC.
   1972 Sacred power and centralization: aspects of political power and adaptation in Africa. In *Population
   Growth: Anthropological Implications*, edited by B.
   Spooner. Cambridge: MIT: 219–44.

Reyna, S. P.
   1990 *Wars Without End: The Political Economy of a
   Precolonial African State*. Hanover: University Press
   of New England.

Sahlins, M. D. and E. R. Service
   1960 (eds.) *Evolution and Culture*. Ann Arbor:
   University of Michigan Press.

Shennan, S.
   1994 Review of Earle, T. (editor), "Chiefdoms: power,
   economy and ideology". *Man* 29 (2): 466–7.

Smith, A. and David, N.
   1995 The production of space and the house of Xidi
   Sukur. *Current Anthropology* 36 (3): 441–71.

Southall, A.
   1954 *Alur Society: A Study in Processes and Types of
   Domination*. Cambridge: W. Heffer and Sons.

Sterner, J.
   1992 Sacred pots and "symbolic reservoirs" in the
   Mandara Highlands of Northern Cameroon. In *An
   African Commitment: Papers in Honour of Peter
   Lewis Shinnie*, edited by J. Sterner and N. David.
   Calgary: University of Calgary Press: 171–9.

Sterner, J. and N. David.
   1991 Gender and caste in the Mandara Highlands:
   northeastern Nigeria and northern Cameroon.
   Ethnology 30 (4): 355–69.

Vincent, J.-F.
   1991 *Princes montagnards du Nord-Cameroun: Les
   Mofu-Diamaré et le pouvoir politique*. Paris: Editions
   Harmattan.

Walde, D., N. David, and S. MacEachern
   1994 Style and the identification of artifact production systems: an explicitly scientific approach. Paper
   presented at the 6th Stanley Conference on African
   Art, Clay and Fire: African pottery in social and historical context (Iowa City, 8 and 9 April, 1994).

Wobst, H.
   1978 The archaeo-ethnography of hunter-gatherers or
   the tyranny of the ethnographic record in archaeology. *American Antiquity* 43: 303–9.

Yoffee, N.
   1993 Too many chiefs? (or, Safe texts for the '90s). In
   Archaeological Theory: Who Sets the Agenda?, edited
   by N. Yoffee and A. Sherratt. Cambridge:
   Cambridge University Press: 60–78.

9

Material culture and the dialectics of identity in the Kalahari: AD 700–1700

JAMES DENBOW

Introduction

A major current issue throughout southern Africa is the manner by which the false convergence of tribal/ethnic allegiance and ideology initiated by Europeans during the colonial era can be unraveled. This requires a new formulation of the history of the subcontinent – one which will rely on archaeological materials to provide a firm historical basis for assessing the trajectory of pre-colonial social and economic formations and their transformations in the colonial period. Yet, until recently, anthropologists and historians have tended to view the entire region before the latter part of the nineteenth century as having been populated by isolated cultural and linguistic entities with few connections among them. Khoisan-speaking people in the Kalahari, for instance, have been represented as foragers unaffected by Bantu-speaking agropastoralists until the twentieth century. All local cultures, however, have been historically constructed through ongoing dialogues with others – dialogues characterized as much by social flux as by stability. As Wilmsen and Vossen (1990: 11) point out, "the resultant constructed ethnicities rarely conformed to a people's prior self-identification."

Current "debates" over the "authenticity" of some Kalahari peoples (Solway and Lee 1990; Wilmsen and Denbow 1990) thus exemplify more general trends in anthropological thought that question the historical utility of ethnographic concepts such as closed cultural traditions, that take on an apartheid-like appearance in the southern African context. Concerns over the affects of ethnographically "static" cultural representations have led authors such as Marcus and Fischer (1986: 78) to conclude that we now need to "revise conventions of ethno-graphic description away from measuring of change against some self-contained, homogeneous, and largely ahistoric framing of the cultural unit toward a view of cultural situations as . . . in a perpetual historically sensitive state of resistance and accommodation to broader processes of influence that are as much inside as outside of the local context."

I take as my starting point the proposition that processes of resistance and accommodation are as characteristic of pre-colonial social formations as they are those of the present. Archaeological data provide a means to situate and analyze the historical dynamics of stability and transformation. In this chapter I analyze changes in social relations by stressing ecological conditions of production and political structures of distribution. It is hoped that in this manner the situational fluidity of social identity in the Kalahari can be historically contextualized.

This theoretical position differs fundamentally from several recent recastings of southern African prehistory and history. There is great value in Huffman's (1989) analytical insights into ceramic decorative variation. But his explanatory concepts of fixed cultural forms (Eastern and Western Bantu) associated throughout time with particular peoples, and his corollary proposition that all changes in material forms are the result of migrations of whole people, are of little value in understanding processes of transformation in social formations. In like manner, Hall's (1990) structural-functionalist interpretation of mode-of-production metaphors is useful in describing material conditions at fixed temporal periods but is overly mechanistic in dealing with the political-economic processes that underlay the conditions he describes. It is also true that Europeans have been major agents in the past 400 years of southern African history. But to focus on Africans through this lens alone obscures the variety of African responses and resistances this engendered. Archaeological materials can help contextualize this long African legacy and are of critical importance to assessments and reinterpretations of that history in terms of modern political realignments. It is to this material that I now turn (see Figure 9.1 for sites mentioned in the text).

The politics of production and distribution

The Central Cattle Complex

For a decade now, archaeologists have postulated that a widespread "Cattle Complex" underlay a structural relationship between settlement patterns and culture across most of the southern African highveld (Denbow 1982,

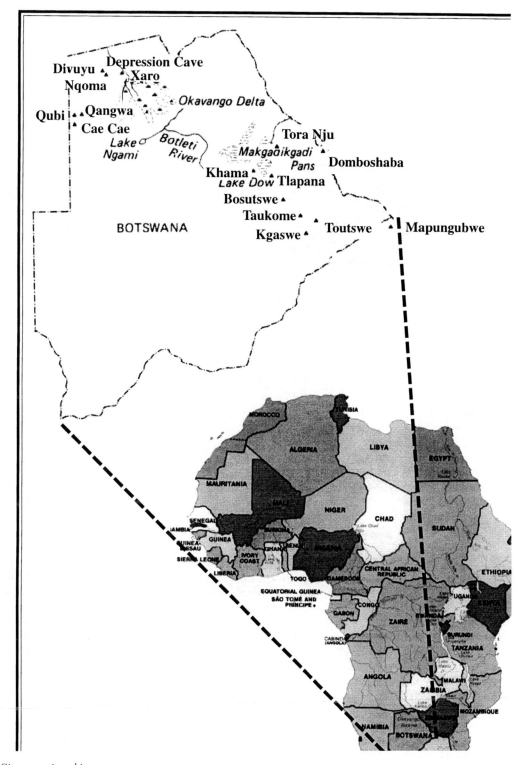

Figure 9.1   Sites mentioned in text.

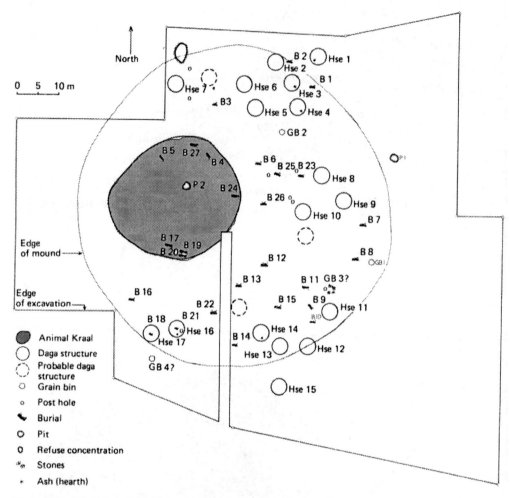

Figure 9.2   Plan map of the Kgaswe excavations.

1983, 1986; Huffman 1982, 1989). A major feature of this cattle pattern is the spatial layout of villages in which thatched pole-and-daga houses are grouped around a central animal kraal (Figure 9.2). Wealth and patriarchal dominance are indicated by the burial of men and boys inside the central byres; women and children were buried in the surrounding housing compounds. Similar practices in the nineteenth century reflected a cosmology where "the ancestors were the domesticated dead of the settlement . . . [they] formed part of the sphere in which men, through the medium of cattle, reproduced the social order . . . [so that] while veneration occurred at the grave sites of both men and women, the Tswana cult provided no acknowledgement of matrilateral ties; the female dead

also spoke in agnatic idiom" (Comaroff 1985: 82–6). The burial of men inside the centrally located animal kraal at Cattle Complex sites may be an earlier manifestation of such beliefs. Political affairs and other important matters were discussed in a men's assembly area adjacent to the central cattle kraal. A large midden next to the kraal at K2, for instance, is thought by some to reflect such political activities (Huffman 1996). In the Cattle Complex, hidden storage pits found under kraal deposits are thought to have been used to store emergency grain supplies that were centrally administered; grain kept in above ground structures adjacent to the houses may have been privately held.

All Cattle Complex settlements share this same basic

layout, though there are variations in detail. Animal kraals and the bones of domesticated animals are common at most sites in southern Africa. It is only at those dating between the ninth and thirteenth centuries in eastern Botswana and adjacent portions of Zimbabwe and South Africa, however, that very deep dung deposits up to 2 meters in depth occur (Denbow 1979). The expansion of herds to numbers large enough to produce such deposits is probably indicative of a fairly common ecological response when new species colonize a favorable environment (Ricklefs 1979: 507–19). A similar period of rapid herd growth, for instance, took place at the beginning of the twentieth century after the Rinderpest epidemic had killed off 90 percent of the domesticated animals in Botswana. Since that disaster, there has been a forty-fold increase in cattle numbers (Fosbrooke 1973).

When agropastoral economies were first established in Botswana climatic conditions were more favorable, with rainfall in some areas as much as 150 percent higher than today (Thomas and Shaw 1991; Tyson and Lindsay 1992). Evidence for a rapid buildup of cattle herds during this period, in the form of deep deposits of vitrified dung, is strong. It is the uses to which such herd increases could be put that are of interest here. While any increase could simply have been consumed, the archaeological evidence indicates that the proportion of wild to domesticated species in faunal assemblages remained about the same through time. Figure 9.3, for instance, shows that there was an inverse relationship between the consumption of livestock and wild game at Kalahari sites. Ethnographic descriptions of African pastoralists, however, indicate they often value animals more as a store of wealth than they do as a source of meat, milk, and hides. Cattle are the principal currency used in bridewealth payments. Such transactions allow lineages to appropriate the innate reproductive capacity of women, while providing for continuity between generations. In this way wealthy lineages may increase at the expense of others. Cattle can also be loaned out to consolidate political support for, as Miller (1988: 49) notes, "control over the 'means of production' in its highest form brought deference rather than storehouses filled with spoiling fish or rotting grain." Furthermore, the dispersal that results from such exchanges is a hedge against catastrophes such as disease, raids, or drought that can more easily wipe out a herd kept in one place.

Today there is considerable variation from household to household in the degree of investment in agriculture, cattle and small stock, hunting and gathering. The precise mix of activities is dependent upon the local structure of risks and opportunities, the age and gender composition

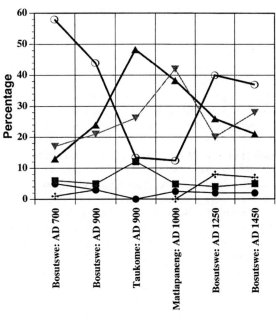

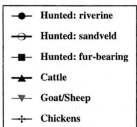

Figure 9.3   Proportions of wild and domestic fauna at some Kalahari sites

of the household, the local characteristics of transport and marketing systems, and variations in the availability of water, grazing, fertile soils, and other productive resources. Pastoralism is a risky enterprise, with regular cycles of boom and bust. While herds can multiply geometrically, they can also suffer catastrophic losses from drought, disease, or raiding. As a result, there exist powerful incentives for herders not to hoard animals, but to spread their risks by using them to broaden social networks, or by converting them into other goods. When herds are small, animals are often used to widen social connections. As herds increase, however, institutions such as bridewealth may be transformed to "sustain a systematic bias in the allocation of wives, in favor of a privileged group . . . [and] in a subtler way to sustain the influence and advantages of the powerful" (Kuper 1982: 164). Such processes undoubtedly informed past as well as present practice.

The eastern Kalahari

A highly reflective grass, *Cenchrus ciliaris,* has colonized the dung enriched substrate of early Cattle Complex - villages in eastern Botswana, making them easily identifiable on aerial photographs. As a result, it has been possible to reconstruct the regional settlement pattern for Toutswe culture sites between AD 700 and 1200 in some detail (Denbow 1979, 1984, 1986). Extensive aerial and ground reconnaissances reveal a three-tier settlement hierarchy dominated by three primary hilltop sites – Toutswemogala, Bosutswe, and Shoshong – each over 40,000 m² in area. Secondary sites such as Taukome and Mmadipudi are half that size, while tertiary sites such as Kgaswe and Maipethwane are about 2,000–5,000 m² in size (Denbow 1984, 1986). One indication of the regional density of such settlements is provided by a partial survey carried out between 1979 and 1984 which located more than 350 Toutswe villages within an 80-kilometer radius of Toutswemogala; hundreds more exist, but have not been systematically examined (Denbow 1982, 1983). The three tiers of sites can be distinguished by the sizes of their cattle kraals, by the area covered with houses and other features, and by their length of occupation. The site of Toutswemogala, which gave the Toutswe complex its name, covers 100,000 m² with over one meter of cultural deposit. The principal period of occupation dates between the eleventh and thirteenth centuries AD, after which it was abandoned except for a brief reoccupation in the sixteenth century. The primary site of Bosutswe, 90 kilometers to the west is of similar size but has a longer sequence of occupation that extends from the eighth to the eighteenth century. Second-tier sites such as Taukome were also occupied for periods of up to 200 years, but their overall area is much smaller, averaging less than 10,000 m². The third tier of settlements includes sites such as Kgaswe and Maipethwane that were occupied for periods of fifty years or less, and were then abandoned when firewood, soils, and grazing lands became exhausted (Denbow 1984b).

The Bosutswe site

Excavations at Bosutswe in 1990 uncovered over 4 meters of deposit, the lowest 2 meters of which produced evidence of 400 years of Toutswe occupation. In the center of the hilltop, these deposits are overlain by a 1.5-meter sequence of hut floors containing Mapungubwe ceramics dating from the twelfth to thirteenth centuries. During this period, Bosutswe became a westward extension of

Mapungubwe hegemony in the Limpopo valley. A Zimbabwean commoner occupation follows in the thirteenth and fourteenth centuries. The shallow deposit, lack of elite ceramics or other artifacts, and insubstantial pole-and-daga houses all suggest that, by the Zimbabwe period, the site had been reduced to a minor position in the regional political economy. The final occupation of Bosutswe was ephemeral and dates to the eighteenth century. It consists of seven small, semicircular stone enclosures associated with clusters of stone grain-bin foundations (Figure 9.4). Similar stone walls occur along the southern fringe of the Makgadikgadi salt pans, but their relationship to the structures at Bosutswe is presently unclear.

Bosutswe's position on the very edge of the sandveld may have facilitated its ability to control trans-Kalahari exchange networks. Its importance in intercontinental exchange is attested by finds of imported cane-glass beads and cowry shells in the Toutswe and Mapungubwe levels. The presence of chickens (*Gallus domesticus* of probable Indonesian origin) and European house rats (*Rattus rattus*) in all levels of the site indicate that trade contacts with the coast affected household economies far into the interior (Plug 1996). These finds, along with the size and length of occupation of the site, indicate that Bosutswe played an important role in the political economy of the eastern Kalahari from the tenth to fourteenth centuries. While chickens and rats do not seem to have crossed the desert, blue cane-glass beads and cowry shells have been recovered at sites from the Makgadikgadi pans to the Angolan border in northwestern Ngamiland. These trade goods probably passed through large centers such as Bosutswe and Toutswe on their way west. Evidence for movements of goods from west to east across the Kalahari has also been found. Sherds from a very distinctive, charcoal-tempered, red-slipped Ngamiland bowl were found in the Toutswe levels at Bosutswe. These pots must have been transferred to Bosutswe along the same networks that carried other commodity and luxury items across the desert. Unfortunately, trade in items such as grain, ivory, salt, and wild game is more difficult to track because products of local origin are difficult to distinguish from those obtained from farther away. As a result, inter-regional trade is probably underestimated in the archaeological record.

Canine teeth from at least eight hyena – animals with well-known ritual associations – were recovered from the floor of a Mapungubwe hut, 130 centimeters below the surface. A cache of over ninety chert and agate pieces was recovered from the same location. Excavations on the hill-tops surrounding Bosutswe indicate that the chert was

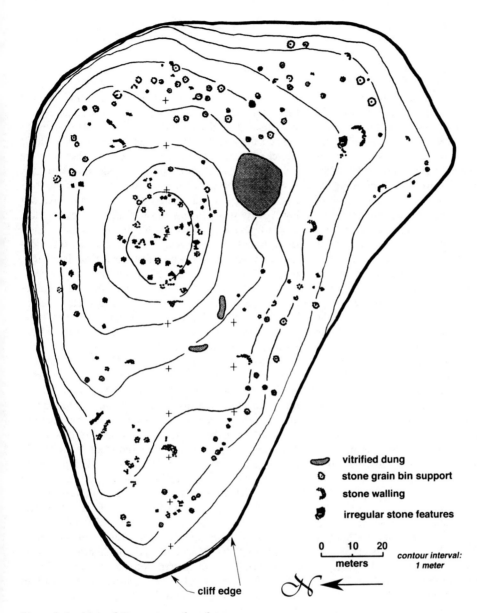

Figure 9.4   Map of Bosutswe surface features.

mined there, worked into cores and blanks of standard sizes, and then brought to Bosutswe where it was cached along with round sections of laminar white agate. The amyadaloidal agate was prized out of a basalt outcrop at the base of the hill. Detailed analyses of the lithic reduction sequence (Weedman 1992) indicate that none of the chert was fashioned into formal tools for use at Bosutswe

– little even shows signs of utilization. Instead it would appear that it was not mined for internal use, but rather for exchange with neighboring stone-using people. The fact that chert was cached on the floor of a hut along with fragments of white agate (a common feature in diviner's kits) and hyena canines, suggests its exchange invoked spiritual as well as material associations. The central location of the "hyena hut" at the highest point of the hill suggests it was the house of an important person. Recovery of several cane-glass beads and a fragment of ivory from this same floor support this contention.

Evidence that stone tool use encoded social distinctions within the Toutswe culture is suggested by the differential distribution of lithics on sites at different tiers of the Toutswe hierarchy. In eastern Botswana, no stone tools or waste flakes were recovered from higher-order sites such as Toutswemogala or Thatswane, despite extensive excavations in these locations (Denbow 1982, 1986; Lepionka 1979). Even at Bosutswe, where thousands of lithic specimens were recovered, few bore signs of modification or use, and none had been fashioned into formal tools. This suggests they were produced for exchange. Backed segments, thumbnail scrapers, blade cores and other stone artifacts have been recovered, however, from third-tier sites including Taukome and Maipethwane. This suggests that use of stone tools was confined to the lower echelons of Toutswe society where access to iron was perhaps more difficult than for the occupants of higher-order sites (Denbow 1982). More extensive excavations are needed before one can determine whether such differences in stone-tool distribution simply reflect intermittent interaction with neighboring hunters and gatherers or whether, instead, some Toutswe farmsteads were multi-ethnic and multicultural communities similar in social composition to many contemporary Kalahari cattleposts.

Sites with deep deposits of vitrified dung disappear in the Toutswe area after approximately AD 1200, indicating that cycles of herd growth and collapse were features of the region's economy for a long time. Between AD 700 and 1200, finding sufficient labor to tend the exponentially growing herds would have been a serious consideration for Toutswe communities. Autochthonous hunters and gatherers constituted one obvious labor reservoir that could be drawn upon in times of expansion; the poor, the misfortunate, and the young constituted another. During times of herd reduction, such non-family labor would have had to contribute in other ways or be cut lose to fend for themselves. Cycles of herd proliferation and decline would thus have affected the dialectic between agropastoralists, pastro-foragers, and foragers in significant ways as relations varied from exclusivity and hostility to congruence and assimilation.

Incentives for accommodation and resistance would have characterized both sides of this relationship, with foragers, for instance, perhaps increasing their production of hunted game during some periods in order to satisfy the demands of settled agropastoralists. Some may have also been drawn to cattleposts and villages to supply the growing need for labor that expanding herds would demand. At the same time, access to domesticated animals would also have provided incentives for some foragers, particularly those with access to good grazing and water supplies, to withdraw their labor and become herders in their own right. Such a reaction could explain why distinctive Khoi ceramics, stone tools, and cattle remains are found at several small sites along the middle stretches of the Botletli. The ceramics from these sites are quite distinct from those of more sedentary Iron Age communities on the eastern and western ends of the river. In the eighteenth and nineteenth centuries, this area was home to pastro-foraging Khoi-speakers. These Botletli pastro-foragers, or Black Bushmen as some have called them, have been somewhat of an anomaly in anthropological circles because, while they speak Khoi languages, they are genetically related to neighboring Bantu-speaking populations and some have been herders for centuries if not millennia (Denbow 1996). This suggests there has been considerable latitude for the construction of new, multidimensional cultural and linguistic identities in the Kalahari. Language changes and new pottery traditions may thus be indexes of a more complex dialectic of resistance and accommodation. Yet the East Coast trade goods and other commodities that were passed through this region from the east to Matlhapaneng and Nqoma in the west indicate there were also accommodations made with neighboring agropastoralists (Denbow 1996). The regional changes in culture and identity exposed in the archaeological and linguistic record suggest that in the past, as today, the construction of fluid social units, rather than the defense of strongly marked unilineal descent groups, was an important strategy for coping with uncertainty and risk in the Kalahari (Comaroff 1985).

The species composition of faunal remains from Bosutswe (Plug 1996) provides additional insight into the political economy of eastern Botswana between AD 700 and 1700. During the Toutswe period from the eighth to the twelfth century, domesticated cattle, goats, and sheep were the most important sources of meat, supplemented by large bovids such as zebra, wildebeest, and eland. While most of this game could have been procured within a short distance of the site, the assemblage also includes fish, lechwe, sitatunga, hippo, and crocodile that must have come from a greater distance. The closest sources for these species would have been to the west at Lake Xau and the Botletli River. Today large herds of game still migrate across the Makgadikgadi grasslands during the dry season to water in these locations. Given the distances involved (over 200 km) some of the large game at

Bosutswe may have been obtained from Makgadikgadi hunters and gatherers or pastro-foragers who would have been in the best position to procure it. Milk, grain, pottery, metal, chert, agate, and other products of Bosutswe could have formed appropriate returns. Springbok remains from Taukome in the hardveld 75 kilometers east of Bosutswe provide additional evidence for inter-regional trade in game meat (Plug 1982). Fish remains from sites such as Gan'nyo in the Makgadikgadi indicate that even small settlements participated in such exchanges between micro-environments.

While cattle were likely to have been a focus of elite investment and a means to acquire social power during the formative stages of the Toutswe culture, the volume of Indian Ocean trade increased significantly after the commencement of gold mining in the twelfth century. A chain reaction of economic and political restructuring ensued, reverberating from east to west across the region. While cattle and other domestic stock continued to provide the greatest proportion of the meat diet, the vitrified dung middens so characteristic of the earlier Toutswe complex now disappear from higher-order sites. This suggests a devaluation in the status of cattle that led to modifications in the *organization* of herding. Instead of keeping herds of cattle as a material manifestation of their political importance, the Mapungubwe elite shifted them from primary centers to lower-order, satellite communities. This change occurred all across the region, from the eastern Kalahari at Bosutswe to the Limpopo valley and adjacent portions of Zimbabwe (Huffman 1996).

The Zimbabwe ceramics from Bosutswe signal a further transformation, this time from elite center to commoner village. With the rise of the Zimbabwean state in the fourteenth century, the political center of gravity shifted northward to the gold fields near Francistown and along the Tati River. A hierarchy of stonewalled settlements arose, with larger centers such as Domboshaba and Vukwe in the gold-bearing districts being surrounded by smaller walled outposts. The westernmost ruins (Figure 9.5) are found along the edge of the Makgadikgadi salt pans at Gan'nyo, Tora Nju, Tlapana and Khama (Denbow 1985a, 1985b; Main 1992–4; Wilmsen and Denbow 1990). Trans-Kalahari trade apparently withered as the value of ivory, rhino horn, and skins diminished relative to salt, gold, and copper. Chert and agate mining at Bosutswe was discontinued at the same time. Thus, it would appear that as the value of hunted products declined, there was a concomitant devaluation of relations with the people further west who produced them.

The northwestern Kalahari

The hierarchical settlement system noted for the Toutswe complex has not been observed in western Ngamiland. Furthermore, while domesticated animals made up a similar proportion of the diet, centralized deposits of vitrified dung do not occur. This suggests that animals were more dispersed and patterns of ownership more decentralized. The burial of men and women together in middens at the periphery of the village, rather than in a central cattle byre, is another contrast with Cattle Complex sites to the east. Such a placement is, however, similar to that found in the "matrilineal belt" of central Africa where ancestors were buried on the outskirts of villages in "mediating" ground between village and forest. To extend Comaroff's earlier metaphor, the joint burial of males and females in middens at the edge of the village, and the absence of central animal kraals, suggests that ancestors at sites such as Divuyu and Nqoma (discussed below) could "speak" in more matrilateral idioms.

The proportions of cattle, small stock, hunted game, and fish in the economies of sites in Ngamiland also varies more widely than was found in eastern Botswana (Denbow 1990). This may be due to a number of factors, including the greater degree of ecological zonation found in the northwest where permanent open water, periodic swamps, semi-arid grasslands, and scrub-covered sand dunes can occur within a few kilometers of one another. Such environmental diversity favors the development of locally specialized exchange economies organized to exploit the production differentials such zonation makes possible. Economic and political bargaining power between communities may thus have been more diffusely apportioned than was the case in the Toutswe region.

Divuyu

The site of Divuyu is located at the top of the female hill at Tsodilo, 180 meters above the surrounding plain. Access to the site is difficult. Radiocarbon dates bracket its occupation between the sixth and eighth centuries AD. Over 200 copper and iron tools and ornaments have been recovered, all apparently imported as finished objects since neither copper nor iron ores outcrop at Tsodilo and no remains of smelting furnaces have been found. Metallurgical analyses (Miller 1996) indicate that the artifacts originated from a variety of sources; most had been extensively reworked. While a few productive tools such as awls, chisels, and arrowheads were recovered, most of the metal was fashioned into items of personal adornment that included beads, bracelets, chains, and pendants.

The confined hilltop location of Divuyu is not suitable for agriculture or grazing, suggesting that defense was an

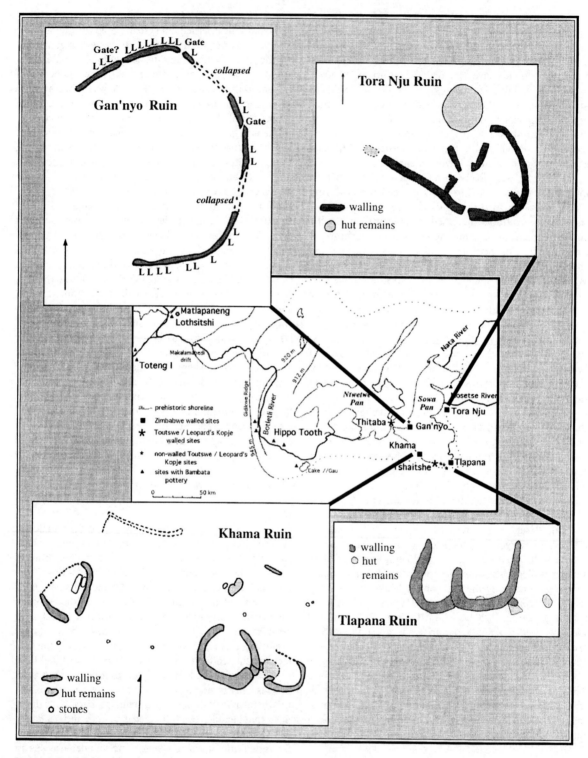

Figure 9.5   Makgadikgadi ruins.

important consideration. Since no earlier Iron Age sites have been found in Ngamiland, it seems likely that this was oriented against autochthonous foragers or pastro-foragers (Denbow and Wilmsen 1986). Divuyu peoples consumed large numbers of wild game that included sandveld species such as duiker, impala, buffalo, eland, and wildebeest, as well as fish, hippo, lechwe, reedbuck, and waterbok that must have been procured from areas of permanent standing water. The bulk of the meat diet, however, was supplied by herds of sheep and goats, supplemented by a few cattle (Turner 1987). Plant foods included gathered mongongo nuts, whose carbonized remains occur in quantity, along with domesticated sorghum and millet. The mongongo nuts and wild faunal remains attest to the importance of foraging at Divuyu. Despite this overlap in resources with hunter-gatherer economies, however, only one backed segment and thirty-three chert flakes were recovered. Thus, in keeping with its pioneer status, Divuyu displays little material evidence for social amalgamation or interaction with indigenous foragers or pastro-foragers. Even salt, a widely traded item, was locally manufactured using specially constructed pots with perforated bases as strainers. These findings contrast with those from the slightly later site of Nqoma, situated on a lower plateau of the same hill.

Nqoma

Nqoma, located about 2 kilometers south of Divuyu, lies on an easily accessible lower plateau of the female hill. The main occupation of the site dates between the ninth and twelfth centuries AD, coterminous with the Toutswe complex discussed above. Twenty-six glass beads and eleven marine shells indicate that the site was sufficiently powerful and wealthy to be able to attract East Coast trade items across the Kalahari. That such items became indicators of status and power is suggested by the discovery of an ivory replica of a conus shell found at the site. More than 2,500 iron and copper artifacts were recovered from Nqoma, making it one of the richest metalworking sites in southern Africa (Denbow and Wilmsen 1986). As at Divuyu, all of this material was imported – with some of the copper artifacts possibly coming from as far away as the Shaba province of southern Zaire (Miller 1996). Almost all of this metal was fashioned into bangles, beads, and other items of personal adornment.

The emphasis on metal jewelry at Nqoma is striking when compared with other Kalahari sites. At Nqoma, iron and copper beads outnumber ostrich eggshell beads by a factor of 4 to 1. In contrast, at Bosutswe there are roughly twenty eggshell beads for every metal one; at smaller sites such as Taukome and Matlhapaneng the pro-

portion drops even further to 100 to 1. Such differences suggest that the occupants at Nqoma intentionally used metal jewelry in their construction of social distinctions between themselves and those with less access to metal, such as the foragers living in rockshelters at the base of the hill. The incentive to import glass beads and other luxury items from the East Coast may have come from a similar desire to construct difference. Thus, while Divuyu provides little evidence for interaction between Stone Age and Iron Age peoples, the data from Nqoma suggest that by the end of the first millennium a more dialectical relationship between foragers and food-producers was emerging. Furthermore, the extensive use of metal and the absence of central cattle kraals suggest that, as in central Africa, iron and copper took the place of cattle as a store of wealth and medium of exchange. As Vansina (1984: 142) concludes, "what cattle are to the eastern Bantu, iron and copper are here."

Figure 9.6 indicates that cattle increased dramatically from Divuyu to Nqoma, where they rival goats and sheep as mainstays of the domestic economy. At the same time, hunted game also increased to 35 percent of the faunal remains (Denbow 1990). While it is possible that Nqoma peoples simply stepped up their hunting activities, this seems unlikely given the findings from other sites in the Kalahari where increases in cattle consumption correlate with decreases in game (see Figure 9.3).

Significantly, the increase in hunting at Nqoma also corresponds with an enormous increase in the number of lithics. Over 7,500 chert flakes were recovered at Nqoma, along with eighty-four backed segments, thirty-one scrapers, fifty-three cores, and sixty-six utilized flakes. Obviously, a scarcity of iron and copper at Nqoma is not the reason for this change. Instead, the lithics, along with the increase in hunted game, suggest that relations between herders and hunters shifted significantly during the two centuries that separated Nqoma and Divuyu. In addition, the evidence that lithic manufacture took place at Nqoma suggests that foragers may have been living, not just trading, there.

Excavations in rockshelters at the base of the hill illustrate the other side of this relationship. At White Paintings Shelter and Depression Cave excavations have uncovered Late Stone Age occupations that contain small quantities of Divuyu and Nqoma ceramics, a few fragments of iron, and an occasional sheep or goat bone (Robbins 1990). According to Robbins and Campbell (n. d.), changes in the lithic assemblage in the first millennium AD indicate that "hide scraping was an important activity during this time. The number and distribution of scrapers hints that something more than the casual

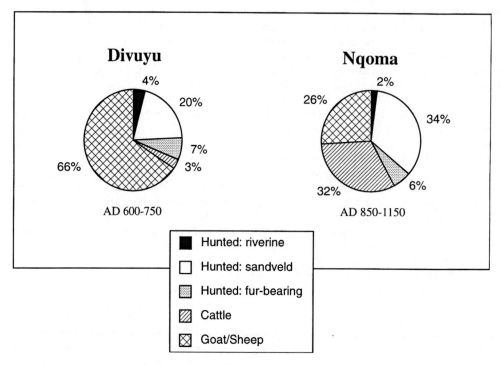

Figure 9.6   Comparison of Tsodilo faunal assemblages.

preparation of a few hides for local use was going on. This finding leads us to believe that the people occupying Depression shelter were processing hides for exchange with the nearby village fold . . . [and] served as 'entrepots' between the peoples and resources of the sandveld and the Early Iron Age villagers who lived on the Female Hill . . . " Another potential indicator of a change in regional social relations may be salt. No perforated pottery salt strainers were recovered from Nqoma, suggesting that this necessary item was now acquired through exchange, perhaps with foragers at distant salt pans, rather than locally produced as it was at Divuyu.

The extraordinary amount of metal jewelry found at Nqoma suggests a social counterpoint to the economic integration and convergence indicated by the lithic and faunal remains. If so, it would mean that aspects of forager and farmer identities were being mutually constructed in dialectical fashion, rather than in isolation. Similar "mixed" assemblages of lithics, iron, and pottery found near the Namibian border indicate that relations between practitioners of differentiated economies were not confined to Tsodilo (Kinahan and Kinahan 1984: 21–2; Wilmsen 1978, 1989; Wilmsen and Denbow 1990; Yellen 1973).

It has been asserted that the small fragments of pottery and iron found at sites far out in the sandveld were simply collected as "curiosities" (Yellen and Brooks 1988) and were of little significance to sandveld life other than as a reflection of infrequent, casual bartering (Solway and Lee 1990). While such artifacts are usually associated with pastoral and agropastoral economies, this does not mean that their function or implicit value in the regional political economy lay solely in the sphere of production. Possession of such artifacts was also a material manifestation of connectedness with wider political, social, and economic networks. Some of the wild game, ivory, ochre pigments, ostrich eggshell beads, and other items recovered at Nqoma represent the other side of such exchange relations. The possible use of metal jewelry at Nqoma to encode differences in status, power, and wealth, however, suggests these relations were complex, not ephemeral, and involved much more than simple, disinterested exchange of decontextualized commodities.

With the rise of Mapungubwe hegemony in the twelfth century, gold and other manufactured items began to replace wild products at the apex of value in the East Coast trade. In concert with these changes, Nqoma was abandoned and the integrative sets of trade and other relations it had established with neighboring peoples were progressively attenuated as the region was reduced to a marginal position in the political economy of southern Africa. No new intercontinental trade reached Ngamiland until the seventeenth century when Portuguese goods, introduced through the Atlantic coast of Angola, were left in the upper levels at Xaro, and at the Alex site in the Kwebe Hills south of Lake Ngami.

Conclusions

The introduction of pastoral and agricultural economies below the Zambezi-Okavango-Kunene rivers brought with it a complex interdigitation of peoples that included foragers and pastro-foragers, as well as agropastoralists. Variations in the distribution of rainfall, surface water, grazing land, and other resources led to diversification of these communities through time. Beginning about the ninth century AD, Bantu agropastoralists gained a dominant position in the eastern half of Botswana. A social hierarchy ensued with foragers relegated to marginal social and economic positions within the Toutswe complex (Denbow 1984, 1986). As population densities rose, formerly autonomous and semi-autonomous foraging and agropastoral communities became situated within a wider constellation of societies that included both independent states and acephalous groups; lateral relations among these polities affected the internal political processes of them all. By the end of the first millennium AD, political and economic networks allowed innovations and transformations to reverberate across the region (Denbow 1990).

One of the critical nodes of production that came to be controlled by an emerging elite was cattle (Denbow 1982, 1983, 1986; Huffman 1982). According to Kuper (1982), the exchange of cattle for the productive and reproductive forces of women was *the* most central social transaction among southern African peoples. A large cattle herd was the currency of political authority, reflecting an owner's ability to mobilize commodity production, people, and spiritual power to his own ends. Another node was control over intra- and inter-regional trade. Exchanges of glass beads, cowry shells, ivory, metal, game meat, and other products linked communities into complex networks of interdependency. In some cases, such as along the Botletli River, autonomy rather than assimilation resulted as principles of kinship, residence, and land tenure were adjusted to accommodate changes in the political and economic landscape. The growth of gold mining after the thirteenth century helped restructure the regional political economy. One consequence was an extension of Mapungubwe hegemony to Bosutswe, far out into the sandveld of eastern Botswana. Whereas cattle had formerly been central to the ideology and political economy, their importance was now marginalized. This was reflected in the dispersal of herds from prominent to small satellite communities. The seeds of the present, ethnically encoded cattlepost-economy may have been sown at this time.

While such transformations were well underway by the beginning of the second millennium AD in the eastern half of the subcontinent, they did not happen to the same extent in the west until the nineteenth century. Here, Khoi and Khoe-speaking herders and foragers dominated the region in the eighteenth century when they were first encountered by Batswana and, later, Europeans (Gordon 1992; Wilmsen 1989). The standard explanation for this difference has been that the west was more isolated by dry desert conditions and could not support agropastoral economies; by extension, variation in the socio-economic status of Khoisan peoples was thought to be a simple product of isolation (Kuper 1969; Lee 1979; Solway and Lee 1990; Yellen 1990). The western environment is as able as the eastern to support livestock, however, and the archaeological data indicate that agropastoral economies go back here almost 1,500 years.

The differences between the two areas must therefore be political and economic in nature, and stem from internal differences in the structure of social formations that began to emerge during the first millennium AD. The clear-cut ecological zonation found in northwestern Botswana, for instance, seems to have favored the establishment of more balanced social relations among economically differentiated communities than was the case in eastern Botswana. The use of metal jewelry at Nqoma to construct social difference appears to have been an inherent feature of these relations. With the rise of Zimbabwe hegemony in the east, the northwest was reduced to peripheral status and political relations of production and distribution that had once integrated diverse communities were transformed into ethnically coded relations of difference and separation.

References

Comaroff, J.
  1985 *Body of Power, Spirit of Resistance: The Culture and History of a South African People.* Chicago: University of Chicago Press.
Denbow, J.
  1979 *Cenchrus ciliaris:* an ecological indicator of Iron Age middens using aerial photography in eastern

Botswana. *South African Journal of Science* 75: 405–8.

1982 The Toutswe tradition: a study in socio-economic change. In *Settlement in Botswana*, edited by R. Hitchcock and M. Smith. Johannesburg: Heinneman.

1983 Iron Age economics: herding, wealth and politics along the fringes of the Kalahari during the Early Iron Age. Ph.D. dissertation, Indiana University, Bloomington.

1984a Prehistoric herders and foragers of the Kalahari: the evidence for 1500 years of interaction. In *Past and Present in Hunter Gatherer Studies*, edited by C. Schrire. Orlando: Academic Press.

1984b Cows and kings: a spatial and economic analysis of a hierarchical Early Iron Age settlement system in eastern Botswana. In *Frontiers: Southern African Archaeology Today*, edited by M. Hall et al. BAR Monographs. Cambridge: Cambridge University Press.

1985a Report on an archaeological reconnaissance of the BP soda ash lease, Magkadikgadi Pans, Botswana. Report prepared for the Botswana Government and British Petroleum. Gaborone: National Museum.

1985b Report on archaeological investigations at Sowa Pan. Report prepared for British Petroleum and the Botswana Government. Gaborone: National Museum.

1986 A new look at the later prehistory of the Kalahari. *Journal of African History* 27: 3–29.

1990 Congo to Kalahari: data and hypotheses about the political economy of the western stream of the Early Iron Age. *African Archaeological Review* 8: 139–75.

1996 Stolen Places: the discourse of identity and the construction of history in the Kalahari. In *Quellen zur Khoisan-Forschung*, edited by E. Wilmsen. Köln: Rüdiger Köppe Verlag.

Denbow, J. and E. Wilmsen
1986 The advent and course of pastoralism in the Kalahari. *Science* 234: 1509–15.

Fosbrooke, H.
1973 An assessment of the importance of institutions. *Botswana Notes and Records* 5: 26–36.

Gordon, R.
1992 *Images of the Bushman: Myth and the Making of a Namibian Underclass*. Boulder: Westview Press.

Hall, M.
1990 *Farmers, Kings, and Traders: The People of Southern Africa 200–1860*. Chicago: University of Chicago Press.

Huffman, T.
1982 Archaeology and the ethnohistory of the African Iron Age. *Annual Review of Anthropology* 11: 133–50.

1986 Iron Age settlement patterns and the origins of class distinction in southern Africa. *Advances in World Archaeology* 5: 291–338.

1989 *Iron Age Migrations*. Johannesburg: Witwatersrand University Press.

1994 Toteng pottery and the origins of Bambata. *Southern African Field Archaeology* 3: 3–9.

1996 *Snakes and Crocodiles: Power and Symbolism in Ancient Zimbabwe*. Johannesburg: Witwatersrand University Press.

Kinahan, J. and J. Kinahan
1984 An archaeological reconnaissance of Bushmanland and southern Kavango. Report to the South West Africa Department of Agriculture and Nature Conservation, Windhoek.

1996 A new archaeological perspective on nomadic pastoralist expansion in south-western Africa. In *The Growth of Farming Communities in Africa from the Equator Southwards*, edited by J. Sutton. *Azania* special volume 29–30. Nairobi: English Press.

Kuper, A.
1969 The Kalagadi in the nineteenth century. *Botswana Notes and Records* 2: 45–51.

1982 *Wives for Cattle*. London: Routledge and Kegan Paul.

Lee, R.
1979 *The !Kung San*. London: Cambridge University Press.

Lepionka, L.
1979 Excavations at Tautswemogala. *Botswana Notes and Records* 9: 1–16.

MacGaffey, W.
1986 *Religion and Society in Central Africa: the BaKongo of lower Zaire*. Chicago: University of Chicago Press.

Main, M.
1992–4 Reports to the National Museum of Botswana regarding archaeological reconnaissances and discoveries along the southern edge of Sowa Pan.

Marcus, G. and M. Fischer
1986 *Anthropology as Cultural Critique: An Experimental Moment in the Human Sciences*. Chicago: University of Chicago Press.

Miller, D.
1996 *The Tsodilo Jewellery: Metal Work from Northern Botswana*. Cape Town: University of Cape Town Press.

Miller, J.
1988 *A Way of Death.* London: James Currey.
Plug, I.
1982 Faunal remains from Taukome. Unpublished report, Department of Archaeozoology, Pretoria Museum.
1996 Seven centuries of Iron Age traditions at Bostuswe, Botswana: a faunal perspective. *South African Journal of Science* 92: 91–7.
Ricklefs, R.
1979 *Ecology.* Sunbury on Thames: Thomas Nelson.
Robbins, L.
1990 The Depression site: a Stone Age sequence in the northwest Kalahari. *National Geographic Research* 6: 329–38.
Robbins, L. and A. Campbell
n.d. The Stone Age at Tsodilo. Unpublished report in posession of the author.
Solway, J. and R. Lee
1990 Foragers, genuine or spurious? Situating the Kalahari San in history. *Current Anthropology* 31: 109–46.
Thomas, S. and P. Shaw
1991 *The Kalahari Environment.* Cambridge: Cambridge University Press.
Turner, G.
1987 Herders and Hunters in northwestern Botswana: the faunal evidence. *Botswana Notes and Records* 19: 7–23.
Tyson. P. and J. Lindsay
1992 The little Ice Age in southern Africa. *Holocene* 2: 271–8.

Vansina, J.
1984 Western Bantu Expansion. *Journal of African History* 25: 129–45.
Weedman, K.
1992 Foragers, pastro-foragers, and agro-pastoralists: lithic use in Botswana from the 2nd millennium BC through the 19th century AD. Unpublished MA thesis, University of Texas, Austin.
Wilmsen, E.
1978 Prehistoric and historic antecedents of an Ngamiland community. *Botswana Notes and Records* 10: 5–18.
1989 *Land Filled with Files: A Political Economy of the Kalahari.* Chicago: Chicago University Press.
Wilmsen, E. and J. Denbow
1990 Paradigmatic history of San-speaking peoples and current attempts at revision. *Current Anthropology* 31: 489–524.
Wilmsen, E. and R. Vossen
1990 Labour, language and power in the construction of ethnicity in Botswana. *Critique of Anthropology* 10: 7–38.
Yellen, J.
1973 Notes to accompany archaeological materials shipped to the National Museum, Botswana. MS, National Museum, Gaborone, Botswana.
1990 The transformation of the Kalahari !Kung. *Scientific American* 262: 96–105.
Yellen, J. and A. Brooks
1988 The Late Stone Age archaeology of the !Kangwa and /Xai/Xai valleys, Ngamiland. *Botswana Notes and Records* 20: 5–27.

10
Seeking and keeping power in Bunyoro-Kitara, Uganda

PETER ROBERTSHAW

Archaeologists have long been interested in the process of state formation. However, attention has recently shifted towards investigation of lower levels of political complexity, particularly chiefdoms. The publication of a recent School of American Research seminar (Earle 1991b) and other research on chiefdoms (summarized by Earle 1987) has led to a fairly radical reinterpretation of our understanding of such "intermediate-level" societies. The functionalist notion that chiefs managed the distribution of resources has been replaced by a realization that chiefs were rather more selfish individuals out to extract a surplus from their followers, who in turn could curb the more despotic tendencies of their leaders by threatening to shift their allegiances elsewhere. This description, albeit superficial, reflects the central role given in recent work to discussion of how chiefs acquired and retained power, the essential components of which were control of the economy, war, and ideology (Earle 1991a: 9).

Chiefdoms are usually viewed in evolutionary models of state formation as the immediate precursors of states. These models have been the subject of a spirited attack by Yoffee (1993). He, *inter alia*, points out the dangers inherent in subverting a taxonomy of recent societies into an evolutionary scheme whereby contemporary chiefdoms, for example, are viewed as representative of the historical precursors of states, allowing archaeologists to flesh out flimsy data with borrowed ethnographic detail. Yoffee (1993) has also cogently argued that states do not normally evolve from chiefdoms. Instead, states may arise from the competition among different nodes of power (economic, political, and ideological) within a society. In fact, successful chiefdoms would appear to be inimical to the development of states. Thus, power is the current

buzzword in the archaeology of complex societies (see also Schoenbrun this volume). Furthermore, the "dual-processual theory" proposed by Blanton and colleagues (1996; see also DeMarrais et al. 1996) offers an epistemological foundation for the archaeological investigation of power that has been applied to Bunyoro-Kitara (Robertshaw in press).

In this chapter I examine the political history of Bunyoro-Kitara in western Uganda. This region is well-known anthropologically for its pre-colonial states, and historically for the debate over the size of the polity that preceded these states. However, the focus on the major Ugandan states, notably Bunyoro,[1] of the nineteenth century has often obscured the fact that hidden in the geographical and political interstices were several smaller polities or chiefdoms (see also Kopytoff, Stahl this volume). Examples of these polities include Buhweju and the relatively autonomous region of Bwera under the stewardship of the Moli clan. Recent historical research has also demonstrated the importance of small-scale polities throughout the pre-colonial history of Bunyoro-Kitara (Tantala 1989). Moreover, this region is surrounded by others that also supported pre-colonial polities of varying size and political hierarchies.

The body of this chapter is divided into two sections: the first addresses the historical evidence and the second the archaeological evidence for the evolution of polities in Bunyoro-Kitara. After a brief review of earlier work, the historical section focuses upon research by Tantala (1989), bringing to it the model of the internal African frontier proposed by Kopytoff (1987, this volume). This model offers some valuable insights into the social processes involved in the later Iron Age settlement of Bunyoro-Kitara. Archaeological evidence reveals that there was scant agricultural settlement in Bunyoro-Kitara prior to *c.* AD 1000 (Robertshaw 1994), warranting application of the model.

The historical research concludes that two major periods of small-scale polities preceded the establishment of the Nyoro state. This conclusion is examined in the archaeological section of the chapter, where I discuss relevant evidence from earthworks and other sites. This exercise is hampered by the scant amount of archaeological research undertaken in Bunyoro-Kitara. The final section offers a brief and tentative reconstruction of the history of political complexity in Bunyoro-Kitara.

Bunyoro-Kitara and its history

Bunyoro-Kitara is situated in western Uganda between the Western Rift Valley and the Ruwenzori Mountains to

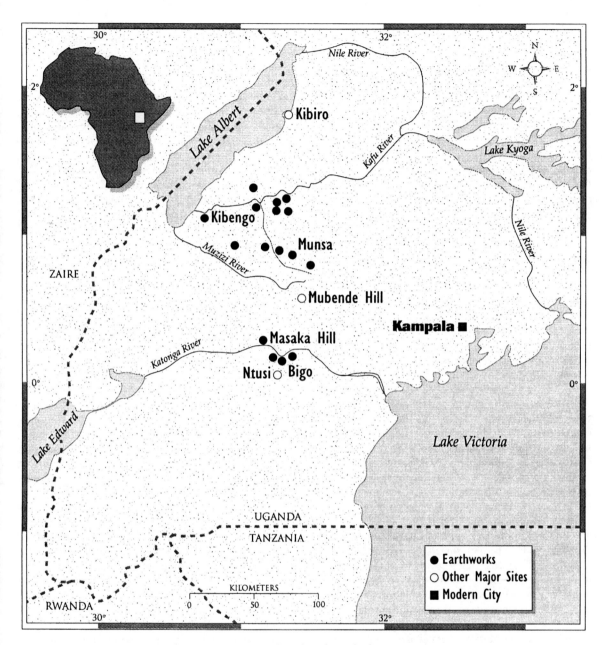

Figure 10.1   Western Uganda showing the location of earthworks and other major sites.

the west, and the low-lying regions adjacent to Lake Victoria to the east (Figure 10.1). Although drier than its western and eastern neighbors, Bunyoro-Kitara has an annual rainfall in excess of 1000 mm, occurring in two extended rainy seasons. The characteristic topographic pattern comprises clearly defined areas of raised ground separated by swampy streams and rivers, which often contain extensive stands of papyrus bordered by moist semi-deciduous forest. Nowadays, homesteads, surrounded by gardens and banana groves, are dispersed over the higher ground. In the absence of cultivation or regular grazing by livestock, the vegetation is luxuriant, containing dense stands of elephant grass (*Pennisetum purpureum*); it is classified as "forest/savanna mosaic" (Uganda Government 1964). Traveling south towards and across the Katonga river, the countryside becomes drier and there are extensive stands of acacia woodland.

At the time of European contact in the late nineteenth century, much of Bunyoro-Kitara lay within the borders of the Nyoro state, whose major ethnographers were John Beattie (1960, 1971), and the missionary-explorer Roscoe (1923). This state was founded upon a pyramidal system of land tenure, with surplus production expropriated in the form of tribute. Wars of succession commonly occurred with the death of the ruler (*mukama*) and the size of the state and the degree of central control waxed and waned through time.

The pre-colonial history of Bunyoro-Kitara has mostly been written from oral traditions recorded at the court. These traditions revolve around the activities of three successive dynasties: the Batembuzi, the Bacwezi, and the Babito, the last of these comprising the ruling dynasty at the time of European contact. Given the context in which these traditions were recited and recorded, it is not surprising that they were generally interpreted as describing the history of former polities, from whom the present Nyoro state drew its legitimacy. Historians generally accept that many events described in the history of the Bito dynasty actually took place. However, there has been some argument over whether the Bito king-list was padded over time to impress British colonial overlords as part of political jockeying between the Banyoro and their Ganda neighbors (Buchanan 1975; Henige 1974). At the other end of the time scale, the Batembuzi have mostly been consigned to the realm of myth, though they have recently acquired some historical recognition as a result of studies of clan traditions (Buchanan 1974). Caught in the middle, the Bacwezi have received intense scrutiny. Were they men, gods or perhaps something in-between?

In the 1950s and 1960s, the great Cwezi debate tended to be polarized between the idea that the Bacwezi were gods (Wrigley 1958) and the view that they were the rulers of an "empire," who were deified after their demise (Oliver 1953). A more cautious middle ground was charted in the 1970s by various historians, notably Berger (1980, 1981), Buchanan (1974), and Schmidt (1978), who tended to conceive of the Bacwezi as leaders of small-scale polities, whose sites later became shrines that served as centers of resistance to the power of the Bito state. Nevertheless, the notion of a Cwezi state was resurrected in both the Cambridge and Unesco histories of Africa. In the former, Oliver (1977: 634) describes the Cwezi state as a "temporary, tribute-imposing overlordship over a series of small

chieftainships in . . . an ecologically coherent area." In the Unesco version, Ogot (1984: 503–4) refers to a "loosely organized empire" extending over a vast area stretching into modern Kenya, Rwanda, and Tanzania.

A thorough analysis of all the traditions – court, clan and local – has been completed by Tantala (1989), whose work reveals that the Bacwezi probably represent one stage in a succession of small-scale polities in Bunyoro-Kitara that are much more akin to chiefdoms than states. The origins of these polities are best understood with reference to the model of the process of settlement of a frontier region proposed by Kopytoff (1987, this volume). According to this model, village fission in well-populated regions results in the expansion of kin-based groups into sparsely occupied (and, hence, frontier) regions. Bunyoro-Kitara in the early second millennium would seem to have been a classic frontier region, being comparatively sparsely inhabited and ecologically less productive than surrounding regions. Clan traditions reveal a complex pattern of multiple immigrations into Bunyoro-Kitara by what appear to be small kin-based groups whose subsistence was based on the growing of cereal crops and the herding of domestic livestock, particularly goats (Buchanan 1974). Once settled, the newcomers would seek to attract followers, since economic security would come from clearing adequate land for cultivation. It was labor rather than land that was in short supply. Furthermore, creation of a sufficient agricultural surplus would permit the exploitation of minerals and other resources by part-time craft specialists. Later immigrants were either incorporated into existing kin groups and/or accorded less status. Coalition was, in principle, advantageous to all parties, since numerical strength equated to economic and military security. The ability to attract and retain followers would transform a successful group into a simple chiefdom. However, such a development was not inevitable since allegiances could easily be transferred to a more powerful neighbor. Therefore, it was advantageous for dominant groups to legitimize their leadership and power through the assumption or co-option of ritual authority, as is explained in Schoenbrun's contribution to this volume.

Subsequent events in Bunyoro-Kitara also conform to Kopytoff's model, though details were shaped by a major drought and its aftermath. Competing small-scale polities, which reproduced on the frontier many aspects of the societies from which they emigrated, are evident in many areas of Bunyoro-Kitara in the period that would seem to correspond with the late Tembuzi epoch of the historical chronology. Some of these polities, including one in the Kitara heartland of Bugangaizi, were evidently more successful than others (Tantala 1989: 476). During this period, several traditions refer to the occurrence of a "Great Drought," which caused considerable population displacement (but see Schoenbrun this volume, note 2). Illustrative of the effects of this drought and of the utility of the frontier model is the case of the emergence of the polity of Kitara kya Nyamenge. Nyamenge and his followers fled from a forest fire during the Great Drought and then established a clan-based (Siita) polity focused on the village of Kitara. Their power and ability to attract supporters seems to have stemmed from their iron-working abilities and control of local iron production (Tantala 1989: 479). Political power was also linked to the possession of ritual authority. The Kitara kya Nyamenge polity was probably no larger than a cluster of villages. Indeed, it was probably one of a number of similar-sized polities – simple chiefdoms – that were focused on locations with boundaries defined by natural features of the landscape (Tantala 1989: 500–4).

After the Great Drought, those groups who emphasized cattle-keeping in their subsistence economies seem to have recovered more rapidly. Cattle pastoralism and its associated values spread (Schoenbrun this volume), changing the political economies of existing polities. The spread of pastoralism was linked to the rise of the Cwezi spirit-possession cult. Traditions of regicide and wars indicate that the replacement of older polities and their ritual authority by the expanding Cwezi polities was achieved in good part through warfare and raiding. It seems that these Cwezi polities were also chiefdoms rather than states, though comparatively little is known of their political institutions. Each polity was centered on a ritual site, generally situated on a prominent hill, where was found the shrine of the spirit who was the patron of the ruling line (Tantala 1989). The distribution of such shrines is shown in Figure 10.2. The map suggests that each polity probably controlled an area of between roughly 250 and 750 km^2 and perhaps a population of several thousand people.

The best-known Cwezi polity is that of Ndahura, who is credited in earlier interpretations of the court traditions with the founding of the Cwezi "empire" (e.g. Oliver 1953). Although certainly not an empire, Ndahura's polity was clearly expansionist; he is reputed to have mounted many raids in which women and cattle were the main booty. He may also have levied a tax on trade. Salt was probably the most important trading commodity during the Cwezi era. Found in quantity only at two locations, Kibiro and Katwe, which are in the Western Rift Valley on the western borders of Bunyoro-Kitara, salt was essential for the health of the cattle that formed the backbone of Cwezi economies. Thus, salt was traded along well-established routes through Bunyoro-Kitara. The location of Cwezi shrine sites in close proximity to these routes is not coincidental (Tantala 1989: 671).

The power of individual Cwezi polities rose and fell through time. This process is reflected in the traditions that recount the transfer of power from Ndahura, whose shrine is at Mubende Hill, to Wamara, whose node of authority lay to the south at Masaka Hill. The collapse of Ndahura's polity is suggested both by the failure of one of his raids and the tradition that one item of booty garnered unintentionally by his warriors was smallpox (Nyakatura 1973: 22).

The Cwezi polities were eventually mostly subsumed or destroyed by the expansion of the Babito and their followers, who entered Bunyoro-Kitara from the north and whose origins lie among the Nilotic-speaking Luo. The success of the Babito and their ability to carve out a tributary state is not easily explained. The explanation may lie in superior military strength (Oliver 1977). It is clear that the Babito sought ritual legitimation for their authority by inventing kinship ties with the Cwezi pantheon. They also appeased the leaders of the Cwezi cults by not only allowing them considerable independence in the vicinity of the shrine sites but also involving them in their own rituals of authority. Thus, for example, Nyoro coronation rituals were held at the Cwezi shrine at Mubende Hill (Lanning 1966) and the *mukama* of Bunyoro sent occasional gifts to the head of the Yaga clan who had inherited the regalia of the Cwezi hero, Mulindwa (Kamuhangire and Robertshaw interview with Zakao Kyanku, August 9, 1994).

In summary, the pre-Bito history of Bunyoro-Kitara, as reconstructed by Tantala, has two major periods of small-scale polities. First, there is the late Tembuzi period with its agricultural polities, where the scale of integration seems to have been simple chiefdoms. Second is the Cwezi period, in which polities were larger, had a greater emphasis upon cattle and raiding, and exercised new forms of ritual authority. How well does this reconstruction[2] fit the available archaeological evidence? Our answer must be equivocal until more excavations have been undertaken, but the archaeological data raise many interesting questions.

The archaeology of Bunyoro-Kitara

Little archaeological research has been undertaken in western Uganda. It was initiated during the colonial period by various government administrators, notably Eric Lanning, and enjoyed a brief period of professional

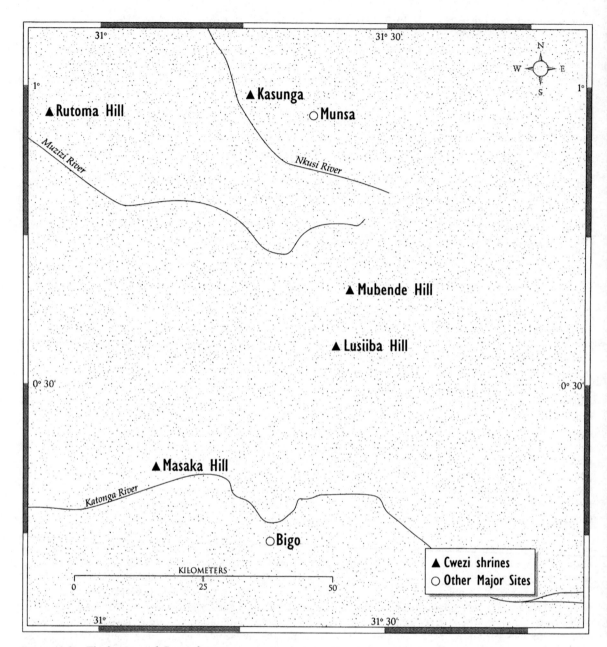

Figure 10.2   The location of Cwezi shrines.

investigation around the time of independence before disruption due to political unrest. A resurgence of research in the last decade was inspired by the British Institute in Eastern Africa and facilitated by internal political stability. Nevertheless, fewer than ten sites have been excavated to date, and excavation reports are available for only a couple of these.

The distinctive feature of the archaeological record of Bunyoro-Kitara is the existence of earthworks (Lanning 1953). These sites comprise systems of one or more trenches, sometimes up to several kilometers in length, which usually encircle an area of higher ground or a rock outcrop that could serve as a natural defensive feature. Bigo, also known as Bigo bya Mugenyi, is the largest of these sites. It is one of two or possibly three earthworks sites located in close proximity to each other on the south bank of the Katonga River. All the other earthworks are further north, with sites extending almost to the shores of Lake Albert (see Figure 10.1).

So far, the investigation and interpretation of the earthworks have revolved around whether or not they can be linked with the Bacwezi and hence provide confirmation of the Bacwezi as the rulers of a supposed medieval empire. Bigo has been posited as the capital of this "empire" (e.g. Posnansky 1966: 5; Oliver 1977: 632). The obvious allure of linking the earthworks at Bigo and elsewhere to a Cwezi empire lay in the apparent archaeological proof of this historical construct, which in good circular reasoning also provided a convenient explanation for the existence of these sites. Moreover, the distribution of the earthworks approximated well with the core region of the Cwezi empire. Pottery and other finds indicated that these sites were occupied by people with a common cultural heritage, prompting at least one author to talk of a "Bacwezi culture" (Lanning 1957: 313). However, later publications were less forthright, referring instead to a "Bigo Culture" with its "characteristic painted pottery" (Lanning 1960: 195). The layout of Bigo bore resemblances to later Nkore capital sites to the south (Posnansky 1966, 1969), while its construction implied the existence of a large organized labor force. Estimates of this force ran as high as 1,000 men laboring for two to three years (Gray 1935). Finally, the radiocarbon dates for Bigo seemed to correlate with those obtained for the Bacwezi by historians counting back through the generations of Nyoro kings.

All these positions have been or can be assailed. The resemblances in pottery from different sites that encouraged the notion of a "Bigo Culture" may be superficial, confined to the use of finger-daubed paint and fiber roulettes. Preliminary analyses by Jeremy Meredith (ms., in author's possession) indicate differences as well as similarities between the pottery assemblages from Bigo and Mubende Hill, suggesting that the "Bigo Culture" may be a heterogeneous tradition reflecting local stylistic variation imposed on a widespread core tradition (see also Desmedt 1991; Robertshaw 1994; and Kopytoff this volume, pp. 93–5, for an historical ethnographic analogy). The architectural reconstruction of Bigo as a capital is disputed by Schmidt (1990: 263), who prefers a different interpretation of the building history of the mounds in the center of the site. In contrast to Gray, Steinhart (1981) offers a more conservative estimate of the labor needed to construct the earthworks, suggesting that voluntary work-parties laboring on a seasonal basis over several years would have been sufficient. Clearly, a crucial question in this regard is the duration of the construction of the earthworks. The Bigo radiocarbon dates range from AD 850 to the present and are hence not incompatible with a model of gradual earthwork construction. However, critical examination of the dating results suggests that Bigo was most likely occupied somewhere between the fifteenth and seventeenth centuries, a period that would be too late for the chronology of the Bacwezi founded upon kinglists (Schmidt 1990).[3] Schmidt (1990) has also argued that there are no oral traditions firmly ascribing Bigo to the Bacwezi (but see Tantala 1989: 207). Similarly, Ntusi, which is a very extensive settlement site several miles south of Bigo (Lanning 1970; Reid 1990; Reid and Meredith 1993), is not certainly associated in traditions with the Bacwezi.

All of the earthworks north of the Katonga River are locally associated with a man named Kateboha, whose name apparently refers to his ability to tie up his enemies. Although attempts have been made to place Kateboha as a member of the Bacwezi (Lanning 1953: 59), he does not figure in any of the major traditions. Tantala (1989: 634) speculates that Kateboha may have been a praise-name used in a pre-Cwezi polity in the Bugangaizi area.

Recent excavations at Munsa have revealed that the earthworks at this site were constructed in the late fifteenth or sixteenth century AD (Robertshaw 1997). Similar dates have also been obtained for the earthworks site at Kibengo (Lanning 1960). Occupation at the center of the Munsa site, however, began much earlier, probably around the ninth century. Burials with imported glass beads and copper jewelry also precede the construction of the earthworks, as do an iron-smelting furnace and associated slag. Contemporary with the earthworks are several very large pits, probably used for grain storage (Robertshaw 1997). While cattle remains were also found at Munsa, the storage pits suggest that an agricultural surplus may have funded the construction of the earthworks.

If the correlation between Bigo and the other earthworks with the Bacwezi (or at least one historical interpretation of the Bacwezi) is rejected, we may ask what we know from archaeology about the sites of Masaka Hill and Mubende Hill, since these sites are firmly identified in tradition with the Bacwezi; indeed, both were active Cwezi shrines earlier this century. In the case of Masaka Hill, little is known (Lanning 1954), since no excavations have been attempted at this site, access to which is a logistical nightmare (Kamuhangire et al. 1993). At Mubende Hill archaeological materials extend over four or five hectares and appear to belong to two phases of occupation, the latter falling in the late nineteenth or even early twentieth century. The earlier occupation is dated to the late thirteenth or fourteenth century. Although cattle bones are present, numerous grindstones and large pits suggest an economy based on cereal agriculture. No obvious symbols of wealth were found in the excavation of what appears to have been a village. Similarly, there was no evidence of long-distance trade nor of an emphasis on either cattle-keeping or iron-production. Mubende Hill was possibly already a shrine site by the fourteenth century (Robertshaw 1988, 1994: 108).

Two other sites merit discussion: Ntusi and Kibiro. Ntusi, the southernmost excavated site in Bunyoro-Kitara, possesses an earthen-walled reservoir (Sutton 1985) but no other earthworks. Midden material occurs at Ntusi both as mounds up to 5 meters high and as scattered trash extending over more than 100 hectares (Reid 1990, 1991). These features prompted John Sutton (1993: 52) to refer to Ntusi as a town, but it is not known how much of the site was occupied at any one time. Radiocarbon dates for the site span the period from about the tenth to the sixteenth centuries, though the major mounds seem to have accumulated between the eleventh and thirteenth centuries. Recent excavations have produced vast quantities of bones, predominantly of cattle, as well as pottery and numerous grindstones, but the relative importance and social relations of the pastoral and agricultural modes of production is not known. Nevertheless, Ntusi is crucial to an understanding of political and economic developments in Bunyoro-Kitara; it is not only the earliest but also the largest settlement in the region, as judged by the size and extent of its middens. Ntusi is located only a few miles south of Bigo, where construction of the earthworks may have begun about the fifteenth century, just after the major phase of settlement at Ntusi.

The existence of long-distance exchange networks reaching to the East African coast by about the thirteenth century is indicated by the discovery at Ntusi of several imported glass and cowrie shell beads. Also, in one area of the site, ivory was manufactured into beads, perhaps for export (Reid 1990, 1991). Two ivory beads were excavated at Mubende Hill, but elephants were eradicated from this region only in the colonial period. A fourteenth-century date has been suggested for a burial associated with imported glass beads and a copper ring at the salt-working site of Kibiro (Connah 1996: 93), while glass beads and copper are present at Munsa at an even earlier

date (see above). Control of trade in exotic goods may have provided a means to the accumulation of wealth, perhaps most cogently in cattle (Schoenbrun this volume), which was instrumental to social and political stratification. However, it is notable that no glass beads have been found in archaeological contexts that are contemporary with any earthworks. Thus, external long-distance exchange networks may have waned in importance towards the end of the fifteenth century.

Kibiro, located on the shores of Lake Albert at the opposite end of Bunyoro-Kitara from Ntusi, was the major salt-producing center for the entire region. Salt is required by both people and cattle, and control of the distribution of salt was an important facet of the later Nyoro kingdom (Connah 1996: 20 quoting Mounteney-Jephson 1890: 36). It may have been a factor also in the success of some earlier polities in the region (Tantala 1989). Excavations at Kibiro indicate that salt production began here early in the present millennium (Connah 1996), an age that fits well with the frontier phase of settlement of the larger region reconstructed from archaeological survey data (Robertshaw 1994). It would be interesting to know whether the scale of salt production at Kibiro increases in subsequent centuries, for Tantala (1989: 671) suggests that increasing cattle populations in the period of Cwezi polities would have stimulated the regional salt trade. She also notes that Cwezi individuals are sometimes described in traditions as traders and that many of the Cwezi shrine sites are located on trade routes (Tantala 1989: 671). Therefore, we might speculate that there is a connection between the decline of Ntusi about the end of the thirteenth century and the rise of the pastoral Cwezi polities (but see below). The demand for salt may have distracted the attention of Cwezi rulers away from Ntusi and towards Kibiro and the trade routes from the north.

While Kibiro appears to provide confirmation of the importance of intra-regional trade in salt, iron may also have been a valuable commodity, both in the Cwezi period (see Tantala 1989: 670) and especially among the pre-Cwezi polities. The importance of iron in pre-Cwezi polities is evident from the account of the Siita polity of Kitara kya Nyamenge (Tantala 1989: 479) and from the continuing identification of the Siita clan as knowledgeable iron-workers (Buchanan 1974: 102–104; Robertshaw 1991 fieldnotes). The archaeological evidence for iron-working at Munsa may also be relevant here.

Further archaeological evidence is provided by a preliminary season of surveys in 1991, the results of which are, however, tentative because of various sampling and analytical problems (Robertshaw 1994). There is very little evidence for agricultural settlement in Bunyoro-

Kitara prior to the tenth century, supporting the notion of a sparsely populated frontier region. Moreover, early sites were small. However, by the fourteenth century or thereabouts, large settlements without earthworks were located on or just below ridge tops or in areas that abut on prominent rock outcrops which may have served as defensible terrain. Earthworks themselves began to be constructed in about the late fifteenth or sixteenth century. Site size hierarchies appear to remain a feature of the archaeological record until European contact in the nineteenth century, though after about 1700 most of the population abandoned village sites in favor of more dispersed homesteads (Robertshaw 1994).

If we ignore efforts to link oral traditions of the Bacwezi with earthworks sites such as Bigo, we can return to the question of the degree of fit between the historical reconstruction outlined in the previous section and the archaeological evidence. The archaeological surveys and excavations support the hypothesis that Bunyoro-Kitara was a sparsely populated agricultural frontier at the beginning of the second millennium AD. The leaders of small farming communities sought to attract followers and did so before about AD 1400 by enhancing their prestige through the establishment of long-distance exchange networks, by the control of iron production and distribution, and by claims to ritual authority. This archaeological reconstruction fits reasonably comfortably with Tantala's history of the pre-Cwezi polities.

However, our attempt to blend seamlessly the archaeological and historical reconstructions comes woefully undone in the face both of the Cwezi shrine site at Mubende Hill and of the earthworks. The excavations at Mubende Hill do not support the historical hypothesis of a pastoral Cwezi polity based at the site; rather they suggest a small agricultural polity of the thirteenth or fourteenth century, supported by ritual authority, akin to the pre-Cwezi polities described by Tantala. Construction of the earthworks at Munsa, Kibengo, and probably Bigo dates to about the fifteenth or sixteenth century and may have been financed by agricultural surpluses, though cattle were also kept at these sites. It seems difficult to justify a correlation between these earthworks and the Cwezi polities, since the former are not the shrine sites that mark the apparent centers of these polities. A separation of political and ritual power in these polities is possible though at odds with both the historical interpretation and the available dating evidence. Furthermore, pastoralism is emphasized in the historical reconstructions of the Cwezi polities, but the archaeological evidence indicates the importance of agriculture. Finally, local oral traditions identify many of the earthworks with Kateboha, a persona not listed among the Cwezi pantheon. A tradition of this individual's demise refers to his having "kept his people busy . . . cultivating the land" (Lanning 1959: 187), further strengthening the argument that the earthworks were part of agricultural, rather than pastoral, polities.[4]

We may also ask whether or not the earthworks were the centers of competing regional polities. If they were the centers of competing polities, it seems strange that most of them are linked in tradition with a single individual, Kateboha. Moreover, when we plot the earthworks on a map (see Figure 10.2), it is noticeable that they occur in clusters, which would not seem to match predictions based on the hypothesis of competing polities. In this instance sampling errors may distort the data, since the earthworks were recorded by colonial administrators in the course of their other duties. Indeed, many sites are suspiciously close to major roads. Yet the 1991 surveys, albeit limited in extent, did not reveal any previously unrecorded earthworks. The earthwork sites are also of different sizes and complexity; some, such as Bigo and Munsa, comprise numerous trenches with a total length of several kilometers, whereas others, such as Karwata and other northerly sites, consist of a single trench enclosing an area less than 500 meters in diameter (Lanning 1953). Therefore, it is possible that there existed several polities of different sizes, but these doubts cannot be resolved until there is dating evidence for each site.

What about the Great Drought that may have been instrumental to the creation of polities, such as that of Kitara kya Nyamenge? The increased emphasis on pastoralism that may have presaged the rise of Cwezi cults may also have resulted from this drought. Is there palaeoenvironmental evidence for such a drought? Historians of Uganda have mostly relied upon the chronology of droughts reconstructed by Herring (1979) from studies of the Rodah Nilometer in Egypt. However, Herring's work is founded upon an earlier erroneous interpretation (see Harvey 1982 for details). The correct dates are provided by Hassan (1981), who argues that Nile levels are an accurate reflection of rainfall in the Lake Victoria region. Nile levels were very low between AD 1180 and 1350, and very high between 1350 and 1470. After a brief low between 1470 and 1500, records are missing for the period from 1500 to about 1725. These records are insufficiently fine-grained to allow the identification of a "Great Drought," but it seems reasonable to infer that it may have occurred in the 1180 to 1350 period of low Nile levels (but see Schoenbrun this volume, note 2). However, traditions of drought may serve as metaphors for a whole suite of calamities, so caution is needed before accepting the historical veracity of a remembered drought (Henige 1982: 89). Moreover, detailed palynological research is required to reconstruct the climatic and vegetational history of Bunyoro-Kitara.

In summary, archaeological evidence offers only tentative support to parts of Tantala's historical reconstruction of two periods of small and competing polities prior to the establishment of the later Nyoro kingdom. Both archaeology and history (Schoenbrun this volume) demonstrate the utility of applying Kopytoff's model of the internal African frontier to the peopling of the region. Both disciplines also provide evidence of small-scale polities, akin to chiefdoms, in the first centuries of the second millennium AD that were founded on various forms of religious and economic power, including control of long-distance exchange and iron production. According to historical reconstructions, these small polities were succeeded by the larger pastoral polities of the Cwezi. It is at this juncture that archaeology and history appear to diverge, for the Cwezi shrine site of Mubende Hill seems to have been a small agricultural settlement, while some, at least, of the earthworks seemed to have been founded upon an agricultural economic base. However, more surveys and excavations are required to establish the size, scale, and economies of the polities that may have been centered upon earthworks and shrine sites. Developments in regions surrounding Bunyoro-Kitara, many of which supported chiefdoms or states, are also poorly known from archaeology. Situating Bunyoro-Kitara's political history in the broader context of the Great Lakes region will further clarify the role of long-distance trading networks, warfare, and other patterns of regional interaction.

Conclusions

Hierarchical polities developed in Bunyoro-Kitara after settlement of an internal African frontier early in the second millennium. The success or failure of particular polities was founded upon the ability to attract and retain followers, who provided labor to clear and cultivate land and to manage livestock. Followers also constituted military strength that could be used to subdue neighboring polities, acquire women and cattle in raids, and control regional and long-distance exchange networks in salt, iron, and prestige goods. Economic and military might also went hand-in-glove with ritual power. The wild cards in this system were drought and disease, with the former perhaps hitting agricultural production harder than it did livestock. In addition to diseases afflicting the people of the frontier, others, such as rinderpest and trypanosomia-

sis, could decimate a herd of cattle. In Bunyoro-Kitara early polities based on agriculture, iron production, and local religious cults were superseded by somewhat larger polities founded upon pastoralism, raiding, and the Cwezi cults. A major drought may have precipitated this transformation. Many of these later polities were eventually displaced or incorporated into the Nyoro state in a process that is poorly understood.

Available archaeological evidence indicates that aspects of this historical reconstruction require modification. In particular, the earthworks suggest the existence of contemporary polities of possibly different sizes that are not clearly delineated in oral traditions. Furthermore, the construction of earthworks implies a concern with the possession and control of agricultural land rather than livestock, since pastoralists usually take their livestock elsewhere when threatened by raiding. If the earthworks indicate a focus on agricultural production, then they should be correlated with either the predecessors or the successors of the pastoral Cwezi polities. Equating the earthworks with the pre-Cwezi polities implies that these polities were much larger than the historical interpretations would suggest. Moreover, such a link is contradicted by the available dating evidence for Mubende Hill and for several earthworks. Currently, the pastoral Cwezi polities reconstructed by historians seem curiously invisible in the archaeological record. Indeed, given the emphasis on land tenure which permeates the Nyoro state, the earthworks may be linked with the establishment of Bito authority, though the lack of mention of earthworks in the traditions recorded at the Nyoro court weakens this argument. Resolution of these problems should result from current archaeological investigations of earthworks and Cwezi shrine sites.

While many of the details of the political and economic history of Bunyoro-Kitara in the last thousand years remain to be clarified, there are some general lessons to be learned from this work in progress. First, a critical and dialectical approach to the integration of historical and archaeological research will advance our understanding far more than will efforts to employ the results acquired from one discipline to verify interpretations within the other discipline (see also Schmidt 1990; Stahl 1993). Second, application of terms such as "tribe" and "chiefdom" with all their anthropological baggage may force historical and archaeological data into interpretive straitjackets, thereby condemning the past to be forever a ghostly reflection of the ethnographic present. Third and likewise, the use of unilinear evolutionary schemes to explain the origins of states is ill-advised. The history of Bunyoro-Kitara and the encompassing Great Lakes region is replete with numerous and contemporary polities at different levels of scale and integration. We must embrace, rather than ignore, this complexity to explain the development of states. Finally, discarding the notion of the state as the goal of political evolution permits exploration of the diversity of non-state, rather than pre-state, polities. This is an important issue for those concerned with the politics of the past and of the present in developing countries (Robertshaw 1996; see also Stahl this volume). Many Ugandans are turning to the pre-colonial past in an endeavor to forge a sense of national pride and identity; they should discover a rich and remarkable heritage.

Notes

1 The following conventions are used for Bantu prefixes: Bunyoro refers to the region occupied by the Banyoro, who in adjectival form are simply Nyoro.

2 I have chosen to focus upon Tantala's reconstruction since her analysis of the traditions is the most thorough historical treatise yet written about Uganda. Thus, disagreements between the evidence from the archaeology and Tantala's reconstructions should not be read as an attack on the latter's research. Other historical reconstructions could also be subjected to criticism, but shortage of space does not permit me to evaluate the reconstructions proposed by all the historians of pre-colonial Bunyoro-Kitara. It should also be borne in mind that my summary of Tantala's reconstruction is a too brief synopsis of a closely argued dissertation of almost 1,000 pages.

3 This argument is, however, undermined by the fact that one of the radiocarbon dates (GX-0519) was misprinted in the excavation report (Posnansky 1969: 135): the result was AD 1370 (Posnansky 1966: 5), not AD 1570. This misprint, brought to my attention by John Sutton, was overlooked by Schmidt. However, construction of the Bigo earthworks around the fifteenth to seventeenth centuries, as posited by Schmidt, correlates well with the dating of the construction of the Munsa and Kibengo earthworks (Robertshaw 1997).

4 There are no recorded traditions linking Kateboha with Bigo, a site whose location south of the Katonga river is in a drier region than the more northern earthworks and therefore perhaps more suitable for pastoralism than for agriculture.

References

Beattie, J.
1960 *Bunyoro: an African Kingdom*. New York: Holt, Rinehart & Winston.
1971 *The Nyoro State*. Oxford: Clarendon Press.

Berger, I.
1980 Deities, dynasties and oral tradition: the history and legend of the Abacwezi. In *The African Past Speaks*, edited by J. C. Miller. Folkestone: Dawson: 61–81.
1981 *Religion and Resistance*. Tervuren: Musée Royal de l'Afrique Centrale.

Blanton, R. E., G. M. Feinman, S. A. Kowalewski, and P. N. Peregrine
1996 A dual-processual theory for the evolution of Mesoamerican civilization. *Current Anthropology* 37: 1–14.

Buchanan, C. A.
1974 The Kitara Complex: the historical tradition of Western Uganda to the sixteenth century. Ph.D. dissertation, Indiana University.
1975 Of kings and traditions: the case of Bunyoro-Kitara. *International Journal of African Historical Studies* 7: 516–27.

Connah, G.
1996 *Kibiro: The Salt of Bunyoro, Past and Present*. Nairobi: British Institute in Eastern Africa Memoir 13.

DeMarrais, E., L. J. Castillo, and T. Earle
1996 Ideology, materialization, and power strategies. *Current Anthropology* 37: 15–31.

Desmedt, C.
1991a Poteries anciennes décorées à la roulette dans la Région des Grands Lacs. *African Archaeological Review* 9: 161–96.

Earle, T.
1987 Chiefdoms in archaeological and ethnohistorical perspective. *Annual Reviews in Anthropology* 16: 279–308.
1991a The evolution of chiefdoms. In *Chiefdoms: Power, Economy and Ideology*, edited by T. Earle. Cambridge: Cambridge University Press: 1–15.
1991b (ed.) *Chiefdoms: Power, Economy and Ideology*. Cambridge: Cambridge University Press.

Gray, J. M.
1935 The riddle of Biggo. *Uganda Journal* 11: 226–33.

Harvey, C. P. D.
1982 The archaeology of the Southern Sudan: environmental context. In *Culture History in the Southern Sudan*, edited by J. Mack and P. Robertshaw.

Nairobi: British Institute in Eastern Africa Memoir 8: 7–18.

Hassan, F. A.
1981 Historical Nile floods and their importance for climatic change. *Science* 212: 1142–4.

Henige, D. P.
1974 Reflections on early interlacustrine chronology: an essay in source criticism. *Journal of African History* 15: 27–46.
1982 *Oral Historiography*. New York: Longman.

Herring, R. S.
1979 Hydrology and chronology. In *Chronology, Migration and Drought in Interlacustrine Africa*, edited by J. B. Webster. London: Longman: 39–86.

Kamuhangire, E. R., J. Meredith, and P. Robertshaw
1993 Masaka Hill revisited. *Nyame Akuma* 39: 57–60.

Kopytoff, I.
1987 The internal African frontier: the making of African political culture. In *The African Frontier: The Reproduction of Traditional African Societies*, edited by I. Kopytoff. Bloomington: Indiana University Press: 3–84.

Lanning, E. C.
1953 Ancient earthworks in western Uganda. *Uganda Journal* 17: 51–62.
1954 Masaka Hill – an ancient center of worship. *Uganda Journal* 18: 24–30.
1957 Protohistoric pottery in Uganda. In *Third Pan-African Congress on Prehistory*, edited by J. D. Clark. London: Chatto & Windus: 313–17.
1959 The death of chieftain Kateboha. *Uganda Journal* 23: 186–8.
1960 The earthworks at Kibengo, Mubende District. *Uganda Journal* 24: 183–96.
1966 Excavations at Mubende Hill. *Uganda Journal* 30: 153–63.
1970 Ntusi: an ancient capital site in western Uganda. *Azania* 5: 39–54.

Meredith, J. N.
n.d. Preliminary pottery report on the 1987 Mubende Hill excavations. Manuscript on file with the author.

Mounteney-Jephson, A. J.
1890 *Emin Pasha and the Rebellion at the Equator: A Story of Nine Months' Experiences in the Last of the Soudan Provinces*. 2nd edn. London: Sampson, Low, Marston, Searle & Rivington.

Nyakatura, J. W.
1973 *Anatomy of an African Kingdom: A History of Bunyoro-Kitara*. Edited by G. N. Uzoigwe. Garden City, NY: Anchor Press/Doubleday.

Ogot, B.A.
1984 The Great Lakes region. In *General History of Africa IV: Africa from the Twelfth to the Sixteenth Century*, edited by D. T. Niane. Unesco: 498–524.

Oliver, R.
1953 A question about the Bacwezi. *Uganda Journal* 17: 135–7.
1977 The East African interior. In *The Cambridge History of Africa, vol. 3: from c. 1050 to c. 1600*, edited by R. Oliver. Cambridge: Cambridge University Press: 621–69.

Posnansky, M.
1966 Kingship, archaeology and historical myth. *Uganda Journal* 30: 1–12.
1969 Bigo bya Mugenyi. *Uganda Journal* 33: 125–50.

Reid, D. A. M.
1990 Ntusi and its hinterland: further investigations of the Later Iron Age and pastoral ecology in southern Uganda. *Nyame Akuma* 33: 26–8.
1991 The role of cattle in the Later Iron Age communities of Southern Uganda. Ph.D. thesis, Cambridge University.

Reid, D. A. M., and J. Meredith
1993 Houses, pots and more cows: the 1991 excavation season at Ntusi. *Nyame Akuma* 40: 58–61.

Robertshaw, P.
1988 The interlacustrine region: a progress report. *Nyame Akuma* 30: 37–8.
1994 Archaeological survey, ceramic analysis and state formation in western Uganda. *African Archaeological Review* 12: 105–31.
1996 Knowledge and power. *African Archaeological Review* 13: 7–9.
1997 Munsa Earthworks: a preliminary report. *Azania* 32: 1–20.
in press Explaining the origins of the state in East Africa. In *New Approaches in Later East African Archaeology*, edited by Chaprukha Kusimba and Sibel Barut Kasimba. Philadelphia: University of Pennsylvania Press.

Roscoe, J.
1923 *The Bakitara*. Cambridge: Cambridge University Press.

Schmidt, P. R.
1978 *Historical Archaeology: A Structural Approach in an African Culture*. Westfield: Greenwood.
1990 Oral traditions, archaeology and history: a short reflective history. In *A History of African Archaeology*, edited by P. Robertshaw. Portsmouth, N. H.: Heinemann: 252–70.

Stahl, A. B.
  1993 Concepts of time and approaches to analogical reasoning in historical perspective. *American Antiquity* 58: 235–60.
Steinhart, E. I.
  1981 Herders and farmers: the tributary mode of production in western Uganda. In *Modes of Production in Africa*, edited by D. Crummey and C. C. Stewart. Beverly Hills: Sage Publications: 115–55.
Sutton, J. E. G.
  1985 Ntusi and the "dams". *Azania* 20: 172–5.
  1993 The antecedents of the interlacustrine kingdoms. *Journal of African History* 34: 33–64.
Tantala, R. L.
  1989 The early history of Kitara in Western Uganda: process models of religious and political change. Ph.D dissertation, University of Wisconsin Madison.
Uganda Government
  1964. Vegetation map of Uganda. Entebbe: Government Printer.
Wrigley, C. C.
  1958 Some thoughts on the Bacwezi. *Uganda Journal* 22: 11–17.
Yoffee, N.
  1993 Too many chiefs? (or, Safe texts for the '90s). In *Archaeological Theory: Who Sets the Agenda?*, edited by N. Yoffee and A. Sherratt. Cambridge: Cambridge University Press: 60–78.

11

The (in)visible roots of Bunyoro-Kitara and Buganda in the Lakes region: AD 800–1300

DAVID L. SCHOENBRUN

Introduction

Between 1600 and 1800, in eastern Africa's Great Lakes region, the states of Bunyoro-Kitara and Buganda formed and began to export their bureaucratic, militaristic, and religious hegemony to neighboring societies. They did so with little or no connection to intercontinental or maritime trading systems. They did so in wet, dry, highland, and lakeshore environments. They did so using metals, cattle, bananas, grains, fishing, and hunting, in varying combinations, as their technological and agricultural bases. But they also did so with less visible resources, with funds of meaning and concepts of power and with sometimes abstract units of social organization. This essay will argue that the history of these visible and invisible roots of these two states between the Great Lakes reveals that any sort of evolutionist model for state formation must take these factors into account.

Exploring these issues begins with the evidence from Great Lakes societies which diagnoses their own analytical categories for social life. If scholars choose to settle on chiefdoms as important units of study they must understand their importance to those who lived in them. Such a condition highlights the necessity of interdisciplinary scholarship. Archaeologists, comparative linguists, and comparative ethnographers generate information on the varieties of chiefdoms and, more importantly, these scholars may suggest what other sorts of social and material relations – family structure and gender – may be implicated in the development of chiefdoms. For historical linguists, such data emerge from the comparative study of retention[1] and innovation in the vocabulary (material and lexical) of power, settlements,

social relationships, and gendered identities (see Appendix). But only careful survey and excavation by archaeologists will confirm these sequences of innovation and reproduced continuity.

For the period after 800, researchers in the Great Lakes region will find fairly detailed records of change in three vital arenas: environment and climate (Hassan 1981; Schoenbrun 1994b), agriculture and settlement (Reid 1991, 1995; Robertshaw 1994; Schoenbrun 1993) and technology and material culture (Childs 1991; Connah 1991, 1996). Though few studies have addressed themselves to all these matters, the evidentiary base for exploring the roots of states between the Great Lakes is enviably dense.

This chapter builds on this evidence to summarize the regional agricultural histories of two geographical-linguistic zones within the larger Great Lakes region: Rutaran and North Nyanzan. These agricultural histories reveal some of the material bases of wealth and power. The chapter turns next to some thoughts on the opening and closing of an "internal frontier" in the Central Grasslands. Following on this, I consider the semantic histories of some words which describe forms of power. A final section recounts the historical development of units of social organization and gender relations in the context of the emergence of the internal frontier. I conclude by reflecting on how these findings require modifications to evolutionist paradigms of state formation.

Regional agricultural history

Between 800 and 1300 agricultural and technological specializations took distinctive regional forms across the Great Lakes zone. They included specialized pastoralism (Reid 1991; Schoenbrun 1993), intensive banana farming (Schoenbrun 1993; Wrigley 1996: 60–1), an entirely novel form of pottery decoration and shape (Connah 1991; Desmedt 1991; Robertshaw 1994; Stewart 1993), and the increasingly widespread practice of iron smithing (Robertshaw 1994; Sutton 1993). These developments left permanent impressions in the palaeo-environmental record from parts of the Great Lakes region. They also heralded an entirely new set of related changes in political scale, the notions of power which gave life to this new politics, and the forms of settlements which encoded intimate parts of the new politics of power (Reid 1995, 1996; Robertshaw this volume; Schoenbrun 1996a, 1996b; Tantala 1989).

The linguistic data reveal a remarkable simultaneity in the timing of the development of both specialized pastoralism and intensive banana farming. Cattle had been part of the legacy of Great Lakes food systems from very early on, and the span of time between the development of a breeding taxonomy and a color taxonomy is fully two millennia (Schoenbrun 1993: 45–50). When the banana arrived it seems to have been taken up at a somewhat faster pace with no more than 600 years separating the innovation of the first varietals from the development of generics and plantation terms (Schoenbrun 1993: 50–3). However, these slightly different rates of change harmonized after 1000 to 1200, with the explosion in terms for cattle colors and the development of generic terms for bananas. Reid's study of cattle bones from Ntusi and associated sites (1991, 1996: 10) strongly supports placing the emergence of specialized pastoralism in the central grasslands, probably after the twelfth century.

These changes occurred together with two other transformations recognized in the archaeological and palaeo-environmental records: the spread of a distinctive rouletted style of pottery decoration, the complete removal of secondary forests (matched by an expansion of grasslands), and a notable decrease in rainfall which the Roda Nilometer dates to between 1200 and 1350 (Robertshaw this volume, p. 131, discussing Hassan 1981). Rouletted pottery traditions rather quickly developed distinctive facies (Connah 1991; Desmedt 1991) and a distinctive seriation (Robertshaw 1994). From this sequence, Robertshaw suggests a correlation, in Bunyoro-Kitara, between seriated rouletted potting traditions and emerging site-size hierarchies (Robertshaw 1994, this volume).

The internal frontier between the Great Lakes

Distinct emphases on cattle or bananas generated conditions in which people crafted new links between religious and political forms of power. Because religious and political specialists were deemed reponsible for ensuring the health of food production systems,[2] changes in the social relations of power accompanied radical changes in food production. Between the Great Lakes these processes heralded the earliest struggles over people and wealth recognizable in parts of the region's oral historiography, archaeology, and the comparative linguistic and ethnographic records (Berger 1981; Connah 1991; Newbury 1991; Robertshaw 1994; Schoenbrun 1995; Tantala 1989). They form the groundwork on which later political edifices were to stand, however uncertain their tenure may have been.

People chose to emphasize bananas or cattle as a response to new social pressures as well as a response to tensions within the agricultural ecology visited on them

by climatic and vegetational changes. Dispersal and renewal of people and power appear to have been signatures of the history of the Great Lakes region, indicating thus the frustration of pursuing purely evolutionist paradigms for the progress of political centralization. While it is true that political scale grew over linear time, it is also true that its centers were precarious and fleeting.

These qualities of Great Lakes institutional history characterize a historical process protrayed elegantly by Igor Kopytoff's notion of the internal frontier (Kopytoff 1987: 3–84). Kopytoff's formulation models the development of internal tensions in older areas of settlement, their roles in ejecting members from their ancestral communities into areas of lower population density, the eventual re-establishment on this internal frontier of portions of the social and cultural codes of the ancestral areas, and the later sculpting of these codes into ideologies of firstcomer-status and of patrimonial control of both land and ritual practice. Robertshaw (this volume) has linked this process to a two-stage development of political complexity in one part of the Great Lakes region, Bunyoro, where mixed-farming communities initially settled the lands north of the Kafu River and where the development of pastoralism improved the range of environments and forms of material wealth available to leaders for use in their community-building strategies.

Between Victoria-Nyanza and the central grasslands (Figure 11.1), this process appears to lead, inexorably, into an evolutionist historical narrative. The spiral nature of the narrative, the seeming expansion of territorial reach for each new sort of settlement, follows from the successive additions of "elements of complexity" to the villages or chiefdoms. These expansions of political scale appear out of the dialectical interaction of scarcity in labor and land with the abundance of pasture and trade in salt, iron, barkcloths, and foodstuffs. The spiral straightens into a line when empty lands cease easily to be within the reach of marginalized or otherwise disaffected members of ancestral communities. No longer able to vote with their feet, the subjects of erstwhile chiefs who increasingly demand tribute (in kind and in labor) and allegiance (at court and in contract relations), must stand and negotiate. With this development, the story reaches the threshold of state-formation: the once-empty interstices between zones of ancient and dense settlement become the frozen frontiers over which the leaders of centers of population and political complexity begin to struggle for control and over which they began to deploy coercive elements of instrumental power. It is a short step from these competitions to military expansionism. And Robertshaw (this volume) has shown how oral histori-

Figure 11.1   The Great Lakes region, showing language groups mentioned in text and archaeological sites.

ographies from the Bito kingdom of Bunyoro-Kitara tell of such expansions and contractions. Examples quickly multiply (for example, see Wrigley 1996: 192–206).

Such stories crop up continually because their governing questions require them to take one of two characteristic shapes: linear evolutionism or a dialectical process of expansion and constriction. In neither of these genres has there been much room for historical discussions of either organizing principles of social life, like gender-relations (but see Reid 1993), or for analyses of cognitive systems which both conditioned and responded to new opportunities for creating forms of wealth and power. Archaeologists and pre-colonial historians, however, are well on their way to redressing these inequities (McIntosh 1993; Newbury 1991; Ray 1991; Wrigley 1996: 79–121).

The argument now must turn to consider the extent to which long-neglected aspects of pre-colonial African political history, like intellectual histories of power, constitute some of the visible and invisible roots of African states. This tack leads the story back to the agency of people – men and women at the edges of chiefly or state power – too-often left out of the arguments about the origins of states.

The two powers: instrumental and creative

Power takes a variety of forms but seems to break down into two types: instrumental and creative. Instrumental power secures outcomes through the control of people's actions (Blanton et al. 1996: 2–3; Roscoe 1993: 112–14). Creative power manipulates and invents forms of meaning (Bourdieu 1990: 112–21). These meanings possess several capacities. They can legitimate instrumental power, they can help people renegotiate their social relationships, or they can help groups establish and superintend the boundaries between disorder and order. The two forms intersect repeatedly because one is not epiphenomenal on the other. Since instrumental power is crafted within the semantic universe of moral agency – precisely that universe in which creative power works – the two forms must be studied together. For example, chiefship and healing each brings together aspects of both sorts of power.

The fusions of instrumental and creative power achieved by persons in these institutions, and the borders they draw around the two sorts of power may be studied historically by pursuing the semantic histories of words which represent important distinctions in Great Lakes theories of power (Table 11.1). The following terms will be discussed: *kupánga* "create," *kudèma* "order," *kugàbá* "give out, apportion," *kukída* "surpass, over-

come," *mâna* "capacity to create life," and *-gàlá* "physical principle of life." The semantic histories of these terms lack chronological precision,[3] but the forgiving reader will be rewarded with a sense of the historical development of the visible and invisible contents of the state.

Relations between the two powers

Great Lakes Bantu societies understood that one axis along which they could negotiate their social lives connected the capacity for creating order to the capacity for life. The ancient verbs *kupánga* and *kudèma* expressed this first principle and the nouns *imáàna* or *imáànyi* and *-gàlá* expressed the latter idea (Cf. Table 11.1).

The most widely distributed meaning for *kupánga* is "to act, create or make something corporeal" (see also Wrigley 1996: 81–2). This ancient meaning narrowed to "to seize by magic, control by powerful speech plus a material item" and narrowed further still in the Proto Great Lakes Bantu noun meaning "supernatural creative power, including the creator personage." From this meaning, Western Lakes and West Nyanza communities derived terms for "bloodpact," "to prevent rain," and "to shine intensely (of the sun)," respectively (see Table 11.1).

The verb *kudèma* carries two meanings with tantalizing hints at a common origin. The very same phonological and tonological shape means both "to become heavy" and "to create a corporeal thing (like making a drum or stringing a bow)." Both meanings may be reconstructed for Proto Savanna. In the latter meaning, the verb overlaps with *kubumba* "to fashion a pot" (in some languages the two are synonyms [i.e., in Haavu]). These two meanings produce interconnected semantic histories. In Proto Mashariki the meaning "to overwhelm, fail" appears to have been derived from "to become heavy." In Proto Western Lakes the noun "creator, maker (an attribute of the creator personage)" appears to have been derived from the Proto Savanna meaning "to create a corporeal thing." In Proto Rutara this meaning narrowed further in the verb "to control, govern, dominate." The interrelationship between the two fields of meaning comes in Rutaran times. By adding to a verb for creative power the meanings of legitimate political power, Rutaran communities brought into existence the claim that both the King and the Creator ruled by overcoming obstacles and thus ruled by creating power from their acts of domination.

Great Lakes societies built other semantic bridges from creative power to instrumental power. In the meaning "physical life force," the ancient noun *-gàlá* (class 5/6) reaches its widest meaning. It came also to mean (class

Table 11.1 *A semantogram for five terms for power in Bantu*

	*kupánga	*kudèma	*kugàbá	*-mànIa	*-gàlá
Proto Savanna ¬ ¬	"Act, create something"; Creator"	"Become heavy"; "Put in order"	"Give out, distribute"	"Think"	"Physical principle of life"
Proto Mashariki ¬ ¬	"Seize by magic; Give power to object via speech"	"Overwhelm, fail"	"Make decisions, command"		
Proto Great Lakes Bantu ¬ ¬ ¬	"Super-natural creative power; name for agent of creation"; "shine (of sun)"	"Creator, maker (attribute of creator)"	"Divide up, distribute"	"Life force, capacity to give the life force"	
Proto Rutara Bantu		"Control, govern, dominate"			
Proto Western Lakes	"Blood pact"; "Prevent rain"	"Creator, maker [retained]"	"Gift exchange of cattle [Proto West Highlands]"		"Rich person, leader"; "Sons [Proto Forest]"

Explanatory guide: Read the semantogram from top to bottom in order to move from the past towards the present and thus to follow that linear course of semantic retention and shift. Blank squares indicate retention of earlier meaning. Words with asterisks preceding them ("starred forms") are proposed phonological reconstructions of the sound shapes as they existed in the Proto Savanna (or earlier) communities. Rules of regular sound correspondences underlie these proposals.

1/2) "rich person or leader" and (class 5) "sons (those whom a single wife bore and who will stand to inherit a father's property)" in the Western Lakes Bantu-speaking communities of the Great Lakes region. As well, the ancient verb *kukída "to pass over, surpass" narrowed to mean "to heal, cure" before Western Lakes-speakers added the meaning "to become rich." Finally, the Proto Great Lakes noun *mâna "life force, capacity to give the life force" appears to have been derived from the Bantu verb *-mànIa "to think" (Schoenbrun 1997). The derivation means that, late in the dissolution of the Proto Great Lakes dialect chain, people understood a direct connection to exist between knowledge and creative power. And they understood that such a connection served as a central feature in legitimizing the instrumental power of politics.

Not all terms which spoke of power redrew the boundaries between the instrumental and the creative. Some never crossed this semantic divide. The verb *kugàbá, in its widest meaning, expressed the act of giving away something, of dividing something up between two or more individuals. Languages from Cameroon (Duala) to Natal

(Zulu) express this action with a reflex of the verb *kugàbá. In Proto Mashariki, the meaning narrowed to "to exercise power, execute decisions." Proto Kivu society felt the necessity to distinguish acts of giving things from acts of distributing things by having added a prepositional suffix to the ancient verb root to express the latter meaning. A later step in the elaboration of gift-exchange ideology occurred in Proto Rutara society, where the Proto Kivu prepositional verb *kugàbúlira came to mean "cattle contract" in a class 14 deverbative form.

Great Lakes Bantu-speaking communities classified the powers in their world in part by fashioning discursive distinctions between instrumental and creative powers. Instrumental power involved getting people to do things. It included conceptions of warfare and violence. The main division in this field separated the power of order from the power of conquest or domination. This sort of divide within instrumental forms of power represents a classic means to establish political legitimacy – a leader is a civilizer, a conqueror, or a civilizing conqueror. A leader bridges this divide between conquest and order. On the other hand, creative power involved the mysteries of the life force and the quest for balance and health. The main division in this field lay in distinguishing the capacity to give life (**mâna*) from the force of life itself (**-gàlà*). This phenomenological construction enabled the art of healing through acts of empowering words (such as the words spoken over medicines or as the words spoken in divination). The conceptual separation of the gift of life from the force of life itself meant that people expected or hoped that healers possessed a practical knowledge which could have bridged that gap. Healers, through their knowledge and their speech, made possible the maintenance or re-establishment of a link between the sources of life (rain, blood, milk, semen, etc.) and its different manifestations (crops, children, cattle, etc.).

People transformed what had been instrumental power into creative power, and vice versa, by reapplying terms for the one to qualities of the other. Redrawing the divides between one or the other sort of power may represent social processes of metonymy. For example, when Proto Rutara-speakers added the meanings "control, govern, dominate" to the verb **kulèma*, which had meant before "to create or make a corporeal thing," they expressed both an attribute of chiefship and an attribute of **imâna*, the force which gives life. Proto Rutaran society brought into discursive existence a metonymic joining of king and spiritual force, and they made it possible thereby to pose moral hypotheses about the conditions of the one by reference to the actions of the other. The familiar dyad of "sacral kingship," where a king represented his people and his kingdom and possessed moral responsibility for the health and fertility of both, comes partly into existence through the kind of semantic extensions and colonizations of hitherto distinct sorts of power which the example of Proto Rutara **kulèma* illustrates.[4]

The dispersed creative powers so far discussed probably were the prerogatives of internal frontiersmen who sought through them to set up ritual and hegemonic control over the land. But they were also the nemeses of would-be centralizers of instrumental power (and, later, of the coercive form of state power) because they and their practitioners were so difficult to supervise (Tantala 1989: 674–9) and because they so easily formed bases for armed revolt. Familiar figures in this regard come to us through oral historiographic representations of rebellious or innovative healers like Nyabingi, Ryángombe, Kiranga, and certain Cwezi figures. In this regard, the historical development of "powers" cannot be studied apart from the historical development of the units of social organization and gender relations in and through which "power" had life.

Social organization and gender

To grasp the elusive qualities of divides in the semantic fields of words for "power" we must review the history of some Rutaran and North Nyanzan units of social organization and gender relations. These institutional and ideological dimensions to the social history of the region, before states formed, represent key locations for the generation of divides and connections between creative and instrumental power. Thus, together with agricultural histories, the social history of institution and gender must be integrated into any social history of the roots of state-formation.

Some visible contents of power: space, gender, and food
Among the many interconnected semantic fields that bear traces of the history of the social organization of space in Rutara and North Nyanza, five will be discussed here: "clan," "lineage," "agnates," "valuable farmland," and "courtyard."[5] The etymology for one of these terms, **-kika*, reveals its earlier meaning to have been limited to that of "homestead," where it has now taken on the meaning of "clan" in North Nyanza. Another, **-gàndá*, has an important residential dimension to its meanings elsewhere in Bantu, but has come to refer to the highly dispersed exogamous, totemic, and (rarely) corporate clans of Rutaran societies. A third term, *ssiga*, refers to a maximal patrilineage in Ganda (and in Kuria). Another term, **-dá*, in the meaning "family" (Ganda) or "lineage" (Haya, Soga, Nande), seems to have been derived from the Proto Bantu root for "womb, interior (of the body)." The noun **-bánjà* means "building site, place of authority," in its widest distributions. It came to mean, as well, "dispute" and "debt," in Great Lakes Bantu before West Nyanza-speaking farmers added the meaning "valuable farmland (especially with bananas)." The last term for which a reconstruction and an etymology may be offered here is **-buga*. This means "courtyard" (in class 7/8) and "Queen Sister" (in class 11) in Ganda and Nkore. All these terms express histories of the social relations of power. And the histories of the development of new meanings for each of them reflect the development of social complexity and the creation of institutional locations for the deployment of creative and instrumental powers (Table 11.2).

Changes in gendered identities drove these historical processes. For example, ethnographic evidence exists to define the hearth (**-higa*) and the house (**-ka* and **-ju*) as female domains (Ehret 1998: 151). On the face of it, this suggests that the extension of meanings for these terms, in Rutara and North Nyanza, to include patrilineage and

Table 11.2 *A semantogram for five terms for social organization and space in Bantu*

	*-ka 5/6, 7/8	*-gàndá 11/10	*-pɪga 5/6	*-buga 7/8, 11/10	*-bánjà 5/6, 7/8, 11/6
Proto Bantu, Savanna, or Mashariki ¬ ¬ ¬	"House-hold, homestead" [Mashariki]	"House, village, leader's compound" [Bantu]; "Clan or matriclan" [Mashariki]	"Firestones" [Bantu]	"Free land near home" [Bantu]	"Building site" [Bantu]; "Place of authority" [W. Bantu]
Proto Great Lakes Bantu	"Homestead or house (possibly patrifocal)"[6]	"Relatives, family of agnates"			"Building site" 7/8; "Dispute" 5/6, 11/6; "Debt" 5/6
Proto West Nyanza Bantu ¬ ¬ ¬ ¬	"Homestead or house"	"Agnatic descent group, possibly patrifocal"; ["Dispersed patrilineage" in Western Lakes].	"Eponymous patrilineage"		"Valuable farmland, Debt, Dispute"; ["Building site and Dispute" retained in Western Lakes]
Proto Rutara Bantu	"Patrifocal household" 5/6, 7/8	"Dispersed patriclan"	"Clan settlement" [S. Rutara]	"Courtyard; large open space; village, town"	"Valuable farmland, developed farmlands (esp. with bananas)" 7/8
Proto North Nyanza Bantu	"Homestead" 5/6 "Clan" 7/8 [Class 7/8 normally augments size]	"kinship, relatives, family" 1/2, 9/10	"Branch of patriclan"	"Chief's residence" 9/10 "Royal capital" 7/8	"Valuable farmland, developed farmlands, (esp. with bananas or potential for them)" 7/8

patriclan can be expected to reflect the outcome of a struggle over the gendered control of material and cultural resources referred to by the new meanings added to the old words: children, productive lands, livestock, and jural process (Håkansson 1989). Even though the material contexts in which such struggles took place in North Nyanzan and Rutaran societies, before 1500, are fairly well known, the plain fact is that we can have no hope of recovering the precise social contexts for the initial use of metaphors based on the house and on the female body to express various sorts of units of social organization.

We can, however, recognize that the contexts for their use were not infinite. They were located within wider but

finite fields of production, reproduction, and cognition (S. Feierman, personal communication, 1994). If it is safe to say that a limited number of forms of production and reproduction strongly suggest a limited number of possible forms for house or lineage metaphors, then we may make some headway toward social histories between the Great Lakes. If such a generative approach proves untenable, we had better stop here and admit the futility of searching for the spatial contexts of social and economic life, contexts which we rightly suspect to have been as fundamentally important in the past as was "the environment." Considering the ethnographic evidence for some of the distinctive features of the social space expressed by house and lineage metaphors offers a way to proceed

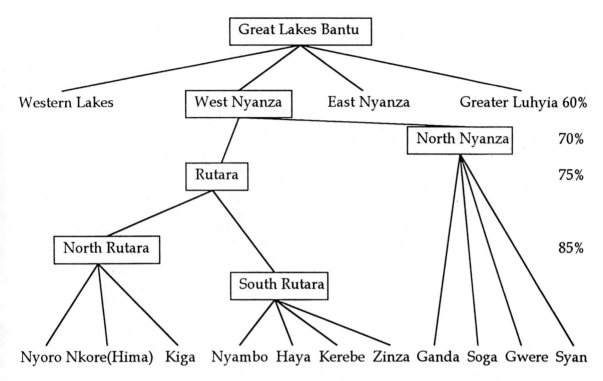

Figure 11.2   Great Lakes Bantu and its subgroups: glottochronology reckoned at a shared retention rate of 86% per 500 years.

(Schoenbrun 1996b). Because of restrictions on space, I can offer here only a summary of this social history for two geographical-linguistic portions of the Great Lakes region: Rutaran and North Nyanzan societies (see Figure 11.2)

Between 800 and 1300, families changed their structure by emphasizing patrilineality over undifferentiated descent or an older matrilineality (Ehret 1998: 149–55; Schoenbrun 1995: 8–13). The linguistic evidence for this consists in the fact that individual terms for undifferentiated or bilateral forms of descent are more widely and discontiguously distributed in Bantu than are individual terms for lineality. These latter terms are more numerous and have narrower and more densely packed distributions. Together, the distributional evidence and semantic histories suggest that explicitly gendered lineality, whether matrifocal or patrifocal, is the more recent (though still quite ancient) social innovation (Ahmed 1996; Ehret, 1998; Vansina 1990).

Complex levels of patrilineality, which held explicit claims to landuse rights, emerged during the period when Rutara and North Nyanza groups formed. With these developments, fertility came to be controlled jurally by males and ritually by both men and women (Berger 1995; Tantala 1989: 674–9). The jural control wielded by men perhaps assisted them in concentrating people and their descendants on productive property (*-bánjà*), in the contexts of growing economic specialization and competition.

These developments formed part of a response to an environmental crisis near Lake Victoria and in the highlands east of the Kivu Rift (Schoenbrun 1994b; Robertshaw this volume, pp. 126–7) and to social conflict in those same areas. They also formed part of a response to the new challenges to homesteads which lay in the open savannahs (Reid 1991, 1993; Sutton 1993) and in the dense banana gardens (Schmidt 1978: 32–5; Schoenbrun 1993; Wrigley 1996: 60–1). The emphasis on lineality grew to include the control and distribution of new forms of surplus, like cattle (in North Rutara society, controlled by the homestead head, the *nyineka*) and perennial croplands (*-bánjà* and **-taka*) rich with the invested labor of wives (in North Nyanza society, controlled by the family head, the *mukulu*, or by the lineage head, the *mutaka*).

Above all, this was a dialectical process of historical change which included environmental parameters, the deploying of power, innovations in the character of units of social organization, and profound changes in gendered social relations. It was not determined by any one of these factors, as the differing histories of units of social organization charted below reveal.

In North Nyanza, the word *ekika* replaced the word *orugàndá* in the meaning "dispersed patriclan." It did so at the same time that North Nyanza societies innovated a host of new words (including *-bánjà*) which reflected agricultural experiments with intensive banana farming. During this period (between 1000 and 1300) the concentrations of population around the best banana-bearing lands made local collections of homesteads the new foci of the social relations of clanship. This differed from the widely dispersed character of clans (sing. **-rugàndá*) elsewhere in West Nyanza societies like Rutara. Land for bananas was indeed plentiful in Buganda, but the best plots were then, as they are now, not often contiguous. They were separated by swamps and tongues of barren, rocky hilltops. Moreover, this era coincided with a period of reduced rainfall amounts (Hassan 1981), very likely rendering the best banana gardens less numerous than they have been at any time since. What seems an environmentally determinist argument must not obscure the dialectical relations between the physical locations of the discontiguous, relatively rare lands best for bananas and the instrumentality of local collections of homesteads in providing the labor required to convert these "better" lands into banana gardens. Localities did not provide labor automatically. They did so through marriage ties and through gendered divisions of labor. As wives, women were the knot in the marriage tie between patrilineages. Why all this should have taken place may become clearer if we consider the role of the cognatic family group (sing. *olulá*; pl. *endá*) in this scenario.

The center of *olulá*'s semantic domain is "inside" the body, and quite often the womb itself. The North Nyanza referents specify that cognatic family groups (pl. *endá*) rarely attain the status of lineages capable of establishing legal claims to the land based on first-comer status (and, later, as granted by the king). Nor did family groups succeed in establishing ritual claims to productive land, a right normally achieved by burying three or four generations of its members on the same plot (Mair 1934: 164; Roscoe 1911: 134). In Ganda society, the cognatic family group (sing. *olulá*) is generally fewer in number than the maximal patrilineage (sing. *ssiga*). This contrast reveals the central challenge to reproducing groups through time:

because one womb cannot achieve this alone, others must be brought *inside* as wives or husbands and their children must be given legal status as insiders, as "us" not "them," as agnates not affines. Why North Nyanzan-speakers came to draw this line around those sharing real or putative patrilineal descent and not around those sharing matrilineal descent cannot now be known.

To the west and south of North Nyanzan societies, Rutaran societies manipulated these combinations of environmental realities and social change very differently. In the Rutaran lands, the development of pastoralism had radically changed the conditions under which Hima women could improve their positions as wives. In the central grasslands, specialized pastoralism began as early as AD 1100 (Reid 1991: 255–69, 1993: 22–4). One of the possible outcomes of struggles for control over pastoralist knowledge may have been the exclusion of women from herding. This exclusion perhaps followed on from men having succeeded in developing control over cattle, in the first place, through an ideology of patrilineal descent and inheritance. This would have put livestock in male hands at the sort of mixed farming sites, such as Ntusi (and, later, Bigo), around which experiments in specialized pastoralism flourished (Reid 1991; Robertshaw 1994; Sutton 1993).

On the closing internal frontiers, formed by the specialists in herding or in banana farming who had settled just beyond or within nodes of ancient mixed-farming communities, clan heterogeneity had an enduring nature. With respect to perennially cropped banana gardens (*kibánjà* or *lusuku*), small families (pl. *endá*) would not have been able to conserve their holdings as consistently, from generation to generation, as larger ones might have been able to do. With fewer members, the holdings of an heirless departed member of a small family (sing. *olulá*) would have more often reverted to the "homestead or patrilineage head" (sing. *mukúlú*[7] in Rutara and West Highlands) or to the "person holding lands in the name of the clan" (sing. *mutaka* in North Nyanza), for reassignment to strangers. Where larger cognatic families (pl. *endá*) lived, heirless plots would have been rarer because it would have been correspondingly more likely that when a brother died another member of the succession lineage (an adelphic group in North Nyanza society) would have been approaching adulthood (Fallers 1956: 84ff).

On the early internal frontier, where land was plentiful but labor scarce, a leader of a small family (sing. *olulá*) or clan (sing. *ekika*) would thus have been in a position more often than leaders of larger families or clans to remake the content of their group by allocating land to outsiders. This condition would have had the effect of emphasizing unequal amounts of instrumental power over land and people because the Rutaran lineage head (sing. *mukúlú*) or the North Nyanza clan lands holder (sing. *mutaka*) both held potential reallocation rights to much of the land. Wherever the most desirable lands were in short supply, as around North Nyanza and Southern Rutara banana gardens, the only way a cognatic family (sing. *olulá*) could grow was through having more children, hence the value of marriage and wives. And it is precisely in these contexts that the house and belly metaphors emerged together to represent small and large patrilineages. Where lands or pastures were abundant (as, perhaps, at Ntusi) an enterprising homestead head (sing. *nyineka* or sing. *mukúlú*) could add potential land-holding strangers to its group, as recipients of reallocated rights to cleared land or new rights to clear new fields. In these homesteads (pl. *amaka*), wives' fertility provided the ultimate insurance against a clan's or a cognatic family's disappearance.

Conclusion: the invisible contents of political society before the states

In an excellent article on practice theory and state formation, Paul Roscoe argued that the potential for political centralization – the concentration of power over others – exists "wherever humans have wants that can best or only be satisfied through the agency of others, since these conditions promote struggles for dominion to satisfy these wants" (Roscoe 1993: 114–15). The functional logic of the North Nyanzan cognatic family (sing. *olulá*) and of the Rutaran homestead (sing. *eka*), in their historically variable forms, constitute such conditions. But the struggle for dominion follows more than one path because the resources – the forms of power – also differ. Differences between, for example, the sizes and character of clans and lineages, reflect outcomes of "the creativity of interested humans operating both within and on these and other, non-material circumstances to augment their power and satisfy their wants" (Roscoe 1993: 115). Material circumstances condition the human capacity for manipulating redistributions of wealth, engineering shortages of key goods (including wives or husbands), and deploying surplus as forms of political entrepreneurship.

Between AD 1000 and AD 1500, the conditions of specialization constrained some and facilitated others' ability to "remove themselves entirely from the oppressive power of others . . . through relocation" (Roscoe 1993: 115). To some degree, the communities which first relocated to the central savannahs were forced to do so by circumscribed access to the mixed farming lands in the old core nodes of ancient settlement. Those who remained in the core nodes converted to intensive banana farming. Those who fled re-established the old mixed farming system at sites like Ntusi, only to release into specialization a range of persons who became herders. These latter communities effectively "closed" the internal frontier which their ancestors had opened.

Evidence from the Later Iron Age sites discussed by Robertshaw (this volume) add flesh to this skeletal outline. Ntusi's excavators, principally Andrew Reid, have unearthed evidence of an ivory atelier together with a few cowrie beads (Reid 1991: 217). The still rarer finds of glass beads, at sites some distance from Ntusi itself, surely suggest exchanges with the coast (Reid 1991: 216; Wrigley 1996: 87) and hint at novel forms of adornment. While no firm argument may yet be offered for a chief's or a healer's having monopolized trade "routes" (but see Tantala 1989: 671–9), the clear links between these artefacts, Ntusi and its surrounding sites, and the challenges faced by those who pioneered the internal frontier invite reflections on the correlation between new powerful people, new forms of power, and new forms of adornment.

At Kibiro, Graham Connah discovered a pottery sequence which reveals settlement there from the tenth century. Connah also believes that production of high quality salt is nearly as old, beginning perhaps early in the present millennium (Connah 1991: 491). Robertshaw's excellent work brings us to the verge of some compelling correlations between archaeology, comparative linguistics, and oral historiography. Though he feels uncertain that heterogeneity in rouletted pottery traditions from earthworks sites reveals those sites to have been "centers of small and competing regional polities" (Robertshaw this volume, p. 145), the evidence offered here for changes in gendered units of social organization in Rutaran communities means that we may interpret his and Reid's findings at Ntusi to represent the earliest phases of the opening of the internal frontier. At that stage a homestead's principal challenge lay in the struggle for followers. This challenge may well have generated the still-poorly understood presence of bead ornamentation at Ntusi. Perhaps the gift-exchange of beaded items marked early patron–client relations.

However, the size and complexity of polities are not the same thing. If leaders must guarantee the safety, fertility, and fecundity of the land and people under their rule as well as distribute resources so as to create and maintain social relationships, then the size of a chiefdom or kingdom will be a function of the combination of productivity and the proximity of neighboring competitors. Wrigley argues that this point means that early Ganda political power could well have been based on very small territories and populations (1996: 84).

Telling the story of the development of monarchy thus depends as much on cognitive codes for instrumental and creative power as it does on material conditions for prosperity and threat. The joining of creative and instrumental powers in the persons of chief and healer, during the West Nyanza eras, echoes Wrigley's argument, and marks "chiefship" or "royalty" as having existed during periods well before 800. The initial movement into an internal frontier, then, offered the potential to change the character of this joining of the two powers. To be sure, Rutaran images of leadership redrew boundaries between the two powers, boundaries perhaps initially described by the creative healers who enjoyed successes in meeting the challenges of life in the drier zones surrounding places like Ntusi. Both Rutaran and North Nyanzan societies participated in this first movement at the same time as they generated an internal frontier within the wetter zones just inland from Victoria Nyanza. In the latter case, North Nyanzan conceptions of royalty looked familiar to Rutaran views. Both, however, lacked a set of institutions to create a state from a king (Wrigley 1996: 241–51). These institutions developed around service and loaning, to bind together far-flung communities in debt-relations using the institutional ideology of kinship and clanship as exclusionary means to generate a hierarchy of first-comers and newcomers withing the structures of service and clientship.

The two powers, then, were made to serve the interests of corporate groups (whose leaders held control of land, cattle, and ritual sites) in the era of the closing of the frontier. During the period after 1300 communities recognizable as Ganda, Nyoro (or Rwanda, Nyambo, and Haya) formed. And they ushered in a sea change in social life, gender relations, conceptions of the two powers and of divides between them and they joined these changes to agricultural and environmental changes to render their descendants capable of building monarchies which connected the vision of the Monarch to the vision of the State (Carlson 1993: 322–8; Wrigley 1996: 84–9).

The historical development of the central elements of this complex revolved around tensions between ideologies of lineal descent and inheritance and the opportunities for political aggrandizement offered by institutions of clientship and blood-brotherhood. This pitted patrifocal families against offices of chiefship, on the one hand, and between chiefship and healing specialists, on the other hand (Schoenbrun 1995; Tantala 1989: 671–9). The contest circled around concerns with fertility and fecundity as the moral grounds on which chiefs accepted the

offer of their right to redistribute wealth and to exercise ritual control over production. Concerns with fertility and fecundity also formed the moral grounds for the power of healers to restore social balance and to exercise ritual control over reproduction. The patrifocal family seems to have been constructed around gendered divisions of labor and around differing rights to labor and property, rights determined by both gender and by an individual's particular position in the stages of the human life-cycle.

Moral economies of health and politics were encoded in theories of redistribution and fertility, theories whose historical existence emerges from comparative semantic studies and from the posing of etymologies for the relevant terms. Because vital dimensions of gender relations and of divisions of labor appear in the gendering of parts of Rutaran and North Nyanzan homesteads, and in the semantic histories of the words which name these spaces, a discussion of these data should reveal to archaeologists that studying settlement patterning offers them more than the chance to construct site-size hierarchies. It offers the chance to see possible ways in which such hierarchies were understood by their makers to operate. And, more importantly for the themes of this volume, it offers insights on the ways in which hierarchy was reorganized and subverted inside distinct forms of agriculture. The historical study of social space thus links archaeology, comparative linguistics, and comparative ethnography. It also presents data which modify sweeping evolutionist theories of "state formation" and which restore to different groups their differing relations to the "state" embodied in the form of their roles in contesting and renegotiating the terms and conditions of political and social power.[8]

Appendix

History from linguistics between the Lakes

Historical relationships between Great Lakes Bantu languages emerge from comparisons between core vocabulary lists which allow the provisional establishment of regular sound correspondences and the recognition of cognates (Schoenbrun 1994a). By counting rates of cognation in core vocabulary, for each pairing of the languages under study, a preliminary subgrouping of Great Lakes Bantu takes shape. Higher percentages reveal more recent divergence while lower numbers show earlier divergence. For example, Nkore and Ganda have a 59 percent cognation rate; they share 59 out of the 100 core vocabulary items. But Nkore and Nyambo have a 81 percent cognation rate. All three tongues are related, but Ganda began to diverge from its ancestral speech community, proto-North Nyanza, long before Nkore and Nyambo began to diverge from theirs, proto-Rutara (see Figure 11.2).

Just how long ago people spoke Proto Rutara Bantu may be surmised from glottochronology, a subset of lexicostatistics. Glottochronology uses the empirical finding that random change in basic vocabulary tends, over periods of centuries, to accumulate at a regular pace, and thus differences in cognate percentages can be given extremely rough chronological value.[9] About sixteen out of 100 items will be replaced each 500 years, either by semantic shift, by morphological analogy, or by borrowing from another language (Ehret 1988: 564–6; Vansina 1990: 9–16). Thus, using the rate given above, Nkore and Nyambo lost their easy mutual intelligibility a little more than 500 years ago. On the other hand, North Nyanza, the speech community ancestral to Ganda, lost its easy mutual intelligibility considerably earlier, say 1,200 or so years ago. Dialects of Proto-West Nyanza, the speech community ancestral to both North Nyanza and Rutara, lost their easy mutual intelligibility in the still more distant past, well over 1,500 years ago. Figure 11.2 depicts the historical relationships between several intermediate groups of Great Lakes Bantu and offers rough chronologies for their development.

The existence of these intermediate speech communities and their historical relationship to each other, and to their ancestral and descendant forms, implies a process of cultural spread across a geographical region. This process may be described by charting the geographical extent of modern languages and, then, attributing equal strength first to modern tongues, and then to their ancestral speech communities, as they must have moved across the geographical plane in order to account for the current distribution (Sapir 1916 [1985]: 410–25). Thus, in the Figure 11.2, because the bundle of modern languages constituting the North Nyanza branch of West Nyanza Bantu centers on the northwest corner of Victoria Nyanza and because the corresponding group of languages making up Rutara Bantu centers on the area south of the mouth of the Kagera river (see Figure 11.2), these all must have developed out of a zone midway between these two areas; the West Nyanza territories must, then, have lain around the Victoria Nyanza shore and inland along the Kagera river.

The question of how languages spread is both historical and sociological (Cooper 1982: 5–62). Therefore, the principle of least moves represents only one sense of the historical regions in which emerged different Lakes proto-linguistic identities. Social, environmental, and economic factors all shaped the spread of Lakes Bantu speech. For example, the early spread of proto-Great Lakes Bantu certainly was facilitated by settlement along the lakeshores and riverbanks and by the use of canoes. What is more, processes of language shift may have lain at the heart of the entire story. Pre-existing communities of farmers, hunters, gatherers, and fishers may have gradually shifted the choice of a first language to Bantu speech from Sudanic, Cushitic, or the unknown tongues of ancient food collectors. Such possibilities remind us that languages may spread without the movement of people and that they may spread by the sometimes discontiguous settlement of the niches preferred by each community.

Reconstructing vocabulary and documenting its retention and its transformation follow the work of genetic classification. The fruits of these labors provide precisely what archaeologists desire most: evidence for the all too often invisible parts of social and economic change. If the historical linguist can reconstruct a word for "cattle" or "banana" to the chronologically and geographically defined West Nyanza Bantu speech community, then archaeologists may search fruitfully in those areas for material evidence of these food sources. If the historical linguist can reconstruct, for West Nyanza Bantu, words for "govern" or "courtyard," archaeologists can begin to search as well for evidence of those social and spatial relationships. Their search will offer the possibility of confirming or denying inferences from comparative linguistics and comparative ethnography.

But words like "banana" and "govern" carry referents which differ widely in the social contexts for their use in daily life. We may feel confident that a reconstructed word for "banana" reflects the existence of knowledge of that fruit in the lives of West Nyanza Bantu speakers. Together with other words for varietals, banana gardens, tools, and cultivating techniques, we may even feel confident that such knowledge existed not from mere familiarity with banana fruit but from its actual production. Yet words for "govern" and for different parts of a settlement emerge in contexts of negotiation and contest. The semantic histories of words for "govern" and for "homestead" bear traces of the social contexts in which their makers moved, disputed, and agreed with each other. Because they do not exist as isolated bits of practical knowledge, they must be reconstructed as pieces of interlocking sets of semantic fields, the content of which describes the dimensions of thought on such matters as government and social space. Retrieving interlocking sets of semantic fields proceeds through uniting ethnographic description with the rigors of lexical reconstruction and of etymology (Vansina 1990: 9–16; Schoenbrun 1997: 10–18).

Notes

The author is grateful for permission to reproduce material from the following articles: "Gendered histories between the great lakes: varieties and limits." *International Journal of African Historical Studies* (1996) 29: 461–92. "An intellectual history of power: usable pasts from the Great Lakes region." In *Proceedings of the 10th Congress of the Pan African Association for Prehistory and Related Studies*, edited by G. Pwiti and R. Soper (1996). Harare: University of Zimbabwe Press: 693–702.

1 It should be pointed out that "retention" must not be confused with "static." It will be obvious that where innovation occurs its effects cannot be limited in any rigorous way to a specific part of social life. Retained words for "homestead" will not have had the "same" contexts of usage where one community builds its homesteads next to perennially cropped fields and the other builds its homesteads into cattle kraals.

2 Tantala (1989: 462) develops this for cattle, employing a perhaps too-literal interpretation of a drought metaphor that recurs in regional oral traditions.

3 The genetic classifications inside of which I build these histories come from Ehret (1995) and Schoenbrun (1994a).

4 The example of *kuhánga* expresses this process as well: note its meaning extensions in Proto West Nyanza and in Proto Western Lakes to include what individuals can do with properly superintended creative power.

5 For full treatment of the linguistic evidence for these, and other terms, please see Schoenbrun 1997.

6 Kuria has *eka*; *icika* "patricentered family, dispersed and exogamous."

7 In class 1/2, the word also means "elder" more widely in Bantu.

8 For historians working with Great Lakes oral traditions this is not a novel insight. See Berger (1981); Newbury (1991); Ray (1991); Tantala (1989); and Wrigley (1996).

9 For generally favorable views on this vexed question see Anttila (1989: 396–8); Ehret (1988: 566–9); Swadesh (1955: 121–37). For an unfavorable view see Bynon (1977: 266–72).

References

Ahmed, C. C.
   1996 *Before Eve Was Eve: 2200 Years of Gendered History in East-Central Africa*. Ann Arbor: University Microfilms International.

Anttila, R.
   1989 *Historical and Comparative Linguistics*. Amsterdam: John Benjamins.

Berger, I.
   1981 *Religion and Resistance*. Tervuren: Musée Royal de l'Afrique Centrale.
   1995 Fertility as power: spirit mediums, priestesses and the precolonial state. In *Revealing Prophets: Prophecy in East African History*, edited by D. Anderson and D. Johnson. London: James Currey: 65–82.

Blanton, R. E., G. M. Freinman, S. A. Kowalewski, and P. N. Peregrine.
   1996 A dual-processual theory for the evolution of Mesoamerican civilization. *Current Anthropology* 37 (1): 1–14.

Bourdieu, P.
   1990 *The Logic of Practice*. Oxford: Polity Press.

Bynon, T.
   1977 *Historical Linguistics*. Cambridge: Cambridge University Press.

Carlson, R. G.
   1993 Hierarchy and the Haya divine kingship: a structural and symbolic reformulation of Frazer's thesis. *American Ethnologist* 20 (2): 312–35.

Childs, S. T.
   1991 Style, technology, and iron smelting furnaces in Bantu-speaking Africa. *Journal of Anthropological Archaeology* 10: 332–59.

Connah, G.
   1991 The salt of Bunyoro. *Antiquity* 65: 479–94.
   1996 *Kibiro. The Salt of Bunyoro, Past and Present*. London: British Institute in Eastern Africa. Memoir 13.

Cooper, R. L.
   1982 (ed.) *Language Spread: Studies in Diffusion and Social Change*. Bloomington: Indiana University Press.

Desmedt, C.
   1991 Poteries ancienne décorées à la roulette dans la Région des Grands Lacs. *African Archaeological Review* 9: 161–96.

Ehret, C.
   1988 Language change and the material correlates of language and ethnic shift. *Antiquity* 62: 564–74.
   1995 Bantu subclassification revisited. Unpublished ms.
   1998 *An African Classical Age: Eastern and Southern Africa in World History, 1000 BC to AD 400*. Charlottesville: University Press of Virginia.

Fallers, L.
1956 *Bantu Bureaucracy*. Chicago: University of Chicago Press.

Håkansson, N. T.
1989 Family structure, bridewealth, and environment in Eastern Africa: a comparative study of house-property systems. *Ethnology* 28 (2): 117–35.

Hassan, F. A.
1981. Historical Nile floods and their importance for climatic change. *Science* 212: 1142–5.

Kopytoff, I.
1987. The internal African frontier: the making of African political culture. In *The African Frontier: The Reproduction of Traditional African Societies*, edited by I. Kopytoff. Bloomington: Indiana University Press: 3–84.

Mair, L.
1965 [1934] *An African People in the Twentieth Century*. New York: Russell and Russell.

McIntosh, R. J.
1993 The pulse model: genesis and accommodation of specialization in the Middle Niger. *Journal of African History* 34 (2): 181–220.

Newbury, D. N.
1991 *Kings and Clans: Ijwi Island and the Kivu Rift, 1780–1840*. Madison: University of Wisconsin Press.

Ray, B.
1991 *Myth, Ritual, and Kingship in Buganda*. Oxford: Oxford University Press.

Reid, D. A. M.
1991 The Role of Cattle in the Later Iron Age Communities of Southern Uganda. Ph.D. dissertation, University of Cambridge.
1993 Changing social relations and their contribution to the development of pastoralism in the interlacustrine region of eastern Africa. *Tanzania Zamani* 1 (3): 20–34.
1995 Social organisation and settlement in the interlacustrine region. *Azania* 29/30: 303–13.
1996 Ntusi and the development of social complexity in southern Uganda. In *Aspects of African Archaeology: Papers from the 10th Congress of the PanAfrican Association for Prehistory and Related Studies*, edited by G. Pwiti and R. Soper. Harare: University of Zimbabwe Press: 621–7.

Robertshaw, P. T.
1994 Archaeological survey, ceramic analysis, and state formation in Western Uganda. *African Archaeological Review* 12: 105–31.

Roscoe, J.
1911 *The Baganda: Their Customs and Beliefs*. Cambridge: Cambridge University Press.

Roscoe, P. B.
1993 Practice and political centralization. *Current Anthropology* 34 (2): 111–40.

Sapir, E.
1916 [1985] Time perspective in aboriginal American culture: a study in method. In *Edward Sapir: Selected Writings in Language, Culture, and Personality*, edited by D. G. Mandelbaum. Berkeley and Los Angeles: University of California Press: 389–462.

Schmidt, P. R.
1978 *Historical Archaeology*. Westport: Greenwood Press.

Schoenbrun, D. L.
1993 Cattle herds and banana gardens: the historical geography of the Western great lakes region, ca. AD 800–1500. *African Archaeological Review* 11: 39–72.
1994a Great lakes bantu: classification and settlement chronology. *Sprache und Geschichte in Afrika* 14: 1–62.
1994b The contours of vegetation change and human agency in Eastern Africa's great lakes region: ca. 2000 B.C. to ca. A.D. 1000. *History in Africa* 21: 269–302.
1995 Social aspects of agricultural change between the great lakes: 500–1000. *Azania* 29/30.
1996a An intellectual history of power: usable pasts from the Great Lakes region. In *Aspects of African Archaeology: Papers from the 10th Congress of the PanAfrican Association for Prehistory and Related Studies*, edited by G. Pwiti and R. Soper. Harare: University of Zimbabwe Press: 693–702.
1996b Gendered histories between the great lakes: varieties and limits. *International Journal of African Historical Studies* 29 (3): 461–92.
1997 *The Historical Reconstruction of Great Lakes Bantu Culture Vocabulary: Etymologies and Distributions*. Köln: Rüdiger Köppe Verlag.

Stewart, K. A.
1993 Iron Age ceramic studies in great lakes Eastern Africa: a critical and historiographical review. *African Archaeological Review* 11: 21–37.

Sutton, J. E. G.
1993 The antecedents of the interlacustrine kingdoms. *Journal of African History* 34 (1): 33–64.

Swadesh, M.
1955 Towards greater accuracy in lexicostatistical

dating. *International Journal of American Linguistics* 21: 121–37.

Tantala, R. L.
1989 The early history of Kitara in Western Uganda: process models of religious and political change. Ann Arbor: Ph.D. dissertation, University of Wisconsin-Madison University Microfilms International.

Vansina, J.
1990 *Paths in the Rainforests: Toward a History of Political Tradition in Equatorial Africa.* Madison: University of Wisconsin Press.

Wrigley, C. C.
1996 *Kingship and State: The Buganda Dynasty.* Cambridge: Cambridge University Press.

12

The power of symbols and the symbols of power through time: probing the Luba past

PIERRE DE MARET

Introduction

With its many shared linguistic, symbolic, and ideological characteristics, the Bantu-speaking population of central, eastern, and southern Africa offers an exceptional opportunity for comparative studies. How, with a common background, they managed to expand and adapt to the various local conditions they encountered in this gigantic area over a period of probably more than three millennia is fascinating. Although two-thirds of Fortes and Evans-Pritchard's seminal book *African Political Systems* (1940) was devoted to Bantu political organization, the potential contribution of this part of the world to the recent debate on chiefdoms, intermediate level societies, and the rise of early states has been almost completely overlooked in favor of Oceania, America, and, to a lesser extent, Europe (Earle 1987).

Bantu Africa offers not only side-by-side examples of major kingdoms, such as the Kuba, and autonomous villages with collective leadership, such as the Lele, but also hundreds of societies exhibiting a wide range of intermediate political systems. Considering only the Bantu living in the rainforest, Vansina (1989) notes

> One can go from one end of the scale of complexity to the other by setting up a model of transformations that takes all the cases into account. When this is done it becomes clear that kingdoms can grow out of chiefdoms, or out of a single big man's house, or out of government by an association, encompassing many settlements, where leaders move from rank to rank. As soon as the highest rank is limited to a single incumbent, a kingdom emerges. Kingdoms can result from the transformation of the institution whereby wealthy

men take titles, publicly acknowledged by their communities during sumptuous festivities and accompanied by emblems and subsidiary titles given by the big man to his spouses and followers . . . All the political systems of the peoples of the forest can be fitted into a single diagram showing multiple pathways going from simple to complex systems and vice versa. These various developments can be traced over centuries, if not millennia, providing a rare opportunity to achieve a true political history.

As Vansina (1989, 1990) convincingly demonstrated, reconstruction can be achieved by combining mainly linguistic and ethnographic data with oral tradition. Part of the resulting hypothesis can then be tested by archaeology. Alas, before independence, the recent African past was considered hardly worth excavating, and since then, the very difficult political and economic situation prevailing in Central Africa has prevented the development of archaeology. Thus, for example, the early history of the most famous kingdoms (Kongo, Mbundu, Teke, Lunda, Luba, Kuba) remains virtually unknown. Excavating the core area of these major kingdoms has been on the agenda of the few active archaeologists in the area, but so far very little has been achieved (Clist 1991; Maret 1990, 1991; Pinçon 1991). However, the Upemba depression, in the Luba heartland, has yielded a wealth of archaeological evidence with few equivalents elsewhere in sub-Saharan Africa.

Furthermore, in a stimulating book, Nooter Roberts and Roberts (1996) explore the relationships of memory, history, and art among the Luba, and how various objects and performances used as mnemonic devices were manipulated in the context of kingship and political relation. They successfully demonstrate that "since precolonial times, the recounting of history has been a specific and highly valued form of intellectual activity among Luba; and that visual representation has been and is a primary vehicle for the making of Luba histories of kingship and center/periphery political relation" (Nooter Roberts and Roberts 1996: 17).

All this provides an excellent opportunity to combine archaeology, ethnography, and history in an attempt to shed light on the development of the Luba state, one of the most famous of Central Africa.

The Upemba Depression: geography, ecology, and settlement

Halfway between the Atlantic and the Indian Oceans, Upemba is situated more than 1,500 km from the nearest coast. Sheltered from any direct influence from the coast-lines, it constituted a perfect setting for a truly indigenous development. It was not entirely isolated, however, due to the presence of the Zaire River,[1] which flows through the entire length of the Depression (see Figure 12.1) and then towards the equatorial forest, some 400 kilometers downstream. Upemba's ecology presents a clear contrast to that of the neighboring savannas. The basin is a rift valley boxed in by a mountain range on the east and the Kamina plateau on the west. It is also a vast flood plain (210 km long and 20 to 45 km wide), dotted with scattered lakes and irrigated by the Zaire River and a few tributaries. Their waters are rich with fish and their banks are alive with a multitude of wildlife. The loam deposited by the annual floods keeps the soil fertile.

Collective action was often needed to build dikes to keep rising water out of settlements, to clear artificial channels through the floating vegetation, to control lake levels for fishing, and to restrict fishing in order to avoid depletion of this resource (Reefe 1981: 79). The waterways in the Depression form also a unique communication network for dugout canoes. This assures close ties between the inhabitants. The rich natural resources of the Upemba basin both attract and support a dense population, in contrast with the surrounding savannas.

Archaeological data

Of the fifty or so archaeological sites documented throughout the Depression, only six have been excavated so far: Sanga in 1957 (Nenquin 1963) and 1958 (Hiernaux, Longree, and De Buyst 1971), 1974 and 1988; Katongo in 1974; Kamilamba, Kikulu, and Malemba-Nkulu in 1975 (Childs and Maret 1996; Maret 1978, 1985b, 1992) and Katoto in 1958 (Hiernaux, Maquet, and De Buyst 1972).

Much information has been revealed by the more than 300 graves that have been excavated, principally in the northern, more accessible, part of the basin. In this area, four main traditions were identified and a formal chronology was established, extending from the seventh century AD to recent historical times (Figure 12.2) (Geyh and Maret 1982; Maret 1977, 1979, 1992). This chronology was further confirmed by fifty radiocarbon and four thermoluminescence dates (Maret 1982, 1992).

The wealth of grave goods discovered has provided valuable information on these societies; nonetheless their interpretation from a socio-political point of view is problematic as it is based on data retrieved mainly from burials. A major objective of the 1974 excavations was to locate settlement structures, which would provide a

greater frame of reference than the graves alone for the study of these Iron Age societies. Several sites did indeed reveal settlement levels and made it possible to confirm the relative chronology, but it was impossible to map significant structures since the levels were not sufficiently preserved. The rare places in the basin that were suitable for the establishment of villages have often been in continuous use since the Stone Age for various purposes – fields, refuse-pits, huts, or cemeteries. The mixing of deposits due to these disturbances destroyed most structures. In addition, the majority of these constructions were made from reeds, which leave hardly any trace.

Due to the extended crisis that Zaire has endured since then, it has not been possible to organize a large-scale research project aimed at diversifying our database.

The Kamilambian

In Upemba, the Iron Age begins in the seventh century AD, with the Kamilambian. The ceramics of this period are stylistically related to those of a larger tradition, the Copperbelt Early Iron Age, and constitute so far its most northerly point of extension. Although copper has been recovered from contemporaneous sites in Zambia (Bisson 1976: 129–30) and elsewhere in Zaire (Anciaux de Faveaux and Maret 1984), it was not found in the Upemba sites. The small-scale regional copper trade in the Copperbelt had not yet reached the Upemba Depression by AD 800, nor had the coastal trade, which was developing on the Indian Ocean shores at the same time. These lacunae correspond to observations made by Phillipson (1968) and Clark (1974: 62) on their sites in Zambia. At that time, the Early Iron Age communities of inland equatorial Africa probably lived in autonomous villages.

The thick layer of rich cultural material excavated at the eponymous sites of Kamilamba reveals a long and dense period of occupation (Maret 1992). The dwellings were made of daga and branches. Interestingly, iron was found only in a funerary context (fourteen iron tools and weapons) in the single grave from this phase that has been excavated.

Compared to later periods, the Kamilambian remains are sparse throughout the Depression. This is due either to their age or to the fact that settlements were relatively few in number. There is a certain homogeneity in shape and decoration among their ceramics but nothing to the degree found in the subsequent Kisalian group, where many aspects, not only of pottery, but also of the rest of material culture and rituals, point to high levels of cultural homogeneity.

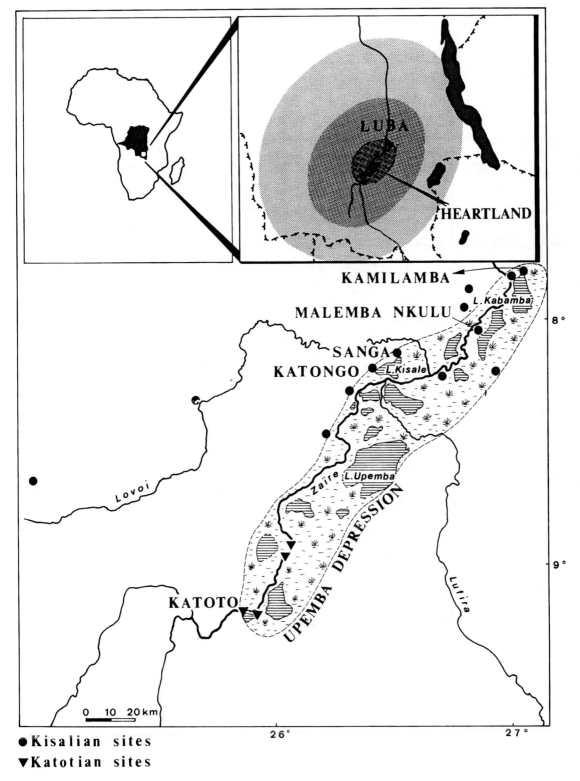

Figure 12.1 Tthe Upemba Depression: archaeological sites mentioned in the text.

NORTHERN UPEMBA DEPRESSION ARCHAEOLOGICAL SEQUENCE

AD	Phase (Number of graves)	Grave goods	Trade	Population density
500				
600	Kamilambian (1)	Only iron implements and weapons. No pots.	No evidence	Low
700 800	Ancient Kisalian (19)	Few pots, iron weapons, and implements. Copper beads and bangles. Very few ceremonial axes and one anvil as status symbols; ranking instituted. Autonomous leaders?	Copper ornaments, trade with Copperbelt	Increasing
900 1000 1100	Classic Kisalian (142)	Abundant pottery in some graves, along with ivory, copper and, iron ornaments. Gravegoods differ according to gender, but graves of women and children among the richest; status inherited, but no sharp division between the wealthy minority and the rest. Small discs of shell in strings, used for social payments into associations? High homogeneity in pottery and ritual.	Expansion of trade with Copperbelt. Coastal trade items such as cowries appear.	High
1200 1300 1400	Kabambian A (54)	Metal grave goods decline but copper crosses common. Local variation in pottery and burial ritual more pronounced. No symbols of power except one conus shell disc. Greater contrast between wealthy and poor.	Trade with Copperbelt, mostly unstandardized H-type copper crosses, used as special purpose currency? Long distance trade expands: cowries, conus, glass beads.	High
1500 1600	Kabambian B (15)	Few pots, with thick red slip. Initially numerous very small H-type copper crosses, decreasing to one or two per grave.	Trade with Copperbelt, H-type copper crosses become smaller and standardized, used as money?	High
1700 1800 1900	Modern Luba (6)	No pots or metal, glass beads only.	Smoked fish exported. Arabo-Swahili, then European traders and raiders. Numerous European glass beads.	High

Figure 12.2   Archaeological sequence for the northern Upemba Depression.

The Early Kisalian (eighth–ninth century AD)

The Early Kisalian phase is recognized from the eighth century. Excavated graves are rare, possibly indicating that population densities were relatively low compared to subsequent periods. But fragments of grindstones and two iron hoes were found in a domestic context, confirming that farming was practiced.

Judging from the ceramics, the initial phase of Kisalian arises from the Kamilambian. The most informative studies of the early Kisalian have been concentrated along the shores of Lake Kisale, but its range no doubt extended from the outset over the northern part of the basin, progressively replacing the Kamilambian.

Large curved knives typify the Kisalian but spearheads are also common in this period. The latter were probably not hafted since they were found in a heap and may very well have been considered as valuable objects or even currency, as was the case in many other Central African societies (Maret 1981). It seems quite plausible to propose that the other metal objects found (weapons, tools, and jewelry) were destined for use by the dead in the "afterlife." They may also have been placed within the grave for their intrinsic value in order to display the wealth of the defunct's group, or even used as posthumous "currency." It is difficult from the archaeological record to be categorical about their precise postmortem symbolic function, but Luba believed in an afterworld. Whatever their precise role, the ritual consumption of a large number of metal objects must have contributed to maintaining a high value for them in the world of the living.

In equatorial Africa elaborate axes were often symbols of political and religious power and this is well documented among Luba (Van Avermaet and Mbuya 1954: 70; Womersley 1975: 82). Two elaborately decorated ceremonial axes were retrieved, one from an Early Kisalian grave at Katongo (Figure 12.3) and another from a slightly more recent Kisalian grave at Kamilamba. This evidence indicates that this society already made use of elaborate symbols of religious or political authority. It is certainly not a coincidence that out of 161 Kisalian graves (both Early and Classic) the wealthy Kisalian grave from Kamilamba with the ceremonial axe was also the only one containing an iron anvil, placed next to the skull. The multiplicity of symbolic and ritual ties between traditional ironworking and leadership, particularly among the Bantu of Central Africa, has received much attention (Childs and Dewey 1996; Dewey and Childs 1996; Herbert 1993; Maret 1980, 1985a). This connection stems from both symbolic and economic processes since there is a very important homology between the symbolic functions of the ironsmith and those of the chiefs and kings.

In the Upemba basin, next to the Kamilamba site, an iron anvil was found at the beginning of this century among the regalia of Chief Mulongo (Boterdal 1909). Symbol of the blacksmith's activity, iron anvils were used during the coronation ceremony of Luba kings, one of the most important moments of which was called "striking the anvil" (Womersley 1975: 82–3). Two anvils were also found placed against the skull of a Rwandese king (Van Noten 1972, fig. 8) confirming that an anvil found among grave goods can be an authority symbol making the deceased a symbolic blacksmith rather than a real one. In Rwanda, as in many other kingdoms of Central Africa, mimicking the blacksmith was a part of enthronement rituals and the king was a kind of ritual blacksmith (Maret 1985a).

Besides iron objects, the tombs contained pottery and artifacts made of copper, a very rare metal in Upemba at that time. The large arm and ankle bracelets of copper suggest that the Upemba basin had then been absorbed into the widening commercial networks that distributed the metal produced in the Copperbelt. As Bisson has shown (1976: 67–92), copper was used there principally for adornments. It was much more in demand than either salt or iron, which were also traded in those days (Fagan 1969). Stemming from the previous Early Iron Age tradition, the Early Kisalian marks the start of major political and economical processes in the area.

The Classic Kisalian (tenth–twelfth century AD)

Towards the tenth century both the number of Kisalian graves in the cemeteries on the northern shore of Lake Kisale and the great number of sites from this period in the northern half of the Upemba Depression seem to indicate a marked demographic increase compared to the Early Kisalian tradition, of which only three sites have been discovered so far. But the northern part of the Depression is only the best studied area of a larger Classic Kisalian distribution. Classic Kisalian potsherds and even graves have been found on the plateau southwest of the Depression as well (Vansina, personal communication, and 1994: 35–6), but this area has thus far not been the focus of systematic surveys.

This phase corresponds to the 130 classic Kisalian graves which have been excavated at Katongo and Sanga. After a period of acclimatization to the favorable environment of the Upemba Depression it seems that the population began to increase rapidly, due to an enriched and varied diet of fish, agricultural produce, cattle and fowl breeding, and game (antelope, hippopotamus, elephant, etc.).

Traces of fish found in the pottery and various hooks

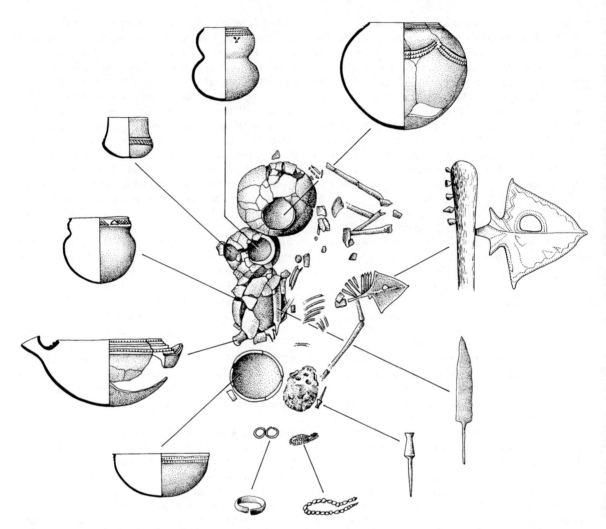

Figure 12.3   Early Kisalian burial of a man with ceremonial axe and anvil, an iron machete, and copper jewelry.

and harpoon heads illustrate the major role of fishing in daily life. A trilobate vessel used as a brazier first appeared at this time. Even today, identical utensils are used by fishermen in central Africa for cooking in their dugout canoes. The presence of hoes, grinding stones, and gourd-like pottery as well as vessels possibly used for fermented beverages all indicate that farming was practiced by the villages, which were located at a small distance from the lakes and waterways. There might have been at this time already a certain complementarity between the fishermen and the farmers, as is the case today in the Kindondja chieftaincy.

The various grave goods of the Classic Kisalian period are sumptuous. The masterful execution of artifacts in metal, bone, ivory, and ceramics indicates the existence of skilled artisans. Ceramic material abounds, typically featuring contoured shapes and a delicate decoration. Some pots were even produced in series for interment, as they show a marked uniformity in shape, size, and decoration, and no sign of use-wear. While iron objects were basically the same as in the preceding period, copper was used much more extensively not only for ornaments but, exceptionally, also to make fish hooks, needles, nails, and small knife blades. The quality of the jewelry shows that wire-drawing and laminating techniques were fully mastered by the artisans (Childs 1991). Finely engraved copper and bone jewelry were found. Women wore cowries and teeth as necklaces and the men carried a jawbone on their belt. Basket weaving was also known.

There was a complicated funeral ritual which took into account social status. Grave goods differed between men and women and also seem to indicate the existence of a hierarchy of wealth and status. If one considers the number of pots in the graves as an indication of wealth at Sanga, out of 114 Classic Kisalian graves, only nineteen contained more than twenty pots (16.6 percent of the graves) and only seven graves contained more than thirty pots (6.1 percent). The graves containing the most pots also contained most of the unusual and probably valuable objects, such as ivory pendants, bells, cowries, human jaws, tortoise shells, and leopard canines. The same graves also contained copper ornaments and iron objects in abundance. Small discs of shell in strings were also found, similar to the ones used until recently downstream as a common currency for social payments, especially in socio-political associations (Vansina 1990: 179–80, 354 nn. 40–3). Several symbols of political authority in Central Africa (Vansina 1973–4) have been discovered in Kisalian graves, among them the leopard canine, the smithing anvil, the bell, and the ceremonial axe. Although a wealthy minority certainly existed, the difference between them and the rest of the population was not so striking since many tombs of intermediate wealth were also found.

Membership in the rich minority was apparently inherited; several of the more luxurious tombs belonged to children. This implies well-defined social stratification, as does the presence of the ceremonial axes. The presence of a miniaturized ceremonial axe in a small child's grave further suggests inherited status. The grave with the anvil at Kamilamba and another grave, among the richest, contained a second skeleton. Human sacrifice is likely, as was the case at the death of Luba chiefs (d'Orjo de Marchovelette 1950; Womersley 1984: 83–5). The existence of small bells with clappers can be considered as a sign of social hierarchy. Van Avermaet and Mbuya (1954: 11) write that in certain areas of the Luba kingdom, the chief invested by custom to this office has the right to ring a bell when his women go to bathe. Vansina (1973–4: 357) tells us that these bells are a symbol of authority among several Central African peoples. However, contrary to what Vansina (1969) believed, to date no bell of the other type, the large bells without clappers, whose relation with power is much stronger, has been excavated in Kisalian context.

Such factors can only be explained by admitting the existence of a relatively well-developed social and political organization, resulting from a remarkable combina-tion of circumstances in which it is difficult to distinguish the causes from the effects. Environmental conditions seem to have been one of the key factors. The exceptionally high demographic density stemmed not only from the wealth of the basin but also from the collective effort that was necessary to exploit resources optimally. As Reefe (1981: 69–71) rightly points out, this could have been at the origin of the political development of the Upemba, as early as the end of the first millennium. Similar situations have existed in the vicinity, e.g., the Lozi kingdom of the Upper Zambezi and the Kazembe kingdom along the lower Luapula (Cunnison 1959; Reefe 1983; Roberts 1973). Conversely, much farther downstream along the Ngiri River in the midst of the equatorial forest, the Libinza, who lived in the flooded forest, have never known political unity although they practiced large-scale collective work (Kuper and Leynseele 1978; Leynseele 1979).

From the Nile and the Niger to the Zaire and the Zambezi, it would be worthwhile to do a systematic comparison assessing the contributions of the continent's flood plains to its political history, but we should refrain from too much environmental determinism. Areas rich in diversified resources attract high population densities and both factors contribute to trade on an increasing scale. All this may provoke centralization. However, as the Libinza remind us, and as it was convincingly demonstrated by Vansina for many other rainforest Bantu populations, "culture is also crucial both as knowledge and technique and as a value system" (Vansina 1990, 1994). From the outset, the Bantu had a specific construction of ideology and power: "in fact two ideologies coexisted: one that extolled and explained the success of big men and one that stressed the ideal equality of all, which underlies the suspicion of witchcraft" (Vansina 1990: 253).

The importance of the waterway network in the Upemba Depression is at least partially illustrated by the fact that most Kisalian remains are found on the banks of the river and the dead are oriented in relation to it. Today, Luba symbolism still associates death with waterways (Burton 1961: 40–9). The great similarity of ceramics and rituals at the various Kisalian sites reflects a certain political unity as well as the easy communication afforded by the waterway network.

The role of the Upemba's rich environment in supporting high population densities should not be overlooked in a discussion of socio-political evolution. A direct relation between population density and state formation in Africa south of the Sahara has been put forward (Vengroff 1976) for societies capable of producing a stable surplus. The creation of surpluses has generally been linked to the development of agriculture. However, the Kisalian surplus is most certainly derived from fishing. Fishermen have, in general, played a major commercial role in Africa and this may have also created surpluses. In the Kisalian period, if social differentiation was made possible and very often enhanced by the existence of a surplus, the latter is not sufficient to explain the origin of the former. As Sahlins points out: "Too frequently and mechanically anthropologists attribute the appearance of chieftainship to the production of surplus. In the historic process, however, the relation has been at least mutual, and in the functioning of primitive society it is rather the other way around. Leadership continually generates domestic surplus. The development of rank and chieftainship becomes, *pari passu*, development of the productive forces" (Sahlins 1972: 140).

If tombs dating from the Early Kisalian are few, their number increases considerably afterwards. It is quite feasible that the concentration of the population in the Upemba Depression dates back from the Early Kisalian at least. Today, there is still a sharp contrast between the number of inhabitants living in the Depression and in the neighboring savannas. In those less populated areas the need for political integration was not as strong as in the Upemba basin.

The development of trade began in the same period and marked the end of geographical isolation. This factor also probably contributed to the build-up of a progressively more politically organized society. With the Early Kisalian, in the eleventh century, copper became extremely abundant in graves, indicating that trade links were steadily developing with the copper mining area to the south. These commercial relations have been corroborated by the discovery, mid-way between the Upemba basin and the closest copper mines, of a typically Kisalian anthropomorphic flask.

The Classic Kisalian period included the penetration of trade items from the coast. The first cowries from the Indian Ocean are found in graves of that period. At this initial phase, their presence in Kisalian tombs is best explained by hand-to-hand transmission rather than by the existence of a trading network organized and supervised by specialists.

We know from the first explorers to penetrate into those regions in the 1880s that smoked fish, the staple food of the basin, was exported over long distance and bartered for raffia and beads (Bontick 1974: 80–5; Zeebroek 1976: 67–78). This leads us to believe that fish has been the basin inhabitants' wealth since a remote period, and that the barter of their staple food brought them copper and other prestigious products. Other scholars have demonstrated that exchanges took place at an early stage between neigh-

boring groups (Gray and Birmingham 1970). Thus, foodstuffs (salt, smoked fish, honey, palm oil, wine), raw materials (iron, hematite, copper, wax), as well as local products (basketwork, materials, iron tools, ceramics) were bartered.

It seems that during the Kisalian period trade was limited but sufficient to facilitate a certain degree of social stratification. Imported objects of value were manipulated by the wealthiest, probably in order to display and legitimize their power.

The Kabambian A (thirteenth–fifteenth century AD)

The Kisalian was replaced by the Kabambian A at the turn of the thirteenth century, after a relatively short period of transition. The nature of such a transition remains obscure. We still do not know whether a progressive shift of customs in a society subject to growing exterior pressures produced corresponding shifts in material culture or whether new ceramic traditions were the result of population movements. The development of trade and the extension of the zone of these populations could have largely modified their daily practices and accounted for the emergence of Kabambian pottery and rituals, which contrast with former Kisalian customs.

At Sanga, for instance, the orientation of the skeletons is different. Iron grave goods become less numerous. Ceramics dating from the early Kabambian period, (Kabambian A), seem to stem from Kisalian craftsmanship from the manufacturing point of view (shaping, paste, firing, red slip) although the shape and decoration are different. Overall, Kabambian graves and rituals give the impression of much less unity than during the Kisalian period. In terms of pottery, tool shape, and burial position, the Kabambian has more local features. The river probably does not play the same unifying role that it did during the Kisalian period. These considerations may show a weaker integration of Kabambian groups, even a relative cultural disparity. Was Kabambian society encompassed by a larger political structure originating outside the Upemba basin? It is entirely possible that the emergence, at the same period, of kingdoms in the savannas northwest of the basin progressively subdued the Upemba basin's inhabitants hastening the demise of their cultural homogeneity. Greater cultural variability could also be seen as evidence of competing, more autonomous groups in a wider Kabambian complex. An archaeological campaign in the area of Kabongo, the main Luba kingdom's legendary dynastic center, would go a long way toward evaluating this hypothesis.

If Kabambian graves are rarer than Kisalian tombs at Sanga, this is almost certainly because the entire site has not been excavated. In fact, the large number of Kabambian graves in Malemba-Nkulu and Kikulu reveal that population density probably remained stable. Although Kabambian grave goods are generally less abundant, at Malemba-Nkulu a few graves reveal a wealth of goods, especially a unique double burial. This evidence suggests that the social stratification begun during the Kisalian period continued during the Kabambian and was even heightened since the graves of intermediate wealth disappeared. Interestingly, those richest graves lack the distinct markers of socio-political status, such as ceremonial axes or anvils, that were used earlier during the Kisalian period, as well as more recently by the Luba.

One should note, however, the presence of a small clapper bell and, in one instance, of a small fragment of a Conus shell disc (Maret 1985b: 166). This most interesting object, unknown thus far from Kisalian burials, is strongly related to political authority. It was made into necklaces worn by chiefs and prominent notables among Luba and many other savanna peoples (Kawende and De Plaen 1996; Legros 1996). The absence of other power symbols in the Kabambian higher ranking burial remains surprising and suggests that the nature of power had changed. It may well be that regalia were reserved for the most important leaders, who were buried in special locations, like river beds, as has been practiced recently by the Luba.

The Kabambian seems to have developed along with the expansion of long-distance trade – as attested by the presence of cowries and glass beads. But increasing regional trade was a development with perhaps greater ramifications. This view is supported by the presence of cruciform-shaped ingots, the famous small copper crosses (Maret 1995). They first appeared during the final Kisalian and are typical of Kabambian graves. Molds excavated by Bisson (1976: 427) show that very large H-type crosses were smelted further south, in the Kipushi copper mines of the Copperbelt between the ninth and twelfth centuries. They are quite similar to older crosses found in the Upemba Depression. These crosses underwent a remarkable evolution.

During the Kabambian, the form of the crosses was standardized and at the same time they shrank in size. This means a decrease in the actual quantity of copper despite an increase of the number of crosses in the graves. At the same time, the position of the crosses shifts from the chest towards the hips and the hands. In explaining these changes, one could suggest that in the Early Kabambian the crosses were a prestige good whose use was probably restricted to a few mostly social exchange spheres. Later, developing regional and long-distance trade expanded the range of uses to which crosses could be put and turned them into multipurpose currency used for a large number of transactions (Maret 1981, 1995).

Cowries are typical of the grave goods found with female skeletons buried in Kisalian and Kabambian tombs. During the latter period they seem to have acquired a monetary value since we found a series of those shells together with copper crosses in a grave in Malemba-Nkulu. However, crosses were the preferred monetary unit during the Kabambian A period probably because of the scarcity and fragility of other possible exchange media.

The Kabambian B (sixteenth–eighteenth century AD)

In the sixteenth and seventeenth centuries, copper smelting in the Copperbelt increased dramatically (Bisson 1976: 429). This period corresponds to the Kabambian B, whose tombs contain very small crosses but only a few vessels with a thick red slip. The shape of these pots anticipates more recent Luba ceramics. The burial ritual is also modified.

Towards the end of the Kabambian period, in the late seventeenth or early eighteenth century, historians tell us that the Luba state was a vast, politically and economically dominant entity (Reefe 1981). Reefe (1981: 81–4) links the emergence of the Luba state to the control of raw materials such as iron and salt, both of which were found in deposits near the center of the kingdom. Iron and salt deposits are not rare in Shaba and thus their control alone could hardly have fostered political and economic centralization. One therefore wonders if this state did not have its roots in an original and symbolically elaborated social and political organization. It is more probable that this state was at first built on an ideological foundation (Vansina 1996, and personal communication). Thenceforth it developed a political organization capable of incorporating the new chieftaincies conquered during military expeditions (Reefe 1981: 79–114) while gradually taking over the inter-regional trade in which copper played a leading role.

This Luba state expanded during the nineteenth century to become one of the largest states in Central Africa. This development proceeded in step with that of long-distance trade with the Arabs. The Luba took an active part in producing and providing the ivory in response to coastal Arab and European demand (Wilson 1972). Territorial expansion to the east and the increasing trade and cultural contacts of the eighteenth and nineteenth centuries could well explain the replacement of

KAMILAMBIAN	ANCIENT KISALIAN	CLASSIC KISALIAN	KABAMBIAN A	KABAMBIAN B	LUBA

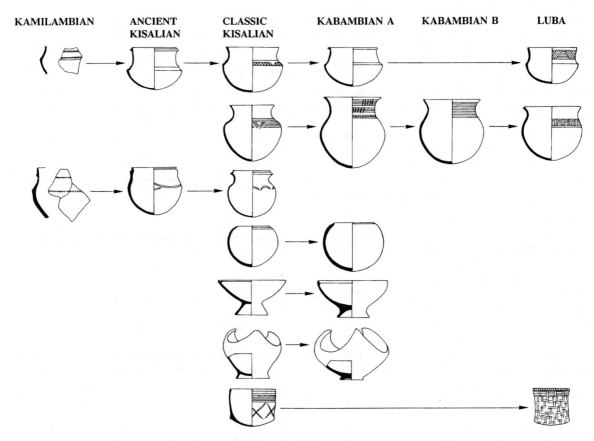

Figure 12.4   Ceramics from the northern Upemba Depression, showing continuity and change through time.

Kabambian ceramics and burial rituals by ethnographically identifiable "Luba" practices.

The recent Luba period
Beads are the only grave goods found in recent Luba tombs, where the body is placed in a flexed position with the hands positioned by the face. This practice corresponds to the Luba ritual as it has been observed in the early part of the century (Burton 1961: 34–5), and fits in with the description given by informants. Villagers declare that copper crosses have not been used in the region for at least four generations. Continuity can be detected, however, between Luba ceramics found in the uppermost deposits and sometimes still used by elderly people and Kabambian B ceramics.

It is thus possible to trace the evolution of the societies which occupied the Upemba Depression over nearly 1,500 years. The striking factor in the string of transformations

that these human groups have created from the Early Iron Age to recent times is, in the end, their remarkable continuity rather than the social, political, economic, and technical changes that occurred over the centuries.

Kamilambian, Kisalian, Kabambian, and recent Luba ceramics developed one from the other, even if it is easy to distinguish them typologically (Figure 12.4). Certain aspects of the pottery reinforce this ceramic continuity, such as the trilobate braziers that existed in the Kisalian and Kabambian A periods. Similarly, though red slip is in evidence since the Kisalian and has therefore existed throughout the evolution of Upemba society, it only became thick in the late Kabambian. Carinated pottery with a step-like shoulder, typical of recent Luba eathernware, appears to be the result of an evolution that began with carinated vessels in the Kamilambian. The ceramics decorated with a human head, rare in Central Africa, but found in the Kisalian period, are still used today in traditional Luba ceramics. As for the headrests of the Kabambian period, they were still used until recently in the region (Maes 1929: 23–4). The shape of hoes remained almost unchanged throughout the Iron Age and certain contemporary baskets are identical to Kisalian skeuomorphic pottery (Maret 1992: 16). A strong link exists between burial rituals and the waterways from the Kisalian until recent times (Burton 1961: 34–9; Theuws 1960: 119, 155). The funerary ritual involving the burial of very young children inside urns has been practiced by the Luba (Van Avermaet and Mbuya 1954: 453) and in Sanga during the Kisalian and Kabambian periods. From the Kisalian until recently, the peoples of these regions filed their incisors to a point. Lastly, the sheer number and size of Classical Kisalian sites tends to show that the currently high level of demographic density is of considerable antiquity (Saint-Moulin 1974: 348).

Conclusion

Archaeological data show that the Luba civilization and state are the result of a cultural process spanning a millennium or longer. This exceptional continuity in the record of material culture provides a sound basis for the use of ethnographic data to interpret the wealth of the archaeological remains and to investigate some theoretical issues.

In the 1970s, when the major archaeological excavations were carried out, the image of the Luba state was that of a kingdom so centralized and powerful that it was known as the "Luba Empire" (Reefe 1981; Van der Noot 1936; Verhulpen 1936). This model was largely a colonial artifact based on literal interpretation of the founding myth of the kingship, on preconceptions about African kingdoms, and on the desire of colonial authorities to foster a sense of "pure" ethnicity and to regroup people in large ethno-political structures that would be easier to subject to the colonial rule (Nooter Roberts and Roberts 1996: 17–29).

In recent years, "Luba" has been shown to be a most ambiguous category, covering many different territories and identities, and ethnonyms more significant at the periphery than in the center (Petit 1993: 30; Roberts 1996). Furthermore, the center itself was mobile, as the capital was moved after the death of each king. Nooter Roberts and Roberts (1996: 20–8) have recently argued that there was no proof that "imperial authority" was militarily enforced and that occasional gifts of deference made by peripheral leaders to heartland kings signified recognition of seniority and of the utility of economical and political exchanges in much the same way that a junior member of a clan or a lineage honors elders. "A royal center then was more an ideological construct than an empirical reality. . . . Luba power rested not with a single dynastic line of kings or with a single 'center', but with a constellation of chieftaincies, officeholders, societies, and sodalities that validated claims to power in relation to what we suggest to be a largely mythical center. The paradox is explicit: there was no real center, yet belief in one allowed cultural integration of an entire region. Identification with a 'center' was in effect a means of legitimizing the 'periphery' " (Nooter Roberts 1991). Vansina (1996) concurs: "The main Luba kingdom was first and foremost a construction of the mind."

Lacking the capacity to maintain a standing army, the power of the Luba kingdom was more symbolic than military. It had thus to rely on ideology and to share its prestige with the heads of largely autonomous regional communities which sought legitimacy and identity through the manipulation of various myths, emblems, and a rich array of regalia. Powerful politico-religious associations, especially the Mbudye, also played an important integrating role at the political, ritual, and cultural level (Nooter Roberts 1996; Nooter Roberts and Roberts 1996: 37; Reefe 1981: 46–8). Through initiation, male and female members of the Mbudye association acquire supernatural powers that allow them to arbitrate conflicts, to dethrone a chief or a king, to guard political and historical precepts, and to disseminate this knowledge. Mbudye adepts danced and performed rituals celebrating the deeds of heroes and kings, spreading to outlying areas the prestige of the kingship. Acting as the memory of the society, they were critical to the internal balance of power in Luba politics. Objects of power and memories were in fact at "the very foundation of the main Luba kingdom, and the gist of a Luba-inspired concept of 'civilized life' for much of southeastern Zaire and nearby Zambia" (Vansina 1996). This is reminiscent of the prestige of the Roman Empire or of the French court in the eighteenth century. Outside of its heartland, the prestige of the Luba was such that people turned to their model authority whenever they wanted more political power. Indeed we know of chiefs making trips to the Luba court in order to acquire sacred royalty symbols and knowledge (Roberts 1996: 228). Luba people thus offer an unusual model of social and political organization which is worth integrating in ongoing theoretical debates.

On the old Bantu ideology oscillating between the prestige of big men and the ideal equality of all, one sees, as early as the eighth century, the Kisalians manipulating various symbols of power. Evidence indicates also that socio-political differentiation and ranking were instituted by the eighth century. It further suggests that individuals buried with important symbols of political and religious power were local, autonomous leaders of villages or groups of neighboring settlements using them to legitimize their authority. The fact that wealth and probably status are passed along inter-generationally is indeed usually regarded as a classic characteristic of chiefdoms (Yoffee 1993). Through various integrating processes this structure will eventually form a huge socio-politically organized society that will be called a "kingdom," and even an "empire." But the power of the ensuing state was based mostly on the use of specific symbols of cultural and political commonality, to use some of Yoffee's (1993) categories. The other dimensions of power, i.e., economic and political (including military power) seem to have had little relevance, and have hardly co-evolved.

The resulting Luba "state" is Bantu's contribution to the variability in models of ancient regional polities. It is likely that control over the various "Luba" communities remained limited because, in the end, the old Bantu ideology of autonomy prevailed. The study of Luba vocabulary confirms that the word for "chief, notable" is ancestral and older even than the Luba language itself, but the word for "king" is a later borrowing (Vansina 1996). It is thus likely that the Luba polity finds its roots in the five-century-long tradition of manipulating complex symbols of status and power by Kisalian local chiefs and notables. The resulting very sophisticated although decentralized construct was later put to use, around Kabambian time, by rulers who, probably under non-Bantu eastern influence, had a more centrally oriented inclination.

Even if the initial use of military force in subduing chieftaincies and gradually taking over trade is likely, the new sovereign rulers must have soon developed a more civilized way to impose their new order. They must have owed most of their power to the syncretic fusion of the old Kisalian civilization with the new, probably foreign hierarchical structure, much in the way demonstrated by Msiri, the mid-nineteenth-century leader of the Yeke/Nyamwezi immigrants just south of the Upemba (Legros 1996). As head of a small trading band more in search of political than commercial opportunities, Msiri managed to carve for himself and his kin a large state by first establishing alliances with local rulers, gaining some legitimacy in the process, and then by gradually establishing a complex system of economic, matrimonial, and political exchanges in order to assert his domination on the autochtonous population.

Manipulating regalia, emblems, and other objects of memories (Nooter Roberts and Roberts 1996) was central to the legitimization process of those kings and their various titleholders and dignitaries. This may also explain why since Kabambian times these symbols do not end up as grave goods anymore. As memory objects they have become more important to the living than to the dead. Contrary to the general archaeological notion that complex social organizations from chiefdoms through early states have striking wealth differentials in burials, we may have here the case of political organizations becoming increasingly complex but witnessing the disappearance of grave goods.

In Central Africa, political developments hardly fit the standard evolutionary schema of increasing material representation of increasing political and economic power. But by combining the "Words and Things" technique so masterfully used by Vansina (1990) to reconstruct the history of political tradition in the rainforests of equatorial Africa with systematic and well-focused ethnographical and archaeological research, it is possible to make a significant contribution to the reconstruction of the political past of Africa and to various theories of increasing social and political complexity.

Note

1   Since this chapter was written, Zaire has been renamed the Democratic Republic of the Congo, and the Zaire River is now called the Congo River.

References

Anciaux de Faveaux, E., and P. de Maret
    1984 Premières datations pour la fonte du cuivre au Shaba (Zaïre). *Bulletin de la Société Royale Belge d'Anthropologie et de Préhistoire* 95: 5–20.
Bisson, M. S.
    1976 The prehistoric copper mines of Zambia. Ph.D. dissertation, University of California, Santa Barbara.
Bontinck, F.
    1974 *L'autobiographie de Hamed ben Mohammed el-Murjebi Tippo Tip (ca. 1840–1905)*. Brussels: Académie Royale des Science d'Outre-Mer.
Boterdal
    1909 Rapport d'enquête. Chefferie de Mulongo. Unpublished document.
Burton, W. F. P.
    1961 *Luba Religion and Magic in Custom and Belief*. Tervuren: Musée Royal de l'Afrique Centrale.
Childs, S. T.
    1991 Transformations: iron and copper production in

Central Africa. In *Recent Trends in Archeo-Metallurgical Research*, edited by P. Glumac. MASCA Research Papers in Science and Archaeology no. 8.

Childs, S. T. and P. de Maret
1996 Re/Constructing Luba Pasts. In *Memory: Luba Art and the Making of History*, edited by M. Nooter Roberts and A. F. Roberts. New York: The Museum for African Art: 49–59.

Childs, S. T. and W. J. Dewey
1996 Forging symbolic meaning in Zaire and Zimbabwe. In *The Culture and Technology of Iron Production in Africa*, edited by P. Schmidt. Gainesville: University Press of Florida: 145–71.

Clark, J. D.
1974 *Kalambo Falls Prehistoric Site: The Later Prehistoric Cultures*. Cambridge: Cambridge University Press.

Clist, B.
1991 L'archéologie du royaume Kongo. In *Aux origines de l'Afrique Centrale* edited by R. Lanfranchi and B. Clist. Paris: Sépia: 253–8.

Cunnison, I.
1959 *The Luapula Peoples of Northern Rhodesia*. Manchester: Manchester University Press.

Dewey, W. J. and S. T. Childs
1996 Forging memory. In *Memory: Luba Art and the Making of History*, edited by M. Nooter Roberts and A. F. Roberts. New York: The Museum for African Art: 61–83.

Earle, T. K.
1987 Chiefdoms in archaeological and ethnohistorical perspective. *Annual Review of Anthropology* 16: 279–308.

Fagan, B. M.
1969 Early trade and raw materials in South Central Africa, *Journal of African History* 10: 1–13.

Fortes, M. and E. E. Evans-Pritchard
1940 (eds.) *African Political Systems*. Oxford: Oxford University Press.

Geyh, M. A. and P. de Maret
1982 Histogram evaluation of 14C dates applied to the first complete Iron Age sequence from West Central Africa. *Archeometry* 24: 158–63.

Gray, R. and D. Birmingham
1970 (eds.) *Pre-Colonial African Trade: Essays on Trade in Central and Eastern Africa before 1900*. London: Oxford University Press.

Herbert, E. W.
1993 *Iron, Gender, and Power*. Bloomington: Indiana University Press.

Hiernaux, J., E. de Longree, and J. De Buyst
1971 *Fouilles Archéologiques dans la Vallée du Haut-Lualaba 1. Sanga 1958*. Tervuren: Musée Royal de l'Afrique Centrale.

Hiernaux, J., E. Maquet, and J. De Buyst
1972 Le Cimetière Protohistorique de Katoto. In *Sixième Congrès Panafricain de Préhistoire*, Dakar 1967, edited by H. Hugot. Chambéry: Les Imprimeries Réunies.

Kawende Fina Nkindi, J. and G. De Plaen
1996 Pearls of wisdom. In *Memory: Luba Art and the Making of History*, edited by M. Nooter Roberts and A. F. Roberts. New York: The Museum for African Art: 92–7.

Kuper, A. and P. van Leynseele
1978 Social anthropology and the "Bantu Expansion," *Africa* 48: 335–52.

Legros, H.
1996 *Chasseur d'ivoire. Une histoire du royaume Yeke du Shaba (Zaïre)*. Bruxelles: Edition de l'Université Libre de Bruxelles.

Leynseele, P. van
1979 Les Libinza de la Ngiri. Ph.D. dissertation, Leiden University.

Maes, J.
1929 *Catalogues illustrés des Collections Ethnographiques du Musée du Congo Belge, I, 1. Les appuis – tête du Congo Belge*. Bruxelles: Musée du Congo Belge.

Maret, P. de
1977 Sanga: new excavations, more data, and some related problems. *Journal of African History* 18: 321–37.
1978 Chronologie de l'Age du Fer dans la Dépression de l'Upemba en République du Zaïre. Ph.D. dissertation, Brussels University.
1979 Luba roots: a first complete Iron Age sequence in Zaire. *Current Anthropology* 20: 233–5.
1980 Ceux qui jouent avec le feu: la place de forgeron en Afrique Centrale, *Africa* 50: 263–79.
1981 L'Evolution monétaire du Shaba Central entre le 7e et le 18e siècle. *African Economic History* 10: 117–49.
1982 New survey of archaeological research and dates for West Central and North-Central Africa. *Journal of African History* 23: 1–15.
1985a The smith's myth and the origin of leadership in Central Africa. In *African Iron Working*, edited by R. Haaland and P. Shinnie. Bergen: Norwegian University Press: 73–87.
1985b *Fouilles archéologiques dans la vallée du Haut-*

Lualaba, Zaïre – II Sanga et Katongo 1974. 2 vols., Tervuren: Musée Royal de l'Afrique Centrale.

1990 Phases and facies in the archaeology of Central Africa. In *A History of African Archaeology*, edited by P. Robertshaw. London: James Currey: 109–34.

1991 L'archéologie du royaume Luba. In *Aux origines de l'Afrique Centrale*, edited by R. Lanfranchi and B. Clist. Paris: Sépia: 234–41.

1992 *Fouilles archéologiques dans le vallée du Haut-Lualaba, Zaïre – II Kamilamba, Kikulu et Malemba-Nkulu, 1975.* 2 vols. Tervuren: Musée Royal de l'Afrique Centrale.

1995 Croisettes memories. In *Objects: Signs of Africa*, edited by L. de Heusch, Tervuren: Musée Royal de l'Afrique Centrale: 133–45.

Nenquin, J.

1963 *Excavations at Sanga 1957: The Protohistoric Necropolis.* Tervuren: Musée Royal de l'Afrique Centrale.

Nooter Roberts, M.

1991 Luba art and polity: creating power in a central African kingdom. Unpublished Ph.D. dissertation, Columbia University.

1996 Luba memory theater. In *Memory: Luba Art and the Making of History*, edited by M. Nooter Roberts and A. F. Roberts, New York: The Museum for African Art: 117–49.

Nooter Roberts, M. and A. F. Roberts

1996 (eds.) *Memory: Luba Art and the Making of History.* New York: The Museum for African Art.

d'Orjo de Marchovelette, E.

1950 Les funérailles des Chefs Luba: Ilunga Kabale et Kabongo Kumwimba Shimbu. *Bulletin de l'Association des Anciens Etudiants de l'Institut Universitaire des Territoires d'Outre-Mer* 9: 27–31.

Petit, P.

1993 Rites familiaux, rites royaux. Etude du système cérémoniel des Luba du Shaba (Zaïre). Ph.D. dissertation, Université Libre de Bruxelles.

Phillipson, D. W.

1968 The Early Iron Age in Zambia: regional variants and some tentative conclusions. *Journal of African History* 9: 191–211.

Pinçon, B.

1991 L'archéologie du royaume Teke. In *Aux origines de l'Afrique Centrale*, edited by R. Lanfranchi and B. Clist. Paris: Sépia: 242–52.

Reefe, T.Q.

1981 *The Rainbow and the Kings: A History of the Luba Empire to 1981.* Berkeley: University of California Press.

1983 The societies of the Eastern Savanna. In *History*

of Central Africa, edited by D. Birmingham and P. M. Martin. London: Longman.

Roberts, A. D.

1973 *A History of the Bemba: Political Growth and Change in North-Eastern Zambia before 1900.* London: Longman.

Roberts, A. F.

1996 Peripheral visions. In *Memory: Luba Art and the Making of History*, edited by M. Nooter Roberts and A. F. Roberts. New York: The Museum for African Art: 211–43.

Sahlins, M.

1972 *Stone Age Economics.* Chicago: Aldine-Atherton Inc.

Saint-Moulin, L. de

1974 La répartition de la population au Zaïre en 1970. *Cultures et Développement* 2: 331–49.

Theuws, T.

1960 Naître et mourir dans le Rituel Luba. *Zaïre* 14: 115–73.

Van Avermaet, E. and J. Mbuya

1954 *Dictionnaire Kiluba-Français.* Tervuren: Musée Royal de Congo Belge.

Van Der Noot, A.

1936 Quelques éléments historiques sur l'empire Luba, son organisation et sa direction. *Bulletin des juridictions indigènes et du droit coutumier congolais* 4 (7): 141–9.

Vansina, J.

1969 The bells of kings. *Journal of African History* 10: 187–97.

1973–4 Probing the past of the Lower Kwilu Peoples (Zaïre). *Paideuma* 19/20: 332–64.

1974 Long-distance trade-routes in Central Africa. *Journal of African History* 15: 375–90.

1989 Deep down time: political tradition in Central Africa. *History in Africa* 16: 341–62.

1990 *Paths in the Rainforests: Toward a History of Political Tradition in Equatorial Africa.* Madison: The University of Wisconsin Press.

1994 *Living with Africa.* Madison: The University of Wisconsin Press.

1996 From memory to history: process of Luba historical consciousness. In *Memory: Luba Art and the Making of History*, edited by M. Nooter Roberts and A. F. Roberts New York: The Museum for African Art: 12–14.

Van Noten, F.

1972 *Les tombes du Roi Cyirima Rujugira et de la Reine mère Nyirayuhi Kanjogera: description archéologique.* Tervuren: Musée Royal de l'Afrique Centrale.

Vengroff, R.
   1976 Population density and state formation in Africa. *African Studies Review* 19: 67–74.

Verhulpen, E.
   1936 *Baluba et Balubaïsés du Katanga*. Anvers: Edition de l'Avenir Belge.

Wilson, A.
   1972 Long-distance trade and the Luba Lomami Empire. *Journal of African History* 13: 575–89.

Womersley, H.
   1975 *In the Glow of the Log Fire*. London: Peniel Press.

   1984 *Legends and History of the Luba*. Los Angeles: Crossroads Press.

Yoffee, N.
   1993 Too Many Chiefs? (or, Safe Texts for the '90s). In *Archaeological Theory: Who Sets the Agenda?*, edited by N. Yoffee and A. Sherratt. Cambridge: Cambridge University Press: 60–78.

Zeebroek, R.
   1976 La Monnaie dans le Monde Bantou. Le cas des Luba du Shaba. Mémoire de Licence, Brussels University.

13

Pathways of political development in equatorial Africa and neo-evolutionary theory

JAN VANSINA

The main evolution of societies in the standard neo-evolutionary sequence is seen as a progression from quite small-scale totally autonomous groups called "bands" towards very large-scale and highly centralized social formations called "states" through still ill-defined intermediary stages labeled "tribe" and "chiefdom." The whole progression then is defined in terms of political organisation (Yoffee 1993). It is in this context that the long-term history of political organisations in Equatorial Africa (Figure 13.1), described in a recent study (Vansina 1990), is relevant to test the theory. Equatorial Africa designates the northern part of Central Africa – an area as large as the United States east of the Mississippi, mostly covered by various tropical rainforests. Anthropologists have recognized some 450 ethnic groups there, and it is possible to distinguish about twenty-five different political regimes in the area (using the distinctions common in social anthropology and disregarding a special "band" status for foragers such as pygmies since these constituted only a part of a society, the other part being that of their farmer hosts). These political institutions are based on the most diverse ideological principles and range in size from single villages, such as Libinza (Ngiri area, Zaire) comprising as few as a hundred or so inhabitants, to kingdoms encompassing well over 100,000 inhabitants. If one includes the kingdom of Kongo in its centuries-long heyday, there was even a polity of 500,000 people. The range includes the "tribe," "chiefdom," and "state" rungs on the neo-evolutionary ladder. In addition, equatorial Africa is especially interesting because all these political regimes developed out of a single ancestral political system, existing 5,000 years ago. Moreover, they did so largely in isolation from the outside world. Influences

from eastern Africa played a role only in the easternmost part of the area and influences from the world economy began only after AD 1500. Nearly all of the populations in the entire area speak Bantu languages, a family of languages which has benefitted from over a century of comparative historical study. It has been possible in this case to apply a technique called "words and things" which allows one to reconstruct the histories of objects, institutions, customs, values, and ideas over the whole period involved and to link such data to the still scanty archaeological record (a detailed discussion of the "words and things" method can be found in Vansina 1990: 9–31).

The ancestral system

It all began with the political organisation of ancestral Bantu speakers in westernmost Cameroon and southern Nigeria *c.* 2000 BC (Vansina 1990: 71–100). These people lived in "houses" (i.e., households) directed by a big man (probably not a woman) and comprising most of his close relatives and their dependents as well as servants and hangers-on. Big men competed with each other to increase the size, the labor force, and the security of their houses by attracting people from other houses. Despite this competition, a few of these Houses clustered their residences together into a village for economic and security reasons. The village was jointly governed by its big men. Four or five villages of equal importance formed a district, the largest territorial unit, which was united only by the preference of its constituent villages to exchange goods, services, and people (such as marriage partners) preferentially among themselves. They also cooperated in their mutual defense. Most districts probably counted around 500 inhabitants. Of the three units of house, village, and district, the village was the most ephemeral. Competition between its big men continually produced tensions and easily led to secession and the break up of the village, all the more so because the village moved to a new site at least once every ten years or so for economic reasons. The existence of stable alliances between houses living in different villages, probably within the same district but occasionally across districts, makes good sense in this context. Such alliances are known as clans. Certain signs such as slogans, food interdictions, and facial scars were used to express such alliances, and a myth of past common experience (genuine or not) was also elaborated to justify them.

This political organization was based on two contradictory ideological principles at once: one asserting the supernatural powers of leaders and the other the equality of all people (in practice, all married men, it appears). The

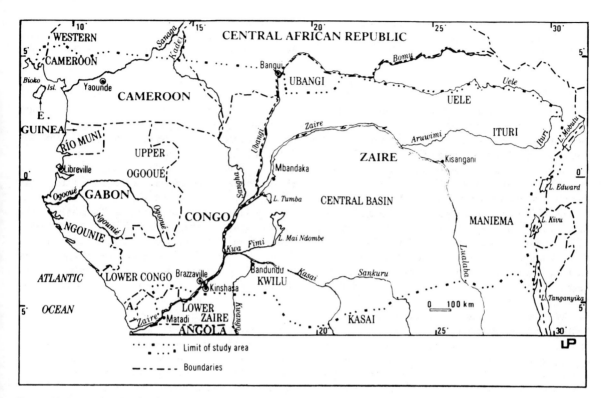

Figure 13.1 Equatorial Africa

first one was to lead, among other avatars, to the ideologies of sacred kingship; the other is still buttressed by the ideology of witchcraft because any exceptional achiever is suspected of being a witch. The political organization cherished extreme autonomy at every level beyond the house, but celebrated personal leadership within it. Tasks requiring larger groups than the house were successfully carried out through cooperation, limited to a few situations and limited in time, but effective nevertheless.

An organization that was grounded in such contradictory ideologies and which looks so haphazard may appear to be quite transitory. In fact, it was extremely stable because its balance of power was based on competition and cooperation between leaders of roughly the same strength. Houses were dependent on the talents of their individual leaders and often did not outlast them, which meant that it was truly rare for a house to become durably bigger and stronger than others, while the fact that each house was too small to be secure in a settlement of its own meant that alliances both through common residence in villages and through clan alliances were necessary. If one house became too strong, several other Houses could rally

against it. Finally, competing leaders both within the house and between houses could always opt out and found a new village on unclaimed lands. The system worked well then, as long as population density was low. In sum, the very flexibility of this organization explains its inherent stability during many centuries until some of the basic underlying enabling conditions such as population density and economic way of life became different.

Even under changing conditions, however, the twin ideologies and the tension between local autonomy and centralization continued to exist. They have done so throughout all of the successor regimes of the original organization until recent times. The desire to safeguard autonomy allied to the recognition of the need for cooperation have only rarely led to the absolute preponderance of either centralization (genuine states have been extremely rare in Central Africa) or total autonomy (societies reduced to a simplified version of the original house are also extremely rare). Hence during the last 4,000–5,000 years we do not find any overall evidence for a clear progression towards greater centralization as neo-evolutionary theory would lead us to expect. Nor does an examination of the various pathways of transformation from the original social organization to recent social organizations suggest such a progression.

Pathways of socio-political change

The original political organization eventually spread from its lands of origin over the whole of Central Africa including equatorial Africa as part of the phenomenon known as the Bantu expansion (Vansina 1995). Much later it underwent a series of transformations, which one can pick up from about AD 1000 onwards. The first of these occurred independently in as many as ten different cradles. We do not know exactly what drove districts in these areas to innovate. Certainly the most direct and precipitating cause was the ambition of gifted leaders and their invention of new institutions to enlarge and perpetuate their power – an activity that was legitimized by the development of new facets of the two familiar ideologies. Beyond this, however, there are indications in some cases for demographic increase (itself interrelated with other factors), an accumulation of wealth resulting from increased trade (again interrelated with other factors) and an increase in food surpluses. In some cases new military technology seems to have played a major role. Wealth, a gift to arbitrate, or superior wisdom seem to have been the usual qualities that allowed leaders to rise above their peers. Superior military talent is rarely in evidence, nor is there in this area – *pace* Frazer – much evidence for gaining political power from any priestly status. Whatever the causes, in most cases a district where a transformation process occurred became significantly more powerful than its neighbors and thus upset the balance of power, destabilizing the region around it. This imbalance created insecurity and forced neighboring districts to attempt to restore the balance either by adopting the original institutional innovation or by inventing a counter-innovation of their own. This in turn created insecurity among their neighbors, who were then forced to react in a similar way. Thus a chain reaction began which could cover a huge area before it petered out when it reached either an area of very low population density or an area where transformations emanating from another cradle had already strengthened its districts. In many cases this was not the end of it, for an escalation of innovations now developed among the districts near the epicenter, locked, as they were, in competition, and as every one of these still tried to achieve a definitive advantage over others. This escalation then maintained the impetus of the original chain reaction for centuries.

It is not possible within the compass of a short chapter to even sketch the sequence of all of the transformations which have stemmed from the original cradles (for more extensive discussion, see Vansina 1990). I will summarize only two sequences. The first of these is a tale of relentless territorial centralization from big man to king which seems to confirm familiar views about the origin of the state and to conform to neo-evolutionary views (Vansina 1990: 146–65). It began with the development of principles of succession within a house whereby the number of potential challengers to the position of big man was reduced. This innovation limited the chances that a House would disintegrate as a result of the struggles for power which followed the demise of its big man. Concurrently the head of one house, usually the house which founded a village first and then attracted other houses, came to be accepted as the recognized leader of the whole village. This increased the stability of the village. The position of this leader was sanctioned by a ritual in which he, as founder of the village, erected the collective village charm for the defense of all its inhabitants.

The next step consisted in accepting one of the village leaders in a district as a *primus inter pares*. This person was given the title of *nkani* or "arbitrator" which indicates his role. That development seems to have occurred during the first millennium AD. This step was decisive in turning the district gradually into a chiefdom. That in turn broke the balance of power in a large area around that chiefdom because its military potential exceeded that of neighboring, less well-coordinated units. The creation of a chiefdom thus acted as a catalyst in the area surrounding it. Everyone adopted it. Soon the institution came to be enriched with rules of succession, rituals of installation, chiefly perquisites, and detailed ideologies which arose in a competitive dialogue between emerging chiefdoms over a large area. All the notions and institutions necessary for larger territorial units were thus created in embryo.

They blossomed when principalities appeared. These resulted from the conquest of one chiefdom by another and the creation of a two-tiered territorial system in which a prince ruled over chiefs. Institutionally, they were also marked by the invention of a corps of political titleholders, with one subset of titles evolving out of functions relating to the large house of the prince and the other out of the territorial political structure as the importance of the main chiefs was recognized through a title. By AD 1200, principalities were set up in at least two different core areas: north of the Lower Zaire not far from the ocean (Kongo), and the plateau west of the Congo/Zaire river upstream of Brazzaville (Teke). Two centuries later, three major kingdoms – Kongo, Loango, and Tio – had arisen out of the continuing competition between principalities. Ancillary sequences to the main sequence sketched here occurred all around them. Among others we mention only two cases: the creation of leagues between autonomous districts in southern Gabon, held together because the participants belonged to a common association, and the creation of very large independent villages in northeastern Gabon, with thousands of inhabitants each.

The whole sequence of development seems to agree very well with neo-evolutionary views. But the later parts do not. For the three kingdoms were very different in crucial respects. Only one of them, Kongo, achieved a high enough degree of centralization to be called a state. Only here did the king and his court control the appointment and dismissal of territorial governors, only here did taxes (in a common currency) flow to the capital, only here did a pyramid of judicial courts exist, and only here was there a significant royal armed force. In extreme contrast, the Tio king neither appointed nor controlled his lords, he did not receive regular taxes beyond a small area around his capital, and he did not dispose of a superior military force. The royal judicial court competed with that of any other lord. The kingdom existed mainly in the acceptance by all that the king was superior in title and spiritual power to all because he controlled the national charm which affected the whole territory. Such a decentralized kingdom cannot possibly be labeled a state. Loango's situation was intermediary between the two others.

Moreover the story does not end with the rise of the state of Kongo from 1400 onwards. That state collapsed after 1665 to be replaced by an extremely decentralized political system whose unity was restricted to the common use by all of a single burial center: the residence of a king without authority, something very similar to the Tio kingdom in the last few centuries as well.

Consider also the fact that only two other sequences out of the ten documented in equatorial Africa led directly to the emergence of kingdoms (Mangbetu and Bioko), both of which were quite ephemeral. In three other sequences, a kingdom appeared but merely as one among many outcomes. In one case, a kingdom (Nzakara) grew out of segmentary patrilineal developments; in another (Lega-Sile) it developed out of a government by overarching association and under the influence of the nearby kingdoms of the Great Lakes, while in the last one a kingdom (Kuba) was only one of several outcomes of a sequence starting with coalitions of Big Men. This also happened to become the only

kingdom besides Kongo to turn into a centralized state, albeit a smaller one as it encompassed only 120,000 inhabitants over 30,000 square kilometers. Many pathways toward growing complexity in terms of size of population, size of area, and institutions were involved, and these did not necessarily generate only kingdoms but many other types of political formations. Hence evolutionary theory has no predictive value and should not be used by archaeologists to extrapolate a sequence of developments towards greater centralization.

The second sequence chosen here begins on the northern banks of the great bend of the Zaire river (Vansina 1990: 101–19). Around AD 1000 the house, at least in the inner basin of the river south of its great bend, had grown in size and in importance at the expense of the village – exactly the contrary of what happened in the previous sequence. Some Houses became wealthier and hence more powerful than others because they were better placed for trade. In this context too, and for the same reasons, new succession rules limited competition for its leadership. Soon thereafter, a further innovation occurred. All the villagers began to identify with the founding house in its relations with outside villagers or houses, as if they were junior members of the house. This happened in places where the choice of sites to settle was limited (e.g., along the River Zaire), and where villages stayed in the same general spot for a very long time, thus restricting the option of individual houses to move from one village residence to another. Moreover, some of the sites, especially those commanding confluences of the river, were far more strategic than others because settlers there could control the flow of commerce over considerable distances. As a result of the identification with the leading house of a village, the district soon came to be thought of as cluster of founding houses linked together by marriage alliances. Meanwhile, competition for the most desirable sites fueled military innovations. New weapons and new ways of fighting requiring larger numbers of men drawn up in battle lines, were developed. Villages, prosperous because they controlled nodes of commerce, automatically attracted more young men than others (bilateral descent gave men a wide choice of residences) and hence they grew larger and stronger than others. This new situation in which villages were clearly of unequal strength was then again translated into ideology. Leading houses were no longer thought of as equal allies but as unequal "elder" and "younger brothers," and genealogies were constructed to that effect. The invention of patrilineages was the end result of this process, for the patrilineal image contains both a detailed hierarchy of age and generation and yet a claim to equality as "brethren."

The former district thus turned into a formal structure in which each village retained its autonomy, yet occupied a precise rank in the common genealogy. Thus the genealogy, at least in emic theory, laid out a pattern of collaboration in time of war well in advance of any emergency, a pattern that was expressed by frequent rituals accompanying the disposal of the spoils of the leopard and other "noble game" which showed the exact position of each autonomous unit within the whole.

Districts interpreted as the spatial expression of patrilineal structures became so much better structured and coordinated than their neighbors and gave them such an advantage in times of war that the latter had to either copy the institution or counteract it. Adventurous leaders at the southern edge of the core area discovered that their military power was so overwhelming compared to that of districts further away from the core area that they could easily overwhelm them. A large territorial expansion southwards was the result. It rapidly spread until it was stopped far in the south when the conquerors clashed *c.* 1450/1500 with better organized and militarily strong districts emanating from an entirely different cradle.

To the west of the core area and along the Zaire bend, the Doko people reacted by inventing a counter-innovation. The villages there on banks of the Zaire River, the main artery of commerce, had also become very large. They had participated in the early innovation in which one House dominated each settlement. But they limited the succession to the leadership of the dominant House in a different way. They excluded the descendants of all but one of the wives of the big man and in doing so invented matrilineages. Politically this meant that relationships of allegiance within a town or district were no longer perceived in terms of kinship at all but as territorial relations. The district became a chiefdom ruled by a founding "house." This counter innovation was efficient enough to balance the power of the neighboring patrilineal districts. It also spread itself further westwards as far as the great swamp of the Zaire and Ubangi rivers. There all communication was by water and the new military innovations upstream had little effect.

In the northern part of the core area meanwhile continual small innovations born out of continual competition between adjacent patrilineal districts led to the emergence of a full-scale segmentary patrilineal system based on male primogeniture and hence of a "dynasty," while the territory of sovereign groups became much larger than a single district. This line of development then led to several different further outcomes. To the northwest one group, the Ngbandi, maintained the segmentary patrilineal system and from 1500 onwards spread nearly

as far as the lower Ubangi incorporating older inhabitants as they went. But one of these older populations, the Ngombe, reacted by a counter-innovation that improved their military efficiency. They already lived in fairly large villages but they now reinforced their village structure at the expense of the leading house. They invented the position of village leader independent of the houses that constituted the village. This person was elected on the basis of wealth, talent for arbitration, and physical strength, and his authority was bolstered by ritual, which recalls well-known practices of "divine kingship." At the same time houses were no longer allowed to secede at will. Village endogamy became predominant and age grades cut across the house structures, which reinforced village unity. Finally they created confederations of villages. Even so, the territorially wider segmentary patrilineal system of the Ngbandi gave them more military manpower and in the long run military superiority, so that at least after 1700 they slowly gained ground over Ngombe lands. Thereupon some Ngombe village confederation crossed the Zaire River *c.* 1800 and began to conquer swathes of territory south of the Zaire bend from the much less well-organised local populations there. Due north, meanwhile, a single dynasty strengthened to the point that the Nzakara kingdom arose after 1600. To the northeast a single ruler, the ancestor of the Zande, started a similar expansion *c.* 1700. But he could not control his sons, each of whom started his own expansion. This resulted in a huge expansion of principalities united only by the common belonging of all the princes to the same dynasty and by the establishment of three ranks in society: the royals, original Zande, and conquered people.

An expansion towards the east followed well after the onset of the expansion to the north, perhaps *c.* 1700. Here, nearest the original core, the territories were densely populated but fairly small, with the result that the military power of the handful of units which occupied these lands became extremely strong and these units became both larger and fewer. Their patrilineal ethos was further enhanced through dramatic rituals which now linked all rituals and healing to the relevant ancestor cult, to the point, for instance, that any and all medicines or charms had to incorporate relics from the ancestors. Once this growth in scale (but not in centralization) had been achieved these groups introduced their innovations eastwards until, far to the east, areas of very low population density were reached. Further innovations followed in this expansion area. They included, *c.* 1750, the settlement of a large permanent town, Basoko, and the creation of a type of chiefdom (Angba) with innovative succession practices. A successor was now designated irrespective of his position in the patrilineal genealogy of the leader, but chosen among his sons and during his lifetime. That meant the emergence of a large, if not very centralized chiefdom. By 1880 local dynamics which were still continuing in a part of this eastern area also led to the creation of large chiefdoms based on conquest where the patrilineal legitimation was totally abandoned in favor of territorial legitimacy.

This whole sequence of developments, which covered some three-quarters of a millennium, runs contrary to the expectations of neo-evolutionary theory. For while an increase towards greater cooperation for security reasons and probably also for commercial reasons did occur, the tenacity with which local autonomy was maintained throughout is not foreseen by this theory. These people invented political formations in which increasingly efficient cooperation on specified issues accrued without any genuine centralization at all. Secondly, the diversity and multiplicity of the political formations that resulted could not have been predicted at all. Theoreticians can try to maintain that these political developments are just peristaltic movements, irrelevant to evolution, and that all these groups stagnated on the same rung, but that will not convince since among the various outcomes are structures which have been classified as "tribes," "chiefdoms," and "states"! Theoreticians might claim that only the minority of outcomes which produced chiefdoms and kingdoms represented the next stage, or perhaps two stages. But given the known detail of the developments involved, the evolutionary labels themselves appear to be totally artificial. And what, in any case, is the use of a theory that simply denies most sociopolitical change even over long periods as irrelevant?

The eight other main sequences which one can trace in equatorial Africa are all similar in their unpredictability and in the great variety of their outcomes. So are the known sequences further south in the Central African savannas and woodlands. These include some outcomes that are not reported in equatorial Africa proper, such as various systems based on age grades and one based on the common recognition of a single ritual center for rain-making. The original system of a district, village, and house has therefore yielded a huge spectrum of political systems. In equatorial Africa *c.* 1880, the smallest and most decentralized system was one of dispersed and mobile hamlets in a large area of very low population density, each being the seat of a house with a patrilineal core and all being linked together only by their common participation in one or two brotherhoods concerned with divination and circumcision whose overlapping memberships provided a wider cultural unity. The largest was the

kingdom of Kongo in the seventeenth century with its population of over half a million.

Neo-evolutionary theorists have simply never imagined that such a luxuriance of political formations was possible. The nineteenth-century founders of the theory thought that there were two – and only two – principles of human aggregation: kinship or territory. They imagined that evolution went from a simple community based on kin to a complex society based on territory. What central Africa shows is that this is an oversimplification. The principles of aggregation found there are: residential, kinship, age, association, ritual center subjection, and territory. While most of these principles of aggregation occur together in each political formation, one or two usually dominate them and all the ones mentioned became dominant in one formation or another that sprang from the single original house–village–district system.

Conclusions

The confrontation between neo-evolutionary theory and the evidence from equatorial Africa leads to disastrous results for the theory. There simply is no evidence for an overall increase in centralization. P. Shifferd (1987: 47) had already obtained similar evidence with regard to African cases before but dismissed it by stating that while increasing centralization can be observed in the evolution of human culture in general, it is not inevitable in each case and whether it takes place at all depends on other interrelated causes. But this will not do in the case of equatorial Africa, unless of course one invents an *ad hoc*, unknown factor *x* that only came into play when centralization increased. Barring that, the evidence does refute the theory, at least for its "tribe," "chiefdom," and "state" rungs.

But is it not possible to argue that the damage stems more from an oversimplistic model than from any social evolutionary premise itself? Rather than defining simple to complex as a move from decentralization to centralization and rather than imagining it as a move from kinship to territory, could one not allow the possibilities of cooperation without centralization and the various principles of aggregation? That does not prevent a disaster because the notion of centralization is absolutely crucial to the definitions of the "chiefdom" and "state" rungs on the ladder. They are defined respectively as "regionally organized societies with a central decision-making hierarchy coordinating activities among several village communities" (Earle 1987: 288) and "an independent socio-political organization with a bounded territory and a center of government " (Claessen and Skalník 1978: 637; Claessen 1991: 27). By implication the "tribe" rung is also affected in so far as it is characterized by the absence of centralization. Hence, to abandon "centralization" as the core feature of neo-evolutionary theory is to dismiss most of today's neo-evolutionary literature, which happens to concentrate on chiefdoms and states.

Similarities between processes of social and cultural change can and must be explained in ways other than by an appeal to the spurious analogy of evolution. Such similarities do exist: unilineal descent has been invented many times over and has often led to similar social structures – although similar is never identical. Ultimately the explanation of similarity lies in the sameness of the human identity of the inventors, the sameness of logical processes, the sameness of basic emotions, the sameness of biological requirements. The definition of a human, however, also includes reflexivity and hence culture, and cultures differ because they start from different reflexive premises. That fact explains why the history of different human groups is always different, just as the sameness of humans explains why parts of some processes of development may be so similar. The same wealth of the human endowment thus explains why historical processes are totally unpredictable. Even in very similar circumstances, a rarity by itself, different people perceive different choices and hence act differently, or even if they perceive the same choices they prefer different solutions. Thus, in the end, human nature itself defeats any attempt at an orderly "logical" evolution of human history, and makes spurious any extrapolation from archaeology to obligatory pathways of development.

References

Claessen H. J. M.
  1991 *Verdwenen koninkrijken en verloren beschavingen.* Van Gorcum: Assen.
Claessen, H. J. M. and Skalník, P.
  1978 *The Early State.* Mouton: The Hague.
Earle T. K.
  1987 Chiefdoms in archaeological and ethnohistorical perspective. *Annual Review of Anthropology* 16: 279–308.
Shifferd, P. A.
  1987 Aztecs and Africans: political processes in twenty-two early states. In *Early State Dynamics*, edited by H. J. M. Claessen and P. Van de Velde. Leiden: Brill: 39–53.
Vansina, J.
  1990 *Paths in the Rainforests: Towards a History of Political Tradition in Equatorial Africa.* Madison: University of Wisconsin Press.
  1995 New linguistic evidence on the Bantu expansion. *Journal of African History* 36 (2): 173–95.
Yoffee, N.
  1993 Too many chiefs? (or, Safe texts for the '90s). In *Archaeological Theory: Who Sets the Agenda?*, edited by N. Yoffee and A. Sherratt. Cambridge: Cambridge University Press: 60–78.

Index

Afikpo village group 9, 11
Africa, colonial images of 40, 43, 44
African archaeology
  and decolonization 43
  funding 45
  time–space systematics 40–1
  variability, winnowing of 42, 44, 45, 48, 49
African Political Systems (1940) 1–2, 3, 7, 8, 9, 15, 16, 17, 94, 151
African rice 66, 67, 69, 70, 74, 75
Afrocentrism 45, 48
age-grades 4, 170, 171
Aghem (Wum) polity 19, 88–95
agriculture
  and gender 141, 143, 144–5
  and foraging/hunting 45, 48, 70, 74
  expansion 68
  intensification 5, 66, 68, 73–5, 76, 136–7, 145–6
  Kofyar 74
  origins 45, 66
alliances 17, 76, 166, 167, 169
Alur 14–15, 21, 31–6, 94, 101
  Atyak polity 31, 32
analogy 12, 97, 98, 99, 107
Arens, W. 16–17, 23n.
Arochukwu 11
  oracle cult 7, 11, 12, 23
Ashanti 7, 11, 19
associations 9, 11, 23, 77, 81, 161, 169
Athens 59, 62
authority
  charismatic 61
  political, symbols of 157
  ritual 4, 76, 126, 127

Bacwezi (*see* Cwezi)
Bafut kingdom 80–6
Banda, Ghana 48
Bantu
  expansion 168
  "Houses" 166–7, 168–9, 170

Bashu 17
Big man 4, 21, 161, 166, 168
Bigo 129, 131, 133n.
Boserup, E. 75
Breuil, Abbé H. 40, 41, 42
Buganda 136–50 *passim*
Bulozi kingdom (*see* Lozi)
Bunyoro-Kitara, Uganda 124–33, 136–46
Bunyoro (*see* Nyoro)
  earthworks 129–32
Burg-Wartenstein Symposium 41–2
Burkitt, M. 40, 41, 42

Cameroon 99
  Grassfields 80–6, 88–95
  kingdoms in 80, 81, 82, 94
  montagnard society 99, 101, 104, 106
caste 101, 106
cattle 6, 66, 67, 68, 116, 117, 121, 127, 130, 137
  agropastoralists 113, 126
  Central Cattle Complex 110–13
  pastoralists 127, 132, 136, 144
  pastro-foragers 116, 117
Central (Equatorial) Africa 99, 101, 166–72
centralization 8, 14, 21, 34, 75, 82, 94, 98, 107, 137, 145, 167, 168, 171–2
chief 2, 99, 101–6, 146
chiefdom (*see* political organization)
chieftaincy 88, 90, 92, 93, 94
  sacred 90
Childe, V. G. 41, 42
cities
  and civilization 43
  and monumentality 20, 56, 59, 60, 61, 62
civilization 43, 45, 80
  and cities 43
clan 101, 102, 103, 104, 105, 106, 141, 142, 144, 145, 166, 168
coalitions 126
coercion, coercive power 33, 57, 62, 101, 106